THE INSIDERS' GUIDE® TO METROPOLITAN WASHINGTON D.C.

by
Stephen Soltis
and
Brian T. Cook

Richmond Times-Dispatch

9 780912 367408

Co-published and marketed by:
Richmond Newspapers, Inc.
333 East Grace St.
Richmond, VA 23219
(804) 649-6000

•

Co-published and distributed by:
The Insiders' Guides®, Inc.
P.O. Box 2057 • Highway 64
Manteo, NC 27954
(919) 473-6100

•

FIRST EDITION
1st printing

•

•

Printed in the United States
of America

•

•

ISBN 0-912367-40-7

Richmond Newspapers, Inc.
Supplemental Publications

Director, Marketing Development
Robert J Bowerman

Manager
Ernie Chenault

Account Executives
Heidi Crandall, Adair Frayser Roper, Mike Morrison

Project Coordination
Bonnie Widener

Artists
Susan Reilly, Ronnie Johnson, Sean Contreras, Chris Novelli, Chuck Nilles

The Insiders' Guides®, Inc.

Publisher/Managing Editor
Beth P Storie

President/General Manager
Michael McOwen

Project Manager
Sue Maloney

Manager/Creative Services
David Haynes

Manager/Distribution
Giles Bissonnette

Editorial Assistant
Georgia Beach

Fulfillment Coordination
Gina Twiford

Controller
Claudette Forney

Preface

Setting about the task of writing an *Insiders' Guide® to Metro Washington* is every bit as daunting as it is exciting. Perhaps no other region in the country is as diverse, dynamic, intriguing and, for that matter, misunderstood as the Nation's Capital.

All of us no doubt have strong perceptions of Washington. It is, after all, a city that lives and breathes under an international microscope. The idealist in us views Washington as a great shrine to the American heritage, a beacon reinforcing the beliefs in freedom and democracy for all nations. We are taken aback by the inspiring landmarks, monuments and memorials, the broad avenues, sprawling parks, world-class museums and galleries, and stately embassies.

At the same time, the cynic in us may see Washington as a land of free-wheeling politicians, lethargic bureaucrats, opportunistic lobbyists and petty special-interest groups. We are dismayed by the sight of homeless people sleeping on steam grates within earshot of the White House and alarmed by grave crime statistics.

In the last decade, we all have come to view Washington in a dramatically new light. This once largely one-dimensional government town has blossomed into a premiere national and global business center. For it is in Washington where the rules are made for the complex game of international trade and commerce. The decision-makers are here. The information is here. The communication channels are here. Indeed, these factors may be why you are here or are soon to be headed here.

And you're not alone.

Metro Washington's population now stands at 3.9 million residents, making us the nation's sixth-largest market. If we were an independent country, we would have the world's 22nd-largest economy.

This rapid expansion of business activity and population has created a new dynamic. While Washington always has been known as a transient community, the spiralling growth of the private sector is creating an increasingly stable residential base.. In other words, more and more people are settling here, establishing roots, raising families and getting involved in their communities.

Despite nostalgic tendencies, it's impossible to think of Washington simply as the District of Columbia, the 63-square-mile stretch of federal land bounded by the Potomac River, Virginia and Maryland. "Washington" has come to mean much of Northern Virginia, including Fairfax, Arlington, Loudoun and Prince William counties as well as the City of Alexandria. "Washington" also is the fast-growing Suburban Maryland counties of Montgomery, Prince George's and Ann Arundel.

Some urban specialists now even claim "Washington" stretches as far west as the Eastern Panhandle of West Virginia, as far east as the Eastern Shore of Maryland, as far north as the Pennsylvania border and as far south as Spotsylvania County, Virginia — or about half way between the District of Columbia and Richmond!

For practical purposes, we will concentrate primarily on the District and the aforementioned core counties of Northern Virginia and Suburban Maryland. They encompass what we view as Metro Washington, D.C., or the Nation's Capital.

In the pages to follow, you will find what we hope is a fresh, insightful and comprehensive guide to our region. It is our goal that the Insiders' Guide® to Metro Washington proves to be an invaluable source for newcomers as it sketches the nuts and bolts of relocating, finding a home, getting around, choosing a school and the myriad other tasks that go with the newcomer territory.

In addition, longtime residents and frequent visitors to the region will find the book useful for its extensive coverage of the arts, attractions, hidden and historical treasures, dining, shopping and other facets that make up the "Washington" experience.

Acknowledgements

The Insiders' Guide® To Metro Washington could never have been written without the flood of assistance and encouragement we received along the way. We are especially indebted to Dave Clinger of the Public Relations Council, Inc. in Richmond for his vote of confidence and sage-like advice.

A healthy dose of gratitude is due our tireless editor, Beth Storie, who somehow managed not only to get this book out (as well as several others) but also found time to give birth to a son, Holden. Congratulations and many thanks, Beth.

Sally Scott Marietta of the Greater Washington Board of Trade went above and beyond the call of duty, supplying us with armloads of vital — and irreplaceable — information and never once asking when she was going to get it back.

Reams of helpful information also poured in from the Washington Convention and Visitors Association and the respective tourism, economic development and parks and recreation authorities in Northern Virginia and Suburban Maryland.

Stephen Fuller, director of George Washington University's Real Estate and Urban Development program, provided us with an insiders' perspective on Metro Washington's complex housing market.

Also on the front lines of support were Charlene Duryea and Pat Carbine of *Washington Flyer Magazine*; their encouragement didn't go unnoticed.

Josh Rubin and Todd Behrendt proved to be invaluable clutch players, especially down the home stretch when things got a little crazy. Appreciate it, guys.

Steve would like to extend special thanks to Gordon and Betty Beasley for their constant support and understanding, and Matthew and Deanna Soltis, whose passion for life and love of the written word have nurtured and inspired.

Brian would especially like to thank his parents, Joanne and Mac Cook, for their unyielding encouragement and support (thanks again to Dad for passing along those writing genes!), and to all his friends for their gracious understanding when the usual social commitments could not be met, but book deadlines had to be.

Finally, we'd like to dedicate the labors of this work.

TO

Stacy and Annie Soltis, my left and right arms, whose patience and tolerance never cease to amaze this proud husband and dad. Oh, yes, and to Dewey, my trusted black lab and nocturnal sounding board.

S.S.

AND TO

Joanne and Mac Cook, for just being the wonderful, generous and loving people that they are; to the late Beth Steude and the late Becky Vest, an aunt and a cousin whose artistic and literary talents were enviable and whose generous words of praise through the years were uplifting if undeserved; and to Sonny and Riggo, my two much-loved feline housemates who kept me company (and sometimes happily distracted) during many long days and nights at the computer.

B.T.C.

About The Authors

Stephen Soltis came to Washington during the height of the Iran-Contra hearings, although he admits he "knew absolutely nothing" about the affair. He began his writing career at a daily suburban newspapers in Dallas after receiving a journalism degree from the University of North Texas.

A contributor to a number of national and international newspapers and magazines, he began his Washington career at *John Naisbitt's Trend Letter*, a global business publication that monitors management, marketing and societal trends. Since 1990, he has worked as a business and regional travel editor for *Washington Flyer*, the nation's first in-airport magazine.

A newcomer or a seasoned Washington veteran, depending on who you talk to, he lives in the cozy but cosmopolitan Northern Virginia suburb of Centreville with his patient wife Stacy, also a writer, and baby daughter Annie Carol, a future scribe. He recently received a masters degree in liberal arts from Mary Washington College in Fredericksburg, Virginia.

The self-proclaimed "Californian by birth, Virginian by the grace of God" has developed a deep-seated love and respect for all things Washingtonian, including crazy commutes on the Beltway, Maryland-style crab cakes, D.C. breakfast briefings, sunrises over the Chesapeake and camping in the nearby Blue Ridge.

Brian T. Cook just can't seem to get enough of Washington, having lived in the area since coming into the world more than 30 years ago. (His attachment to the region might have something to do with the presence of his beloved Washington Redskins.) Born in the District of Columbia, he grew up in nearby Vienna, Virginia, and today makes his home in Alexandria. When he's not busy rooting for the Redskins, he earns a living as editor of *Washington Flyer*, the official magazine of Washington National and Dulles International airports. It was his knack for English studies and love of the written word — both proudly inherited from his talented father — that made him vulnerable to the journalism bug which indeed bit him during high school. After entering Radford (Va.) University, he headed straight for the student newspaper office where he logged enough time to become editor-in-chief. Journalism degree from Radford in hand, he began his professional career in 1983 as a beat reporter with the *Reston* (Va.) *Times*, part of a chain of weekly newspapers in Northern Virginia. He subsequently spent four years in another part of suburbia, Great Falls, Virginia, as an editor and reporter with the Gazette Newspaper Group, and in 1988 received 1st- and 3rd-place awards from the Virginia Press Association for Lifestyle and Sports Feature writing. He has managed the editorial operations at the *Flyer* since its inception in 1989.

Table of Contents

Directory of Maps

Inside
Metro Washington

Inside the District of Columbia

In a city where give and take is a way of life, where political concessions are arguably its raison d'etre, it shouldn't come as a surprise that Washington, D.C., was born out of compromise.

During the years immediately following the Revolutionary War, Northerners and Southerners raged fierce debates over where to put the permanent capital city. A deal finally was struck in 1790. It was a concession forged between two of the greatest political leaders in America — Alexander Hamilton, a New York Federalist and fiscal conservative, and Thomas Jefferson, a Virginia agrarian liberal. The terms were straightforward: Jefferson's Southerners agreed to support Hamilton's proposal that the federal government assume the war debts of the 13 original states if, and only if, Hamilton's Northerners would agree to move the capital city

Vital Stats for Washington, D.C. and Environs

🏛 Washington, District of Columbia, was named for George Washington and Christopher Columbus.

🏛 D.C. became the nation's capital on December 1, 1800.

🏛 The District originally included Arlington County and the City of Alexandria, but both jurisdictions were ceded back to Virginia in 1846.

🏛 District population is 607,000: Metro D.C. population is 3.92 million.

🏛 Location: Wedged between Maryland and Virginia along the Potomac River.

🏛 Terrain: Mostly flat but rolling to the north and west. Elevation: 30 feet; highest point in D.C. is Tenleytown, 410 feet.

🏛 Climate: Temperate. Average maximum temperature in the summer is 88 degrees, minimum is 70. Average maximum winter temperature is 43 degrees, minimum is 32. Average annual rainfall: 39 inches; snowfall: 16 inches. Clear days: 101; precipitation days: 111.

🏛 D.C. government consists of a mayor and a council; Mayor: Sharon Pratt Kelly. Election: November 1994. Many political leaders in D.C. are lobbying for statehood.

(which then was in Philadelphia) to the South, to a veritable wilderness along the banks of Potomac River.

The so-called Compromise of 1790 set into motion the creation of what would ultimately become one of the leading cities of the world, a capital that commands global influence but is also touched significantly by every state in the union and by virtually every nation on earth.

Fittingly, Washington grew up with America. It shared the wounds of the Battle of 1812 and the Civil War. It celebrated the arrival of the Second Industrial Revolution and the success of the great barons that transformed the nation's economic landscape. It teemed with energy and a sense of sacrifice during the World Wars I and II. It grew wary and then outright divided over the Korean and Vietnam wars. It became a tad cynical in the wake of Watergate, a bit pessimistic during the Carter years, and somewhat greedy during the Reagan/Bush tenure. And now, as the Clinton era begins to unfold, Washington — and the thousands of newcomers who have arrived with the new administration — just seems plain anxious.

Like the presidential administrations that come and go, Washington is in a perpetual state of transition. It's a markedly different creature today than it was just 10 years ago, let alone 50. But to really understand where the District and its surrounding suburbs are today and where they're headed in the 21st century, it's helpful to go back a few decades, to at least the beginning of the post-World War II years.

As the 1940s gave way to the '50s, Washington's population soared. In the nearby countryside of Maryland and Virginia, forests of oak and pastures of blue grass began yielding to subdivisions and shopping centers. Business was booming. The future looked bright. As the federal government continued to grow dramatically during the '60s and '70s, so did the physical size (and, some may say, the ego) of the region. Washington's leisurely Southern pace began to break down under an urban briskness more common to the great cities of the Northeast. The suburbs ballooned farther out. Traffic increased exponentially. The Redskins became a feared opponent, even in Dallas.

Perhaps no decade transformed Metro Washington more than the '80s, however. Big government began getting strong competition from big business for the hearts and minds of Metro D.C. residents. (In reality, they were both feeding off of each other like there was no tomorrow.) The once-solely government town was now home to 10 Fortune 500 companies, the 11th-highest concentration of such firms in the U.S.

The '80s also introduced a new dark side to Washington. Drug trafficking, primarily in crack cocaine, began paralyzing neighborhoods throughout the inner city. Consequently, by 1988, the District of Columbia had become the "Murder Capital of the World." Two years later, the city's mayor at the time was arrested for possessing and using the same drug that was devastating so much of his city. His actions,

Ford's Theatre is where President Lincoln was assassinated in 1865.

which were captured on film by police using a hidden camera, severely scarred, perhaps terminally, Washington's national and international image.

The late '80s saw a decline of sorts in Washington's perceived political standing. Pundits declared it was no longer all that significant, at least not in a newsworthy sense. After all, the new "hot spots" were Berlin and Moscow, where communism was being dismantled, and Bonn and Tokyo, where the new world economic order was being crafted.

Of course, the '90s so far have debunked a lot of the Washington-in-decline myth. Berlin and Bonn are fumbling over social and economic woes, ditto with Moscow, and Tokyo is still feeling the side effects of an overheated economy. No, for better or for worse, Washington remains the single most important political center in the world. We saw that quite clearly in Iraq and more recently in Somalia.

As a newcomer, you're probably already aware of the fact that if you ask 10 people their impressions of Washington, you're likely to get 10 different answers. Bureaucratic city. Ceremonial city. Beautiful. Dangerous. The list goes on. If there's one thing Washington doesn't evoke from people it's indifference.

And, quite frankly, that's what makes this city and this region so interesting to live and work in.

Inside Northern Virginia

The Monolith that is Fairfax County

One of the nation's most populous and economically vibrant

suburban areas, Fairfax County is the driving force of Northern Virginia and, for that matter, much of Metro Washington. With some 820,000 residents, it's larger than several states and is 35 percent larger than the District of Columbia. Moreover, nearly one in seven Virginians lives in the county.

Steeped in history — this is, after all, the home of George Washington and George Mason (father of the American Bill of Rights) — Fairfax County is defined by a sense of civic orderliness and a commitment to a high standard of living. When English explorer John Smith (the first European to set eyes on the present-day Washington, D.C., area) ventured into the county in 1608, he was taken aback by the amount of wildlife and natural resources that graced the area. Bounty he would later help claim for England.

If Smith were in Fairfax County today, he would also want to claim some of the finest public schools in the nation, a work force that is among the nation's most educated and affluent, and a public safety record that is the envy of most suburban jurisdictions.

In recent years, aggressive economic development efforts have yielded a number of corporate relocations and expansions into the county, including the landing of the world headquarters of Mobil (which moved from New York City) and General Dynamics (St. Louis). Along the Dulles corridor, a legion of global high-tech and aerospace firms including Airbus Industrie, Rolls-Royce and British Aerospace have set up shop, enticed by proximity to the power structure of Washington and the rapid expansion of air service at Washington Dulles International Airport.

Equally alluring to newcomers are the county's vast park lands, myriad shopping malls (including one of the nation's largest in Tysons Corner), upscale neighborhoods and abundance of historical and recreational attractions.

The flipside to the county's fortunes is an infrastructure that lags behind the pressures of a booming population. No matter what time of day, you can usually find a traffic jam somewhere in Fairfax County. Home costs here are among the highest in the metro area, with affordable housing in dangerously short supply.

While the local government is largely responsive to these and other problems, Fairfax, especially to the uninitiated, must seem like a congested and hectic place. That aside, the county continues to be one of the region's most popular relocation sites. So much so that by century's end, the county's population could eclipse 1 million people.

Urban Cousins: Arlington County and the City of Alexandria

Arlington County and the City of Alexandria are the alter egos to suburban Fairfax. Much more in tune with the urban pace of Washington (they were in fact part of the District of Columbia at one time), Arlington and Alexandria command

Photo: Carol Highsmith Photography

Pennsylvania Avenue is the main thoroughfare of the Nation's Capital.

a great influence on the nation's capital.

In Arlington, the self-proclaimed "Virginia Side of the Nation's Capital," you can find such Washington icons as the Pentagon, Arlington National Cemetery, the Iwo Jima Memorial and Washington National Airport. As in Alexandria, economic activity in Arlington historically has been tied to the federal government. In addition, both cities house hundreds of national and international associations, lobbyists and special-interest groups.

Over the years, Arlington has assumed somewhat of a multiple personality. Self-contained communities such as Ballston, Crystal City, Pentagon City and Rosslyn, each with its own central business district, seem to compete against each other with their glitzy shopping centers, towering apartments and condo units, and inexhaustible supply of hotels and restaurants. The northern edge of the county contains upscale single-family homes, many on large lots with views of the Potomac and the District beyond, while the extreme southern end borders on seedy, with crime being a major concern. All told, nearly 175,000 people now call Arlington home.

Mention the word "Alexandria" and most people immediately think of Old Town, the city's charming and super-chic historic district that's nestled along the banks of the Potomac. And for sure, history is a way of life in Old Town. Settled in 1749 by Scottish merchants, the city blossomed into one of the leading ports of Colonial America, driven in good measure by a lucrative trade in Virginia-grown tobacco. George Washington conducted a lot of business here and Robert E. Lee grew up in Alexandria before later moving to Arlington House, now part of Arlington National Cemetery. Alexandria's venerable Christ Church has been visited by almost every president. The Revolutionary and Civil wars played out on Alexandria's streets, many of which look much the same today as they did in the early 19th century.

Walk around and you'll find block after block of painstakingly restored Federal-style homes interspersed between curio shops, inns, bars, restaurants, parks, churches and museums. Old Town wasn't always so gentrified, though. From the 1940s through the early '70s, hard times set in and much of the area was blighted with boarded-up shops and dilapidated homes. When the revitalization bug kicked in 20 years ago, entire blocks of houses could have been purchased for a fraction of the present-day cost of a single home here. As you can imagine, many a fortune was made in Old Town.

Alexandria is more than Old Town, though. Most of its 111,000 residents live in diverse, outlying neighborhoods, like the West End, with its many high-rise apartments, and Beverly Hills, an established community of shaded streets and large homes.

Prince William County

With more than 40% of its working-age residents commuting

out of the county to their jobs, Prince William County is pretty much a vintage bedroom community. In the last decade the county's population surged from 145,000 to 216,000, a jump of nearly 50 percent, making it one of the nation's biggest gainers.

Newcomers arrive in masses here to live in nice, relatively affordable neighborhoods with improving schools and a surprisingly large amount of cultural and recreational diversions. Prince William is home to sprawling national and state parks, a minor-league baseball team, and several community theater groups and museums. Manassas National Battlefield, one of the most important sites of the Civil War, is here as is the FBI Academy, Quantico Marine Base and Quantico National Cemetery, which is actually larger than Arlington National Cemetery.

Prince William has been extremely proactive in efforts to lure more employers to the county. Some of the larger corporate names here are IBM and GTE, which have offices in Manassas, as well as Dynatech and Virginia Power, with locations in Woodbridge. Easily the biggest attraction in Prince William, though, is Potomac Mills, one of the biggest outlet centers in the U.S. and the single largest tourist attraction in Virginia.

The Virginia Exurbs: Loudoun, Fauquier and Stafford counties

The outlying Virginia counties of Loudoun, Fauquier and

Photo: Washington Convention and Visitors Association

The Washington Monument, a 555-foot obelisk, honors America's founding father.

Stafford are at a crossroads as Metro Washington continues to expand in its radial fashion. Not quite totally suburban but neither completely rural anymore, the counties are what may be termed "exurban."

In a way, we're hesitant to lump Loudoun County into this category, since it is easily one of the fastest-developing outer jurisdictions in either Virginia or Maryland. Nevertheless, with a population of 86,000, or almost one-tenth of Fairfax County's size, Loudoun is still mostly wide open spaces. And both natives and newcomers would like to keep it that way. That's why you'll see the heaviest concentration of commercial and residential activity kept to the eastern stretches of the county, from Leesburg to the Fairfax County line. Here is where you'll also find Washington Dulles International Airport (although a small piece sits in Fairfax), a major catalyst behind the county's growth. To the south and west of Leesburg, the county seat, is a sprawling patchwork of farms, orchards and horse pastures. It is here where Virginia's famed Hunt Country begins.

South of Loudoun is Fauquier County, with its equally beautiful horse farms and country estates. New housing developments in and around Warrenton, the county's largest community, are attracting more and more Metro D.C. commuters and even a growing number of retirees. Fauquier contains some of the most scenic land in the Old Dominion and consequently, like Loudoun, there is a considerable anti-growth movement here (or as local government officials like to put it, "controlled growth").

Stafford County is a bit of a different story, however. Located just south of Prince William, it is actively wooing new residents and businesses with affordable land prices, the promise of relaxed living and easy access to Interstate 95. Folks are responding to the offer. During the '80s, the county's population jumped to 61,000 and recorded one of the highest percentage gains in Virginia. Stafford enjoys a close proximity to both Washington and Richmond and is bordered immediately to the south by the City of Fredericksburg, one of the most charming and historic communities in the commonwealth.

Inside Suburban Maryland

The State of Montgomery County

Although die-hards on both sides of the Potomac would probably never admit it, Montgomery County is to Maryland what Fairfax County is to Virginia. In other words, it's an aberration of sorts. As Maryland's largest and most affluent county, one could argue (as do many lawmakers in Annapolis) that Montgomery is its own separate state. That might be overdoing it a bit, but this mega-county of 750,000 residents is far more aligned, socially and economically, with the District and Northern Virginia than with

Baltimore or any other part of the Free State.

At the same time, Montgomery in many ways is Metro D.C.'s most diverse jurisdiction. The southern half of the county is overwhelmingly white collar, ethnically diverse and decidedly urban. Here you will find the impressive campus of Bethesda's world-renowned National Institutes of Health, the posh homes and estates of Potomac and Chevy Chase, the retail meccas of White Flint and Montgomery malls, the international cuisine of Silver Spring, and the brainstorm of high-tech and communication firms that have sprouted along the I-270 Technology Corridor.

The northern portion of Montgomery, or the "Up-county" as locals emphatically refer to it, moves to a gentler, less-urban beat. Here, it's not unusual to see large dairy farms abutting business parks, or commuters coming to a halt at cattle crossings and creeping slowly behind tractors in the spring. A few years ago, a black bear cub emerged from the woods of Seneca Creek State Park and onto a heavily trafficked road. The cub returned to the wilds unscathed but not before setting off one of the region's more memorable traffic jams. While the Up-county is proud of its efforts to preserve open space (Montgomery has set aside more farmland than any other suburban county in the nation), the tenor of the place is rapidly changing. Subdivisions now extend to the north of Gaithersburg, transforming once-sleepy areas like Germantown and Damascus into bustling bedroom communities favored by young professionals seeking affordable housing. One-time apple orchards and wheat fields increasingly are sprouting single-family homes and shopping centers.

The Melting Pot of Prince George's County

About four years ago, one of the largest commercial developers in Metro Washington broke ground on an ambitious project that came with the promise of virtually reinventing the image of Prince George's County. The huge development was to be called Port America, a stately, multi-purpose business and residential community that would grace the banks of the Potomac River, within earshot of the busy Woodrow Wilson Bridge. But the national recession set in, legal hassles ensued, and today Port America remains largely a hole in the ground, a dream that has yet to materialize.

While it would be unfair to draw too much of a parallel between the fate of Port America and the county it may someday call home, it's probably safe to say that Prince George's has still not yet totally arrived, at least not to the same degree as its more prosperous neighbors to the north and west. A chronic crime problem in the urban areas closest to Washington, coupled with some highly publicized criminal cases involving local government officials, have taken their toll on the county's image. Don't count "P.G.," as it's commonly called, and its 730,000 residents out of the picture, however.

The positives far outweigh the negatives. P.G., among other things, has always been the region's — if not one of the nation's — most established multi-racial communities. Black, white, Hispanic and Asian Americans live side by side and largely in harmony in Prince George's. Affordable housing isn't a catchy buzzword; it's a reality. The county's public school system has made tremendous inroads in recent years, and its multilingual education program serves as a model for the nation.

P.G. is home to the University of Maryland, the state's flagship university with more than 30,000 students and a tradition-rich athletic program. The federal government's presence is also profound. Andrews Air Force Base (used by the president and many other government officials), the National Agricultural Research Center, NASA's Goddard Space Flight Center and the U.S. Census Bureau all call P.G. home.

If you're into spectator sports, chances are you'll be spending some time in Prince George's. USAir Arena (home of the Washington Bullets basketball team, the Washington Capitals hockey team and the Georgetown University Hoyas basketball team) in Landover, Rosecroft Raceway (harness racing) in Oxon Hill, and the Prince George's Equestrian Center in Upper Marlboro entertain tens of thousands of Washingtonians throughout the year.

A Sense of Place in Anne Arundel County

There's a certain feeling that pervades Anne Arundel County. Maybe it's due to Annapolis, the gorgeous Maryland capital city, with its Colonial waterfront homes, 221-year-old State House (the oldest in continuous use in the U.S.) and imposing campuses of St. John's College and the United States Naval Academy. Maybe it's the quiet coves and inlets of the Magothy, Severn and South rivers. Or maybe it's the broad, sweeping views of the Chesapeake Bay afforded from atop hilly pastures dotted with wooden tobacco barns and Thoroughbred horses. Whatever it springs from, it's hard not to feel an acute sense of place in Anne Arundel, a county as beautiful as its name suggests.

Not too many decades ago, Washingtonians built summer homes here and the county's economy was associated largely with the state government and the fishing and sailing trades of the Chesapeake Bay.

Today, Anne Arundel is grappling with a new identity. The past decade ushered in a surge in population, fueled in large part by the well-documented economic fortunes of nearby Baltimore and Washington. Many of the county's 430,000 residents now make the 25-plus mile commute into the District and other parts of Metro Washington — a development virtually unheard of 20 years ago. Rapid suburbanization has had its share of nasty side effects like increased crime and housing costs, but all told, Anne Arundel retains a remarkably high quality of life. Indeed, this is its main selling point. And while long-time residents vehemently resist the notion of being part of Metro D.C. or Baltimore, there is an accommodating attitude toward newcomers that are drawn to this enchanting, history-filled corner of Maryland.

Maryland's Exurbs: Frederick, Howard and Charles counties

As suburban Maryland continues to creep farther out into the countryside, it's markedly changing the face of at least three outlying communities — Frederick, Howard and Charles counties.

Bounded by Pennsylvania to the north and Montgomery County to the south, Frederick County offers the perks of a relaxed country setting (this is the land of covered bridges, vineyards and roadside produce stands) but with an undeniable air of big-city sophistication. In downtown Frederick, the county's principal city, one can nosh on blue-corn tortillas and other "exotic" fare before taking in a gallery opening or browsing through dozens of antique shops. From here, you're about equal distance from Gettysburg, Penn., and downtown Washington, although the commute north is much easier. Still, Frederick is less than an hour's drive from much of Metro D.C. and housing prices won't send your heart rate through the roof.

Howard County, lodged between Montgomery and Baltimore counties, is easily the most established Maryland exurb. Columbia, its largest community, is a planned city developed by the same folks responsible for revitalizing the inner harbors of Baltimore and Norfolk. In Columbia, one can find the comforts of suburbia and the home-investment security that goes with intense zoning regulations. Columbia may be a tad sterile for some, but its numerous tree-lined parkways and quiet residential areas give the impression of country living just 25 miles from either Washington or Baltimore. Merriweather Post Pavilion, one of the nation's first outdoor concert venues, brings top-name entertainment to the county throughout the warm-weather months.

South of Prince George's County, and just 20 miles from the District line, lies Charles County, a place where not too long ago tobacco and truck farming reigned supreme. An influx of new housing developments, especially along the Route 301 corridor between Waldorf and La Plata, and the opening of the county's first shopping mall are helping to create a bona fide suburban atmosphere. The challenge of the future for Charles County inevitably will be forging a balance between development and preservation of its long-cherished rural lifestyle.

(Note: For information about independent cities within the above mentioned counties, consult chapters on neighborhoods and government services.)

Photo: Richmond Newspapers

The Canal Walk in Georgetown.

Inside The Nation's Relocation Capital

Humorist Dave Barry once called Washington, D.C., the "home of the brave" on account of all the crazy political and social posturing that's supposedly part of everyday life in the Nation's Capital.

As a newcomer, you too may feel like a brave soul, a pioneer who has ventured into the lost frontier of an urban landscape that at times seems to move to its own unorthodox, even bewildering, beat. But no matter how you feel as a recent transplant, just remember one thing: You're not alone here.

In fact, you might as well can the pioneer bit. Each year, tens of thousands of newcomers come to call the Washington area home, a phenomenon that has been playing out steadily since the city's founding in 1792.

In just the last decade, the region's population has ballooned 21 percent, from 3.25 million to 3.9 million residents. On average, that's a net gain of nearly 1,200 new faces each week, or 170 people every day! So you see, you're hardly alone.

It's safe to say that Washington was built on the ideal of transience. A political concession of sorts, the capital city was fashioned from the swamps of the Potomac River—at nearly the midpoint along the eastern seaboard — in order to give equal access to the urbanity of the Northeast and the more agrarian cultures of the South and West.

While the nation's complexion has changed dramatically since, Metro Washington is still a region of newcomers, perhaps evidenced even more sharply in this, a year of a new presidential administration.

Don't mistake transience with indifference, however. The Washington area, as you'll soon discover, is a community that cares. Few metropolitan regions offer the sheer volume of social services and health, educational, cultural and recreational amenities as does Metro D.C.

Even the whole notion of Washington's so-called hyper-transient nature has come under fire in recent years. Mobility studies conducted by the U.S. Census Bureau now show that Washington is no more "transient" than Cleveland, Chicago, Houston or any other large American metropolitan area. What is happening, however, is that while newcomers continue to flood into the nation's capital, more and more are staying put once they're here. It's a testament, no doubt, to the area's favorable quality of life as well as its viability as an international business center.

To further debunk the transient myth, Allied Van Lines, the giant Chicago-based household moving company, claims that inbound moves account for nearly 72 percent of all of its relocation activity in the Washington area, the highest such figure in the country.

This stabilizing pattern of mobility, spearheaded by an influx of corporate relocations (the biggest being Mobil's 1987 move to Fairfax County, Va., which brought in 4,000 employees and their families), is reshaping the region's psyche. Washington is evolving into a "community" in the truest sense of the word. Newcomers are putting down roots here, raising families and getting involved in their communities.

Needless to say, not everyone who moves here is going to feel like a part of the community from day one. Relocating, after all, is one of the most stressful events that will occur in one's lifetime. It's right up there with death of a loved one, divorce and loss of a job.

In the next few pages of this chapter we will try to highlight some of the relocation services and consultants available in our region, and programs and organizations that can help alleviate much of the anxiety associated with a major move. We'll follow that up with a list of relocation tips that we've culled from numerous discussions with relocation experts.

Area Relocation Services

• Employee Relocation Council: A national organization headquartered in Washington that extends a clearinghouse of ideas, options and services for the relocating professional. Publishes a related monthly magazine, *Mobility*. Call (202) 857-0857.

• The Relocation Counseling Center: A one-stop-shopping type of service that provides a multi-media guide to Washington newcomers. Among other things, newcomers get a relocation packet containing maps, tables on area taxes and settlement costs, breakdowns of neighborhoods and commuter mileage guides. It's operated by Long & Foster, one of the region's largest real estate agencies, and they have three locations. Call (703) 359-1850.

• Quixsearch: A free, computerized service designed specifically for relocating to Metro Washington. Includes listings for single-family homes, apartments, townhomes and short-term housing. It's located in area Woodward & Lothrop department stores. Call (800) 486-EASY.

• *New Homes Guide*: Washington's leading directory of new housing. An invaluable tool for newcomers. Includes maps, useful buying tips, community directories complete with price-range guidelines, and helpful mortgage charts and real estate tables. Published monthly. For a free copy, call (301) 588-0681.

• Operation Match: A home-sharing service for the Metro area that is sponsored by the Metropolitan Washington Council of Governments. Matches singles, single parents with one child or small families to those who have space to rent in their homes. Ideal for those who

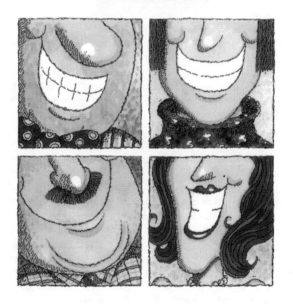

wish to "test the waters" before making a long-term buying or renting decision. Call (202) 962-3716 for a recorded list of locations.

• *Smart Moves . . . For the Relocating Family*: A workbook offering practical advice on personal, business and family issues involved in a major move. It's written by two authors who have experienced "major" transfers. Call Runzheimer International at (800) 942-9949.

Selected Relocation Consultants

Management Alternatives, Inc., 1420 K St. NW, Suite 500, Washington, D.C. 20005, (202) 842-4300

ORS Associates Inc., 1355 Beverly Rd., Suite 320, McLean, Va. 22101, (703) 821-1224

Relocation Professionals LTD, 1350 I St. NW, Suite 870, Washington, D.C. 20005, (202) 408-8112

Carol Paris Brown Inc. Relocation Specialists, 1980 Gallows Rd., Suite 210, Vienna, Va. 22182, (703) 556-8656

The Corporate Relocation Services Network, 933 N. Kenmore St., Arlington, Va. 22210, (703) 528-1535

Guardian Relocation Group, 6824 Elm St., McLean, Va. 22101, (703) 356-0330

Managing Corporate Mobility/ MCM Associates, 112 S. Pitt St., Alexandria, Va. 22314, (703) 549-0787

PHH Homequity Destination Services, 8500 Leesburg Pike, Vienna, Va. 22182, (703) 827-4137

Prudential Preferred Properties, 101 Lake Forest Blvd., Gaithersburg, Md. 20877, (301) 948-9750

Roberts & Lloyd Inc., 10300 Eaton Place, Fairfax, Va. 22182, (703) 448-5590

Valley Relocation Services, 9224 Gaither Rd., Gaithersburg, Md. 20877, (301) 258-7776

Ten Tips For The Recently Relocated

We're assuming, since you're reading this book, that you've already made the move to Metro Washington or are at least deep into the process. Therefore, we're not going to harp on the actual planning and moving stages. Instead, the following tips are intended for recent arrivals to the area.

1. Keep family involved in all discussions: Although the biggest decisions already have been made, it is imperative that even the youngest family members continue to feel like they are part of the relocating process, that they have a say as a newcomer.

2. Sever the moving ties — unpack: Sounds so simple, but you'd be amazed how many people are still living out of boxes six months, sometimes even a year, after their move. Stories abound of young Capitol Hill staffers who come to Washington, work for two years and leave

without ever unpacking all their belongings. The quicker the boxes are emptied, the sooner your new place actually feels like a home.

3. Move into the culture: Don't drop long-held interests or traditions just because you've moved. If the kids were in Cub Scouts in St. Louis, get them in Cub Scouts here. If you were a member of a garden club in Boston, join one here. If you were into whitewater rafting in Colorado, investigate the opportunities in these parts. At the same time, explore the myriad new possibilities indigenous to the Washington area.

4. Get out and see the city and the region: It's somewhat natural to hibernate after a move, given all the unpacking and home-maintenance logistics that loom. But try to budget time, even if it's just for an hour or two on weekends, to play tourist. You'll find that this will do wonders for reducing stress and at the same time will likely inspire a sense of pride in your new hometown.

5. Drop the guilt trip about uprooting the kids: Although relocating can be traumatic for youngsters and teens, they're much more malleable than we give them credit for being. For instance, it used to be that parents were advised to wait and move during the summer, so the kids wouldn't have to be uprooted during the school year. Now, conventional wisdom has it that kids do better if they move into a new area during the school year, even if

it's just a few weeks before the summer break. They'll have a chance to get a feel for their school, their teachers and classmates. When fall rolls around, many of the pent-up anxieties will have disappeared.

6. Stock up on regional and local maps: Coming to grips with Metro Washington's patchwork of roads and highways can be as trying as advanced calculus. Maps are required reading here and the best in the land can be had through the ADC map company of Alexandria, Va.

You'll see their maps in virtually all the area's bookshops as well as in most grocery and convenience stores. For more information, call ADC at (703) 750-0510.

8. Make trial runs to place of work, school, etc.: A little planning here will greatly improve your mental health. Make the trial commutes during normal rush hours or the approximate times you'll be going to these places. Experiment with different routes and always have a contingency plan. We can't stress enough the importance of following this step.

9. Subscribe immediately to a community newspaper and *The Washington Post* and/or *The Washington Times*, the region's two largest daily newspapers. We may be biased here, but there's still no better information access to Metro Washington than through the printed word. Tapping into the Fourth Estate is really the first step in becoming part of the community.

10. Get involved with state societies, alumni groups, or embassy cultural-outlet programs. Homesickness is a natural consequence of relocation. Fortunately, the Washington area has a plethora of remedies. Virtually every state has a state society — a social and networking group—based in Washington. (The Arkansas State Society is all the rage these days.) Chances are your alma mater also has an alumni chapter in Washington. If they don't, you may consider organizing one. For international newcomers, most all the embassies offer some type of cultural programming, whether it's through open houses, lecture series or social clubs. (See related information in the "International Washington" chapter.)

Inside What You Should Know About Crime and Cost of Living

Time for a reality check.

Metro Washington's attributes are many and of such an enviable quality as to make some otherwise wonderful regions seem perhaps inadequate by comparison: a rich history, abundant cultural and recreational opportunities, natural and created beauty, a lofty standard of living, a robust economy and a highly educated and skilled work force. But for all the other features that could be added to this list, there are two that many people (nonresidents especially) also associate with the area and would likely nominate to top a less-inviting list: crime and cost of living.

Don't worry. While it's neither pleasant nor easy to delve into such subject matter, our intent here is not to shock you. Instead, we want to offer a little straight talk about crime and cost of living and also take the opportunity to debunk some of the myths and dispel some of the unpleasant rumors you may have heard.

So repress that urge you may be feeling about now to thumb past this chapter and on to one with a more pleasant-sounding title.

Crime

Like any major metropolitan area, Washington has its ugly side. There's no way to sugar-coat it or try to explain it with fancy euphemisms. We have crime and, barring a major breakthrough in controlling human behavior, it's probably here to stay in some form or another. From the routine to the heinous, some sort of crime is an everyday reality somewhere in Metro Washington. And it's not easy to keep from being made aware of it, whether the messenger is the newspaper, the radio or the brutally graphic reality of color TV.

Now the good news. Metro Washington's social ills are really no different than those of any other metropolitan area of a similar size and character and the situation is not nearly as bad as some people would have you believe. In fact, Washington's violent crime rate ranks far below that of many cities including Atlanta, Dallas, Houston, Miami and New Orleans.

By using the same common sense and caution that would be appropriate in like environments, you can greatly reduce your chances of becoming a victim. Certainly there are no guarantees, and we'll leave it to the outstanding local police departments to recommend specific ways to protect yourself, your family and your property. But suffice it to say that people who unnecessarily place themselves at risk will all too often pay the price, as they would virtually anywhere. And unfortunately, the realities of modern American society have invaded even some of the most bucolic of places, so major cities are by no means alone in their suffering.

Indeed, Washington, DC, has one of the highest murder rates in the nation, but what conveyors of such information often fail to mention is that the great majority of these crimes are related to the drug trade or some other illegal activity and take place in parts of the city that are notoriously dangerous. As with any big city, you know to stay out of bad areas. Random acts of violence in usually quiet areas are of course a reality too, yet, by simply using everyday street smarts, locals and tourists alike should feel perfectly comfortable in Washington's main tourism and business sectors.

The nation's capital is one of the greenest, most photogenic and accessible cities in America and should, when practical, be explored on foot. So always use your head and stay alert, but don't let the criminal element succeed in scaring you away and keeping you from enjoying the many delights that Washington has to offer.

Washington's suburbs enjoy a far lower crime rate than their urban neighbors. By no means are we implying that the 'burbs don't have their share of problems, but in some cases the environment is remarkably sedate. Take Fairfax and Montgomery counties, for example, the two largest and wealthiest jurisdictions in the region and among the most affluent anywhere. Yet, with more than 750,000 residents each and significant portions of high-density development, they are among the safest for their size of any counties in the nation. Violent crime in particular is not at a level that might be expected for such huge jurisdictions that sit so close to an urban core.

We don't want to bombard you with numbers. However, a few might prove informative nonetheless. The Metropolitan Statistical Area of Washington, Maryland and Virginia, with a population of nearly four million, recorded a total of just over 234,000 "violent" and "property" crimes in 1991 (the most recent year for which figures were available as this was being written),

Insiders' Tip

Insiders...
Know that all local police departments are an excellent source of information on personal, home and business security and that many offer free home-security inspections.

according to the FBI's annual Uniform Crime Reports. That works out to about 5,898 crimes per 100,000 people. Interpret as you see fit.

On a national level, the news from the FBI was outwardly positive: For the first half of 1992 (again, the latest information that was available to us), "crime known to law enforcement," as the feds put it, decreased two percent in volume as compared to the same period in 1991, the first decrease in the Crime Index of selected offenses since 1984.

And to wrap up this numbers blitz, here's a brief look at the 1991 crime scene in Metro Washington's major jurisdictions, according to figures compiled by the FBI. We've listed the communities from lowest to highest in terms of their overall crime rate, listed the total number of "offenses known to the police" for 1991, and also given the jurisdiction's approximate population as determined by the 1990 census.

- Fairfax: 28,625 crimes; population 819,000.
- Prince William: 8,821 crimes; population 216,000.
- Anne Arundel: 17,728 crimes; population 427,000.
- Montgomery: 33,769 crimes; population 757,000.
- Prince George's: 45,568 crimes; population 729,000.
- Arlington: 11,872 crimes; population 171,000.
- Alexandria: 8,500 crimes; population 111,000.
- District of Columbia: 64,319 crimes; population 607,000.

Always bear this in mind when you ponder the crime factor in Metro Washington: The people patrolling the streets, conducting the investigations and making the arrests are among the finest police forces anywhere, whether the category is training, personnel, equipment, techniques, facilities or technology. And something to remember if you're feeling a bit jittery about the District: it's home to more law enforcement agencies than any city in the world, combining the local and assorted federal departments. Talk about a police presence.

But that doesn't mean citizens can't do their part. Neighborhood Watch, the popular and highly successful nationwide anti-crime program, is well-established in residential communities throughout Metro Washington. Some programs may use a different name, but they all share a common goal of preventing crime by using citizens to patrol neighborhoods and report suspicious persons and activities to the proper authorities. Call your local police department and/or your

Insiders' Tip

Insiders...
Know that Virginia has the death penalty and ranks fourth on the short list of states that have carried it out the most times since it became legal again in 1976.

community association for information on joining or forming a local Neighborhood Watch program.

The bottom line with crime: Be aware, be smart, but be realistic. And don't let fear get the best of you.

Cost of Living

Let's get to the point on this one. Metro Washington is an expensive place to live.

Whether it's housing, groceries, gasoline, clothing, whatever the product, sticker shock is an all-too-common affliction for people who move here from many of the more reasonably priced areas of the nation. But what you may lose in the pocketbook you gain in quality of life. We know, it sounds like a cruel paradox: How can you enjoy a higher quality of life when you have less money to spend? Well, quality isn't always measured by buying power. It's often things that people value even more such as outstanding school systems, police and fire protection and medical care, responsive and sound local government, and virtually unparalleled cultural and recreational amenities.

Local and state taxes? Some people may feel they're getting a tax cut compared with other high-tax areas of the nation, others may feel just the opposite. But again, the return on the tax dollar in Metro Washington is unusually high. (See previous paragraph for specifics.)

There's one particular tax that Virginia jurisdictions and the District of Columbia collect (Maryland does not) from residents that some people find downright appalling. We're not going to try to convince you to like it, mind you, but rather tip you off before you get that first bill. It's the Personal Property Tax. And yes, as the name indicates, it's personal. The tax is typically assessed on automobiles, trucks, motorcycles, motor homes, trailers, campers, boats, outboard motors, airplanes and business personal property. It is a major source of revenue for local government, ranking right up there with real estate, business and sales taxes.

The tax rate varies from area to area. In Fairfax County, for example, the 1992 rate was $4.57 per $100 of assessed value. But of course there are exceptions. Again using the Fairfax example, the following are taxed at a rate of only one cent per $100: antique automobiles, certified van pool vehicles, vehicles equipped for transporting disabled persons, and some vehicles owned by members of volunteer fire and

Insiders' Tip

Insiders...
Know that driving too fast is an especially risky action on the heavily traveled Capital Beltway and that Maryland police in particular are notorious for their tenacity in nabbing speeders. They also know that radar detectors are illegal in Virginia and the District of Columbia.

rescue squads.

Fortunately for taxpayers, as the property ages, its assessed value tends to decrease as does the amount that must be paid. But beware. Some pieces of property, such as certain "classic" cars (as defined by the jurisdiction), can become more valuable with time and thus be subject to an increasing amount of tax. So you may want to check into this further before buying that '67 Mustang you've had your eye on.

But housing prices tend to cause the biggest financial panic for newcomers. And it's easy to understand when you realize that a monthly mortgage payment on a nice three-bedroom house in, say, greater Dallas, is less than the monthly rent — yes, *rent* — for a high-rise, one-bedroom apartment in some of Metro Washington's close-in suburbs.

The average price of a new single-family home in the Washington area is approximately $205,000; resale properties average about $195,000. Those figures easily place us in the top 10 of all metro areas in the nation. And bear this in mind while you get up off the floor: at any one time there are probably a few hundred $1 million-plus properties for sale here.

With Metro Washington's housing market still emerging from the doldrums brought on by the national recession, experts say that the price range for new homes has narrowed somewhat, a sure sign that builders are finally beginning to cater to a wider audience. The trend now it seems is for new homes to be a bit smaller and less luxurious than before, but at the same time more affordable. Yet costs, of course, are still based largely on the three principle factors of location, location and location. So generally, the farther away from Washington you get, the farther your housing dollar goes. Unfortunately for many working people, that often means an arduous daily commute on traffic-clogged roads, a hardship that many people choose to endure in return for being able to realize the American dream of home ownership.

Metro Washington is inarguably an affluent area overall with a remarkably high standard of living. But don't think that's indicative of a lack of bargains, discounts and good deals. Savvy shoppers find out soon enough. There's much to offer here in terms of enjoying life, but just know that it may take a little more work to get the most from your hard-earned dollars.

Inside

The Beltway Scramble: Getting Around the Metro Area

Natives of Los Angeles or New York may chuckle at this notion, but getting around Metro Washington can be an intimidating experience for newcomers. Even some longtime residents will concede that negotiating the network of often-congested highways, byways and bridges that serves 3.9 million people isn't the most pleasant of tasks.

On an average day, the sheer volume of traffic can make an ordinary non-rush hour journey aggravating. Toss in an accident (even a fender-bender that's been moved to the road shoulder!), a few snowflakes, some rain, a holiday weekend or a Friday afternoon during the summer and you've got the makings of a potentially harrowing ordeal that can leave you longing for the solitude of the Australian Outback. In another respect, though, we have it made when you compare our highway systems with those in some other regions. With a few exceptions, Metro Washington's roads, as incredibly busy as they may be, are generally clean, well-maintained, well-patrolled by police (leadfooted drivers beware) and in some areas motorist-assistance vehicles, and downright scenic in places (we offer the George Washington Memorial Parkway and even the unusually "green" Capital Beltway as prime examples).

While the region has grown dramatically over the past 30 years or so in both population and the rate of commercial and residential development, the transportation infrastructure — due to a combination of political and bureaucratic stagnation, fiscal belt-tightening and an acute case of shortsightedness — has unfortunately not kept pace. As shopping malls, housing tracts and office parks sprouted on the landscape, road, mass-transit and other transportation improvements all too often became an afterthought. Subsequent changes in commuting patterns further challenged planners as more and more suburban residents began driving to a neighboring suburb to go to work instead of into the District. Now, some 60 percent of commuters are traveling from suburb to suburb, which has taken some of the strain off downtown but at the same time resulted in rush-hour problems never envisioned in the 1960s.

Still, some notable progress has been made in improving Metro Washington's transportation infrastructure: major stretches of roadway have been widened; once-nightmarish intersections have been transformed into the safer and more efficient under/over ("separated grade" in engineering parlance) configuration; the designation of HOV (High-Occupancy Vehicle only) lanes has encouraged carpooling; several new roads (Dulles Toll Road, Franconia-Springfield Parkway, Fairfax County Parkway) have been completed or begun; the Metrorail system has continued to expand toward its ultimate length of 103 miles; and interjurisdictional communication and cooperation have been improved in areas such as accident response and snow removal.

Another significant advancement was the launching of the Virginia Department of Transportation's (VDOT) high-tech Traffic Management System, or TMS, a computerized highway surveillance and control program that oversees 30 miles of Interstates 66, 395 and 495, helping detect and clear accidents and disabled vehicles and keep traffic flowing smoothly. This is one instance where it's nice to know Big Brother is watching. Except with TMS, it involves using closed-circuit cameras to keep an eye on traffic conditions, traffic counters embedded in the pavement to convey important information, ramp meters to regulate the number of vehicles entering the roadway, and variable message signs that alert motorists to accidents and other traffic-related events ahead. The amazing system is monitored by VDOT personnel at a control center in Arlington from there they communicate not only with the public, but also the Safety Service Patrols, state police and area traffic reporters. By 1996, VDOT plans to extend TMS coverage 17 additional miles on I-66 from Nutley Street (at the Vienna Metrorail station) to Gainesville and 19 more miles on I-95 between Springfield and Quantico Creek.

In Maryland, a similar traffic-management system called CHART (Chesapeake Highways Advisories Routing Traffic) also uses state-of-the-art technology (message signs, cameras and detection devices as well as patrol vehicles) to provide quick response to accidents and other road emergencies and help reduce congestion. When fully completed by the late 1990s, the statewide program will cover some 400 miles of highway and another 400 miles of major arterial roadways in the state's eight heavily traveled traffic corridors. The system currently covers roadways primarily in the Metro Washington and Baltimore areas.

Major transportation-improvement proposals for the future, including constructing bypasses to the Capital Beltway, widening or perhaps even double-decking bridges, and expanding rail systems and other means of getting people out of their single-passenger vehicles, have been hotly debated at

Photo: Washington Metropolitan Area Transit Authority

The Metrorail, the metropolitan area's subway system, is the most convenient way to get around the city.

times, but nevertheless are cause for optimism.

In the meantime, you've got to deal with the situation at hand, and that's where this chapter comes in. There's no substitute for experience, and that's particularly true when it comes to driving in and trying to find your way around unfamiliar territory. We hope that the information that follows will give you a feel for the region's overall transportation system and perhaps make those initial journeys somewhat less intimidating.

A couple of suggestions first, though. Before tackling Metro Washington from behind the wheel or from any other perspective, we strongly suggest that you get a good map and keep it close at hand. We can't recommend highly enough the book-style variety produced locally by Alexandria Drafting Company, or ADC, "The Map People," as they proudly bill themselves. And they truly are. ADC's detailed, easy-to-use and frequently updated maps of cities, counties and the region are an invaluable resource as well as a great provider of peace of mind. They're available at area convenience stores, drugstores, supermarkets and bookstores. For more information, call ADC at (703) 750-0510.

What if even a map doesn't help you in certain situations? Don't hesitate to ask someone who should know. Despite any negative things you may have heard about the character of the local populace, most Washingtonians are more than happy to lend a hand when they're able. And that includes giving directions.

And always keep an ear tuned to the radio for the latest traffic information, both before you leave and while in the car. All it takes is one nightmarish backup that could have been easily avoided and you'll soon become a devout listener. Most local stations broadcast traffic reports frequently during the morning and evening rush hour, and a few offer updates throughout the day. Some of the most comprehensive coverage is on WMAL (AM-630), WTOP (AM 1500) and WLTT ("W-LITE," 94.7 FM).

Now, fasten your seatbelt and let's hit the road.

Conquering the Beltway and Other Major Arteries

Ah, the Capital Beltway (Interstate 495), that 66-mile, 55-interchange ring of asphalt so many people love to hate. Although originally envisioned as a bypass to Metro Washington, it became instead the area's "Main Street," at once a transportation lifeline and the bane of our existence. We curse it for legendary traffic jams, ill-conceived interchanges and entrance/exit ramps (though many of these have been dramatically improved) and that confusing "Inner Loop" and "Outer Loop" business (we'll clear this up shortly). But we also can't imagine living here without the Beltway. Circumnavigating the District of Columbia like a giant lasso with numerous appendages, it slices through Fairfax County and the City of Alexandria in Northern Virginia, and Prince George's and Montgomery counties in Maryland. It crosses the Potomac River twice, via the American Legion (Cabin John) Bridge and the Woodrow Wilson Bridge, and offers access to numerous thoroughfares including I-66, I-95, I-270, I-295, I-395, the Dulles Toll Road and the parallel Airport Access Road, Routes 1, 29, 50, 123 and 236, the George Washington Memorial and Baltimore Washington parkways, and numerous secondary roads. No other highway in the area carries as much clout or can get us to so many places in so short a time.

And while we're mentioning the two bridges, we'd better point out that they're the site of some of the worst Beltway backups. Maryland and Virginia finally wised up and began stationing tow trucks at either end of each span during the morning and evening rush hour so disabled vehicles could be removed quickly. The American Legion Bridge has seen great improvement through widening, but the narrower Wilson, a drawbridge with one less lane than the Beltway itself, remains a prime bottleneck and major source of irritation. Drawbridge openings (always off-peak hours) are much more closely regulated than in years past, but we needn't tell you the ferocity of the tie-ups that can still result. And another thing to keep in mind about bridges. Remember, coming from Virginia, you MUST cross a bridge to get into the District. (If you manage to accomplish this otherwise, let us know and we'll put together an amazing magic act.) Your five choices, starting north and working our way south, are Chain Bridge, which links the McLean/Arlington area with Canal Road and upper northwest; Key Bridge, named for the author of our "Star-Spangled Banner," Francis Scott Key, joins Rosslyn and Georgetown; Roosevelt Bridge, in the shadows of Rosslyn, is where I-66 runs into Constitution Avenue NW; stately Memorial Bridge, perhaps the most picturesque of them all, runs from Arlington National Cemetery over to the Lincoln Memorial at Rock Creek Parkway; and the 14th Street Bridge, where I-395 winds past the Pentagon and crosses the Potomac adjacent to the Tidal Basin and the Jefferson Memorial.

Back to our discussion of the Beltway, the road opened in stages beginning in 1957, with the federal government picking up 90 percent of the $189 million tab for construction costs; the four- and six-lane version that was completed in 1964 was subsequently widened to eight

Insiders...

Avoid getting stuck in Beltway tie-ups by plotting out alternative routes to take. Even if it involves driving more miles than normal, who wouldn't rather go a bit out of their way as long as they can keep moving and avoid the nightmare of sitting in bumper-to-bumper traffic?

Insiders' Tip

lanes. No matter the number of lanes, at times it never seems to be enough. One workday soon after opening, the Beltway carried about 48,000 cars; today, the daily figure tops 600,000, with vehicles logging some 8 million miles in any 24-hour period. The experts tell us that if we think Beltway traffic is bad today, it's only going to get worse unless more people start carpooling (Metro Washington already boasts the nation's highest proportion of ridesharing) and using mass transit, and an outer bypass is built to take non-local traffic off the road. The consequences of inaction: estimates say that by the turn of the century, the average Beltway commuter will spend almost two more hours in the car each week, and congestion will cost users up to $180 million annually in time, gas consumption and accident losses. Sobering thoughts indeed.

Virginia and Maryland state police have jurisdiction over the Beltway and maintain a very high profile in both marked and unmarked cruisers. Flashing lights that are less likely to send your blood pressure skyward are yellow and found atop special pickup trucks and four-wheel-drive vehicles that come to the aid of stranded motorists. The free state-run service aims to prevent ordinary breakdowns from becoming extraordinary backups.

Tractor-trailers account for only about 6 percent of the traffic on Beltway, yet studies have show that they're involved in nearly 20 percent of the accidents. Truckers, of course, are not always at fault. In fact, they're among the safest drivers on the road since drive is what they do for a living. As a precaution, the big rigs are restricted to the far right lanes of the Beltway, and those vehicles that transport hazardous materials (gasoline, chemicals, etc.) are encouraged, whenever possible, to do so in the wee hours of the night and early morning when traffic is light and the risks of a mishap are greatly reduced.

Sooner or later you'll hear and/or see the terms Outer Loop and Inner Loop, used to describe the two portions of road that comprise the Beltway. Discerning which is which is actually pretty simple. Using the District of Columbia as a reference point (better yet, refer to your map), the Inner Loop is physically closer to the city, and traffic travels in a clockwise motion. The Outer Loop, naturally, sits a bit farther out and traffic moves counterclockwise. Easy, right? Well, you don't have to think about it as much as you used to. To help alleviate some of the confusion, Virginia and Maryland state highway departments several years ago posted signs that state exactly which loop of the Capital Beltway you're traveling.

If you drive to work, keep in mind that the morning "rush hour" in Metro Washington can begin as early as 5 or 5:30 along the some stretches of the Beltway and other heavily traveled routes such as I-66, I-95, I-270 and I-395 and as early as 3:30 in the afternoon. Factor in even longer crunch times during inclement weather, Fridays in general and holiday weekends in particular.

If you can get a couple of people to ride with you, the HOV

Photo: Washington Metropolitan Area Transit Authority

The Metro Center Station.

(High-Occupancy Vehicle) lanes can often — but don't always — get you to home or work faster. And don't take HOV restrictions lightly, because the police don't. Scofflaws face a healthy fine plus several "points" on their license for a moving violation. And forget about putting a mannequin or some other human substitute in your car to get around the HOV requirements. The police have seen it all and don't take kindly to motorists trying to pull one over on them. Here's a summary of the local HOV scene.

• I-395/I-95: HOV-3 northbound, 6-9 AM, southbound, 3:30-6 PM; from the 14th Street Bridge to Woodbridge (Route 1). Currently 17 miles of HOV; barrier-separated lanes along the 10 miles from the 14th Street Bridge to Springfield, and "diamond" (so-called due to the large diamond-shaped pavement markings) lanes for the seven miles from Springfield to Woodbridge. By 1996, a total of 30 miles will exist along I-395/I-95; 19 miles of barrier-separated lanes are being added between Springfield and Quantico Creek.

• I-66: HOV-3 eastbound, 5:30-9:30 AM; westbound, 3-7 PM; from the Roosevelt Bridge to the Capital Beltway. Currently 10 miles; eight more are under construction and 11.5 additional are planned; a total of 30 by 1996. Presently, the entire roadway (two lanes in each direction) is HOV from the Roosevelt Bridge to the Beltway; diamond lanes will ultimately run from the Beltway out to Route 234 in Manassas, with the opening taking place in stages.

• Dulles Toll Road (Route 267), the region's only toll road: HOV-3 restrictions on this popular thoroughfare were implemented in September 1992, then — following strong public opposition — rescinded a short time later. As this book was going to press, plans were to try to implement HOV again at some point; proposed restrictions are for HOV-3 eastbound, 6:30-9 AM, westbound, 4-6:30 PM; the 12 miles' worth of diamond (left) lanes would run from Route 28 to Route 123.

The tolls still very much exist, however. The popularity of the Dulles Toll Road quickly exceeded all expectations almost immediately after opening in 1984. And despite today's heavy traffic burden, commuters in the corridor, primarily from western Loudoun County and the Fairfax County communities of Herndon, Reston, Tysons Corner, Vienna and McLean, are much better off with the road than they were before it was built. The Toll Road runs parallel to the airport-only Dulles Access Road and feeds into I-66. Beginning in the west and working east, the entrances and exits are located at Route 28/Sully RoadParkway, Wiehle Avenue, Hunter Mill Road, Route 7, Spring Hill Road and the Capital Beltway. An extension of the road from Dulles to Leesburg is underway and completion is scheduled for 1996. The main toll plaza, located between Spring Hill Road and Route 7, is staffed 24 hours a day. Booths at other entrances and exits are attended 16 hours a day (5:30 AM to 9:30 PM Monday-Friday); outside of these hours, automatic toll machines operate and motorists need exact change. The toll is 50 cents at the main plaza except for Spring Hill Road commuters who ride through a designated lane and pay 25 cents. The fee is 25 cents at all other gates except Route 28 where it costs 35 cents. For more information on using the Dulles Toll Road, call the administration building at (703) 734-1666.

For any questions relating to highway travel in the region, contact the public affairs offices of the Virginia Department of Transportation (703-934-7350), the Maryland State Highway Administration (410-333-1111), or the District's Department of Public Works (202-939-8000).

For information on carpool and vanpool opportunities, call your county or city office of transportation, or the regional Ride Finders program at (202) 783-7665 (POOL).

So now that you know a little bit about Washington's Main Street and other major thoroughfares, there are a number of things to keep in mind to help lessen the aggravation and enhance the safety for you and other Beltway motorists. The following tips were gleaned from "The Capital Beltway Owner's Manual," produced by the DO IT (Develop Outer Interstate Thruways) Coalition.

• Leave Earlier and Know Where You're Going—Allow plenty of time (it usually takes longer than you think it will) to get to your destination. Delays are common and sometimes impossible to avoid, and speeding is not only illegal, but can be dangerous as well as costly. Know your exit by name and preferably also by number, and watch for signs as you approach it. Rapid lane changes by surprised drivers often cause accidents.

• Gas Up Before You Go — Traffic jams can gobble up fuel and leave you stranded, an embarrassing as well as potentially hazardous predicament on the Beltway. Among the most notorious Beltway traffic "hot spots" are the interchanges at I-270, I-395/I-95 (long ago dubbed the "Mixing Bowl"), the stretch between Braddock Road and Route 7, the aforementioned American Legion and Wilson bridges, Wisconsin/Connecticut/Georgia avenues, and I-95/U.S 1/Baltimore-Washington Parkway.

• Try Driving Courteously — Not only will you score a few points with fellow citizens, you'll also give police one less reason to pull you over. Use turn signals, don't tailgate, stay to the right lanes unless passing, don't brake when simply letting up on the accelerator will safely slow you down for a brief moment (this does wonders for preventing chain-reaction collisions caused by panicked drivers), stay in line on exit ramps (few things tick off a driver as much as people sneaking by — illegally — on the shoulder), and give trucks plenty of room. Just as they take longer to get up to speed from a standing start, so too do they need more time to stop.

• Learn Alternate Routes — When the Beltway is backed up and you can avoid it, do so. Forget about a route being longer in miles if it will keep you moving. Anything's better than sitting in gridlock. You'll get where you're going and arrive in a much better frame of mind than if you have to endure traffic hell.

• Don't Rubberneck! — Incredibly, people slowing down to look at an accident scene (often on the opposite loop) can cause more of a delay than the mishap itself.

And also, remember that the same road can have several different names. So don't be confused. Route 7, for example, is called Leesburg Pike in the Tysons Corner area, Broad Street in the City of Falls Church, and King Street in Alexandria. Route 236 is known as Duke Street in the Alexandria area, Little River Turnpike in Annandale, and Main Street in Fairfax City. Route 123 is Ox Road in southern Fairfax County, Chain Bridge Road in the Fairfax City area and again in Tysons Corner, Maple Avenue in the Vienna town limits, and Dolley Madison Boulevard in McLean.

A D.C. Driving Primer

While Washington is indeed one of the most beautiful and best-planned cities anywhere — with its broad avenues, abundant parks and open space and visually pleasing low-profile character — that doesn't mean it's a pleasure to drive in, especially for newcomers.

Insiders...

Know they can avoid traffic hassles at the airport — especially around the frenzied Thanksgiving and Christmas holidays — by dropping passengers off in the satellite parking lots, far from the madding crowds. From there, travelers can hop a free shuttle bus to the terminal.

Insiders' Tip

Confusing one-way streets, traffic circles, a critical shortage of on-street parking spaces and other nuances can make for a confusing time for the uninitiated. Finding a place to park can be both costly and aggravating, and police don't hesitate for a moment to hand out tickets. Ignore those pieces of paying paper and you may find your car towed or perhaps wearing a "boot," a heavy steel clamp attached to one of the front wheels that prevents the car from being driven. All of this underscores the beauty of walking and using public transportation such as Metrorail, Metrobus or one of the 9,000 or so taxicabs. But fortunately, the city's comparatively small size and its grid system of street layout are helpful to newcomers. With a good map, some patience and a bit of practice, Washington is actually not that tough to navigate. And don't be bashful about asking directions. You'll learn that natives and other longtime residents of the Metro area do the very same thing.

When pondering Washington's street system, remember that the U.S. Capitol is the geographic center. The city is divided into four sections — Northwest, Northeast, Southwest and Southeast — with the dividing lines being North Capitol Street, South Capitol Street, East Capitol Street and the National Mall, radiating like spokes of a wheel from the Capitol building. The NW, NE, SW and SE used in addresses are very important. An address on M Street NW could also be found on M Street SE, so bear this in mind when mailing something, much less trying to find a particular place.

Streets that run north-south (14th, 15th, 18th, etc.) bear numbers, while those going east-west are identified with letters (H, R, M and so forth) in alphabetical order. There are no J, X, Y or Z streets. Streets with state names (Pennsylvania, Connecticut) are all diagonals. Circles and squares occur at the intersections of diagonal avenues and numbered and lettered streets.

If you do opt for a taxi, you'll likely be pleasantly surprised by the cost. The fares are based on a zone pricing system instead of the traditional meters that are still used in Virginia, Maryland and most other locales.

The Metro System and Other Ground Transportation Networks

Metro Washington is blessed with a first-rate rail and bus system, Metro, short for the Washington Metropolitan Area Transit Authority (WMATA). The award-winning Metrorail is clean, safe, efficient, inexpensive and attractive to boot. "America's Subway" first opened in 1976 and has grown to link a large portion of the National Capital Area. It's especially loved by commuters and tourists as it offers superb access to the major business district as well as such popular destinations as the Pentagon, the National Zoo, RFK Stadium, Washington National Airport and Arlington National Cemetery.

Members of the Metro Board include representatives from the District, Maryland and Virginia. Area jurisdictions served by Metro pay a subsidy to the system, and residents pay a few cents extra per gallon of gasoline to help fund Metro's operation, maintenance and expansion. But believe us, it's money well spent.

Each of Metrorail's five lines — Orange, Red, Green, Blue and Yellow — passes through the District at some point. The Green Line (the shortest, with most of it still to be built), never leaves the District, but it will, once fully extended into Prince George's County. The Orange Line stretches from Vienna, Va., to New Carrollton, Md.; the Red, from Shady Grove, Md. to Wheaton, Md., but that will change to Glenmont when the line is completed; the Green, from U Street-Cardozo to Anacostia (upon completion, it will begin and end in Maryland, linking Greenbelt with Branch Avenue); the Blue runs from Addison Road in the District to Van Dorn Street in Alexandria (until the Franconia-Springfield station is completed); and the Yellow goes from the Huntington area of Fairfax County to Mt. Vernon Square-UDC in the District. Once fully developed, Metrorial will boast 87 stations along 103 miles of track.

Metrorail operates from 5:30 AM to midnight, Monday through Friday, 8 AM to midnight Saturday, and 10 AM to midnight Sunday. The last trains leave some stations prior to midnight; refer to signs in stations for details. Trains as well as buses run on a reduced schedule on certain holidays.

Large brown pylons topped with Metro's distinctive "M" logo mark all station entrances. There's also very good signage along roads for those stations accessible by auto. Instead of cash or tokens, Metro operates on a farecard system (all passengers must have a farecard to enter and exit), which may seem a bit confusing at first but it's easily mastered with just a few minutes of study. Farecard machines, located in every station, accept nickels, dimes, quarters and $1 and $5 bills while some machines also accept $10 and $20 bills. Fares are based on the time of day and distance traveled, with the base price being $1. Peak (rush) hours of operation are 5:30 to 9:30 AM and 3 to 7 PM, Monday through Friday. Off-peak is all other times and on federal holidays. While the system is far busier during the peak periods, the trains also run more often. But the wait any time of day is rarely longer than about 15 minutes. To avoid having to run to an "Addfare" machine to get into or out of a station, it's a

Insiders...

Heading out during the morning or evening rush hours always keep an ear tuned to the traffic reports broadcast on many area radio stations. The valuable eye-in-the-sky information can mean the difference between a pleasant drive and a jaw-clenching, time-consuming delay.

Insiders' Tip

good idea to purchase a little more fare than you think you might need for a roundtrip.

Metrobus goes everywhere the rail system does, and then some, reaching far into suburban areas as well as the inner city. Routes and schedules for the 1,600-bus fleet are timed with rail routes and schedules to provide a comprehensive transportation system. Individual bus routes are detailed on brochures available at Metrorail stations and in various town, city and county transportation offices. Exact change is required for bus fare; drivers do not carry cash and cannot make change.

For general Metrorail and Metrobus information and timetables, call Metro at (202) 637-7000; TDD (202) 638-3780. Operators are on duty daily from 6 AM to 11:30 PM. Transit Police can be reached at (202) 962-2121; Lost and Found, (202) 962-1195.

In addition to Metrobus, several other smaller local bus systems are in operation. One of the largest, the Fairfax Connector system, serves the southeastern area of the county with 14 routes connecting the Huntington and Pentagon Metrorail stations. Route and schedule information, (703) 339-7200; TDD, (703) 339-1608. Timetables are available at food stores, post offices, libraries, drugstores, governmental centers and the Huntington and Pentagon Metrorail stations.

Other local bus lines include Alexandria's DASH system (703-370-3274), Fairfax City's CUE (703-385-7920), Montgomery County's Ride-On (301-217-7433 or 301-217-6434), and two in Prince George's County, Call-A-Bus (800-899-2287) and The Bus (800-486-9797).

Washington's Greyhound station is at 1st and L streets NE; there are numerous stations in the suburbs as well. (301) 565-2662.

Beyond Metrorail, the region is served by several other passenger trains.

AMTRAK: Metroliner Express weekday service runs between Washington's Union Station (Massachusetts Avenue and N. Capitol Street NE) and Baltimore. Regular service is offered from Union Station to Philadelphia, New York City, Boston, Richmond and Atlanta. (800) 872-7245 (RAIL); TDD (800) 523-6590.

MARC: Maryland Rail Commuter service operates Monday through Friday between Washington and Baltimore (including Oriole Park at Camden Yards for you baseball and Inner Harbor fans) as well as Martinsburg, W.Va. (800) 325-7245 (RAIL); TDD (301) 850-5312.

Virginia Railway Express (VRE): The region's newest commuter rail service opened in 1992. It's a unique transportation partnership and one the area will hopefully see more of as a way to offer convenient, economical alternatives to car commuting. VRE is a joint effort of the Northern Virginia Transportation Commission, the Potomac and Rappahannock Transportation Commission, and the citizens of the commonwealth. VRE operates two lines: the Manassas Line, between Manassas and Washington, and the Fredericksburg Line, from Fredericksburg to the District.

Manassas Line stations are located in Manassas (2), Manassas Park, Burke (2), Springfield, Alexandria, Arlington and the District (2). Fredericksburg Line stations are in Fredericksburg, Falmouth, Stafford, Quantico, Woodbridge (2), Alexandria, Arlington and the District (2). As with Metro, VRE has easy-to-spot roadside directional signs to help guide travelers to the stations, four of which are just a short walk from easy connections with Metrorail at L'Enfant Plaza and Union Station in the District, and at Crystal City and King Street (Alexandria) in Northern Virginia. For convenience, single-ride, 10-trip and monthly-trip tickets are available. For general information about VRE, call (703) 497-7777; for details on local transit connections in particular areas, call: in Fairfax and Arlington counties, the City of Alexandria and Washington, (703) 271-4287, TDD (800) 833-3232; in Prince William County, and the cities of Manassas and Manassas Park, (703) 490-4422, TDD (800) 828-1120; and in Stafford and Spotsylvania counties and the City of Fredericksburg, (703) 373-2890, TDD (800) 828-1120.

Airport Options: National, Dulles and BWI

When traveling requires you to leave the ground — something you'll likely relish after enduring a few Beltway traffic nightmares — you'll be glad that Metro Washington is served by not one, but three major airports: Washington National and its sister facility, Washington Dulles International, and Baltimore-Washington International, better known as just BWI. This enviable situation that few regions can match offers area travelers some real advantages in terms of choices in scheduling, carrier selection and, to a lesser degree, airfares. Combined, the three airports handle about 35 million passengers annually and are served by nearly 50 scheduled airlines. But people aren't the only things being flown in and out of here. The region is a major cargo hub as well, with some 534 million pounds of air freight being transported annually.

While BWI is state-owned and operated, National and Dulles are managed by the Metropolitan Washington Airports Authority (MWAA), a quasi-public agency created by an act of Congress in 1987. Before the dawn of MWAA, whose Board of Directors features equal representation by Virginia, Maryland and Dis-

Insiders...

Know that Union Station is more than just a place to catch a train. The historic and beautifully restored building offers dozens of options for shopping and dining. You can even catch a movie.

Insiders' Tip

trict residents, National and Dulles were the only two civil airports in the nation run by the federal government. Fortunately for the traveling public and the airline industry, Uncle Sam decided to get out of the airport business. Contrary to public perception, MWAA is self-financed; no state or local tax revenues are used to fund airport activities or construction. Oh yes, and don't forget, National and Dulles are very much located in Northern Virginia, despite the announcement you may hear on the plane flying in, or the occasional Washington, D.C., address or phone number you may see. The latter are just vestiges of the days of federal control.

If you want a fourth air-travel option, keep in mind that Metro Washington is only about 100 miles from Richmond International Airport (804-226-3000), located just east of the commonwealth's gracious capital city. We won't delve into any details other than to say this. It's a safe bet that many Metro Washington residents overlook Richmond when it could be the solution to their dilemma. You will find a comparatively limited selection of carriers and destinations served, but the manageable and convenient airport is one to consider if you're having trouble booking a flight out of National, Dulles or BWI that meets your needs. We recall the story of a friend who was trying to get to New Orleans for Mardi Gras and couldn't find so much as an empty seat on a southbound train from Washington, much less anything aboard a regularly scheduled airline. So, as he happily discovered, his best alternative was driving to Richmond and hopping a flight to Charlotte, N.C., and from there, making a connection to the Big Easy. It certainly wasn't as convenient as a nonstop from here, but he says it sure beat missing out on the world's biggest block party.

Returning to our own backyard, Washington National is the region's close-in, short-haul airport, handling domestic traffic only; nonstop flights from National are limited to 1,250 miles. Located in Arlington County just off the George Washington Memorial Parkway and abutting the Potomac River (from which much of National's land mass was claimed), there's probably no other airport in the nation, perhaps even the world, that is so close to the heart of a major city. Under normal traffic conditions, it's about a 10-minute ride from the airport, up the parkway, and over the 14th Street Bridge and into the District. It's only about another five minutes to Capitol Hill. Although much-maligned for being crowded, cramped and hard to negotiate, 52-year-old National is unbeatable for convenience. Just ask a member of Congress or anyone who works or lives in nearby Crystal City, Rosslyn or Alexandria. National is served by all the major domestic carriers and their commuter subsidiaries, as well as the popular USAir and Delta shuttles that ferry passengers hourly between Washington, New York and Boston.

It's true about what you may have heard: getting around National can be an exercise in frustration, particularly for first-timers. The limited parking, maze-like road system

Photo: Metropolitan Washington Airports Authority

Dulles International Airport, located 26 miles from downtown, offers domestic, commuter and international flights.

and overall compact conditions can fluster even the most seasoned traveler. But things are getting better. Much better. The Metropolitan Washington Airports Authority is in the midst of a nearly $2 billion modernization and improvement program for both facilities. Cornerstones of the National refurbishment include the construction of a new main terminal designed by Cesar Pelli (the present terminal, with its graceful Colonial facade reminiscent of Mount Vernon, will be renovated and see far less activity), three parking garages (one has already opened), and a completely redesigned road network that will offer far better access for pedestrians, motorists and Metrorail riders alike. Metro's Blue and Yellow lines serve the airport station. (Traffic problems were reduced considerably about two years ago with the opening of a garage where taxicabs are held and dispatched as needed; up until then, an entire section of road was consumed by a long line of waiting and no doubt frustrated cabbies). With its borders already confined, National will only get better, not bigger, as airport officials like to say. You will see a remarkably different and more efficient airport by the late 1990s, when all work is scheduled for completion.

For general airport information, call (703) 685-8000. Both National and Dulles are served by the airports authority's Washington Flyer Ground Transportation System (703-685-1400), a network of buses, taxis and limousines. Regular bus service is offered between each airport, to and from the Downtown Terminal at 15th and K streets NW, as well as to and from the West Falls Church Metrorail station.

Dulles, located at the end of the airport-only access road 26 miles (about 45 minutes) from downtown Washington, is a different story altogether. The area's full-service domestic and international hub, it's only about 30 years old and was the first airport built for the jet age. Finnish-born architect Eero Saarinen even sought to convey the movement of flight in his design of the stunning main terminal which the American Institute of Architects has recognized as one of the greatest architectural achievements of the 20th century. But beauty wasn't a harbinger of immediate success. Plagued by a "white elephant" label virtually from day one, Dulles languished severely until the mid-1980s when a concerted effort was made to market and promote the airport and its rich untapped potential. Airlines and passengers have since been flocking to Dulles in increasing numbers as the airport further establishes itself as a major player in international aviation. All major domestic airlines (United has a substantial presence) and 10 foreign carriers serve Dulles, with more on the horizon. The airport is one of only two U.S. gateways for the supersonic Concorde and has emerged as an East Coast hub for travel to Europe and the Far East. Its 10,000-acre site on the Loudoun/Fairfax border, a broad expanse of meadows and forest adjacent to established residential areas and a booming business corridor, provides growth room that few airports in the world can match.

And grow it will as Dulles prepares to meet the challenges of the 21st century. While some work has already been completed — including a new International Arrivals Building and expanded parking — the focal point of the airports authority's efforts at Dulles will be the doubling of the current length of the main terminal to 1,240 feet. Also in the blueprints are continued road improvements, still more parking, new midfield concourses linked to the main terminal by underground walkways, and two additional runways. Some projects won't come to fruition until the early 21st century.

And with any luck, a rail line will be constructed in the median of the airport access road just as was intended when the property was purchased by the federal government in the late 1950s. Such a line would conceivably link up with Metrorail's West Falls Church station, providing Dulles with access that has long been needed and is befitting of a world-class airport that's billed as the world's gateway to the nation's capital.

For general airport information, call (703) 471-7838.

Insiders' Tip

Insiders...
Commuting by Metrorail get their farecards ahead of time to avoid having to stand in line at the machines on busy weekday mornings and evenings.

Baltimore-Washington International, meanwhile, often seems overshadowed by National and Dulles, but there's no reason for it. BWI is modern, easy to get to, easy to use and ably serves both of its namesake markets with service by all major domestic airlines (Arlington-based USAir in particular offers extensive service including flights to London and Frankfurt) and seven foreign carriers including El Al Israel Airlines and Icelandair. In fact, talk to many area residents — Marylanders in particular — and they'll tell you BWI is only way to fly. The fact that BWI is so user-friendly, boasts ample parking and is served by both the AMTRAK and MARC rail lines gives the airport added clout with travelers.

Count on nearly an hour's drive from downtown Washington. The airport is located in Anne Arundel County just off the Baltimore-Washington Parkway, but is also easily accessible from I-95. Ample signs are posted along the Maryland portion of the Capital Beltway that clearly show you which exit to take for BWI, a particular help for some of us provincial Northern Virginians who don't wander into the Free State very often except for the occasional sporting event or concert.

For general airport information, call (410) 859-7111. Ground transportation: (301) 859-7545.

Metro Washington also has numerous smaller airports serving primarily private aircraft. Among the busiest are Manassas (703-361-1882), Leesburg (703-777-9252) and, in Prince George's County, College Park Airport (301-864-5844), which also boasts a museum dedicated to its storied past. College Park is the world's oldest continuously operating airport and plays nearly as important a role in aviation history as does Kitty Hawk, N.C. In 1909, Orville Wright came here to teach the first Army officers how to fly, and between 1909 and 1934, it was the site of many aviation firsts.

Eastern U.S.

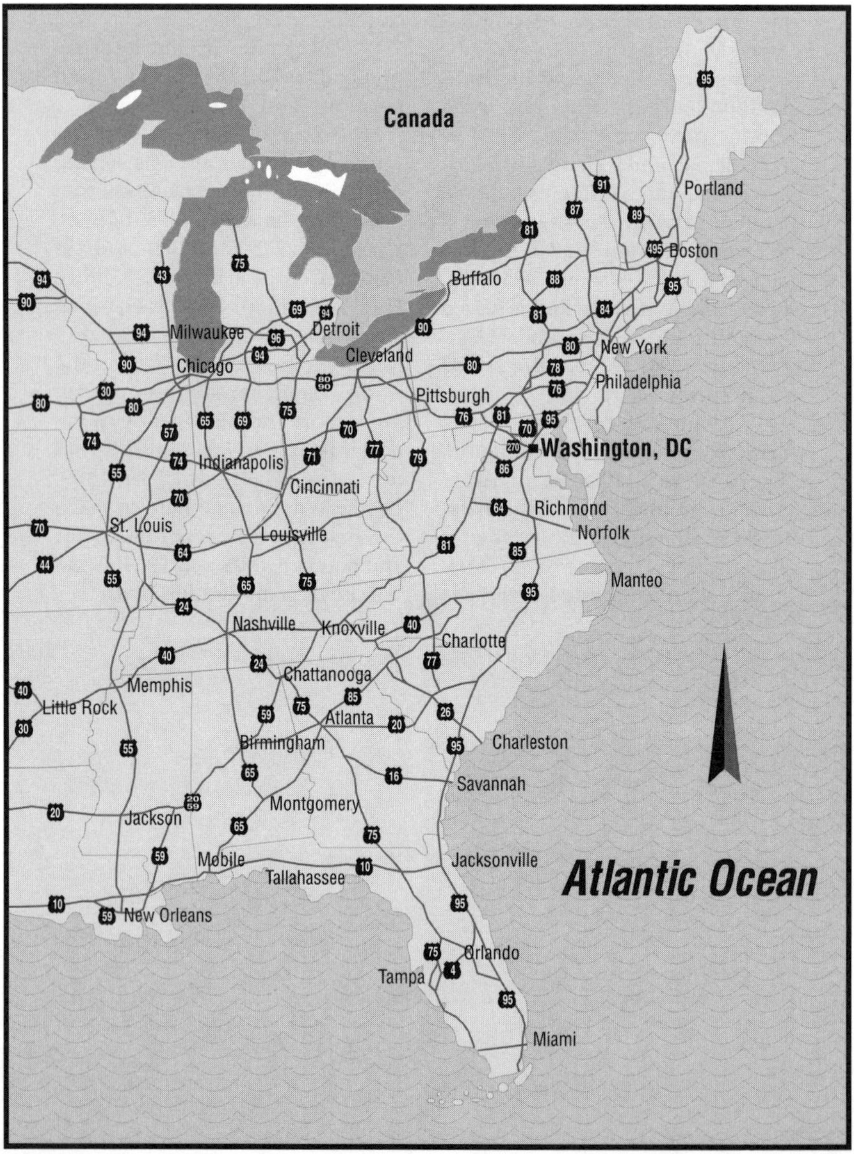

Canada
Portland
Boston
Buffalo
Milwaukee
Detroit
Chicago
Cleveland
New York
Philadelphia
Pittsburgh
Washington, DC
Indianapolis
Cincinnati
Richmond
St. Louis
Louisville
Norfolk
Manteo
Nashville
Knoxville
Charlotte
Memphis
Chattanooga
Little Rock
Atlanta
Birmingham
Charleston
Savannah
Montgomery
Jackson
Jacksonville
Mobile
Tallahassee
Atlantic Ocean
New Orleans
Orlando
Tampa
Miami

Washington, DC and Surrounding Counties

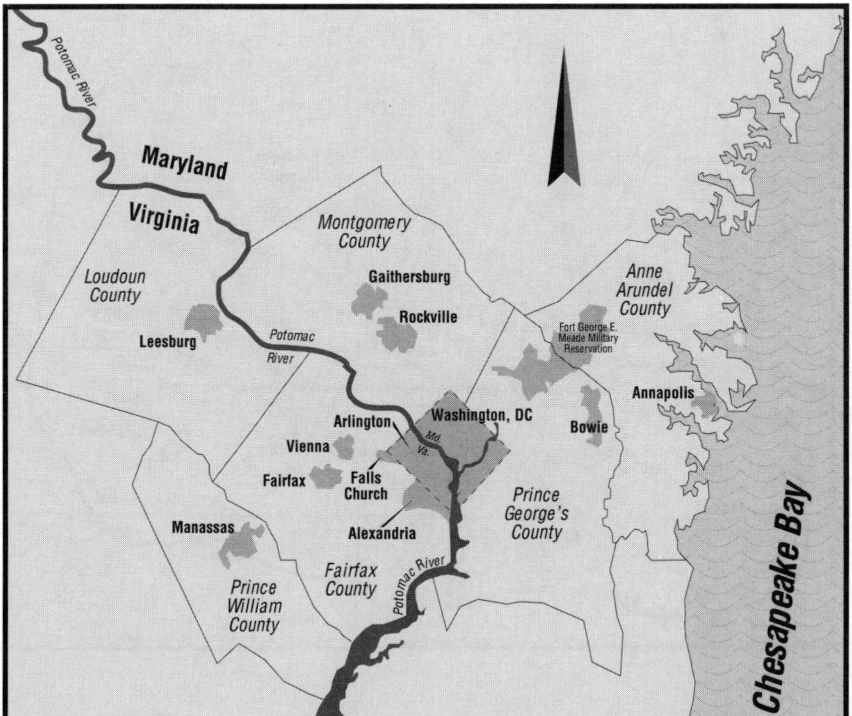

Metro Washington, DC

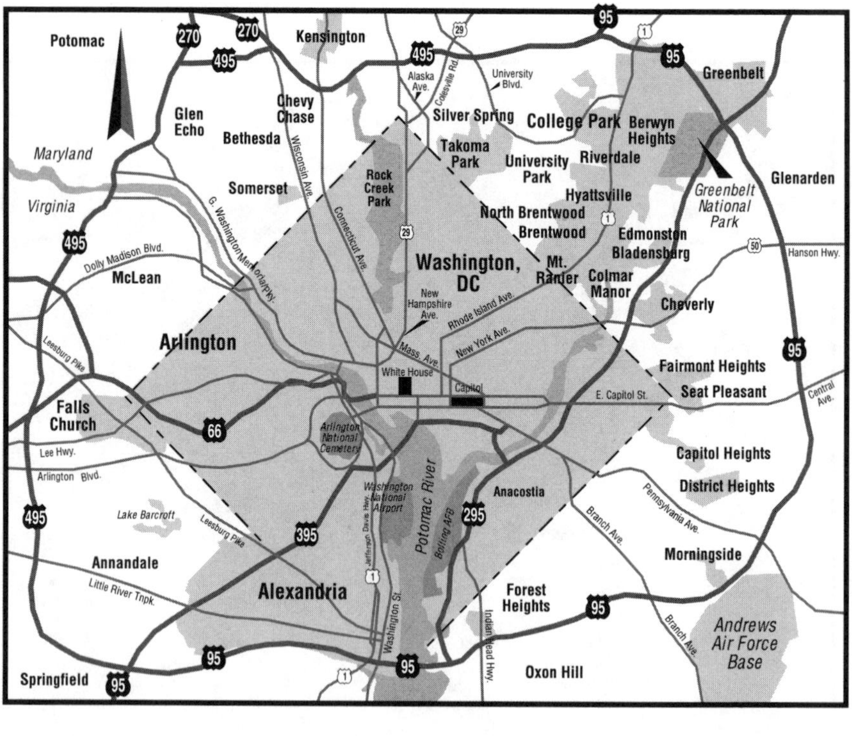

The Mall and Vicinity

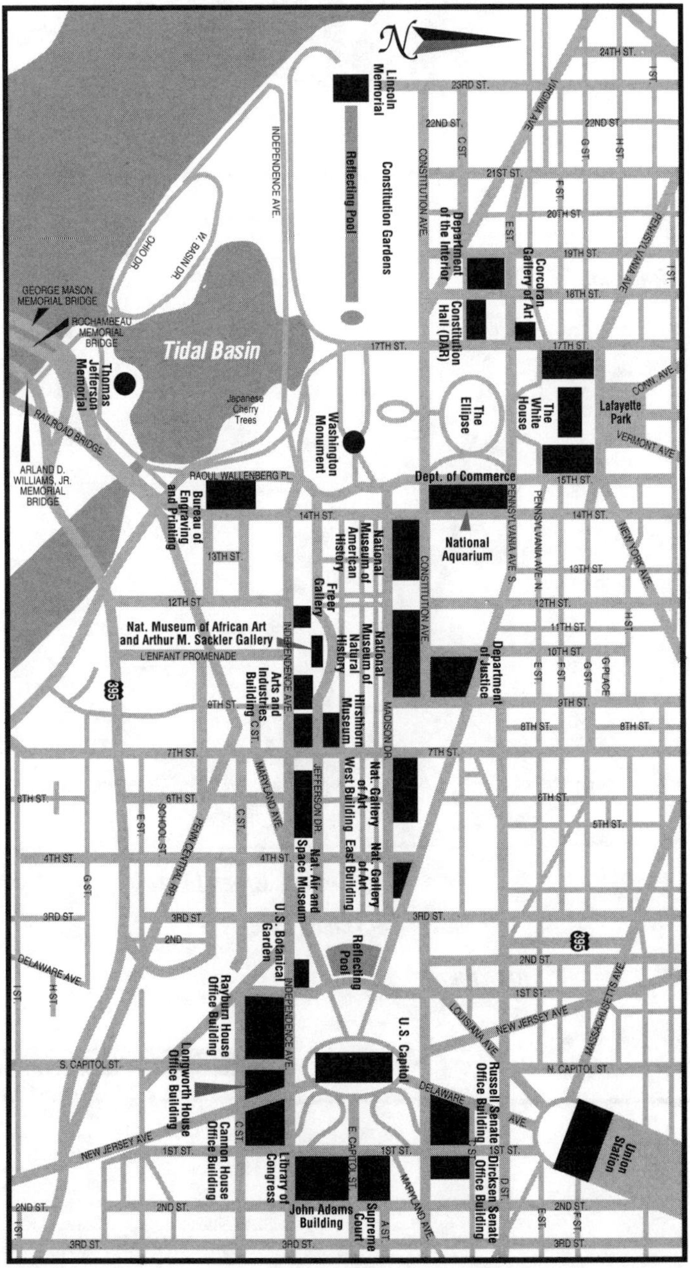

Metrorail System

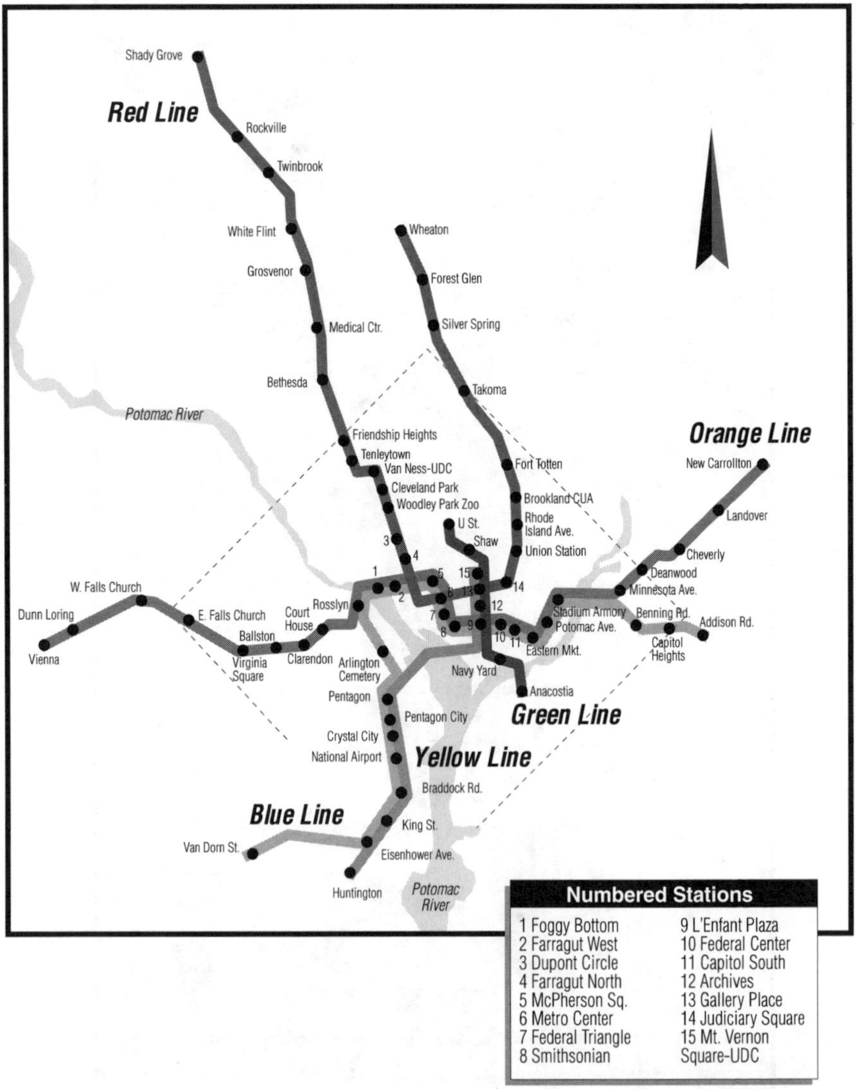

Numbered Stations

1 Foggy Bottom
2 Farragut West
3 Dupont Circle
4 Farragut North
5 McPherson Sq.
6 Metro Center
7 Federal Triangle
8 Smithsonian
9 L'Enfant Plaza
10 Federal Center
11 Capitol South
12 Archives
13 Gallery Place
14 Judiciary Square
15 Mt. Vernon Square-UDC

Inside
The Washington Economy and Job Market

The economy. It has been the national obsession of late. If you're one of the fresh faces in town with the new administration, it's responsible, at least indirectly, for you being here.

Given the high-profile the economy — and that dreaded "R" word — have received over the past couple of years, we thought it appropriate to discuss what is happening right here in the nation's capital.

Back in the booming days of the mid to late 1980s, local business development officials used to talk of Washington's "recession-proof" economy. They touted the fact that the federal government's employment and spending base had a stabilizing effect on the economy, and that the diversity of business here was too great to allow for any major slowdowns.

Well, things didn't quite turn out that way. Washington, like everywhere else, was hit hard by the recession. Commercial real estate, already dangerously overbuilt, took a beating in 1990 and '91. Defense contractors awoke to a post-Cold War new world order and an anticipation of scarcer federal outlays. Banks failed. Engineers, architects, technicians and journalists, among others, were handed pink slips faster than Congress writes checks. Unemployment jumped. Local governments wrestled with fiscal problems. Those accustomed to the fat-cat days of the '80s were thinking the world was coming to an end.

In reality, though, Metro Washington fared much better than most other parts of the U.S. The recession surfaced later here, had far less of a sting, and was quicker to leave. Unemployment never got much beyond 4 percent, a figure most communities would love to have during the best of times. Granted, we're not totally out of the dark yet, but the economy is improving, folks are going back to work, new houses are being built and more office space is being absorbed.

While the business-development people may have blown their recession-proof theory, they were on target as far as the diversity of the economy is concerned. The region's broad mix of industry is one of the great untold economic stories of the past decade.

Plenty of Horses

If you've always thought of Washington as a "one-horse town" — that "horse" being the federal government — you're in for a surprise, pardner.

Maybe we should put it another way. Incumbents and challengers aren't the only ones distancing themselves from Washington these days. Washington itself has moved away from its traditional image as a bureaucratic, red-taped government town. Only thing is, many people, especially newcomers and visitors, still don't know about it. Stick around a while; it will all come clear.

Since 1980, a staggering 98 percent of jobs created in the metro area, or 588,000 new positions, have been attributed to the private sector, in areas like high-tech and biotech, telecommunications, finance and construction. To be sure, federal employment has remained steady but now is only 16 percent of the total workforce compared with 25 percent at the beginning of the Reagan/Bush era. On top of that, even when you factor in the thousands of jobs supplied by local and state governments, the private sector still comes out way ahead of the game. All told, big business employs 74 percent of Washingtonians. Big government, 26 percent.

So what does this tell us? A couple of things, actually. First, we'd be kidding ourselves to dismiss the economic importance of the government's presence. Nobody spends money like federal Washington and no one feels the effects of those shopping sprees more than our local economy. Last year, the feds spent more than $41 billion in the region, accounting for 65 percent of Metro D.C.'s gross regional product.

At the same time, Washington's growing stature as an international business center has come with the benefit of a sounder, more flexible economy. As mentioned in other parts of this book, it also has had a stabilizing effect on the region's psyche. We're no longer all that transient. Businesses and people are staying put and it's redefining the social and economic character of the region. Chances are, as a newcomer, you're probably part of this new dynamic.

The remainder of this chapter is intended to give you a feel for the forces shaping Metro D.C.'s economy, with special emphasis on the diversity and strength of area employers as well as the unique and somewhat intimidating characteristics of the Washington workforce.

Winds of Change

Washington's transformation from a government- to a private sector information-driven economy mirrors one of the most pervasive trends in our global society. The international marketplace of the late 20th century is fueled first and foremost by information. Information is power, and Washington is a wellspring of both commodities.

In the District of Columbia, information and power spring not only from regulatory agencies and Capitol Hill but also from global financial institutions such as the World Bank and the International Monetary Fund. Equally vital are the city's 150-plus embassies that provide instant access to commercial and government representatives from nearly every nation.

These are some of the reasons why, for instance, that 75 percent of the world's multinational corporations already have a foothold here, and why a third, or nearly 2,500, of the U.S.'s national trade and professional associations are headquartered in Metro D.C.

The Washington area claims more than 200 telecommunications and information giants, including MCI, Bell Atlantic and COMSAT. Journalism is big business here as there are some 4,100 correspondents, newspapers, wire services, news agencies and radio and television networks (the highest concentration of journalists in the world are here). Fortune 500 companies as diverse as Mobil, Gannett, General Dynamics, Martin Marietta and Marriott also call the metro area home.

The region's inordinate supply of research institutions and business incubators bodes well for firms aiming to diversify away from federal purse strings and into the commercial sector. Indeed, this so-called "technology transfer" remains one of the biggest challenges facing the region as it heads into the new millennium.

Where the Businesses Are: A Regional Profile

As you already know, the District of Columbia accounts for a very small percentage of the physical area and population of Metro Washington. Population-wise, it contains a mere 16 percent of the region's 3.92 million inhabitants. Area-wise, it's an infinitely smaller percentage — roughly 63 square miles of a metropolis that sprawls over more than 3,000 square miles. What is amazing, though, is how this small strip of land commands such an enormous economic impact on the neighboring states of Maryland and Virginia.

In Maryland, the suburban counties that wrap around the District contain 33 percent of the state's population, 41 percent of its buying income and 37 percent of its retail dollars. Across the river in Virginia, the D.C. suburbs account for 24 percent of the Old Dominion's population, 34 percent of its buying income, and 30 percent of its retail dollars.

The point here is that there's a tremendous amount of business

Insiders...

Religiously read the employment classified section of the Sunday *Washington Post*. Not only is it essential for those seeking work, but it's a good, albeit unscientific, barometer of the metro job market.

Insiders' Tip

and federal activity going on inside and outside the District line. The synergistic relationship between Washington and its suburbs is intense and growing, and it's creating one of the world's most fertile business climates.

Since 1980, the suburbs have claimed 80 percent of Metro Washington's employment growth. Two-thirds of these new jobs have been placed in Northern Virginia, principally Fairfax County. All told, there are now more than 818,000 jobs in Northern Virginia, compared with the District's 730,000 and suburban Maryland's 719,000.

Fairfax County, which encircles the self-governed municipalities of Falls Church, Vienna, Fairfax City and Herndon, houses some of the biggest employers in the metro area including Mobil, AT&T, BDM International, EDS Corp. and Mitre. General Dynamics recently moved its national headquarters here from St. Louis. Fairfax County also claims the largest share of international firms in Metro D.C. Among the 100 foreign-based or affiliated companies here are France's Lafarge Corp., Japan's Canon USA, Britain's BT North America and Canada's and Australia's Molson Breweries USA.

Arlington County, though much smaller than Fairfax, serves as national headquarters for USAir and Gannett Corporation. Other large employers include MCI, Bell Atlantic American Management Systems and, of course, the Pentagon, the world's largest military complex (not to mention the world's largest office building). Next door in Alexandria, one of the nation's oldest port cities and business centers, are the headquarters for the Public Broadcasting System, Crown Life Insurance USA, Time-Life Books, Inc., Softech and the Independent Insurance Agents of America. In Loudoun and Prince William counties, businesses are lured by availability of affordable office space and land and proximity to Washington Dulles International Airport. IBM and Atlantic Research are big players in Prince William, while United Airlines, with over 5,000 employees, is a gigantic presence in Loudoun.

Historically, Maryland's close-in suburbs have benefited from the spillover of federal activity from the District. It's here you'll find such large federal employers as the National Institutes of Health, the National Institute of Standards and Technology, and the U.S. Food and Drug Administration, all in Montgomery County, as well as the National Agricultural Research Center and the Goddard Space Flight Center, in Prince George's County. Montgomery County has emerged as the region's telecommunications and biotechnology hotbed, with names like COMSAT, Fairchild Industries, Vitro Laboratories and Hughes Network Systems all calling the county home, as does the defense and aerospace firm Martin Marietta. Prince George's County is putting a lot of stock in the new University of Maryland Science & Technology Center to help lure more high-tech firms. Anne Arundel County, meanwhile, has witnessed rapid growth in regional headquarters. Some 11 million square feet of office space has been built around Baltimore-Washington International Airport just in the last five years. Big names in the county include Westinghouse, Electronic Systems Groups, ARINC, Nevamar Corporation and ITT Research Institute.

The Washington Workforce

If you're looking for a job in Metro D.C., or even if you've already landed one, it's good to know a few vital stats about your colleagues, the Washington workforce. Besides, a few provocative figures here and there will go a long way on the Washington cocktail-party circuit.

Let's start with the big picture: Some 2.2 million people are employed in the Washington area, 72 percent working in white-collar jobs. That's the highest such percentage in the nation and a full 15 percent higher than the U.S. average.

Sounds impressive enough, but wait, it gets even more striking. The region claims the largest percentage of executive, administrative, managerial, professional and technical workers among the nation's largest metropolitan areas. The proportion of scientists and technicians working in Metro D.C. is unsurpassed and the number of computer specialists is greater than Boston and San Francisco combined. Employment in communications, finance and retail has increased 47, 43 and 39 percent respectively since 1980. The service industry overall has gained 73 percent more jobs during that period, to roughly 760,000 positions.

If you're a woman, you're in good company here. A full two-thirds of working age women are employed in greater Washington, 25 percent of them in professional and managerial positions. Again, on both accounts, the highest such percentages in the U.S.

With three out of five of its residents African American, the District of Columbia has long been the nation's most influential and affluent black city. Today, the entire region boasts the leading percentage of black executives, administrators and managers. In recent years, Washington also has experienced a surge in entrepreneurship among its growing Asian, Hispanic, Middle Eastern and Indian communities.

Of course, at the root of Washington's white collars is education. The metro area inarguably has the best educated workforce in the U.S. Nearly 40 percent of area adults 25 and older hold college degrees, almost twice the national average.

Insiders...
Routinely join industry groups, such as the Press Club of Washington and Women in Advertising and Marketing/ Washington, to network and keep abreast of latest employment and business trends.

Insiders' Tip

In addition, 55 percent have some college experience, and enrollment in continuing-education programs in local colleges is among the highest anywhere.

Beyond all the hyperbole, however, are some very down-to-earth implications. More and more young people are launching their careers in Metro Washington despite the intensely competitive nature of the labor force, especially among entry-level positions. Maybe even more important, less are packing their bags after a couple of years. A full 45 percent of the region's population is between the ages of 25 and 49, making the Washington workforce the youngest in the U.S.

Where the Jobs Will Be

Good show, newcomers. Your timing couldn't have been better. Although it's unlikely we'll ever see the kind of economic expansion we had around here in the '80s, Metro Washington is well positioned for long, sustained growth over the next two decades. As the shift from federal to private sector employment continues unabated, it's estimated that there will be 1.3 million more workers out there by the year 2010, the vast majority in highly skilled service occupations.

The recession aside, we'll see a steady climb in the ranks of high-tech, bio-tech and telecommunications workers, as well as in manufacturing and clerical positions. By the end of the decade, the region will have nearly 32,000 more elementary and secondary school teachers than in 1985, 20,000 more college educators, 14,000 more nurses, 23,000 more computer specialists and 9,000 more electrical engineers. We'll also see 37,000 more secretaries, 10,000 more accountants, and, yes, even 9,000 more lawyers.

In a nutshell, the job market is wide open.

Suggested Readings

An entire publishing sub-industry has cropped up dealing with finding a job in Metro Washington. Among the better books in the genre are:

How to Get a Job in Washington, D.C., by Thomas Camden and Karen Tracy Polk., Surrey Books, Inc., 101 E. Erie St., Suite 900, Chicago, Ill. 60611, (312) 751-7330

An A to Z approach to landing a job in the metro area, including tips on resumés, locating the right contacts, dress and making yourself noticed.

How to Be Happily Employed in Washington, D.C., by Janice Benjamin and Barbara Block, Random House,

Insiders' Tip

Insiders...
Looking for information on international business activity both here and abroad often begin their search at one or more of Washington's 150-plus embassies.

New York, NY

Outlines trends in employment, job options and overviews of Washington industries, including the government, tourism and hospitality sectors.

The Metropolitan Washington Job Bank, edited by Carter Smith, Bob Adams Inc. Publishers, 260 Center St., Holbrook, Mass. 02343

A popular job hunters guide to D.C. area, with comprehensive listings of companies and contacts selected by trade.

1,001 Great Opportunities for College Graduates: Jobs in Washington, D.C., by Greg Diefenbach and Phillip Giordano, Impact Publications, 9104-N Manassas Dr., Manassas Park, Va. 22111, (703) 361-7300

Great graduation gift/survival tool for those hoping to tap into entry-level Washington. Interesting chapters on finding jobs in the media, health, education and environmental industries, plus working on Capitol Hill.

Find a Federal Job Fast!, by Ronald L. Krannich and Caryl Rae Krannich, Impact Publications, 4580 Sunshine Ct., Woodbridge, Va. 22192, (703) 361-7300

Excellent resource to help you cut through the red tape that is so ubiquitous in federal Washington.

Federal Career Opportunities, Federal Research Services, Inc., P.O. Box 1059, Vienna, Va. 22183-1059, (703) 281-0200

This regularly updated booklet, found in virtually every bookstore in Washington, lists all current job openings in the federal government, plus qualifications, contacts, salary structure and responsibilities.

Suggested Contacts

If you'd like to receive more specific information about the Metro Washington economy and/or labor market, we encourage you to contact the following agencies:

District of Columbia Department of Employment Services, Labor Market Information Research Staff, 500 C St. NW, Room 200, Washington, D.C. 20001, (202) 639-1642

The Greater Washington Board of Trade, Employment/Education Bureau, 1129 20th St. NW, Suite 200, Washington D.C. 20036, (202) 857-5970

Maryland Department of Economic and Employment Development, Office of Labor Market Analysis & Information, 1100 N. Eutaw St., Baltimore, Md. 21201, (410) 333-5000

Virginia Employment Commission, 703 E. Main St., P.O. Box 1358, Richmond, Va. 23211, (804) 786-8223

Insiders' Tip

Insiders...
Are aware of the important role of tourism in the Washington economy, accounting for $4 billion in annual revenues.

Selected Economic Development Authorities

If you're interested in starting or expanding a business in Metro Washington, or simply want to know more about companies in specific jurisdictions, we recommend that you contact the following economic-development groups:

D.C. Office of Business & Economic Development, 111 E St. NW, 7th Floor, Washington, D.C. 20004, (202) 727-6600

Montgomery County Office of Economic Development, 101 Monroe St., Suite 1500, Rockville, Md. 20850, (301) 217-2345

Prince George's County Economic Development Corp., 9200 Basil Court, Suite 200, Landover, Md. 20785, (301) 386-5600

Anne Arundel County Office of Economic Development, Arundel Center, Room 418, Annapolis, Md. 21404, (410) 280-1122

Fairfax County Economic Development Authority, 8300 Boone Blvd., Suite 450, Vienna, Va. 22180, (703) 790-0600

Alexandria Economic Development Program, 99 Canal Center Plaza, Suite 4, River Level, Alexandria, Va. 22314, (703) 739-3820

Arlington County Economic Development Division, One Courthouse Plaza, 2100 Clarendon Blvd., Suite 608, Arlington, Va. 22201, (703) 358-3520

Prince William County Office of Economic Development, 4349 Ridgewood Center Dr., Suite 100, Prince William, Va. 22192, (703) 792-6680

Inside Metro Washington Neighborhoods, Homes and Retirement

Finding a home — whether it be an apartment, condominium or a detached house — can be one of the most stressful activities you'll ever confront.

It's tough enough if you're already familiar with the market, but for most newcomers this isn't the case. We jump in blindly and too often come out a little battered and scarred from the experience.

The Metro Washington real estate scene is one of the most intimidating anywhere, given the physical expanse of the region, its exorbitant housing costs, and the subtle but important differences (political, social, demographic) that exist among the District of Columbia, Virginia and Maryland.

This chapter doesn't promise any easy remedies for evading the house-hunting blues. Our point is simply to introduce you to the residential real estate market, the types of neighborhoods and homes available here, and the major players in the home brokerage and construction industries.

We've also included a brief section on retiring in the Washington area, a trend that's catching on with more and more retirees who crave the perks of urban living and value the proximity to varied recreational opportunities.

The Residential Real Estate Market

There are two fundamental truths about the Metro Washington housing market. One, we will never, ever, see the kind of price appreciation that took place around here in the gold rush days of the mid '80s. In some neighborhoods, a less than auspicious rambler that was priced at $90,000 in 1980 could go as high as $130,000 in 1986 and $155,000 in 1988. Twenty-percent-plus annual appreciations were not uncommon in several areas!

Two, Metro Washington, while not exactly recession proof, still traditionally fares much better than the national economy and it's a pretty sure bet the residential real-estate market will never crash through the floor like it did in Denver, Houston and other metro areas during the '80s.

Today, sales of new homes in the Washington area are up 48 percent since 1990, a year most economists now are calling the abyss of the most recent national recession. Home values are appreciating at 3 percent a year and the outlook for the remainder of the decade is for 3 to 5 percent annual gains, well above the national average.

The bad news is that housing is still awfully expensive in the Nation's Capital and we doubt that will ever change. The average price of a home here is $198,200; for a new home it's $205,000. Steep numbers when you consider the national average price of a new house is about $150,000.

With that said, the Washington area still commands a high home ownership rate. About 80 percent of householders own their homes, compared with 65 percent nationally. The implication is that while Metro D.C. homes are expensive, a whole lot of people can still afford them.

About 38 percent of owners live in detached single-family houses, while 40 percent live in townhouses and 22 percent in condominiums.

For those 20 percent who don't own, the fair market rent for a one-bedroom apartment is about $620. For two bedrooms expect to pay $730, and for three bedrooms about $915. House rentals can range from $700 a month for a townhome in the outer suburbs to $3,000 for a plush Georgetown dwelling.

One thing to keep in mind whether you're going to buy or rent is that the pricing rationale here is similar to other large urban areas. In other words, expect to pay a premium to be close to the District and near major commuting links like I-66, the Capital Beltway and Metrorail stations. Prices drop as you move outward; commute times increase. It's the age-old trade-off.

Photo: Virginia Division of Tourism

Blocks of quaint old row houses built like those in English and Scottish seaport towns can be found on Prince Street in Alexandria, near the Potomac River waterfront.

Neighborhoods and Homes

District of Columbia

People tend to forget that Washington, beyond the monuments, is a city of neighborhoods—communities with their own dynamics, history and sense of place. Most of these enclaves are close-knit and largely self contained. The whole effect is something akin to a patchwork of small towns, albeit connected to an urban core.

In a city tagged for its transience, it may come as a surprise that the majority of the District's neighborhoods are home to several generations of families.

Washington neighborhoods too often are categorized by their racial makeup. And for sure, like most inner cities, the District has its lines of racial and economic demarcation. Broadly speaking, the expansive area west of Rock Creek Park is highly affluent and white, while the bulk of the rest of the city is primarily black and middle class. Of course, pockets of dire poverty and crime transcend all four quadrants, but nowhere are they more concentrated than in troubled Southeast D.C. But even here, islands of tranquility and prosperity

Photo: Virginia Division of Tourism

Waterford was founded as a Quaker village and is one of Loudoun County's oldest communities.

can be found along with the slow but determined progress of urban renewal.

As a place to live, the District offers proximity to all major employment centers, including those in Suburban Maryland and Northern Virginia. Virtually no one here commutes longer than 30 minutes to work. Washington's prized Metro mass-transit system, famed nightlife and cultural opportunities, miles of parklands and forests, stately homes and shaded streets, plus its allure as the nation's capital, will always make it a desirable address.

That desirability comes with a price, however. The average price of a home in D.C. is $218,942. The median rent is $441, although rents of $800 to $1,200 are more the norm in prime neighborhoods.

The vast majority of newcomers who relocate to the District settle in Northwest, so we'll begin our neighborhood tour here.

Adams Morgan, which radiates from Columbia Road and 18th Street NW, is Washington's largest and most celebrated ethnic neighborhood. Its global-minded eateries are famous in these parts (see dining chapter) and it's here where you'll find African clothiers next to Spanish bridal shops and Turkish shoe stores. Adams Morgan and neighboring **Mount Pleasant** have attracted a growing number of young professionals, including many tied to the new administration who live in gentrified townhouses and large apartment buildings. A few years ago, Mount Pleasant experienced an unfortunate riot, but the tensions have cooled and the neighborhood seems determined to carry on as one of Washington's most integrated communities.

Immediately to the south of Adams Morgan is **Dupont Circle**, Washington's answer to Greenwich Village. Interspersed among the cafes, art galleries and boutiques are grand old brownstones and row houses. Gays, artists, young progressives and aging bohemians all call Dupont home. While claiming many of the same attributes as Adams Morgan, Dupont is decidedly more established and thus housing prices and rents tend to be higher here.

Closer to downtown, and wrapping around the campus of George Washington University, are the highly urbanized neighborhoods of **Foggy Bottom** and the **West End**. Both are apartment and condo dense, with the former consisting mostly of students and professors and the latter primarily single professionals who commute by Metro or walk to nearby offices. The neighborhoods are wedged between Georgetown to the west and downtown to the east, a consolation to the area's overall lack of restaurants and nightlife.

Downtown living is enjoying somewhat of a renaissance thanks to the continued revitalization of the Pennsylvania Avenue corridor. Several older buildings, including the historic Lansburgh, have been revamped and now house some of the most exclusive condo units in Washington.

By most measures, Washington's toniest address is still **Georgetown**, with its famed M Street nightlife, stylish federal townhomes and secluded estates. West of Wisconsin Avenue is dominated by Georgetown University and its students; east of the avenue is markedly quieter, with bigger homes and well-healed residents. For those with money — tiny townhouses can demand as much as $500,000 — and patience to bear the weekend crush ofpartiers, there is simply no other close-in neighborhood that can match the charm and convenience of Georgetown.

Immediately to the north, in **Glover Park**, a more down-to-earth atmosphere pervades. Brick townhomes and duplexes cluster around small parks and green spaces all within a short stroll of Wisconsin Avenue. Young families, middle-aged empty nesters and long-time residents live side by side and in harmony in this civic-minded and politically progressive neighborhood.

Moving farther north puts you in the land of milk and honey. The neighborhoods of **Foxhall Road**, **Spring Valley** and **Wesley Heights** are the stuff of *Better Homes and Gardens* photo shoots. The neighbors tend to be older than those who reside to the south, politically more conservative and measurably wealthier. On some streets, million-dollar homes are more the rule than the exception.

To the east, in the heart of Northwest, are **Cleveland Park** and **Woodley Park**, a checkerboard of beautiful but modest Victorian homes, older apartment buildings and remodeled townhouses. Easy access to Massachusetts and Connecticut avenues, Metro and such attractions as the National Zoo give the neighborhoods a certain prestige with up-and-coming professionals.

In the far stretches of upper Northwest, neighborhoods like **Tenleytown**, **American University Park**, **Barnaby Woods** and **Chevy**

Chase (not to be confused with neighboring Chevy Chase, Md.) glow with a sense of Small Town America charm, complete with quiet tree-lined streets, beautiful spacious lawns and kids on bicycles. Along the upper western edges of Rock Creek Park, **Forest Hills** unfolds with palatial homes and tucked away streets that allow maximum privacy for the rich and powerful.

East of Rock Creek, along upper 16th Street NW, **Shepherd Park**, **Brightwood Park** and **Crestwood** move to a relaxed suburban beat. Homes are substantially more affordable than similar dwellings to the west of the park, and 16th Street provides a mostly hassle-free link to downtown and points south.

Two Northwest neighborhoods that are rebounding from years of neglect are **Shaw**, which straddles 14th Street above downtown, and **LeDroit Park**, just to the south of Howard University. The new Metro Green Line stop at Shaw/Howard University comes with the promise of further revitalization of these Victorian neighborhoods, but crime is still an ongoing problem.

In Northeast, another neighborhood on the rebound is **Brookland** which houses an interesting mix of students, professors and elderly middle-class residents who reside in well-kept rowhouses and Cape Cods. Catholic University and its rolling wooded campus dominate much of the neighborhood and bring a sense of respite from the clamor of the inner city.

The most sought after address in Northeast is **Capitol Hill**, which also spreads into Southeast. As you might imagine, Capitol Hill teems with young congressional staffers, lobbyists and members of Congress. Huge brownstones and smaller townhomes are the mainstays but a few apartment and condo units can be found. As a rule, those areas closest to the Capitol command the highest prices and are considered the safest.

In Southwest, the neighborhood of choice is the **Waterfront**, located north of the Anacostia River. A haven for federal employees, much of the Southwest Waterfront is within a short walk of Capitol Hill and L'Enfant Plaza, the massive government complex. The area boasts some fine restaurants, theaters and pricey townhomes. High-rise condo and apartment buildings, however, make up the bulk of housing, which is typically more affordable than similar close-in units found to the north of the National Mall.

Anacostia, on the opposite side of the river, contains the District's largest concentration of public housing. This portion of Southeast continues to battle with widespread poverty and violent crime, the worst in D.C.

Northern Virginia

Alexandria

Sharing ranks with Arlington County as Northern Virginia's closest-in suburb, Alexandria has strong historical and cultural ties to the

District of Columbia. But make no mistake, Alexandria may be a suburb of Washington, but this is a Virginia city first and foremost.

Alexandria is immersed in an almost overpowering sense of place. How can it not be with George Washington and Robert E. Lee once calling it home? The municipality is also characteristically Virginian in the way it is run — efficiently and pragmatically.

During rush hour no part of Alexandria is more than 25 minutes from Washington. Metrorail has three stations within the city limits. These are just some of the reasons why the average price of a home ($240,000) is higher than in the rest of Northern Virginia.

Most newcomers' impressions of Alexandria is that it's a lot like Georgetown but without the urban glitz and posturing. And they're right, sort of.

Old Town, the city's most visible neighborhood, could stand double for its northern counterpart on a number of accounts. It's also pricey: Townhouses start at $200,000, but you're more likely to see them up in the $350,000-$500,000 range, especially as you progress east toward the handsomely restored Potomac waterfront. Since Colonial-era homes weren't designed with the automobile in mind, on-street parking is almost always the rule here and on weekends things can get a little sticky. But Old Town is, well, Old Town and that's the biggest selling point of all, especially among the young up-and-coming crowd that tends to migrate here.

Though some would be hard pressed to admit it, there's more to Alexandria than Old Town. Not too long ago **Del Ray**, which wraps around Route 1 and Potomac Yards (a massive train switching yard), was solely a blue-collar neighborhood. Gentrification has set in and some bungalows and Cape Cods now command $200,000 and more.

Alexandria communities that most resemble suburbia are **Rosemont**, **Seminary** and **Beverly Hills**. A lot of the homes were built in the early 1960s on large lots; prices run from $200,000 up to over $1 million, with the greatest concentration in the $300,000 range.

Along the western edge of town are the self-contained neighborhoods of **Park Fairfax** and **South Fairlington**. The majority of housing is townhomes and apartment buildings, many of which sprang up after World War II to house federal workers. Now they're popular with single professionals and first-time buyers.

Also out in the West End is **Landmark**, an area of high-rise condos, apartment buildings and shopping centers located off I-395. Condos start at $75,000 for a one-bedroom unit and can run upwards to $200,000 for deluxe models.

Arlington County

Arlington looks and acts a lot like a city. Its 26 square miles is a collage of satellite business districts, high-rise apartment complexes and tucked away residential neighborhoods. The county has more Metro stations per capita than any other suburb and its population is decidedly middle aged.

Arlington is the most urban county in Metro D.C. and it's a bit unique in that there are no incorporated cities or towns within its borders. Like Alexandria, it was once part of the District of Columbia and many residents here are closer to downtown D.C. and Capitol Hill than are most Washingtonians. Needless to say, Arlington is a convenient and especially attractive area for single, workaholic professionals who like being less than 15 minutes from most of the area's employment centers.

The county is usually identified with its massive business/residential corridors — **Crystal City**, **Pentagon City**, **Clarendon**, **Ballston** and **Rosslyn**. Apartments and condos are the most plentiful housing options here, with the former ranging from $560 to $1,000 a month and the latter commanding $75,000 to $200,000.

The northern tier of the county is almost exclusively residential neighborhoods, some of the most stately areas in Metro Washington. Single-family homes in communities like **Country Club Hills** run from $250,000 for older brick colonials to $800,000-plus for estate homes.

Despite its dense nature, Arlington has set aside hundreds of acres of parklands, and its riverfront bike path, which affords stunning views of Washington and the Potomac, is a source of intense civic pride.

Fairfax County

Northern Virginia's largest jurisdiction runs the gamut on the types of neighborhoods and living options available to newcomers. In Fairfax County you'll find two-story colonials on quiet cul-de-sacs, modest Cape Cods and ramblers in older neighborhoods, lakefront townhomes in new developments, California contemporaries in planned communities, giant estate homes in wooded parklands and turnkey condos in high-rise buildings.

If there is a common thread that runs through this massive county, it is that it's overwhelmingly middle to upper middle class.

Fairfax is among the top five counties in the nation in average household income ($56,600) and

Insiders' Tip

Insiders...

Keep in mind that housing values in Metro Washington are closely tied to access to transportation links. Find out what types of transportation infrastructure are in place (or soon will be) in the neighborhoods you're interested in. City and county government planning offices are good places to begin your investigation.

in the top 15 in median housing values. The average price for a new house is $225,000. Apartments average $700 a month. Those are values if you're coming from the urban areas of the Northeast or parts of the West Coast but a shock if you hail from virtually any other part of the U.S.

One affordable neighborhood inside the Beltway is **Annandale**, an area that has long been a magnet for federal workers and their families. Annandale's signature red-brick ramblers and comfortable ranch homes are priced in the $150,000 to $250,000 range. The community is one of the oldest suburbs in Northern Virginia and is centrally located next to several busy road arteries and I-495.

To the north, **Falls Church**, an independent municipality, comes with a small-town charm and a mix of older stately homes and new townhouse developments. Single-family homes start at $140,000 and work their way up to over $500,000. Route 7 (Leesburg Pike) cuts through the center of the city, offering easy access to Washington and most of Fairfax County. The average commute time to downtown D.C. is 25 minutes.

Great Falls, located in the gorgeous bluffs that tower above the Potomac River in northern Fairfax, is a community of large houses situated on expansive lots of a half-acre and more. Most of the homes here are colonial in design, and $300,000 to $500,000 price tags are the norm. Great Falls and neighboring **McLean**, an even more upscale community, are known for their great schools and serene, wooded surroundings. While only a 20- to 30-minute drive to D.C., the morning commutes along Chain Bridge Road and the George Washington Memorial Parkway can be trying at times.

Moving outside the Beltway, the fast-growing community of **Burke** attracts suburbanites looking for newer houses, plenty of parks for the kids and proximity to major shopping centers. The typical single-family home starts at around $200,000; townhouses run from about $150,000. For all its pluses, Burke commuters face a challenge each day along Braddock and Old Keene Mill roads. Expect a 35- to 50-minute commute into the city.

Wedged between Burke and Annandale is **Springfield**, another older community of modest ramblers on large lots mixed with newer and larger homes on small lots. Like Annandale, Springfield is home to thousands of government and military workers. A large stock of detached homes falls into the $125,000 to $300,000 range. Townhouses begin at around $100,000 and condominiums start at $80,000. Although only 15 miles south of Washington, Springfield's major link to the District is I-95, one of the region's most congested arteries. In all fairness, however, the Virginia Department of Transportation has done miracles in recent years improving existing roads and constructing convenient new secondary roads such as the Franconia-Springfield Parkway.

Mount Vernon, in southeastern Fairfax County, retains a sense of exclusiveness because of its proximity to George Washington's venerable riverside estate. Detached homes on large lots are the backbone of this beautiful neighborhood located between Route 1 and Mount Vernon Memorial Parkway.

It wasn't long ago that **Oakton** and neighboring **Vienna** were considered Fairfax County's far-western suburbs. Located off of I-66, just a couple of miles outside the Beltway, these two communities are now right in the heart of the county, a factor that bodes well with commuters, many of whom use the nearby Vienna Metrorail station. Oakton is mostly a maze of sprawling subdivisions, although parts resemble Great Falls in both topography and opulence. Vienna, an incorporated town settled by the Scots in the early 1800s, has a more established feel. Homes in both areas range from $180,000 to $600,000.

Farther west along I-66, the **City of Fairfax**, another independent municipality, boasts a fine old historic district and an ample supply of moderately-priced homes. Single-family units start at $125,000 while townhouses are available from $100,000. Fairfax is at the junction of several busy roads; commutes into Washington range from 40 to 60 minutes.

In the far western reaches of the county, the rapidly growing communities of **Centreville** and **Chantilly** attract first-time homebuyers with a plentiful variety of townhomes and condominiums. Move-up buyers can purchase large colonials ($170,000-$220,000) for 20 to 30 percent less than comparable homes closer in. Commuting times into downtown can run 45 to 60 minutes.

Out near Washington Dulles International Airport, **Herndon**, an independent town, and **Reston**, a lake- and tree-rich planned community, are populated with young professionals and their families. Detached single-family homes ($130,000 to $300,000) are the residences of choice, but a sizeable number of townhouse and condo developments offer first-time buyers $80,000 and up alternatives. Most commuters use the Dulles Toll Road, heavily trafficked but nonetheless functional.

Prince William County

In a metropolitan area where the term "affordable housing" seems like an oxymoron, Prince William County has become a sanctuary for suburbanites seeking value and space at prices that don't raise blood pressure.

At $135,160, the county's median-price home is about 30 to 50 percent lower than those in jurisdictions to the north, explaining why more first-time buyers and homeowners in the move-up market have settled in Prince William over the last decade. Simple demographics partly tell the story of the county's widespread appeal to young families: Nearly a third of Prince William's 215,000 residents are under age 18 and more than half are under 35, according to the U.S. Census Bureau.

The sprawling bedroom community is one of the fastest-growing areas in the nation. In 1980, less than 150,000 residents were spread across the county's 350 square miles. By 1995, Prince William officials expect 300,000 people to call the county home and by century's end, 350,000.

Neighborhoods along the I-95 corridor such as Lake Ridge, Woodbridge and Montclair have been the biggest gainers so far, with most single-family homes selling between $120,000 and $265,000. Townhouses start at $100,000 and seldom exceed $150,000, while condos typically start at $70,000. The next area pinpointed for growth is the western part of the county near Manassas and I-66, where large single-family homes in new subdivisions can be purchased for $170,000.

The rapid transformation from a quiet exurb to thriving suburb has come with its share of growing pains. Road congestion, while getting better, is still pretty chronic. Prince William commuters spend more time on the road than anyone else in Metro Washington. The recently opened Virginia Railway Express, a commuter train service with six stops in Prince William, will hopefully lure some motorists off the road.

Loudoun County

The fortunes of this beautiful county 30 miles northwest of

Washington are closely tied to the development of Washington Dulles International Airport.

Dulles' renaissance over the last 10 years has played out nicely for Loudoun, helping bring in new aerospace and international high-tech firms and boosting population from 57,000 to 90,000. Most of the county's population lies in and around **Leesburg** and points east along Route 7. Homes in diverse communities like **Sterling, Ashburn** and **Sugarland** run between $110,000 to $275,000. The average townhouse costs about $108,000.

As one moves west and south of Leesburg, the graceful county seat, you enter **Virginia Hunt Country**, a land of blue bloods and stone fences, breathtaking country estates, Kentucky Derby-winning stables and rolling vineyards. The most modest of homes in communities like **Middleburg, Upperville** and **Bluemont** will cost about $140,000 and these are easily eclipsed by the number of million-dollar horse farms that criss-cross the pretty countryside.

Suburban Maryland

Montgomery County

Montgomery County was the first "true" suburb of Washington, D.C. Virginia, after all, was across the river; to get to Montgomery all you had to do was cross Western Avenue. Manmade borders, as Marylanders will tell you, are easier to penetrate than physical borders.

Go up to Montgomery County today and real estate agents will be the first to remind you of this. And indeed, getting into Washington is likely to be less of a hassle from here because of the absence of bridges. That and the fact that Maryland has been very progressive in updating its roadways. A decade ago, I-270, which runs north to Frederick County, was a commuting nightmare. In the past few years, major improvements, including new lanes and upgraded feeder roads, have resulted in a stretch of highway that is among the best-moving in the region, if not *the* best.

These kinds of factors sit well with commuters, many of whom can now find more affordable homes in the Up-County (the northern part of Montgomery) without the worry of sitting half the day on the interstate.

Montgomery isn't just about good roads, though. Like Fairfax, it has every type of housing and neighborhood option under the sun. And like its Virginia cousin, housing doesn't come cheap — about $228,000 for the average home. Renters can expect to pay $670 for a one-bedroom apartment and $770 for a two-bedroom unit.

The quintessential Montgomery County community has got to be **Bethesda**, a residential sanctuary for thousands of government officials and industry leaders. **North Bethesda**, convenient to the Beltway and Metro, is the denser section of town, chock full of townhouse developments and mid-rise condo units. To the south, in neighborhoods like **Chevy Chase**, you'll find vintage suburbia, with large Victorians and colonials situated on impeccably-manicured lots. Single-family homes range between $200,000 and $500,000. Condos start at around $85,000. Commuting time into the city seldom exceeds 20 minutes.

The equestrian set is still holding on in Suburban Maryland, and nowhere is it more evident than in posh **Potomac**. In some areas, subdivisions have chopped down once-magnificent farms into gaudy 5-acre horse "farmettes," but the overall atmosphere remains largely pastoral. Townhouses — the few that are here — start at $200,000, while single-family abodes range from $400,000 to $4 million. River Road, Potomac's lovely link with the outside world, is a wending two-laner that wasn't designed for express commuting. But then again, most of the folks who live in Potomac can probably set their own hours, thus rendering rush hour irrelevant.

Hovering the District line east of Rock Creek Park are **Silver Spring** and **Takoma Park**, two established and quite different residential areas. Silver Spring is probably Montgomery's most ethnic community and of late its downtown corridor has witnessed a renaissance of sorts, boasting some of the region's best international restaurants. Single-family homes start at $140,000 and rarely go above $300,000.

Takoma Park, immediately to the south, is Metro Washington's answer to Berkeley, Calif., or Boulder, Colo. Almost beyond politically correct (the entire city is designated a Nuclear Free Zone), the town, which straddles the Montgomery/Prince George's border, is a flashpoint of community activism. A nice mix of young free-spirits, middle-aged bohemians and long-time elderly residents live in older and mostly modest Cape Cods and Victorians, and the prices pretty much mirror those in Silver Spring.

The village of **Kensington**,

Photo: Reston Land Corporation

The natural beauty of Northern Virginia surrounds this new home.

eight miles north of D.C. and a mile north of the Beltway, defies its highly suburban location. Less than 2,000 people live in this half-square mile community that is among the oldest suburbs in Metro Washington (incorporated in 1894). Many of the Victorian homes date back to the 1890s, adding a nostalgic air to the place. Houses start at $150,000 and work their way up to over $275,000.

Most of the people north of the Beltway live in or around the communities of **Wheaton, Rockville** and **Gaithersburg**. Metrorail and Georgia Avenue connect Wheaton with Washington. Rockville, the county seat, and Gaithersburg, its fast-growing northern neighbor, were once serene little dairy towns whose pastures are now dotted with townhomes and single-family developments. Wheaton and Rockville have the majority of detached housing ($200,000 to $300,000) and are family oriented. Gaithersburg has a large population of single young professionals who tend to migrate toward moderately-priced townhomes ($120,000 and up) in areas like Montgomery Village, a planned residential area.

Two Up-County communities in transition are **Germantown** and **Damascus**. Germantown is the denser of the two, with its rolling hills carpeted by new condominiums, townhouses and shopping centers. About 10 miles up Route 27, once-sleepy Damascus is evolving into a bedroom community of first-time homeowners who are just as likely to commute to Baltimore as Washington.

Prince George's County

The average price of a home in Prince George's County is $135,900, about $80,000 less than a comparable house next door in Montgomery County. Rents are much cheaper, too; the median is about $610 for a two-bedroom apartment unit.

Why the sizeable price difference? Perception. Prince George's could use some good spin doctors. The county's reputation as a blue-collar haven with sub-par schools and too much crime is largely unjustified. Yes, it's more working-class than Montgomery and Fairfax and yes, it's had its share of crime problems, especially in neighborhoods close to the District border. But Prince George's is also the most racially integrated county in Metro Washington and its schools have made tremendous progress in recent years.

Progressive communities like **College Park** and **Takoma Park** teem with college students, artists, writers and aging activists. **University Park** and **Greenbelt** have high concentrations of academicians, scientists and engineers, while **Bowie, Mitchellville** and **Upper Marlboro** attract white-collar professionals and families. Waterfront living gives **Fort Washington** a distinct panache, and this is where you're likely to find some of the most expensive real estate in Prince George's.

Several major road arteries, including Route 50, I-295, Branch Avenue and Pennsylvania Avenue, connect the county with nearby Washington, helping make commuting times here among the lowest in Metro D.C.

Anne Arundel County

Metro Washington's ongoing romance with the Chesapeake Bay is partly the reason why Anne Arundel has become a bonafide suburb of D.C. Commuters choose to live here. For those who must travel to Washington to work every day, it's not a place of incredible convenience, at least not in the same vein as Montgomery and Prince George's.

Although the recent widening of Route 50 has done wonders in curbing logjams, Anne Arundel residents still face 40- to 60-minute commutes into the District every morning.

That's not enough to keep new residents from flocking in, though. More than 400,000 people reside in the county, which stretches north to Baltimore and south into the rural countryside of Southern Maryland. Beside its 1,800 miles of streams and rivers and over 400 miles of Bay shoreline, Anne Arundel offers another strong incentive — affordability. The average-priced home here is $155,000, and the property tax bite is the lowest in Suburban Maryland.

The nerve center of the

county, of course, is **Annapolis**, the quaint capital city that's a strong aphrodisiac for boating and water enthusiasts.

Water-privileged communities also abound on nearby Broadneck Peninsula, offering suburbanites a peaceful tonic to the bustle of the densely populated Washington-Baltimore megalopolis. Washington commuters are also a common site in the county's Western Corridor, an area that fans out from Route 3 north of Route 50 and which includes communities like **Crofton** and **Odenton** where residents can catch the rail line to Washington and Baltimore.

A Few Words About Property Taxes

In the District of Columbia and Virginia, homes are appraised at 100 percent of their market value. Homeowners in D.C. also get an exemption for the first $30,000 of their property's value. In Maryland, 40 percent of the house's value is taxed but at a much higher rate.

For a $200,000 home, about the average price in Metro D.C., this is roughly what you'd pay in property taxes in the following jurisdictions:

District of Columbia	$1,662
Northern Virginia	
Alexandria	$2,090
Arlington County	$1,640
Fairfax County	$2,326
Prince William County	$2,720
Loudoun County	$1,920
Suburban Maryland	
Montgomery County	$2,480
Prince George's County	$2,788
Anne Arundel County	$2,136

When you look at these figures it's important to keep in mind the type of property you're being taxed for. A $200,000 home varies from being a condo in a premium Washington neighborhood to a modest townhouse in Old Town Alexandria to a spacious colonial on a large lot in Prince George's and Prince William counties.

Real Estate Resources

For more information on the local real estate market, licensing practices, ethics and other issues involving buying or renting a home, we suggest you call one or more of the following agencies:

Washington D.C. Association of Realtors, (202) 628-4494

District of Columbia Real Estate Commission,(202) 727-7849

Northern Virginia Board of Realtors, (703) 207-3200

Virginia Real Estate Board, (804) 367-8526

Maryland Association of Realtors, (301) 261-8290

Maryland Real Estate Commission, (410) 356-8120

Real Estate Firms

The following are some of the major real estate brokerage firms doing business in Metro Washington. Most of these agencies are also good sources of newcomer information and services.

LONG & FOSTER REAL ESTATE INC.

11351 Random Hills Rd.
Fairfax, Va. 22030 (703) 359-1500

Long & Foster, a dominant player in the region, handles about $4 billion in sales in Metro Washington each year. The firm's forte is in new-home sales, relocation and property management. It's also ubiquitous: Some 4,400 licensed agents work out of 140 offices scattered throughout the area. The company is affiliated with the Genesis Realty Referral Network.

THE PRUDENTIAL PREFERRED PROPERTIES INC.

7830 Old Georgetown Rd., Suite 100
Bethesda, Md. 20814 (301) 718-7200

Like its name implies, Prudential Preferred handles a large chunk of the upscale market for new homes and resales. Though only in the D.C. area since 1990, the company has 2,500 agents in 37 offices. Annual sales hover around $3 billion. Prudential is part of the Prudential Relocation Management referral network.

RE/MAX REGIONAL SERVICES INC.

6404 Ivy Lane, Suite 502
Greenbelt, Md. 20770 (301) 982-4684

From starter homes to mansions, RE/MAX has one of the largest listings in the market. It has 60 offices throughout Washington, Northern Virginia and Suburban Maryland and is part of the RE/MAX International Referral Roster System.

WEICHERT REALTY

6410 Rockledge Ave.
Bethesda, Md. 20817 (301) 718-4111

The Maryland-based firm recently bought out a portion of D.C.'s Shannon and Luchs Co. and Virginia's Mount Vernon Realty and overnight became one of the largest and most powerful residential brokerage firms in Metro D.C. The company is particularly noted for its large inventory of luxury homes and estates.

Century 21 of the Mid-Atlantic States

1951 Kidwell Dr., Suite 200
Vienna, Va. 22182 (703) 821-3121

This national agency posts annual sales of about $2 billion in the Washington area, and has 110 offices here. Century 21 is part of the VIP Referral network.

Coldwell Banker Residential Real Estate

1953 Gallows Rd., Suite 340
Vienna, Va. 22182 (703) 556-6100

One of the most established brokerages in Metro Washington, Coldwell Banker is another billion-dollar sales producer, with 20 offices and 750 licensed agents. The company has its own referral network service.

ERA Real Estate

4900 Seminary Rd., Suite 204
Alexandria, Va. 22311 (703) 671-6668

ERA is probably best known for its extensive military relocation work, but it's by no means confined to that niche. About 1,000 agents handle virtually every type of residential property, and they sell about 4,000 houses a year.

Lewis & Silverman Inc. Realtors

6701 Democracy Blvd., Suite 401
Bethesda, Md. 20817 (301) 493-4566

This Bethesda-based firm has a major presence in Montgomery County and is recognized for its exclusive listings. The company is affiliated with the All Points Relocation Service.

Town & Country Properties Inc.

8318 Arlington Blvd.
Fairfax, Va. 22031 (703) 698-8222

A full-service brokerage, Town & Country is also involved in the mortgage, insurance and property-management business. The firm has more than 1,000 agents working out of 38 offices. It is part of the RELO referral network.

Carol Taylor & Associates

11000 Picasso Ln.
Potomac, Md. 20837 (301) 483-2000

The majority of Carol Taylor & Associates' listings are in Montgomery County, but the Potomac-based realtor has properties spread throughout Suburban Maryland, Northern Virginia and the District.

Residential Real Estate Builders

The following are some of the largest residential home builders in Metro Washington.

NVR LP

7601 Lewinsville Rd.
McLean, Va. 22102 (703) 761-2000

This giant Washington area builder specializes in garden condos, townhouses and single-family homes, ranging from $100,000 to $350,000. NVR is less than 10 years old but already assumes the leader position in the marketplace.

Pulte Home Corp.

10600 Arrowhead Dr.
Fairfax, Va. 22030 (703) 934-9300

Pulte builds the works, from $85,000 condos to $750,000 Hunt Country classics. The firm has been on the scene since 1956 and is known for its reliability.

Winchester Homes Inc.

6701 Rockledge Dr., Suite 700
Bethesda, Md. 20817 (301) 897-0170

Winchester builds $130,000 to $400,000 single-family homes and condos, and has a large presence in Suburban Maryland.

Washington Homes Inc.

1802 Brightseat Rd.
Landover, Md. 20785 (301) 772-8900

A mid-range builder of townhouses and single-family homes, with prices ranging from $75,000 to $275,000, Washington Homes is also becoming a leading builder in exurban areas of Maryland and Virginia.

Richmond American Homes

3701 Pender Dr., Suite 200
Fairfax, Va. 22030 (703) 352-0800

Another exurban powerhouse, Richmond American builds $95,000-$400,000 condos, townhouses and single-family homes. The Ashburn Farm development in Loudoun County is one such project.

Harkins Builders Inc.

12301 Old Columbia Pike
Silver Spring, Md. 20904 (301) 622-9000

Harkins is one of the region's premiere condo and townhouse developers, covering the spectrum from $80,000 garden units to $1.5 million luxury penthouse properties.

Ryland Homes

10221 Wincopin Cir.
Columbia, Md. 21044 (301) 730-7222

Ryland is aggressive in the exurban townhouse and single-family home market. Properties tend to be competitively priced and therefore popular among first-time buyers.

American Residential

1738 Elton Rd.
Silver Spring, Md. 20903 (301) 431-0001

American Residential has 62 offices nationwide and is a growing player in the Metro Washington home building scene. The builder has projects in all three of the area's jurisdictions.

Retirement Living

Pervasive national lifestyle trends are working in the favor of dynamic urban areas like Metro Washington. Urban retirement is gaining steam today as more seniors look to metropolitan areas for their health care, transportation, recreation and education needs.

As America's 77 million baby boomers age, they bring with them new expectations. More want to be near family and close to business and volunteer activities. Retiring in the desert of Arizona or the beaches of Florida, while still viable options, isn't for everyone in this new generation of seniors.

The implications of urban

retirement are especially profound in the Nation's Capital, a region that's saturated in diversions and opportunities so craved by active seniors. The fastest-growing segment of the metro population is the 55-60 age bracket, which is projected to increase by nearly 24,000 between 1990 and 1995.

Nationwide, people over 65 will make up 13 percent of the population by century's end. That's 35 million people, more than the population of California.

A number of Washington area retirement communities are well positioned for growth in the '90s. They include Silver Spring, Md.'s **Leisure World** (301-598-1000), the region's first planned retirement village, and Annapolis's **Heritage Harbor** (301-261-8650), a US Homes-developed community on the South River that offers moderately-priced single-family homes and condominiums, a nine-hole golf course, and tennis and swimming facilities.

One national survey found that 35 percent of those contemplating retirement preferred to purchase properties one hour from their current location. That distance makes new planned communities such as **Lake Manassas** and **Virginia Oaks**, both in Prince William County, attractive to active retirees in the Washington area.

For older retirees yearning to be pampered, there is **The Jefferson** (703-516-9455) in Arlington, a Marriott-run retirement condominium community. It offers the double perks of home ownership and a plethora of senior services.

A similar residential community, **Sunrise at Bluemont** (703-536-1060) in Arlington, is operated by Oakton, Va.-based Sunrise Retirement Homes and Communities and includes personal touches like private transportation, elegant dining rooms with fireplaces, a beauty salon, exercise rooms and an on-site medical care.

The breadth and depth of urban retirement options will surely multiply in the coming years, making Washington one of the most preferred locales among upscale retirees.

A number of Washington area retirement communities are well positioned for growth in the '90s, including Silver Spring, Md.'s **Leisure World** (301-598-1000), the region's first planned retirement village, and Annapolis's **Heritage Harbor** (301-261-8650), a US Home-developed community on the South River that offers moderately priced single-family homes and condominiums, a nine-hole golf course and tennis and swimming facilities. In addition, such traditional, full-service retirement centers as Manassas, Va.'s **Annaburg Manor** (703-335-8300), Alexandria's **Washington House** (703-379-9000) and Mitchellville, Md.'s **Collington Community** (301-925-7706) are showing signs of growth, proving that the suburbs are viable options for metropolitan retirees.

Inside Metro Washington Education

Ask any business, political or economic development official in Metro Washington what the primary ingredient is that shapes the region's inordinately high quality of life and you're likely to hear the word "education."

When people here wax proudly about the outstanding educational infrastructure, they're not bragging. They're simply telling the truth. Few metro areas in the country — or the world for that matter — can claim the quality and diversity of public and private schools, or the concentration of internationally renowned colleges, universities and research institutions as can the Nation's Capital.

Indeed, education is the fabric that holds this cerebral community together. The region relishes its reputation as the most educated community in America and it places a premium on the learning resources available to its children. Moreover, life-long learning is a trend that has taken hold of Metro Washington, and that's why you'll find that the area is among the nation's leaders in participation in continuing-education programs.

This chapter highlights the educational opportunities found throughout the area, beginning with

Photo: Mary Washington College

Monroe Hall, Mary Washington College, houses academic offices and classrooms.

the public school systems and then moving on to some of the select private institutions. The final section briefly describes the area's major colleges and universities, nearly all of which offer programs for working adults.

Public Schools

The common theme here is rabid parental interest in quality public education. Citizen involvement in local school districts is helping create new and better programs for students and is spurring efforts to attract the best and brightest teachers.

District of Columbia

District of Columbia Public Schools

Registration *(202) 724-2066*

It's no secret that America's inner-city public schools are experiencing tough times. Budget cutbacks, coupled with chronic absenteeism and increased violence, have left thousands of schools nationwide in sad disarray. The District of Columbia public school system suffers its share of problems, but to paint a picture of total gloom and doom would be inaccurate. The good news here far outweighs the bad.

D.C. schools enroll more than 80,000 students. Testament to the city's international character, students represent over 130 nations and speak at least 90 languages. In recent years there has been a marked increase in scores on national basic skills tests, including an elementary-school performance that now outpaces the U.S. average. SAT scores have also inched up over the last few years and now average about 850.

Bilingual programs in Spanish and Chinese have earned the District kudos from educators around the country. Smaller groups of international students are taught English by itinerant teams of language teachers. There's even a school that teaches foreign adults English and prepares them for U.S. citizenship.

The District's citywide magnet schools have always held their ground for students with special skills or artistic talents. The Duke Ellington School for the Performing Arts has some of the finest dance, theater and music departments in the metro area. Other magnet programs specialize in aerospace and marine science, mathematics and accelerated college preparatory courses.

Washington, of course, is one giant learning laboratory, and the public school system has tapped into it through a motivated-students program called "School Without Walls." Academic help is offered to former dropouts through two "Street Academies" — schools that stress personal and career counseling as much as classroom performance. The District extends child care services for students who are parents, and even runs a special school for young men and women who work as pages in the U.S. Capitol.

Like everything else in Washington, D.C., the public schools are constantly under the national microscope, especially in terms of funding and performance. All education programs, after being approved by an elected school board and the city government, must pass the financial scrutiny of Congress and the White House. Needless to say, not all plans win approval. Budgets and, unfortunately, politics often get in the way of much-needed resources. Teachers' salaries, however, have remained competitive, ranging from $23,000 to $48,000.

Problems aside, the D.C. school system has the unlimited educational resources of Washington in its backyard — resources that are the envy of every school district in the nation.

Northern Virginia

Alexandria Public Schools

Registration *(703) 824-6600*

Small (at least compared with the school districts of its Goliath neighbors) and efficient may be the best way to describe Alexandria's well-respected public school system. About 9,200 students attend 13 elementary schools, two junior high schools and one senior high. The district has an occupational center for students with learning difficulties and one for mentally retarded students ages 2 to 21. Gifted and talented instruction is available as are courses for homebound students.

The city's lone high school, T.C. Williams, resembles a junior college, with cutting-edge academic and vocational facilities. T.C. students average 926 on the SAT. About 76 percent go on to some form of higher education.

Alexandria's per-pupil expenditure of $7,550 is among the highest in Metro Washington. Teachers earn between $25,345 and $55,000.

Arlington County Public Schools

Registration *(703) 358-6000*

Diversity defines Arlington County Public Schools, where students speak more than 50 languages, from Spanish and Vietnamese to Arabic and Farsi. Among the county's 29 schools are a special education center, an international children's learning center and three alternative schools for individualized studies. Summer school programs are offered for remedial and advanced study. The school system also has special classes for students with emotional and learning disabilities as well as programs for the mentally retarded.

The county's innovative Adult Education Program enrolls more than 16,000 students and offers high-school equivalency studies, senior citizens' activities and an array of multicultural programs. A Montessori curriculum for three- and four-year-olds and an extended-day program for elementary school students are available on a fee basis that is scaled to family income.

Arlington spends almost $8,000 per student, while teachers' salaries range between $26,000 and $58,000. The investments are paying off: 85 percent of Arlington high school graduates go on to college. The average SAT score is 952.

Fairfax County Public Schools

Registration *(703) 246-2502*

With more than 130,000 students and 9,000 teachers, Fairfax County Public Schools is the 10th-largest school district in the United States. At last count, there were 129 elementary schools, 19 intermediate, 3 secondary (grades 7-12), 20 high schools, 17 special-education centers and 20 alternative schools. The county's 1,100 school buses handle 90,000 students every day, making it the nation's largest busing system.

To put its size in a more regional perspective, the county accounts for 16 percent of Virginia's high school seniors. These tremendous numbers do not equate to mediocrity or impersonalization in the classroom. Fairfax students consistently score 18- to 36-percentile points above the national average in reading, mathematics, language arts and the sciences. Almost 45 percent of the state's National Merit Scholarship Exam semifinalists come from Fairfax County Public Schools.

The system has countywide programs for the gifted and talented, for students with learning disabilities, as well as for international students who speak English as a second language. The county's prized science and technical magnet school, Thomas Jefferson High School in

Annandale, boasts the highest concentration of National Merit Scholars in the U.S.

Vocational programs include studies in business education, home economics, industrial arts and horticulture. Extended-day care, meanwhile, is offered at 82 elementary schools through the Fairfax County Office for Children. Fees are based on a sliding scale. There are also special day care programs for disabled students.

At the heart of the county's educational success are the teachers, over half of whom have master's or doctoral degrees. Salaries range from $25,000 to $54,000.

Administratively, the district is divided into four geographic areas. As you can imagine, parental involvement is high, and teams of parents, teachers, administrators and students have great influence over budgets, curriculum and the establishment of new facilities and programs.

Within the county, meanwhile, are two separate municipal school districts — one serving the City of Fairfax and one serving Falls Church. Fairfax City's system (703-385-7190) operates under a separate tuition contract between the city and the county. It has its own superintendent of schools and board of education. Falls Church (703-341-7600) enrolls more than 1,200 students in its system, widely considered one of the best in the region. Of special note here are a preschool child development center and a comprehensive day care program for elementary students.

Prince William County Public Schools

Registration *(703) 791-7200*

The tremendous — and often overwhelming — growth that transformed Prince William over the past 15 years never short-changed the county's public school system. If anything, it improved it. Today, surveys show that 85 percent of the parents of school-age children rate the county's education system as good or excellent.

Nearly 80 percent of the county's high school graduates go on to college. The average SAT score is around 900.

In all, more than 43,000 students attend 57 public schools here in Virginia's third-largest district. Prince William utilizes the Curriculum Action Plan that earmarks specific learning objectives by grade level for each subject. There are also extensive programs for gifted students, for students with disabilities, and for those who want to pursue vocational studies. Teacher salaries, meanwhile, range from $25,000 to $48,000.

Public school policy is set by the county school board, which is made up of several members appointed to four-year terms. Public meetings of the school board are held the first and third Wednesdays of each month and are widely attended.

Both independent cities within the county — Manassas (703-361-0166) and Manassas Park (703-335-8850) — have their own school systems, with enrollments of 5,000 and 1,400, respectively. Academically, they tend to mirror the county, including the percentage of students who go on to pursue higher education

Loudoun County Public Schools

Registration *(703) 771-6400*

The 15,000-student Loudoun County public school system is among the best in exurban Metro Washington. The system has 33 elementary, middle and high schools. Each school offers computer education, while science labs are found in all middle and high schools. A vocational-technical school comes with the dual purpose of instructing high school students during the daytime and adults in the evening. Districtwide student attendance averages a stunning 96 percent, and the high school dropout rate is among the lowest in Virginia. SAT scores here average 936.

Suburban Maryland

Montgomery County Public Schools

Registration *(301) 279-3391*

Arguably the best public school system in Metro Washington is in Montgomery County. About 93 percent of the county's high school graduates go on to higher education. SAT scores average 989, highest in the area.

Like Fairfax's, Montgomery's system is gigantic. More than 107,000 students attend 173 public schools, including 21 senior high schools and eight special schools geared for gifted and talented students and students with learning and physical disabilities. The county offers extended elementary and foreign language programs, theater education, family math programs, gender equity initiatives, magnet programs, on-the-job training in business and industry and adult education services.

For more information about Virginia Tech's Northern Virginia Graduate Center, contact the campus at 2900 Telestar Court, Falls Church, VA 22042, (703) 698-6000.

All schools meet basic districtwide standards, but all are influenced by the wishes of the local communities. Some elementary and secondary schools use an "open plan" curriculum, with instruction given by teaching teams. All schools have attendance boundaries, however, there's a voluntary integration policy for students who feel they need to be in a school outside of their community.

The student/faculty ratio here is a low 15 to one. Montgomery County teachers earn between $27,000 and $55,000, making them the best-paid educators in the metro area.

Prince George's County Public Schools

Registration *(301) 952-6000*

Prince George's County Public Schools is recognized nationally for its progressive approach to education — a tack that has given the county the most-improved schools in the Washington area.

New graduation requirements for high school students call for more credits in math and social studies and less in electives. The county has innovative comprehensive reading initiatives, English as a second language programs, schools for gifted students, schools for the learning and physically disabled, evening schools for adults, and even an educational project geared toward the needs of Indian children.

About 109,000 students attend the county's 171 schools. Given the amount of services available, the expenditure per student, $5,000, is on the low side, suggesting a great degree of efficiency. Teachers' salaries range between $25,000 and $49,000.

Anne Arundel County Public Schools

Registration *(410) 222-5000*

Anne Arundel County Public Schools has long been recognized as a leader in education reform and innovation. The district was among the first in the U.S. to build a special school for children with physical and learning disabilities. Today, the county increasingly uses open-space schools that deliver individualized instruction through team teaching, independent study programs, student self-scheduling and small seminars.

Among the county's 119 schools are facilities for children with behavioral problems, two vocational centers and 12 high schools. Some 65,000 students are enrolled in the system. The average SAT score is 907.

Private Schools

Private schools in the region range from traditional liberal arts institutions to alternative programs for gifted or learning-disabled students. Of course, the benefits of such highly personalized and specialized study come with a price tag. Generally speaking, tuition fees here can range from $1,500 to $15,000 a year. Another good clearinghouse for additional information on private schools in the area is the Association of Independent Schools of

Greater Washington (202-362-3665).

District of Columbia

Archbishop Carroll High School

4300 Harewood Rd. NE 20017
(202) 529-0900
700 Students/9th-12th/Coed
$3,150 Catholics; $3,350 non-Catholics

Located near Catholic University, in Northeast, Archbishop Carroll is one of the city's leading Catholic high schools. The school is known for its rigorous academic standards, dedicated faculty and strong athletic and activities programs. Graduates go on to Catholic, Georgetown, the University of Virginia, the University of Maryland and other nationally competitive colleges.

Georgetown Visitation Preparatory School

1524 35th St. NW 20007(202) 337-3350
402 Students/9th-12th/Women
$7,450

Located next door to Georgetown University, on a 27-acre campus, Visitation has been grooming young women for higher education since 1799. The prestigious day school is affiliated with the Roman Catholic Church and boasts outstanding programs in the fine arts, foreign languages and mathematics, among others. Visitation grads go on to a wide variety of colleges,

Photo: Mary Washington College

Mary Washington College students chat between classes on the steps of Monroe Hall.

including some of the top schools on the East Coast.

THE LAB SCHOOL OF WASHINGTON
4759 Reservoir Rd. NW 20007
(202) 965-6600
250 Students/1st-12th/Coed
$15,500

The Lab School is designed for intelligent students with learning disabilities. The elementary school emphasizes an ungraded curriculum; grades 7 through 12 are college preparatory. The school is located in a quiet residential area of upper Georgetown, not far from Mount Vernon College.

MACARTHUR SCHOOL
4460 MacArthur Blvd. NW 20007
(202) 965-8700
K-12th/Coed
$95/day

MacArthur's curriculum is modeled for students with emotional and learning disabilities. Of special note here is the school's chemical-dependency program, which has earned national acclaim. The campus is in Foxhall, one of the city's most affluent neighborhoods.

SHERIDAN SCHOOL
4400 36th St. NW 20008(202) 362-7900
K-8th/Coed
$11,000

Sheridan follows traditional liberal arts instruction for elementary and middle school children. An extended-day program runs from 7:30 AM to 6 PM and includes a variety of extracurricular activities. The campus is in North Cleveland Park, a residential neighborhood not far from Tenleytown Metro.

ST. ANSELM'S ABBEY SCHOOL
4501 South Dakota Ave. NE 20017
(202) 269-2350
180 Students/6th-12th/Men
$7,900

Located in the sprawling academic complex that radiates from Catholic University, St. Anselm's is a college prep school for boys of all faiths. The school is operated by the Benedictine monks of St. Anselm's Abbey and it typically receives the highest percentage of National Merit Recognitions in Metro Washington each year. There are challenging programs in music, drama, visual arts, publications and athletics. The Brookland/CUA Metro is nearby.

ST. JOHN'S COLLEGE HIGH SCHOOL/ MIDDLE SCHOOL
2607 Military Rd. NW 20015
(202) 363-2316
550 Students/7th-12th/Men/Coed
*High School **$5,400**; Middle School **$5,100***

Once an all-male prep school, St. John's upper school went coed in 1991. The middle school remains all boys, however. St. John's is run by the Christian Brothers and is known

Insiders' Tip

One of the best kept secrets in Metro Washington higher education is the Department of Agriculture. Offering a variety of collegiate courses ranging from history to accounting to journalism, the USDA program is both affordable and accessible.

for balancing academics with comprehensive extra-curricular activities, including an Army JROTC program.

St. Patrick's Episcopal Day School

4700 Whitehaven Pkwy. NW 20007
(202) 342-2805
428 Students/N-6th/Coed
$8,255 K-6; $5,235-$8,190

The liberal arts are taken seriously at this traditional Episcopal day school. St. Patrick's touts progressive elementary-school programs in the arts, music, French and science.

The Sidwell Friends School

3825 Wisconsin Ave. NW 20016
(202) 537-8111
1,026 Students/PK-12th/Coed
$10,270

Sidwell Friends, affiliated with the Society of Friends, was founded in 1883 and has since become one of the pre-eminent college prep schools in D.C. The day school follows a demanding liberal arts curriculum, including required studies in fine arts, foreign languages, math and science. Personalized community service programs are required of all graduates. Chelsea Clinton, the daughter of the President, attends school here.

Washington International School

3100 Macomb St. NW 20008
(202) 364-1815
660 Students/N-12/Coed
3 years of age for nursery admittance
3-year-olds $5,000; 4-year-olds $7,500; K-5th $9,050; 6th-12th $10,500

It's only fitting that an international city claim a bold international college prep school. A globalized curriculum, including bilingual studies, is the bread and butter of this independent day school. International Baccalaureates are offered along with a plethora of out-of-classroom experiences.

Northern Virginia

Alexandria

Burgundy Farm Country Day School

3700 Burgundy Rd. 22303(703) 960-3431
250 Students/PK-8th/Coed
PK $7,630; 1-5 $8,030; 6-8 $8,430

Burgundy Farm, situated on a 25-acre campus, offers an extended-day program for elementary and middle school students. All classes are taught by two instructors, with strong emphasis on the liberal arts. Summer day and wildlife camps are popular here.

Episcopal High School in Virginia

1200 N. Quaker Lane 22302
(703) 379-6530
285 Students/9th-12th/Coed
$16,500

One of Virginia's most celebrated prep schools, Episcopal is small, personal and highly demanding. The boarding school follows a tradition-rich Honor System that has created an environment of openness among students and instructors. One of Episcopal's biggest draws is a foreign studies program that utilizes the myriad resources of neighboring Washington.

St. Stephen's & St. Agnes School

Grades K-8th/Coed
400 Fontaine St. 22303 (703) 836-2199
$9,280
Grades 9th-12th
1000 St. Stephen's Rd. 22304
(703) 751-0056
990 Students/Coed
$10,320

The emphasis behind this coed Episcopal day school is balancing challenging academics with community service and other types of extracurricular activities. Interscholastic sports are a vital part of campus life. After-school and extended-day programs are available.

Fairfax County

Flint Hill School

10409 Academic Dr.
Oakton, Va. 22124 (703) 242-0705
425 Students/K-12th/Coed
K-3 $8,910; 4-12 $10,235

Flint Hill is a non-denominational college prep school that is widely known throughout the region for its lofty academic and competitive athletic programs. It's located in the heart of Northern Virginia, close to Interstate 66, in the residential community of Oakton.

The Fairfax Christian School

1624 Hunter Mill Rd.
Vienna, Va. 22182 (703) 759-5100
280 Students/K-12th/Coed
$3,300-$5,000

This coed school, located on the outskirts of Vienna, stresses a traditional liberal arts curriculum

Photo: Washington Convention and Visitors Association

The Library of Congress is the world's largest library — an incredible resource for area students.

in a Christian setting. Some after-care programs are available for youngsters. Boys tend to migrate toward the intramural soccer and basketball programs.

Nysmith School for the Gifted

13525 Dulles Technology Dr.
Herndon, Va. 22071 (703) 713-3332
204 Students/N-6th/Coed
2 1/2 years for nursery; tuition varies
1st-6th $6,800

As the name implies, accelerated academics are the rule here. Among the offerings are courses in Japanese, French, computers, dance and art. Extended-day and summer programs are available. The school is located in the northwest Fairfax County community of Herndon, just a few miles from Washington Dulles International Airport.

The Langley School

1411 Balls Hill Rd.
McLean, Va. 22101 (703) 356-1920
450 Students/N-8th/Coed
3 years by Sept. 30 of admitting year
1/2 day program N-PK $5,460
K-5th $9,220; 6th-8th $9,590

An independent day school for elementary and middle grade students, Langley prides itself on its personalized and accelerated instruction. The school is located in one of Northern Virginia's most exclusive neighborhoods. Extended-day and summer programs are available.

The Madeira School

8328 Georgetown Pike
McLean, Va. 22102 (703) 556-8257
320 Students/9th-12th/Women

Madeira offers young women, grades nine through 12, a challenging academic environment, highlighted by a distinct off-campus internship program. The school's lovely 400-acre campus, one of the largest in Metro Washington, is located in McLean, close to most points in Northern Virginia, Washington and Suburban Maryland.

The Potomac School

1301 Potomac School Rd.
McLean, Va. 22101 (703) 356-4101
800 Students/PK-12th/Coed
$11,080

With a student/teacher ratio of eight-to-one, it's hard to get lost in the crowd at the prestigious Potomac School. The independent day school places a premium on competitive academics and extensive community service. It's situated on a 70-acre campus in McLean.

Loudoun County

Foxcroft School

Route 626
Middleburg, Va. 22117 (703) 687-5555
136 Students/9th-12th/Women
$19,400 boarding; $12,600 day

This prep school for girls is nationally recognized for its academic and athletic programs. Foxcroft is located in the heart of Virginia's Hunt Country, and consequently, riding is a popular extracurricular activity here.

Loudoun Country Day School

237 Fairview St.
Leesburg, Va. 22075 (703) 777-3841
181 Students/PK-8th/Coed
PK (1/2 day) $4,350; K-5th $6,650; 6th-8th $7,800

The mission of Loudoun Country Day is advanced instruction, including accelerated programs in foreign languages and the arts. Sports also play a major role at the school, located in Leesburg, the seat of Loudoun County.

Springwood School

Route 4 Box 50
Leesburg, Va. 22075 (703) 777-0800
K-12th/Coed

Springwood is dedicated to students with emotional and learning disabilities. "Another Path," an after-school chemical dependency program, is making inroads with troubled adolescents.

Suburban Maryland

Montgomery County

Broschart School

14901 Broschart Rd.
Rockville, Md. 20850 (301) 251-4624
100 Students/K-12th/Coed
$95/day

Like Springwood School in Leesburg, Va., Broschart offers the chemical-dependency program "Another Path." The Rockville-based school also extends programs for students with emotional and learning disabilities.

The Bullis School

10601 Falls Rd.
Potomac, Md. 20854 (301) 299-8500
500 Students/4th-12th/Coed
4th-5th $8,200; 6th-8th $9,600; 9th-12th $10,800

Students are immersed in a range of academic and extracurricular programs at Bullis. The coed prep school has an extensive athletic program — one that involves a large percentage of the student body.

Charles E. Smith Jewish Day School

1901 E. Jefferson St.
Rockville, Md. 20852 (301) 881-1400
K-12th/Coed

This coed day school blends a liberal arts curriculum with traditional Jewish studies programs. It's located in downtown Rockville, near the Montgomery County administrative complex.

Georgetown Preparatory School

10900 Rockville Pike
Rockville, Md. 20852-3299(301) 493-5000
380 Students/9th-12th/Men
Day $9,200; Boarding $17,200

Founded in 1789, Georgetown Prep is one of the metro area's oldest private schools. The all-male campus has day and boarding options, with the former more common. Affiliated with the Roman Catholic Church, Georgetown Prep attracts a national student body and is a feeder for Georgetown University as well as other highly competitive schools around the nation.

Holton-Arms School

7303 River Rd.
Potomac, Md. 20817 (301) 365-6014
625 Students/3rd-12th/Women
3rd-4th $10,380; 5th-6th $10,480; 7th-12th $11,015

Holton-Arms is an all-girls college prep school that has a long-held reputation for its excellent liberal arts instruction. The Potomac-based day school excels in athletics and other extracurricular programs. After-school care is available.

Landon School

6101 Wilson Lane
Bethesda, Md. 20817 (301) 320-3200
579 Students/3rd-12th/Men
3rd-8th $9,700; 9th-12th $10,100

An independent college prep school for boys, Landon is structured around rigorous academics and a variety of out-of-classroom opportunities in music, drama and art. Volunteer work and community service are valued traditions here as is an honor code among middle and upper school students.

Prince George's County

Capitol Christian Academy

610 Largo Rd.
Upper Marlboro, Md. 20772
(301) 336-2200
K4-12th/Coed

Capitol Christian Academy offers both traditional and alternative academic programs. Of special note here are the intimate tutoring and counseling programs for special-needs children.

DeMatha Catholic High School

4313 Madison St.
Hyattsville, Md. 20781 (301) 864-3666
800 Students/9th-12th/Men
$3,500

One of the region's true academic and athletic powerhouses, DeMatha is recognized by the U.S. Department of Education as an "Exemplary Private School." The all-male prep school is located in the close-in suburb of Hyattsville, convenient to the District and most points in Suburban Maryland.

Riverdale Baptist Church
1133 Largo Rd.
Upper Marlboro, Md. 20772
(301) 249-7000
1,000 Students/N-12th/Coed
$3,500

Riverdale Baptist is Maryland's largest Christian school. Personalized instruction, however, is the norm as are comprehensive programs in computers, the arts, foreign languages, journalism, broadcasting and music. A wide variety of athletic and extracurricular activities is offered. Extended-day care is also available.

Colleges and Universities

Metro Washington colleges and universities attract students and faculty from all 50 states and more than 125 countries. A dozen of the region's leading schools are linked by the Consortium of Universities of the Washington Metropolitan Area (202-265-1313), a network that allows for extensive cross-study programs and sharing of resources such as libraries, faculty and research facilities. Consortium members include the University of the District of Columbia, American, Catholic, Gallaudet, George Mason, George Washington, Georgetown, Maryland, Howard and Marymount universities, and Mount Vernon and Trinity colleges.

District of Columbia

American University
Washington, D.C. 20016-8001
(202) 885-6000

"AU," as it's commonly known in these parts, is a mecca of sorts for future diplomats and journalists. For good reason: The university's international studies and communications departments are among the best in the nation, and consequently they command the highest enrollments. Highly competitive programs also await students in such areas as the life sciences, computer science, education and economics. Affiliated with the United Methodist Church, American offers extensive study-abroad programs in Europe and Latin America. The campus also makes good use of Washington as a learning lab: AU interns are almost as ubiquitous to D.C. as lawyers and lobbyists.

Student life is surprisingly close knit, with 3,500 of the nearly 9,000 students living on or very near campus, which is located in a beautiful residential section of Northwest. Graduate students make up nearly a third of the enrollment, and various programs are available for working professionals. The university's athletic programs are gaining popularity, spurred in part by the opening of a new on-campus gymnasium.

Catholic University of America
Washington, D.C. 20064 (202) 635-5305

Catholic draws strength from the diversity of its students who come from all 50 states and at least 36 countries. Undergraduate programs are offered through the schools of arts and sciences, engineering and architecture, nursing, philosophy and music. The university is somewhat unique in that graduate students (3,600) outnumber undergrads (3,000). There are nine graduate schools compared with the five undergrad schools. The school's drama department is considered one of the nation's best, having produced the likes of Susan Sarandon and other stage and screen stars.

On-campus housing is guaranteed for freshmen and sophomores, and is available on a lottery system for upperclassmen. Many students commute to the Northeast campus from the suburbs and other parts of the District. Catholic's highly acclaimed library contains over 1.2 million volumes and is often frequented by students from other schools in the metro area.

CORCORAN SCHOOL OF ART

Washington, D.C. 20006 (202) 628-9484

This private professional art college offers fully accredited undergraduate programs for visual artists, photographers and designers. The school is affiliated with the venerable Corcoran Gallery of Art, located near the White House and the National Mall.

GALLAUDET UNIVERSITY

Washington, D.C. 20002 (202) 651-5263

Gallaudet is the nation's only university dedicated exclusively to the hearing-impaired. The private liberal arts college, located in Northeast, awards bachelor's and master's degrees in such areas as business, biology, communications, the arts, computer science, education, engineering and environmental design.

The 2,000-strong student body, representing every state and 35 countries, is active in campus and community life. Fraternities and sororities, student societies and intercollegiate athletics are all vital components of the college. Gallaudet also operates model elementary, secondary and college prep schools for hearing-impaired students.

GEORGE WASHINGTON UNIVERSITY

Washington, D.C. 20052 (202) 994-6040

Like Catholic University, George Washington claims more graduate students (about 9,000) than undergrads (6,000). Graduate programs for working professionals are a growing commodity at GW. Bachelor degree sequences, meanwhile, span the liberal arts and technical spectrum, with psychology, political science, international affairs, international business, finance and electrical engineering garnering the largest number of students. The international MBA program is one of the best anywhere and the health professions school is bolstered by the university's highly acclaimed medical center. GW is a private, independent institution.

Despite an urban setting, in Foggy Bottom, the university maintains a distinctive collegiate atmosphere. Fraternities and sororities are big here as are the more than 200 active student organizations, ranging from international and political societies to literary and theater groups. GW athletics are a growing attraction, especially the men's and women's basketball teams. Only freshmen are guaranteed on-campus housing. GW students are known to be avid commuters.

Georgetown University

Washington, D.C. 20057 (202) 687-0100

Georgetown is undoubtedly Washington's — and one of the nation's — most visible and highly regarded universities. The 204-year-old school, the oldest Catholic college in America, has outstanding programs in the arts and sciences, business, engineering, the health professions, foreign service and nursing, to name a few. Graduate students (5,600) nearly equal undergrads (5,800), and they're drawn to Georgetown's fine law, medical and business schools. The university also has one the area's most comprehensive continuing education programs, including dozens of interesting non-credit courses open to all adults.

Some may argue that the university's raison d'etre is its government department, which each year pumps out scores of budding lawmakers, policy analysts, advisors, researchers and diplomats. To be sure, the government department enrolls more students than any other department. (Fittingly, Georgetown is the alma mater of President Clinton.)

Students come here from all 50 states and 84 countries, giving the beautiful 110-acre campus an unmistakably cosmopolitan air. As you can imagine, campus life is rich and intense. Undergrads tend to be the fashion- and trend-setters for Washington's 20-something set.

Howard University

Washington, D.C. 20059 (202) 636-6200

Howard is the nation's largest predominantly black university — and one of the most respected. Twelve undergraduate and 11 grad schools accommodate nearly 13,000 students. Accounting, finance and engineering are among the largest and best programs here. The university's amazing four-to-one student/faculty ratio allows for highly personalized and accelerated instruction.

Howard students (80 percent African-American) come from 48 states and 103 countries. More than a third live in student housing, while the bulk of the rest live in the neighboring LeDroit Park section of Northwest D.C. The 241-acre campus is just a couple miles north of the Capitol. Virginia Gov. L. Douglas Wilder, the nation's first elected black governor, earned his law degree here.

Mount Vernon College

Washington, D.C. 20007 (202) 331-0400

This private liberal arts school for women was founded in 1875 but has spent the better part of the past decade trying to re-invent itself. In the past, Mount Vernon has been criticized as being "soft" on academics. A new direction, however, seems to be taking root and the changes could have a lasting impact on the school's business, communications and social science programs. Mount Vernon is situated on a gorgeous 26-

acre campus in the city's wealthy Foxhall neighborhood.

Southeastern University

Washington, D.C. 20024 (202) 488-8162

One of the metro area's better-kept secrets, Southeastern is a private commuter college that specializes in undergraduate business programs for working adults. The university extends credit for life, military and work experience and has a number of co-op programs and internships. The campus consists of a single building located in a residential neighborhood of Southwest.

Strayer College

Washington, D.C. 20036 (202) 728-0355

Strayer is a private, independent business college with campuses in the District and Arlington, Alexandria, Woodbridge, Manassas Ashburn and Fredericksburg, Va. The commuter school offers associate, bachelor's and master's degree programs. About 70 percent of the students are working adults, most of whom take classes in the evenings and on weekends.

Trinity College

Washington, D.C. 20017 (202) 939-5040

A private liberal arts college for women, Trinity boasts a personalized learning atmosphere and a certain esprit de corps among its 500 or so full-time undergrads. Business administration, political science and information studies are the most popular degrees. The school has graduate programs, some that are coed.

About 95 percent of Trinity students live on the 26-acre campus located across the street from Catholic University. The college is affiliated with the Roman Catholic Church.

University of the District of Columbia

Washington, D.C. 20011 (202) 282-7300

UDC is the only publicly funded college in the District and therefore its mission is a bit different than that of its neighbors. About 45 percent of undergraduates are from Washington, and 85 percent of all students come from public high schools. The student-to-faculty ratio is eight to one, low for a non-private school. UDC offers bachelor's and master's degrees across the liberal arts spectrum. Business administration remains the strongest academic program and the fine arts claim the most number of students.

Student life at UDC is on the upswing, but this is exclusively a commuter school. There's no on-campus housing. In addition, the university is spread across three separate campuses in Northwest. The vast majority of students are part-timers.

Northern Virginia

George Mason University

Fairfax, Va. 22030 (703) 323-2107

George Mason is the fastest-growing university in the commonwealth and one of the fastest growing in the nation. Since its founding in 1957, the college has undergone the transformation from a fledgling regional institution into a powerful national public university. Mason draws on a diverse and singularly impressive faculty, many of whom come from the public policy, business and political ranks of Washington. Undergraduate programs include studies in the arts and sciences, education, information technology, engineering, fine arts, business and nursing. The graduate school accounts for about 30 percent of the student body and contains rapidly expanding programs in business and international studies, among others.

The vast majority of Mason's 20,000 students attend classes on the main campus, located near Fairfax City. The Arlington campus houses some professional programs and the law school. Almost 90 percent of GMU students are commuters and nearly the same amount are from Virginia. The school can, however, accommodate 3,000 people in university housing. Campus life is what you'd expect from a commuting school: sparse. The addition of a new fine arts center and a growing slate of on-campus entertainment programming come with the promise of invigorating the social scene. But Mason students make no bones about it: They're here first and foremost for an education, and that they are getting.

The University of Virginia-Virginia Tech Academic Center

Falls Church, Va. 22042
UVA (703) 876-6900
Va. Tech (703) 698-6000

This jointly-run center in Falls Church links Northern Virginia with the commonwealth's two largest and arguably most influential universities. In case you didn't know, the main campus of the University of Virginia is in Charlottesville, in central Virginia, while Tech is located in Blacksburg, in the southwestern part of the state near Roanoke.

The Northern Virginia center offers adult students an array of undergraduate and graduate liberal arts and technical courses. Graduate degree programs are offered in urban planning, education and engineering.

Marymount University

Arlington, Va. 22207 (703) 522-5600

Marymount began as a private Catholic college for women. About six years ago it went coed and today it seems to be expanding in every direction. (It even has a branch campus in Loudoun County.) The mission remains the same, though: to provide an intimate and accelerated atmosphere to grow and learn. The university offers undergraduate and graduate programs in such areas as nursing, business, education, human resource development, psychology and liberal studies. Day and evening classes are available for working professionals.

George Washington University Northern Virginia Campus

Ashburn, Va. 22011 (703) 729-8300

This satellite campus of GWU (see listing under District of Columbia) is an innovative venture between industry and education.

Several courses and executive seminars are taught by area business and science leaders outside of academia. Master's and doctoral degree programs are offered in engineering, business, information systems and human resources. The center also conducts a number of non-degree professional development workshops. The campus is located in the sprawling University Center, a corporate and research park that sits in the middle of eastern Loudoun County's rapidly growing Route 7 corridor.

Mary Washington College

Fredericksburg, Va. 22401 (703) 899-4681

Thanks to the Virginia Railway Express and a large stock of affordable housing, Fredericksburg has become an exurb of Metro Washington. That being the case, we thought it only appropriate to include in this list the city's academic pride and joy: Mary Washington College. This publicly funded coed college is consistently rated among the top regional liberal arts schools in the country and one of the best buys in higher education. Undergrads number 3,500, and highly competitive admission standards will likely keep that figure stable in coming years. Students seem to migrate to the school's psychology, business and English departments. Bachelor's and master's degree programs in liberal studies are offered to working professionals. MWC's lush tree-lined campus is a recruiting tool in itself.

Suburban Maryland

Columbia Union College

Takoma Park, Md. 20912 (301) 891-4230

Tiny Columbia Union (enrollment 1,200) is a private liberal arts college affiliated with the Seventh-Day Adventist Church. It's located on a 19-acre campus in Takoma Park, a city known for its grass-roots activism and progressive politics. Business and nursing are the strongest programs here and as such they command the greatest number of students. (There are no graduate programs.) More than 70 percent of students commute to campus.

Bowie State University

Bowie, Maryland 20715 (301) 464-6563

Part of the University of Maryland system, Bowie State is a regional liberal arts institution that boasts strong undergraduate programs in business, education and computer science. African-American students account for about two-thirds of the 3,700-strong student body. A third of all students are enrolled in the graduate school. The 280-acre campus includes four dormitories, a learning-resource center, art gallery, radio and TV station and the Adler-Dreikurs Institute of Human Relations.

Capitol College

Laurel Maryland 20708 (301) 953-3200

This college opened in 1927 as a correspondence school called the Capitol Radio Engineering Institute. Today, the private 725-student college awards bachelor's degrees in communications and engineering, including programs in telecommunications management, computer engineering, optoelectronics and engineering technology. Capitol is situated on a 52-acre campus in Laurel, a Prince George's County community lodged about halfway between Washington and Baltimore.

University of Maryland

College Park, Md. 20742 (301) 454-5550

Maybe it's the proximity to Georgetown, or Baltimore's Johns Hopkins, or even the University of Virginia. Whatever the reason, the University of Maryland has never received the proper share of credit it deserves for being one of the nation's better state universities, and one of the fastest-growing research institutions.

With 35,000 students in its 14 undergraduate and graduate schools, Maryland has been criticized as being too large and impersonal. There may be some truth behind the claims, but with its size comes almost unlimited opportunities for academic and social life. Three-quarters of the students here are undergraduates, and they flock to the university's strong programs in engineering, computer science, physics, Spanish, education and business management. Graduate programs in the physical sciences and engineering are bolstered by expanding research facilities on and off campus.

The University of Maryland's innovative University College was established in 1947 as one of the nation's pioneering adult education programs. Today, it is one of the metro area's most popular continuing-ed programs, offering bachelor's and master's degrees in business, biology, communications, the arts, engineering and health professions, among others.

Campus life at Maryland tends to be pretty traditional. Greeks account for about 10 percent of the students and they are joined by over 400 social and professional clubs. Despite some lean times over the past decade, Terrapins have always been bullish on their sports teams. During an up year, football can take on religious proportions in College Park.

St. John's College

Annapolis, Md. 21404 (410) 263-2371

The classic liberal arts education is still alive and well at Annapolis's St. John's College, where the curriculum is centered around the 100 Great Books. So traditional it's non-traditional, St. John's, which dates back to 1696, extends only one degree — bachelor (or master) of liberal arts. Instruction is carried out through discussion, analysis and argument. Written tests are rare and grades are basically nonexistent. If this sounds like fun and games, think again. Academics are taken seriously, if somewhat introspectively, by the 450 students. Classes are intimate (student-to-faculty ratio is six to one) and rigorous. The majority of entering freshmen score well above 1,200 on the SAT.

United States Naval Academy

Annapolis, Md. 21402 (410) 267-4361

It's hard not to get caught up in the pageantry and traditions of the Naval Academy. The sight of Midshipmen marching through the grounds of this immaculate campus that sits on the edge of the Chesapeake Bay is enough to turn a cynic into a patriot.

The academy awards B.S. degrees in communications, computer and physical science, engineering and environmental design and social science. Annapolis graduates must serve five years on active duty as commissioned officers of the Navy or Marine Corps. A sacrifice indeed, but for those fortunate enough to gain admittance (only about 10 percent of 15,000 applicants are accepted each year) the reward is an excellent and free (government-paid) education. Middies even receive a stipend. Not surprisingly, almost 80 percent of those who enter the academy go on to graduate.

Hood College

Frederick, Md. 21701 (301) 663-3131

This private liberal arts college (originally founded for women) is affiliated with the United Church of Christ and is situated on a beautiful 50-acre campus in the city of Frederick. Most of the school's 2,000 students gravitate to academically strong programs in biology, education, social work and psychology. More than 80 percent of students live on campus. While technically coed, women make up 90 percent of the student body.

Community Colleges

Northern Virginia

Northern Virginia Community College

Annandale, Virginia 22003-3796
(703) 323-3196

Northern Virginia Community College, or "NOVA" in the local vernacular, awards two-year associate degrees in over 130 occupational, technical and college transfer programs. The 63,000- student school, the largest college in Virginia, has campuses in Alexandria, Annandale, Loudoun County, Manassas and Woodbridge. The Extended Learning Institute provides credit and non-credit courses for study at home. Continuing education programs abound on all five campuses and community facilities throughout Northern Virginia.

Suburban Maryland

Montgomery College

Rockville, Md. 20850 *(301) 279-5000*

This 23,000-student community college is spread across three campuses in Maryland's largest county. The Rockville campus, by far the biggest with nearly 15,000 students, offers numerous technical and liberal arts transfer programs. The Takoma Park campus specializes in health studies and professional programs. The Germantown campus offers specialized career programs plus the gamut of arts and science courses. In addition to regular, for-credit courses, non-credit programs are taught at campuses and community sites across the county. These popular classes, ranging from auto maintenance to canoeing, enroll more than 17,000 students each year.

Prince George's Community College

Largo, Md. 20772 *(301) 336-6000*

Another one of Maryland's fine community colleges, Prince George's has an open admissions policy and a menu of over 50 areas of study including accounting, health sciences, education and art. Students are as diverse as the curriculum. It's not unusual to see recent high school graduates, mid-career adults and senior citizens taking classes together. Summer programs, contract training arrangements and extension and telecredit courses are all available here. More than half of all credit students transfer to four-year colleges and universities, with the University of Maryland being the No. 1 destination.

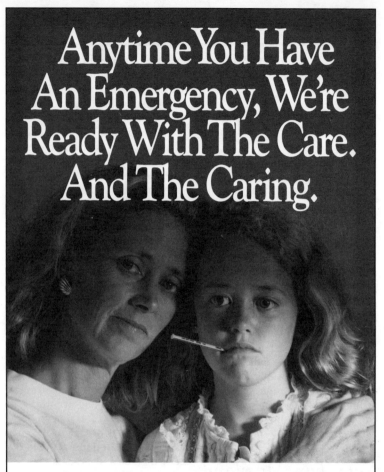

Inside Metro Washington Health Care

The sick, the injured or anyone seeking medical attention can take comfort in knowing that Metro Washington is a health-care mecca.

The National Capital Area is home to some of the world's finest doctors and health-care professionals who have at their disposal some of the world's finest hospitals, research facilities and myriad resources. Perhaps the focal point of the region's health-care establishment is the globally renowned National Institutes of Health, headquartered in Bethesda, in Montgomery County. One of the largest research centers in the world and the chief medical research arm of the U.S. Department of Health and Human Services, NIH is comprised of 24 separate institutes, centers and divisions whose doctors and scientists are front-line soldiers in the relentless fight against sickness, from the common cold to cancer, Alzheimer's disease, AIDS, heart disease, diabetes, arthritis and numerous other devastating maladies. NIH also houses the National Library of Medicine, whose inventory of 3.5 million items ranks it as the world's largest reference center devoted to a single subject. The library has been dubbed the "Fort Knox of health information" because of the richness of its resources.

Looking just beyond Metro Washington for a moment, there are three other major medical resources of note. To the north is Baltimore's prestigious Johns Hopkins University and its expansive health-care complex, and to the south are the University of Virginia Medical Center in Charlottesville and the Medical College of Virginia in Richmond, both acclaimed institutions in their own right.

But this chapter sticks closer to home, offering an overview of 50 or so major hospitals and other medical facilities in Metro Washington including the teaching and research hospitals affiliated with university medical schools that play such a vital role in the training of future doctors, nurses and other health-care professionals. We've also included some mental-health facilities and hospices and touched on the popular walk-in emergency medical centers — many of which are located on the grounds of hospitals — where minor illnesses and injuries can be quickly treated.

Remember that all local governments offer community clinics and other health-care facilities to the local citizenry. Please refer to the "Government Services/Utilities" chapters for government information numbers.

Finding a hospital may be easy, but the same doesn't always apply to finding the right doctor. So before delving too deeply into the hospital world, we've compiled a listing of some free dental and physician referral services, many of which are affiliated with more than one area hospital. In most cases the services can provide access to hundreds of doctors in a wide range of fields and specialties.

One of the most popular referral services, in part by virtue of its easily remembered name and phone number, is Dial Doctors. Just call D-O-C-T-O-R-S; that's 362-8677, with either a 202 or an 800 area code in front.

Other referral lines include: First Call of Reston Hospital Center and Alexandria Hospital, (703) 845-4848; Physician Referral Line of Northern Virginia Doctors Hospital, (703) 578-2294, and Prince William Hospital, (703) 369-8198; Physician Referral and Resource Line of the National Hospital for Orthopaedics and Rehabilitation, (703) 553-2471; Loudoun Physician Referral Service of Loudoun Hospital Center, (703) 771-7300 or (800) 732-3737; Potomac Hospital Physician Line, (703) 221-2500 or (703) 659-1515; Montgomery General Hospital Physician Referral Service, (301) 598-9815; Greater Laurel Beltsville Hospital's HealthMatch, (301) 262-7300; Anne Arundel County Medical Society's Physician Referral Service, (410) 544-0312; Anne Arundel Medical Center's Doctor's Directory, (410) 224-DOCS, or, outside Annapolis, (800) 262-DOCS; and North Arundel Hospital's Physician Directory, (410) 787-4365.

State hospital associations — smaller versions of the American Hospital Association — can be a valuable resource for information on medical facilities in Metro Washington and elsewhere in Maryland, Virginia and the District. Just contact the public relations office at the appropriate organization: Maryland Hospital Association, 1301 York Rd., Suite 800, Lutherville, Md. 21093-6087, (410) 321-6200; Virginia Hospital Association, P.O. Box 31394, Richmond, Va. 23294, (804) 747-8600; District of Columbia Hospital Association, 1250 Eye St. NW, Suite 700, Washington, D.C. 20005, (202) 682-1581.

Most hospitals featured in this chapter offer a multitude of community-outreach health and education programs (CPR, smoking cessation, weight reduction, family planning and child birth, stress management, etc.), many of them free, as well as speakers bureaus, a battery of outpatient testing, surgery and treatment programs and other services above and beyond the usual realm of a hospital's everyday role. Call the individual facilities to find out more.

With one exception, we have not included any of the military or veterans hospitals since they don't serve the general public. And for those people who are entitled to use these facilities, they're already well aware of them.

District of Columbia

Children's National Medical Center

111 Michigan Ave. NW (202) 745-5000

When the young ones are seriously sick or injured, this is one of the top places they could go for treatment. But the patients aren't from just Metro Washington. Children's National Medical Center is recognized as one of the primary providers of medical care and services to infants, children and youth in the entire Mid-Atlantic region. Some 75 percent of pediatricians in Metro Washington have received their training here.

No one enjoys being hospitalized, kids in particular. Children's has been a pioneer in the area of recognizing the trauma of hospitalization for children and since 1910 has had a "rooming in" program for parents so they can stay closeby around the clock. Founded in 1870 — although the present 279-bed facility opened in 1977—Children's is a private, nonprofit hospital with two comprehensive-care branch clinics in the District and several suburban clinics in Maryland and Virginia. Emergency trauma care is perhaps the best-known of its services, but the hospital's expertise extends well into other areas such as cardiology, sports medicine, genetics, plastic and reconstructive surgery, infectious diseases, neonatology, psychiatry and physical therapy. Naturally, Children's is very active in the research field, with special emphasis these days on AIDS, sickle cell and autism.

Columbia Hospital for Women

2425 L St. NW (202) 293-6500

What Children's Hospital is to children, Columbia Hospital for Women is to . . . well, we think the name makes it pretty obvious. Columbia was founded in 1866, and although the present facility opened eight years later, much has changed since. Yet Columbia has never wavered in its commitment to the health needs of women, including the birth of babies, as many occupants of the 154 beds will attest. (One of the authors of this very book, in fact, was born here, as were his three older brothers, so we truly have some first-hand knowledge about Columbia's specialty in obstetrics.)

The hospital's special mission was derived from the federal government's concern for the welfare of women following the Civil War. A former federally supported, charitable institution, Columbia evolved into a private, not-for-profit teaching medical center with a history that involves far more than just the passage of time. Columbia's pioneering physicians are credited with developing lifesaving delivery-room techniques, lowering infant and breast cancer mortality rates, and for making significant advances in reproductive health. The hospital has earned a national reputation for advances in mammography and sonography, gynecological surgery, neonatal intensive care and reproductive endocrinology.

District of Columbia General Hospital

19th St. and Massachusetts Ave. SE (202) 675-5000

Commonly called "DC General," this 404-bed hospital on the banks of the Anacostia River was founded in 1806 when Congress appropriated $2,000 to establish the first institution for care of the poor, disabled and infirm. Like so many of the other older medical centers in Metro Washington, the hospital saw duty as a military hospital during the Civil War. It became the first charitable health institution in the District and also was the city's first training school for nurses. The present facility opened in 1929 and, since the adoption of its present name in 1953, has grown into one of the largest municipal hospitals in the nation.

DC General offers a full range of medical and surgical services and programs including OB-GYN, pediatrics, neurology, orthopedics, internal medicine, ophthalmology, psychiatric services for adults, and physical therapy. With more than 81,000 visits annually, DC General's emergency room is far and away the city's busiest.

The George Washington University Medical Center

901 23rd St. NW (202) 994-1000

One of the area's most comprehensive health care and education centers, 501-bed George Washington University Medical Center was founded in 1844 at the former Washington Infirmary on 16th Street NW. It moved to the present facility, in Foggy Bottom, in 1947. Private and nonprofit, the hospital also includes three other entities: the Medical Faculty Associates, a full-time physician group practice; The George Washington University Health Plan, a health-maintenance organization, or HMO; and the School of Medicine and Health Sciences.

A major teaching and research facility, not to mention a busy 24-hour emergency room, "GW" is involved in research projects totaling over $20 million annually. Special clinical programs include bone marrow transplantation, gallstone lithotripsy and hyperbaric medicine. As could be expected from such a comprehensive health-care facility, an extensive range of services are offered including OB-GYN, neurology, orthopedics, internal medicine, cardiology, psychiatric services for adults, sports medicine, physical therapy, speech pathology and audiology.

Georgetown University Hospital

3800 Reservoir Rd. NW (202) 784-3000

Another of the city's presti-

Insiders' Tip

Insiders...
Looking for a medical specialist often consult one of the numerous — and free — physician-referral services offered by area hospitals and other health-care facilities.

gious university-affiliated medical centers, Georgetown University Hospital was founded in 1898 and went on to break new ground by offering such "modern" conveniences as a special entrance for horse-drawn ambulances. Today's 535-bed facility, which opened in 1948, is located in tony upper Northwest on a residential street lined with gracious mansions and diplomatic residences. The hospital, like its namesake university, is highly regarded internationally; a top-flight team of doctors, nurses and other personnel have access to the most advanced technology in every clinical discipline.

As an ultramodern major teaching facility, Georgetown University Hospital has distinguished itself as a hub of medical research. Pioneering efforts at Georgetown led to later successes with heart-valve implants and hemodialysis, while work today continues in disciplines such as cancer treatment, shock wave lithotripsy, magnetic resonance imaging (MRI) and specialized perinatal and neonatal care. The full range of services includes OB-GYN, pediatrics, neurology, orthopedics, emergency medicine, internal medicine and radiology.

Greater Southeast Community Hospital

1310 Southern Ave. SE (202) 574-6000

Greater Southeast Community Hospital is a study in citizen determination to improve the availability of local health services. It's an effort that began in 1955 and culminated 11 years later with the opening of the 450-bed facility that today serves over 400,000 residents. It's the largest and most comprehensive hospital of its kind in the immediate area and continues to grow, adding equipment and personnel, and enhancing programs and capabilities.

GSCH offers a fairly wide range of surgical and medical services including OB-GYN, pediatrics, neurology, orthopedics, emergency and internal medicine, radiology, family practice, ophthalmology, adult psychiatry, cancer screening, a diabetes management unit, geriatric assessment, oncology, neonatal intensive care, pathology, renal dialysis and cardiology.

Hadley Memorial Hospital

4601 Martin Luther King Jr. Ave. SW (202) 574-5700

Eighty-one bed Hadley Memorial is one of the District's smallest hospitals, but it also is one of the newest, with the present facility opening in 1986, nearly 35 years after the institution was founded. Owned and operated by the Seventh-Day Adventist Church and part of the nationwide Adventist Health System that includes over 70 hospitals and dozens of long-term care facilities, Hadley has a history of compassionate service to anyone and everyone, especially the indigent. Its founder, Dr. Henry G. Hadley, started the Washington Sanitorium Mission Clinic in 1918 to treat the city's working poor and needy; he eventually bought the clinic and donated it to the church before setting out to build a much-needed hospital.

Services offered at Hadley include OB-GYN, pediatrics, surgery, neurology, orthopedics, emergency medicine, internal medicine, radiology, family practice, ophthalmology, psychiatric services for children, adolescents and adults, physical therapy and sports medicine.

The Hospital for Sick Children

1731 Bunker Hill Rd. NE (202) 832-4400

The Hospital for Sick Children is another of the city's smaller (80 beds) health-care centers with a unique role: that of a pediatric "transitional care" facility — the only one of its kind in Metro Washington — that acts as a link between hospital and home. In this case the young patients are being treated for respiratory and chronic illnesses and a host of other disabilities.

Founded in 1883 as a "fresh air" summer home, the present facility opened in 1968. Services focus on a broad range of therapies including physical, occupational, recreational, feeding, respiratory, speech and language.

Howard University Hospital

2041 Georgia Ave. NW (202) 865-6100

The second-oldest of the District's three major university-based teaching and research medical centers, 515-bed Howard University Hospital has come a long way since its founding in 1863 as Freedman's Hospital, a name that in itself speaks of history. The federal government created Freedman's as an emergency facility to treat the thousands of sick and destitute former slaves who poured into Washington after gaining their freedom. The Howard University Hospital of today, opened in 1975, remains synonymous with African American advancement; some of the nation's top black medical professionals, beginning with Dr. Charles Drew, a pioneer in blood plasma preservation, have been trained here. The school itself, meanwhile, ranks as one of the nation's premier historically black universities.

Howard is the third-largest private hospital and one of the four busiest hospitals in Metro Washington, with annual inpatient admissions of some 13,000 and emergency-room visits topping 53,000. Special services for the community include screening and counseling for sickle cell disease, cancer screening, drug and alcohol addiction treatment, and renal dialysis. Underscoring its role as a major health-care provider, the hospital's vast range of services includes OB-GYN, pediatrics, neurology, orthopedics, internal medicine, radiology, family practice, ophthalmology, oncology, dentistry, dermatology, and plastic and reconstructive surgery. Other services, meanwhile, include infectious diseases, neurosurgery, radiotherapy, psychiatric services for children, adolescents and adults, physical and occupational therapy, and sports medicine.

National Rehabilitation Hospital

102 Irving St. NW (202) 877-1000

National Rehabilitation Hospital is something of a godsend for persons who become severely disabled through accident or illness. It is the first and only freestanding facility in Metro Washington dedicated solely to thorough medical rehabilitation with the aim of helping patients to lead active and satisfying lives. Only seven years old, the 160-bed hospital offers a broad range of inpatient and outpatient medical rehabilitation services including driver evaluation and training, social work, neuropsychology, nutrition, physical therapy, speech and language pathology, and therapeutic recreation.

The hospital is designed in particular for persons who are physically disabled by spinal cord and brain injuries, stroke, arthritis, post-polio syndrome, amputation and other orthopedic and neurological conditions; a 40-bed unit is reserved solely for the treatment of the brain-injured. In addition to its role as a rehabilitation center, NRH serves as a strong advocacy voice for the disabled.

Providence Hospital

1150 Varnum St. NE (202) 269-7000

Providence is yet another District hospital with intriguing Civil War roots. Established in 1861 by four Catholic sisters in a renovated mansion, its original role was that of caring for the civilian population as the fighting between North and South raged. As luck would have it, Providence was the city's only medical facility not taken over by the military during the war. It is the sole private hospital in Washington that has remained in continuous operation since.

Established at its present site in 1954, today's 382-bed Providence Hospital specializes in obstetrics and women's health care, geriatrics and a full range of acute and emergency services. Other programs include orthopedics, internal medicine, family practice, ophthalmology, infertility treatment, substance abuse, cardiology, psychiatric services for adults, alcohol/substance abuse diagnosis, and physical and occupational therapy.

The Psychiatric Institute of Washington, D.C.

4228 Wisconsin Ave. NW (202) 965-8200

The first private psychiatric hospital in the District, the 201-bed Psychiatric Institute of Washington was founded in 1967 and moved to its present location in 1973. The facility treats children, adolescents and adults suffering from emotional and addictive illnesses, and even offers an intensive-care unit for especially serious cases. The hospital is an acknowledged center of education and professional development for mental-health professionals. Its presence extends beyond the District line, however, with two affiliated centers in Annapolis, Md., and Woodbridge, Va., offering similar services (see the Anne Arundel County and Prince William County listings, respectively, for addresses and phone numbers).

Saint Elizabeths Hospital

2700 Martin Luther King Jr. Ave SE (202) 373-7034

For nearly 140 years, "Saint E's" has been perhaps the best-known of the District's mental-health care facilities. Its reputation may have something to do with patients such as would-be presidential assassin John Hinckley, who at this writing remains in residence. Located in the same place since its founding in 1855, the massive 1,500-bed hospital actually sits on the grounds of D.C. General Hospital, but you wouldn't know it just by comparing the addresses.

Saint Elizabeths was formerly run by the federal government but today is city-operated under the Department of Human Services. Psychiatric services for children, adolescents and adults are offered in the form of acute care, long-term care, nursing care and residential care. The hospital also deals in forensic medicine. Services are being expanded for children and youth, in-home clients and multicultural and immigrant populations

Sibley Memorial Hospital

5255 Loughboro Rd. NW (202) 537-4000

Sibley is yet another example of a truly "community" hospital, occupying a wooded parcel on a quiet residential street in upper Northwest. The 362-bed hospital is also another example of a District medical center with a 19th-century heritage, founded in 1890 as a nurse training school for deaconesses and missionaries. The hospital itself came later and was named in honor of William J. Sibley, an early supporter of the school's work who donated $10,000 for the construction of the medical center in memory of his wife. The current building and site, however, go back only to 1961. An extensive renovation and modernization program was completed in 1990.

Sibley has made its mark primarily as a surgical center, both inpatient and out. Specialties include eye and plastic surgeries, a wide range of programs for the elderly, and a Sleep Disorders Center. Services include emergency medicine, family practice, internal medicine, neurology, OB-GYN, occupational and physical therapy, ophthalmology, orthopedics, radiology, and psychiatry for adults.

The Washington Hospital Center

110 Irving St. NW (202) 877-7000

Take three separate medical facilities, merge them, and what do you get? In this case, The Washington Hospital Center, the largest private teaching hospital in the District and a hub for research and education. Founded in 1958, the 907-bed facility has developed into one of Metro Washington's top medical

Insiders' Tip

Insiders...
Who for some reason need to seek medical resources beyond what Metro Washington has to offer often look to three nearby cities for help: Baltimore, home of Johns Hopkins University and its expansive health-care complex; the University of Virginia Medical Center in Charlottesville; and Richmond's Medical College of Virginia.

centers with special emphasis on emergency shock-trauma care for the critically ill and injured, many of whom arrive via MedSTAR, the acclaimed air ambulance service.

Washington Hospital Center's expansive list of services includes a comprehensive burn center and cardiology unit, organ transplantation, high-risk maternal fetal care, and treatment for diabetes, cancer and eye disorders. Other services include neurology, OB-GYN, orthopedics, radiology, oral surgery and neurosurgery.

Northern Virginia

City of Alexandria

ACCESS of Alexandria

4600 King St. *(703) 998-4846*

This is what became of the emergency room at Jefferson Hospital after the hospital closed. Please see the listing under the Fairfax County heading for details on the ACCESS story.

The Alexandria Hospital

4320 Seminary Rd. *(703) 379-3000*

The Alexandria Hospital is the primary provider of medical services for city residents. It's also a primary provider of jobs, ranking as the city's largest private employer with 2,000 workers and a staff of physicians numbering about 700. Established in 1872, the hospital occupied five sites before the present 414-bed, not-for-profit facility opened in 1962. As part of its function as a teaching facility, the hospital maintains a partnership with the George Washington University Medical Center.

The hospital boasts a top-rated cardiac surgery unit and a Level II Trauma Center that can handle most life-threatening illnesses and injuries 24 hours a day. Emergency medicine is also a specialty, and for good reason: Alexandria was the first hospital in the nation to staff its emergency department with full-time emergency physicians, a standard practice today at most major medical facilities. For minor emergencies when a private physician isn't available, the hospital offers an Express Care Center, similar to other walk-in clinics but located within the hospital's emergency department. Cancer treatment is also a specialty at Alexandria Hospital, which houses the Northern Virginia Cancer Center offering a variety of treatment programs. Other services include a Birthing Center (one of the authors' daughter was born here), a neonatal intensive-care unit, dialysis, a blood donor center, respiratory therapy and a Same Day Surgery center for outpatients.

Mount Vernon Hospital

2501 Parkers Lane *(703) 664-7000*

Alexandria's other major medical facility, Mount Vernon Hospital is a 235-bed not-for-profit community hospital that opened in 1976. It's a member of the Inova Health System, a not-for-profit, community-based organization that also includes Fair Oaks and Fairfax hospitals (see subsequent entries) as well as home health care, long-term care and behavioral services.

Located just a short ways from

its historic namesake, the hospital provides a full range of medical and surgical services primarily to residents of Alexandria and southeastern Fairfax County. Services include 24-hour emergency medicine, a 23-bed psychiatric unit for adolescents and adults, and a range of programs relating to cardiology, cancer, physical medicine and rehabilitation. Its 350 physicians represent a broad spectrum of the health-care field. Diagnostic services offered include Magnetic Resonance Imaging, digital angiography, ultrasound, echocardiogram, cardiac catheterization, stress tests and mammography. Perhaps Mount Vernon's broadest special service is the Inova Center for Rehabilitation where patients receive comprehensive care and therapy for stroke, orthopedic injuries, head and spinal cord injuries, amputation, Multiple Sclerosis, arthritis, workplace injuries and other neuromuscular disorders. The center includes an inpatient 59-bed acute-care unit.

Arlington County

The Arlington Hospital

1701 N. George Mason Dr. (703) 558-5000

Arlington County's largest and most comprehensive health-care facility is The Arlington Hospital, a 374-bed, nonprofit teaching hospital affiliated with Georgetown University's School of Medicine and several schools of nursing. Open since 1944, it's well-known locally not only for outstanding medical and surgical services, but for being the hospital of the Washington Redskins, primarily due to the affiliations of the team's medical staff.

With over 700 physicians, Arlington Hospital offers a broad spectrum of services including a 24-hour emergency department, adult addiction treatment for alcoholism and other drugs, OB-GYN, high-risk nursery, open-heart surgery, outpatient clinics, physical medicine and rehabilitation, psychiatric treatment, and numerous diagnostic and therapeutic services such as nuclear medicine, radiation therapy and respiratory therapy.

National Hospital for Orthopaedics and Rehabilitation

2455 Army-Navy Dr. (703) 920-6700

Looming over I-395, its name clearly visible on the side of the building, it's hard to miss the National Hospital for Orthopaedics and Rehabilitation, a 115-bed facility that opened in 1951. As its name suggests, the hospital offers services and programs for those who sustain debilitating injuries and illnesses. Services for specific problems are a trademark; the Industrial Medical Services department, for example, deals with the prevention, treatment and rehabilitation of work-related injuries. The hospital also has a large orthotics and prosthetics department and is the only hospital in Virginia to house an orthotics shop.

Services include a complete emergency department, and a sports medicine program at centers at Catholic University in Washington and at branch locations in Herndon, Va., and Landover, Md. Other services include a complete range of specialized procedures including total joint replacement, microscopic hand and foot surgery, arthroscopy, a spine program, and neurologic and traumatic injury rehabilitation.

Northern Virginia Doctors Hospital

601 S. Carlin Springs Rd. (703) 671-1200

Arlington's third major medical facility is Northern Virginia Doctors Hospital, a 267-bed medical/surgical and psychiatric facility that opened in 1961. Located on a beautiful as well as historic piece of property, the hospital offers a full range of medical/surgical and psychiatric services including ambulatory minimally invasive surgery, gynecology, urology, neurosurgery, orthopaedics, gastroenterology and endoscopy, neurology and infectious diseases. There's also an on-campus MRI center, computerized tomography, cardiac catheterization, nuclear medicine and an accredited diagnostic clinical lab service. Besides being open around the clock, the emergency department offers a unique guarantee that seems especially appealing for anyone who has had to wait an inordinate amount of time to be seen by a doctor: if a patient is not seen within 15 minutes of arrival, care is rendered free of charge.

Fairfax County

ACCESS of Fairfax

4315 Chain Bridge Rd.,
Fairfax City (703) 591-9322

ACCESS of Reston/Herndon

11901 Barron Cameron Ave.,
Reston (703) 471-0175

ACCESS is a clever acronym for a very long name: Ambulatory Care Center Emergency Service System. You can see why most people happily use the acronym. Billing themselves as "Prompt, Personal, Caring and Close to Home," these 24-hour freestanding emergency rooms offer a level of care somewhere between the walk-in shopping center facilities and regular hospitals. Part of the INOVA Health System, ACCESS outlets also perform lab and X-ray work on-site.

ACCESS locations typically spring up in former hospital buildings, as evidenced by the locations in Fairfax (the old Commonwealth Hospital) and Alexandria (ex-Jefferson Hospital). The first ACCESS in the chain, in Reston, ironically sits very near one of the county's newest major medical facilities, Reston Hospital Center. Until the opening of Reston Hospital Center and, to a lesser degree, Fair Oaks Hospital, ACCESS of Reston/Herndon was the closest thing many area residents had to a hospital.

Dominion Hospital

2960 Sleepy Hollow Rd.,
Falls Church (703) 538-2872

Dominion is one of Northern Virginia's premier mental healthcare centers for children, adolescents and adults. "First Step," a free, confidential mental health information, assessment and referral service, offers information in various crisis situations including suicide attempts and threats, substance abuse and other addictive illnesses, eating disorders, serious and prolonged depression, acute stress reactions, uncontrollable fears, various behavioral problems in children and adolescents, sexual abuse and childhood trauma, and sleep disorders.

Fair Oaks Hospital

3600 Joseph Siewick Dr.,
Fairfax *(703) 391-3600*

Fair Oaks Hospital was one of two new hospitals to open in Fairfax County in the mid-1980s, in this case, 1987. The other was Reston Hospital Center (see subsequent entry). Its newness is underscored in such design features as bed-mounted telephones and nurse call buttons, wall-to-wall carpeting in patients' rooms, private TVs with free in-room movies, and solariums, gourmet meals and rooms with deluxe amenities called "The Oaks." The 160-bed, 900-employee facility is part of the Inova Health System that includes Mount Vernon and Fairfax hospitals. A western Fairfax location on 47 wooded acres just off Route 50 at I-66 makes Fair Oaks Hospital convenient to many county residents beyond its core service area of Chantilly, Reston and Fairfax.

Over 700 physicians covering 33 specialties have privileges at Fair Oaks, which can handle emergency, medical, surgical, critical care, orthopedic, obstetric and pediatric patients. The 24-hour emergency department offers a helipad located just outside the doors. Two additions made in the past five years focus on the care and treatment of young patients: a 20-bed Maternal and Infant Health Center (1988), which emphasizes a family-centered approach to the birthing process; and a Children's Unit (1990) specially equipped for infants and children through age 18 and staffed by an in-house pediatrician around the clock. Three programs at Fair Oaks Hospital deserve special notice: the International Diabetes Center of Virginia, designed for both inpatient and outpatients; the Pain Management Program — the only one of its kind in Northern Virginia — that incorporates a multidisciplinary approach to the management and treatment of chronic pain; and Geriatric Psychiatric Services, a first-of-its-kind inpatient program in Northern Virginia that provides older persons with rapid diagnostic evaluation, stabilization and transition back to their customary living situation.

Fairfax Hospital

3300 Gallows Rd.,
Falls Church *(703) 698-1110*

This 656-bed, not-for-profit regional medical center, the flagship hospital of the Inova Health System, is Northern Virginia's only Level I emergency and trauma center, meaning it can handle the most critical of illnesses and accidents. Not surprisingly, Fairfax has Northern Virginia's only pediatric intensive-care unit with pediatric emergency medical specialists on hand around the clock.

Opened in 1961, Fairfax Hospital has seen tremendous growth over the years during its emergence as one of Metro Washington's premier medical facilities. It houses the nationally recognized Virginia Heart Center where Metro Washington's first heart transplant was performed in 1986. The hospital was also the site of the region's first lung transplant (1991) and first heart-kidney combination transplant (1992). An amazingly busy obstetrics unit — some 9,000 youngsters are brought into the world here each year, a figure that's among the highest in the Mid-Atlantic — has earned Fairfax its local nickname, "The Baby Factory." And indeed, babies are a specialty here; there's even a unit for high-risk pregnancies along with a neonatal intensive-care unit. Fairfax offers the full range of other medical-surgical services and state-of-the-art technology, but it's also a major teaching hospital, affiliated with Georgetown and George Washington medical schools, the Medical College of Virginia, and nursing schools at George Mason and Marymount universities and Northern Virginia Community College.

Fairfax Surgical Center

10730 Main St., Fairfax City(703) 691-0670

For outpatient surgical services without having to go to an actual hospital, many people opt for a facility such as Fairfax Surgical Center, part of a national network of centers. Offering what it calls "efficient, personal care in a pleasant atmosphere," the center charges a single fee that covers basic medical history, equipment and most supplies, routine drugs and anesthetics that are administered, recovery room services and operating room time. Be aware, though, that the price does not include the professional services of the surgeon and any assistants, the anesthesiologist, radiologist, pathologist, physician consultants and pharmacist.

Reston Hospital Center

1850 Town Center Pkwy.,
Reston (703) 689-9000

With the opening of Reston Hospital Center in 1986, many residents of western Fairfax County, particularly those in Reston, Herndon, Great Falls and parts of greater Vienna, could live life with a little less worry knowing they wouldn't have to travel across the county to Fairfax Hospital to get comprehensive medical care. With 127 beds, it's certainly not the biggest hospital around, but its services are numerous and include most surgical and medical procedures as well as a 24-hour emergency room. Of particular note are the Maternity Center, the Pediatric Center and the Stone Treatment Center, one of only two in the metro area.

Reston Hospital Center was the first hospital in Northern Virginia to offer laparascopic cholecystectomy — gall bladder surgery through minor incisions. The Same Day Surgery department has seen significant growth in recent years, reflecting a national trend toward outpatient services. The traveling public can take heart in that Reston Hospital Center is the "official" hospital of Washington Dulles International Airport due to its proximity, easy access (just a couple of minutes off the Dulles Toll Road and parallel Airport Access Road) and wide range of services.

Urgent Medical Care

6045-KLM Burke Centre Pkwy.,
Burke (703) 239-0300
14151 Saint Germain Dr.,
Centreville (703) 830-5600
6370 Springfield Plaza,
Springfield (703) 569-7554
100 Maple Ave. East,
Vienna (703) 938-5300

Urgent Medical Care and other walk-in centers offering similar services under a different name have become popular alternatives to hospitals for the treatment of minor injuries and illnesses. Often found in shopping centers and other high-traffic areas, they're typically open seven days a week from 9 AM to 9 PM weekdays, 10 AM to 6 PM weekends, although the times can vary from location to location. No appointments are necessary. With a small staff of doctors and nurses, the centers can also perform some lab tests, blood work, sports physicals and other services not requiring the resources or facilities of a traditional hospital.

Loudoun County

Graydon Manor

301 Children's Center Rd.,
Leesburg (703) 777-3485
or (703) 478-8767 (toll-free in Metro D.C.)

You might say that Graydon Manor was founded by people with a unique concern for the future of local health care: Parents of children with psychiatric and other mental difficulties. That was in 1957, but even today, one of those parents sits on the Board of Directors of the private, 61-bed, not-for-profit residential treatment center. Graydon Manor specializes in treating children and adolescents (boys 7 to 17, girls 12 to 17) who have been diagnosed with severe emotional or psychiatric disorders. And while it does not treat those whose primary diagnosis is substance abuse, it can and does serve adolescents with a secondary diagnosis of chemical dependency. Lengths of stay on the 100-plus acre campus, located 12 miles west of Washington Dulles International Airport, range from nine to 18 months, depending on need.

Operated by the National Children's Rehabilitation Center, Graydon offers outpatient services for adults and families throughout the community. An on-site school is accredited by the Virginia and Maryland departments of education.

Loudoun Hospital Center

224 Cornwall St. NW,
Leesburg (703) 777-3300

The county's primary medical facility is the 119-bed Loudoun Hospital Center. Founded in 1912 as a six-room rural hospital, LHC

Insiders' Tip

Insiders...
Going to visit someone in the hospital remember to bring along a few extra bucks since many facilities in the area charge for public parking.

has had five names through the years and today is the flagship facility of the not-for-profit Loudoun Healthcare, Inc., a growing network of affiliated services located throughout the county. LHC offers most major medical and surgical services including 24-hour emergency medicine. Special features include an intensive-care unit, an outpatient surgery department, comprehensive diagnostic imaging services, a birthing inn, a 12-bed mental health services unit, physical, occupational and speech therapy, and business health management services. Its Cardiopulmonary Health Center was one of Northern Virginia's first.

The hospital extends its community-outreach efforts to a new level with Lifeline, an electronic alert system that gives elderly residents or persons with major disabilities a direct connection to the hospital's emergency department (and no doubt provides family and friends with peace of mind). Adjoining the hospital is the Loudoun Long Term Care Center, a 100-bed residential facility.

Affiliated services include the Countryside Ambulatory Surgery Center (703-444-6060) in Sterling; the Loudoun Cancer Care Center (703-444-4460), also located in the Countryside community and offering chemotherapy and radiation therapy; the Medex Immediate Care Center (703-430-7400), a walk-in facility in Sterling for minor emergencies; and the Sterling/Dulles Imaging & MRI Center (703-444-5800) for the diagnosis and treatment of a wide variety of disorders and diseases.

Springwood Psychiatric Institute

Route 4, Box 50, Leesburg (703) 777-0800

Springwood Psychiatric Institute offers comprehensive mental health treatment for adults, adolescents and children on either an inpatient or outpatient basis. The hospital specializes in the treatment of depression, alcohol/drug abuse, codependency, thoughts of suicide, school failure, marital/family problems, and stress and anxiety. Special services include 24-hour admissions, free evaluations, and extensive aftercare programs for patients and their families.

Prince William County

Potomac Hospital

2300 Opitz Blvd.,
Woodbridge (703) 670-1313

Potomac Hospital, established in 1972 with 29 beds, has grown into a 153-bed comprehensive healthcare facility with nearly 800 staff members. The hospital features a fully equipped pediatric unit, maternity unit and neonatology program, 24-hour emergency medicine, magnetic-resonance imaging and radiation therapy, and cardiac catheterization and angiography. Services include allergy and immunology, dermatology, family practice, internal medicine, neurology, OB-GYN, pediatrics, psychiatry, radiation oncology, general surgery, neurosurgery, ophthalmology, oral surgery, orthopedics, plastic surgery, thoracic surgery, urology, anesthesiology, pathology, physical medicine rehabilitation, and radiology and nuclear medicine.

The hospital runs an Urgent Medical Care center in Lake Ridge in cooperation with Fairfax Hospital. (See subsequent listing.)

Prince William Hospital

8700 Sudley Rd., Manassas (703) 369-8000

The county's largest medical facility is 170-bed Prince William Hospital, a private, nonprofit community facility established in 1964. The hospital features comprehensive medical and surgical services and includes a critical-care unit, inpatient and outpatient surgery, oncology, pediatrics, a 24-hour emergency department, a helipad for receiving and transporting the seriously ill and injured, OB-GYN, cardiology, nuclear medicine, radiology and other diagnostic services, dialysis treatment, and physical, speech and occupational therapies.

Urgent Medical Care of Lake Ridge

12449 Hedges Run Dr., Lake Ridge (703) 494-6160

Urgent Medical Care of Lake Ridge offers services similar to those at Fairfax County locations, but this center is open daily from 8 AM to 10 PM.

Woodbridge Center for Mental Health Services

1515 Davis Ford Rd., Suite 6, Woodbridge (703) 690-6419

This is the second suburban branch of The Psychiatric Institute of Washington, D.C. Please refer to the District of Columbia listing for more information.

Mary Washington Hospital

2300 Fall Hill Ave., Fredericksburg (703) 899-1412

Although located just outside the primary focus area of this book, Mary Washington Hospital merits inclusion for its size, services, branch facilities and accessibility to many residents of Metro Washington, particularly those in parts of southeastern Prince William County. As this was being written, the 340-bed hospital was in the midst of a major expansion and relocation. Part of the regional MWH MediCorp health-care organization, the hospital offers private rooms, four intensive-care units (including one devoted to newborns), Labor-Delivery-Recovery-Postpartum suites for new mothers and their babies, neurosurgery, advanced cardiac technology and a 24-hour emergency department.

Affiliated facilities include Snowden at Fredericksburg, a 40-bed psychiatric and addiction treatment center for adolescents and adults; the North Stafford Medical Mall, a free-standing facility that includes the ExpressCare outpatient emergency center; Carriage Hill Nursing Home and Mary Washington Health Center, providers of professional long-term care; Chancellor's Village of Fredericksburg, a retirement community; and Commonwealth Retirement Center, a modestly priced home for adults

Suburban Maryland

Anne Arundel County

Anne Arundel Medical Center

Franklin & Cathedral sts.,
Annapolis *(410) 267-1000*

The county's major medical facility, this 303-bed acute care hospital offers a full 24-hour emergency room and extensive inpatient and outpatient services, support groups and other programs at various locations. Outpatient services include physical therapy, cardiac rehabilitation, multiple sclerosis rehabilitation and intravenous therapy. Walk-In Health Centers are located in Crofton at 1655 Crofton Blvd., Suite 100 (410-721-5100) and in Severna Park at Park Plaza, Suite 580-L, Ritchie Hwy. (410-544-3400). Three diagnostic centers offering radiology and other services are located at 2525 Riva Rd., Annapolis (410-244-2616), 13000 Ritchie Hwy., Arnold (410-647-5380), and 1655 Crofton Blvd., Crofton (410-721-5500).

The hospital's principal outlets include Anne Arundel Magnetic Resonance Imaging, 235 Jennifer Rd., Annapolis (410-266-3328), the Anne Arundel Oncology Center, Jennifer Road and Medical Parkway (410-244-5800), and the Health Education Center, 140 Jennifer Rd. Annapolis (410-224-5777).

North Arundel Hospital

301 Hospital Dr.,
Glen Burnie *(410) 787-4000*

This 320-bed nonprofit hospital focuses on short-term acute care and features a 24-hour emergency room with an Immediate Care Center for treatment of minor injuries and illnesses as well as a center for more severe trauma and injuries. The hospital offers numerous outpatient support programs and services at various locations.

Major extensions of North Arundel Hospital include the Arundel Heart Center, 7649 Crain Hwy., Glen Burnie (410-761-4000), specializing in cardiac rehabilitation; the Life Center, 200 Hospital Dr., Glen Burnie (410-768-6644), featuring a variety of wellness programs; and the Mammography Center, 301 Hospital Dr., Glen Burnie (410-787-4642), featuring state-of-the-art low-dose diagnostic equipment.

Annapolis Center for Mental Health Services

131 Old Solomons Island Rd.,
Annapolis *(410) 224-6400*

This is one of two suburban affiliates of The Psychiatric Institute of Washington, D.C. Please refer to the District of Columbia listing for information on services and programs.

Montgomery County

Chestnut Lodge Hospital

500 West Montgomery Ave.,
Rockville *(301) 424-8300*

Chestnut Lodge is a 132-bed psychiatric hospital serving children, adolescents and adults. Founded in 1910 to care for persons suffering from serious mental illness, today the hospital is widely known for its treatment of schizophrenia, severe depressive and manic disorders as well as borderline conditions. Varying levels of care and a variety of living situations are available, depending on patient needs. The residential program, for example, provides a home-like and family-oriented environment, with all activities geared toward moving the patient toward independent living and a community environment.

Holy Cross Hospital of Silver Spring

1500 Forest Glen Rd.,
Silver Spring *(301) 905-0100*

One of Montgomery County's primary medical facilities, Holy Cross is a 442-bed nonprofit hospital founded in 1963 by a Catholic religious order of women. Not only is this the largest acute-care facility in the county, it is also the only teaching hospital and boasts the largest medical staff in Montgomery with some 1,300 physicians enjoying privileges. It's a good thing; the hospital's chief service area of southern Montgomery County and northern and western Prince George's County is home to nearly 600,000 residents.

Befitting its size and resources, Holy Cross Hospital is a recognized teaching center through affiliations with George Washington University's graduate medical education programs in obstetrics, gynecology, medicine and surgery. The hospital works with G.W. as well as Children's National Medical Center in sponsoring a pediatric teaching program. Holy Cross specialties include critical-care services, emergency medicine, OB-GYN, home care/hospice, pediatrics, psychiatry and a range of surgical procedures. A $24 million improvement program completed in 1992 significantly upgraded the hospital's technology, efficiency and aesthetics.

Montgomery General Hospital

18101 Prince Philip Dr.,
Olney *(301) 774-8882*

Founded in 1920, this 213-bed, nonprofit, community hospital is located in the northern Montgomery County community of Olney, but serves many residents of Howard and Prince George's counties as well. Montgomery General offers a full range of inpatient and outpatient medical and surgical services and programs including obstetrics, pediatrics, 24-hour emergency and cardiac care and cancer care. The hospital offers psychiatric and addiction treatment along with state-of-the-art medical imaging and diagnostic services, health education and screening programs. Some 500 physicians are on staff.

The National Institutes of Health

9000 Rockville Pike,
Bethesda *(301) 496-2351*

Along with the Centers for Disease Control (CDC) in Atlanta, the National Institutes of Health is probably the best known and most widely recognized of the global medical field's distinguished "alphabet" agencies. Still, there's more to NIH than most people probably realize. Internationally renowned for its work, NIH is one of the largest biomedical research centers in the world and the principal medical research arm of the U.S. Department of Health and Human Services. Some 70 buildings, including the 500-bed hospital and lab complex known as the Warren Grant Magnuson Clinical Center, are scattered about the 300-acre Bethesda campus located just 12 miles from downtown Washington.

But NIH had humble beginnings, starting out as a one-room Laboratory of Hygiene in 1887. NIH today is actually 24 separate research institutes, centers and divisions. Special components include the National Library of Medicine — the world's largest reference center devoted to a single subject — more than 1,400 labs with some of the most sophisticated scientific equipment ever developed, and the Fogarty International Center that houses foreign scholars-in-residence. NIH focuses much of its efforts on combatting the major killing and crippling diseases prevalent in the United States today including heart disease, cancer, arthritis, Alzheimer's disease, diabetes, AIDS, neurological diseases, vision and mental disorders, infectious diseases and dental diseases. Other work is involved in studying the human development and aging process and exploring the relationship between the environment and human health.

A few numbers underscore the remarkable impact that NIH has had on the nation's health. As a result of NIH investment in research, mortality from heart disease — the nation's No. 1 killer — dropped 39 percent between 1972 and 1990 while death rates from stroke decreased about 58 percent during the same period. Meanwhile, improved treatment methods have increased the five-year survival rate for cancer patients to 52 percent. Advancements don't come cheaply, though. The $300 annual budget that NIH operated under in 1887 has grown to $10 billion today.

NATIONAL NAVAL MEDICAL CENTER
8901 Wisconsin Ave.,
Bethesda *(301) 295-5388*

Another of Bethesda's healthcare icons, the 427-bed National Naval Medical Center is not open to the general public since its primary role is to provide care and treatment to active-duty military personnel. But it warrants a mention here since the center is, after all, the hospital of the commander in chief of the armed forces, a.k.a. the president. It's here that he usually goes for annual physicals, routine examinations, surgical procedures and the like, so it's not surprising that the full range of medical and surgical services and the latest in equipment, technology and facilities are offered.

The hospital was founded in 1802, but it has been at the present location only since 1942. The site was personally selected by President Franklin Roosevelt who, believe it or not, sketched the design and grounds plans that became the architect's guide. The National Naval Medical Center is among the 10 largest medical facilities in the nation and ranks as perhaps the cream of the crop of all military hospitals. About 17,000 patients are admitted annually while its clinic sees a whopping 725,000.

Psychiatric Institute of Montgomery County

14901 Broschart Rd., Rockville *(301) 251-4500*

This private, 88-bed, short-term acute care hospital has a very specific mission: to help adolescents (13-18 years old), adults (18-geriatric) and families overcome psychiatric and substance-abuse problems. Outpatient services are also offered. Open since 1981, the institute is located adjacent to Shady Grove Adventist Hospital, just off I-270 in the Montgomery County Life Sciences Center. It serves not only patients from Maryland, the District and Virginia but also admits those from other states. The hospital is recognized as one of the first in the nation to develop effective, in-depth treatment for psychiatric problems that have been complicated by chemical dependency. A strong emphasis is placed on interactive group therapy.

Secure Medical Care

803 Russell Ave., Gaithersburg *(301) 869-0700*

Secure Medical Care, like its counterpart operation in Northern Virginia known as Urgent Medical Care, is a quick, convenient alternative to the hospital. Typically found in suburban shopping centers and other busy, high-visibility locations, these and other walk-in facilities are ideal for the treatment of minor illnesses and injuries. They can also perform a limited amount of lab work and diagnostic tests, physical examinations and other services. Most centers are staffed by a small team of doctors and nurses and are open until late in the evening seven days a week.

Shady Grove Adventist Hospital

9901 Medical Center Dr., Rockville *(301) 279-6000*

Shady Grove Adventist Hospital is a full-service facility in transition, with expansions and/or renovations either underway or recently completed in the 24-hour emergency department (Montgomery County's busiest), the critical care and maternity units, and the laser center. Open only since 1979, the 253-bed hospital delivers the second-highest number of babies in the state each year and is the only non-teaching hospital in Maryland to offer kidney transplant surgery. A full range of other inpatient and outpatient medical and surgical services are also offered including a Level II neonatal intensive-care unit and a coronary care unit.

Suburban Hospital

8600 Old Georgetown Rd., Bethesda *(301) 530-3100*

Another of Montgomery

Insiders' Tip

Insiders...
Look to area hospitals and clinics for low-cost or (sometimes) free classes dealing with a broad range of health-care issues.

County's comprehensive community hospitals, 388-bed, nonprofit Suburban Hospital opened in 1943 but has seen some dramatic changes in subsequent years. An extensive renovation completed during the 1980s included the addition of a luxury wing, an Emergency and Shock/Trauma Center, a pharmacy, a cafeteria and restaurant, and an addiction treatment center. A project currently underway and scheduled for completion in 1994 includes two additions that will house new radiology facilities, a medical library, a new main entrance and admitting area, a 260-seat auditorium for medical and community education, and an elevated helipad for air transport of patients.

The more than 850 physicians on staff at Suburban are trained in programs and services as diverse as orthopaedics, cardiology, oncology (Suburban was the county's first comprehensive community cancer center), mental health, dermatology, gastroenterology, infectious diseases, and microvascular and thoracic surgery.

Washington Adventist Hospital

7600 Carroll Ave.,
Takoma Park *(301) 891-7600*

Located in what amounts to nearly a tri-jurisdictional city — Takoma Park is actually located in Montgomery County, but very near the Prince George's and District borders — this 300-bed, acute-care, church-affiliated facility has been in operation since 1907. Offering the most complete cardiac-care services in the county, Washington Adventist has been nationally recognized for innovative treatments in heart catheterization. The hospital's open-heart surgery center performs over 750 such procedures annually.

Other specialties include short-stay surgery (over 5,000 patients annually), maternity, radiation oncology, emergency medicine, rehabilitation medicine and pulmonary medicine. Psychiatric services are available on an inpatient or day treatment basis and include detoxification.

Prince George's County

Doctors Community Hospital

8118 Good Luck Rd.,
Lanham *(301) 552-8118*

Doctors Community Hospital serves a large portion of central Prince George's County, offering all major medical and surgical services except psychiatry and obstetrics. Open since 1975, the 250-bed adult, acute-care hospital underwent a major change in 1990, going from a national, chain-owned facility to a not-for-profit community hospital. The patient units and clinical areas were recently remodeled.

Doctors is well-know for its comprehensive emergency department, which sees some 30,000 patients a year and is the only unit in the county certified to handle victims of hazardous-materials incidents. The hospital also specializes in general and same-day surgery, ophthalmology, cardiology, physical and occupational therapy, and offers complete diagnostic services in radiology and laboratory work. The Home Care Program is available to many patients upon discharge, helping them make the transition from hospital to home and complete their recuperation successfully.

Fort Washington Medical Center

11711 Livingston Rd., Fort Washington (301) 292-7000

Fort Washington Medical Center is an example of multi-jurisdictional cooperation for the betterment of all citizens. The nonprofit, 33-bed facility is an entity of the Greater Southeast Community Hospital Foundation, whose flagship hospital is Greater Southeast Community Hospital, located in Washington. Serving residents of southern Prince George's and Charles counties, the center offers general and surgical services including outpatient surgery, a 24-hour emergency room, home health services, a pharmacy, a complete laboratory, radiology testing, CAT scan and mammography testing, and community education programs.

Greater Laurel Beltsville Hospital

7100 Contee Rd., Laurel (301) 725-4300

Greater Laurel Beltsville Hospital is a private, nonprofit, 200-bed facility located in the heart of the Baltimore/Washington corridor, close to the District line as well as the Capital Beltway and the B/W Parkway. Open since 1978, the hospital offers the full spectrum of medical, surgical and testing services, a 24-hour emergency room that sees some 23,000 patients annually, intensive-care and coronary-care units, alcohol and substance abuse treatment programs, a new Maternal and Child Health Unit, a mental health unit and a comprehensive rehabilitation program. Because of its convenient location, the hospital is able to serve residents of Prince George's, Montgomery, Anne Arundel and Howard counties.

Prince George's Hospital Center

3001 Hospital Dr., Cheverly (301) 618-2000

The county's largest medical facility — and one of its most comprehensive — is 450-bed Prince George's Hospital Center, which opened in 1944 as Prince George's General Hospital. Private and not-for-profit, PGHC is recognized nationwide for its outstanding 24-hour emergency care and is the designated regional trauma-care center for all of southern Maryland. Its Level I Shock Trauma Unit boasts an amazing 97 percent save rate for patients. PGHC also specializes in cardiac care and is the only hospital in the county with an open-heart surgery program. For minor emergencies and non-acute injuries and illnesses, the hospital offers an Express Care Center.

A wide range of obstetric services enables the hospital to handle high-risk pregnancies and difficult deliveries and to care for premature babies. A specialized unit called The Birthplace allows for labor, delivery and recovery to take place all in one area. For outpatient services the hospital offers a newly redesigned Short Stay Center. Other services at PGHC include family practice, gastroenterology, neurology, oro-facial plastic surgery, podiatry, psychiatry, sports medicine and urology. The hospital broke ground in early 1993 on an ambulatory surgical wing that will feature 10 operating rooms. Completion is scheduled for 1995.

Saint Luke Institute

2420 Brooks Dr., Suitland (301) 967-3700

This 24-bed, not-for-profit psychiatric facility was founded by a reverend/doctor and serves priests and other religious men and women active in church ministry. Saint Luke's initially treated only chemical dependency, but today the focus has broadened to include mood disorders, compulsive eating or sexual behaviors, and reactive or chronic depression. The major areas of service are in evaluation, inpatient treatment, aftercare, residential living, outpatient therapy and outreach.

Southern Maryland Hospital Center

7503 Surratts Rd., Clinton (301) 868-8000

"Southern Maryland" is certainly not a misnomer for this full-service, 338-bed facility that serves some 400,000 residents in parts of Prince George's, Charles, Calvert and St. Mary's counties — a big chunk of southern Maryland indeed. Yet the hospital is located just five miles outside the Capital Beltway.

Open since 1977, Southern Maryland Hospital Center is staffed by over 400 physicians representing all the major specialties. Medical and surgical services are offered in a wide range of fields including allergy and immunology, cardiology, dental surgery, dermatology, endocrinology, family practice, gastroenterology, oncology, neurosurgery, pathology, OB-GYN, pediatrics, podiatry, psychiatry, pulmonary medicine, radiology, thoracic/vascular surgery, urology, plastic surgery and emergency medicine.

Hospices

Several hospices serve terminally ill persons and their families throughout Metro Washington. An excellent clearinghouse for information on hospices and the services they offer is the National Hospice Organization, 1901 N. Moore St., Arlington, (703) 243-5900.

District of Columbia

The Washington Home & Hospice, 3720 Upton St. NW, (202) 966-3720

Northern Virginia

Hospice of Northern Virginia (Administrative Offices), 6400 Arlington Blvd., Falls Church, (703) 534-7070

The Hospice Center is located at 4715 15th St. North, Arlington (703-525-7070). Hospice of Northern Virginia also has offices in Leesburg, at 15-B Catoctin Cir. SW (703-777-7866), and Manassas, at 8802 Sudley Rd. (703-257-0048).

Suburban Maryland

Arundel Hospice, 403 Headquarters Dr., Suite 1, Millersville,

(410) 987-2003

Holy Cross Hospital of Silver Spring, Home Care and Hospice Office, 1500 Forest Glen Rd., Silver Spring, (301) 905-1171

Montgomery Hospice Society, Inc., 1450 Research Blvd., Rockville, 301) 279-2566

Shase Medical Foundation, Inc., 11804 Greenleaf Ct., Potomac, (301) 340-9884

Hospice of Prince George's County, 96 Harry S. Truman Dr., Largo, (301) 499-0550

Quality live-in child care...

with a special European *flair*.

- carefully screened European au pairs
- about $170/week for any size family
- AuPairCare counselors in your area

800-4-AUPAIR

AuPairCare

A U.S. Government-designated program.

Inside Metro Washington Child Care

As we have no doubt gushed at least a couple of times by now, Metro Washington is a wonderful place to live and — as many people happily discover — raise children. Few places can match the abundance of stimulating cultural, educational, historical and recreational outlets for youngsters to pursue. Now that we've stoked those maternal and paternal fires a bit, let's take a brief look at the world of child care, an important consideration in an area where the financial realities of life often demand two-income families.

First, a few words about what to expect from this chapter. Like some of the other subjects we've covered, child care is one that could easily be the sole focus of an entire book. There are literally thousands of child-care centers, of every description, available to residents of Metro Washington, and to try and present a complete rundown with descriptions, services and other information is simply not possible here. Instead, what we've tried to provide is a primer on the subject, combining some sound advice on choosing a child-care facility with a listing of numerous organizations (local governments, associations etc.) that are good places to start. The experts there can answer specific questions and help parents in making a decision.

As newcomers might expect, the child-care options in Metro Washington are numerous, diverse and of excellent quality, a reflection perhaps of the region's overall affluence as much as anything else. Whether you're in search of a chain-affiliated commercial day-care center, a small, private in-home operation, a program associated with a school or religious institution, something tailored to the special needs of groups such as the physically challenged, the learning disabled and the non-English speaking, or most any other care option imaginable, you're sure to find it here for infants, toddlers and any other sized young ones who need looking after. A scan through the Yellow Pages, a community phone book or a listing provided by a human-services agency will quickly confirm the wealth of choices available.

The not-so-good news about child care? Well, just as housing, groceries and other necessities tend to cost more in Metro Washington than in many parts of the nation, the same unfortunately holds true for child care. Indeed it can be one of the most potentially worrisome money matters for parents with moderate incomes and who don't have an in-home office, the luxury of a subsidized day-care center at their place of business, or who aren't fortunate enough to have relatives living nearby who are willing and able to help out for free. On average, it costs about $100 to $150 per week for full-time (Monday-Friday) child care, depending of course on the location and type of facility, age of the child, special needs, and other factors that can affect the price. But financial assistance is often available — albeit often unannounced — for qualifying parents who are looking to ease the budgetary burden. Many child-care centers and governmental/social services agencies offer subsidies and even scholarships based on family size, need, income and other determining factors. Plus, private facilities often base their fees on a sliding scale to help those with more moderate means, although such policies are rarely advertised to the general public. So if you find yourself in this situation, it never hurts (and can certainly pay) to inquire.

Child care is a major investment, and like any big-ticket expenditure, especially one that involves a family member, parents are advised to carefully consider the various options and talk with relatives as well as friends, neighbors and coworkers whose opinions you trust and who have experience in this area. It can be a challenge. Few quality-of-life issues have become as important to families in recent years as the availability of top-notch child care, something that experts agree is crucial to a child's well-being and healthy development.

A growing segment of the child-care sector in Metro Washington involves in-home operations, often classified by licensing agencies as Family Day Care Homes. Their popularity is a reflection not only of the region's No. 1 national ranking in the number of working women, but also of the high cost of living here. Many children-loving folks who would otherwise not have to hold a job opt to set up a child-care operation in the home, providing another much-needed source of income without having to commute to a faraway office. Like other child-care facilities, private homes must be licensed, insured, inspected and otherwise held to certain standards for safety, health and sanitation. In addition, persons who care for more than five children (although the number may vary slightly in different jurisdictions) must obtain a special permit and license from local and state authorities.

Keep in mind that the licensing of any child-care facility means that minimum requirements have been met and doesn't necessarily guarantee a high-quality educational experience.

Other types of child care include Day Care Centers, where group care is provided for children typically ages 6 weeks to 5 years. These centers are open for full days year round, and some provide transportation. Nursery Schools and Preschools offer group care for the preschool age child, but are not open all day or year round. Extended Day Care Programs, meanwhile, offer a supervised setting for the school-age child when school is not in session. In addition to before and after school, the programs — much to the delight of parents — often cover snow days and holidays, and some have full-day summer programs.

Nannies — private, full-time and sometimes live-in help — are another option for those who have the means. Costs vary considerably; in some cases the fee is the result of whatever agreement the employee and employer reach. Local child-care agencies often have lists of individual nannies or nanny services, or at least can put you in touch with a source that does.

The au pair (literally, "equal person") program is perhaps the most unusual and interesting child-care option and one that will probably continue to increase in popularity as the global society becomes further pronounced. And it's little wonder that au pairs are big in Metro Washington what with the region's strong multi-ethnic character and well-traveled populace. Au pair is an international youth exchange program organized to create cross-cultural understanding and cooperation between American families and western European young adults. It provides a great opportunity for young people overseas to learn about American culture and family life while living in the U.S. and also serves as a wonderful learning experience for the hosts. Typically, the program involves foreigners between the ages of 18 and 25 who come to the U.S. for a year and care for the children of the host family. There are also reciprocal programs in which American youths serve in the same role with a family in Europe. For information on this unique program, see our contacts listed below.

Whatever child-care facility or program is sought, parents are advised to observe the staff, the other children, and the indoor and outdoor spaces and to ask about such things as the daily routine, nutrition, exercise, learning activities and materials, fees and payment schedules, child/staff ratio, extent of parental involvement, and numerous other factors. For guidance, look to the following organizations.

Locally, the Metropolitan Washington Council of Governments, or "COG" as it's often called, is an excellent source for child-care information and virtually anything else you can think of in which local governments play some sort of role. Contact COG at 777 North Capitol St. NE, Suite 300, Washington, DC 20002-4201 (202-962-3200). As a vast information clearinghouse, COG also refers residents to other organizations, many of them headquartered in Metro Washington, that can be of help.

For accreditation of day-care centers and preschools, contact the National Association for the Education of Young Children (NAEYC), 1834 Connecticut Ave. NW, Washington, DC 20009 (202-232-8777 or 800-424-2460).

For accreditation of family day-care homes, contact the National Association of Family Day Care Providers, 725 15th St. NW, Suite 505, Washington, DC 20005 (202-347-3356).

For information on school-age child care, contact Project Home Safe, American Home Economics Association, 1555 King St., Alexandria, Va. 22314 (703-706-4620 or 800-252-SAFE).

For the scoop on au pairs, contact Au Pair in America (International Exchange), American Institute for Foreign Study Scholarship Foundation, 102 Greenwich Ave., Greenwich, CT 06830 (800-727-2437), or AuPairCare, 1 Post St., San Francisco, Ca. 94104 (800-288-7786).

Other helpful agencies include the National Black Child Development Institute, Inc., 1463 Rhode Island Ave. NW, Washington, DC 20005 (202-387-1281); the National Coalition of Hispanic Health and Human Services Organizations, 1501 16th St. NW, Washington, DC 20036 (202-387-5000); and the National Information Center for Children and Youth with Handicaps, (800-999-5599).

Local Government-based Child Care Resources

For listings of the myriad child-care centers in your area, tips on what to look for in a facility, guidelines, requirements, financial assistance and other information on virtually any facet of child care, contact the appropriate agencies in your jurisdiction.

District of Columbia

Department of Consumer and Regulatory Affairs:
(202) 727-7226
Washington Child Development Council:
(202) 387-0002
Child Day Care Services Division: (202) 727-0284
Office of Early Childhood Development: (202) 727-1839

Northern Virginia

Alexandria

Department of Social Services:
(703) 838-0750
Office for Early Childhood Development: (703) 838-0874

Arlington County

Child Care Office:
(703) 358-5101
Public Schools/Extended Day Programs: (703) 358-6069
Division of Social Services:
(703) 358-5590

Fairfax County

Office for Children/Child Care Resource System:
(703) 218-3700/359-5860
Division of School-Age Child Care: (703) 359-1097
Division of Family and Early Childhood Programs:
(703) 218-3725
Employer Child Care Council: (703) 218-3775

City of Fairfax

Human Services Coordinator:
(703) 385-7894

City of Falls Church
Department of Housing and Human Services: (703) 241-5005
Office of Community Education: (703) 241-7676

Loudoun County
Department of Social Services: (703) 777-0360/0353; (703) 478-8406

Prince William County
Department of Social Services/Child Care Division: (703) 792-4300

Suburban Maryland

Anne Arundel County
Child Care Division/State Department of Human Resources: (410) 514-7850

Montgomery County
Child Care Connection: (301) 279-1773
Child Care Division/Family Resources: (301) 217-1175
Children's Resource Center: (301) 279-1260
Department of Social Services: (301) 468-4012
Child Care Administration: (301) 294-0344

Prince George's County
Locate Child Care: (301) 772-8400
Child Care Resource Center: (301) 772-8420
Child Care Administration: (301) 808-1685
Department of Social Services: (301) 341-3883

The Washington National Cathedral stands as one of the world's largest churches.

Inside Metro Washington Worship

There's an intense spiritual side to the Washington area that doesn't get a lot of attention. Maybe it's the American insistence of separating church and state that has kept the nation's capital from being recognized as an important religious center. Or maybe it's simply the image of ruthless politicians and godless defense contractors running amok.

Nevertheless, behind the power struggles and political machinations, a religious current runs deep here, a kind of hidden moral checks-and-balances mechanism for the folks whose daily decisions affect the way more than 250 million people work and live.

Virtually every denomination under the sun and then some worships in Metro Washington. A quick scan through the Yellow Pages reveals everything from the mainstream to the obscure to the fringe: Catholic, Baptist, Jewish, Episcopal, Mormon, Quaker, Lutheran, Charismatic, Christian Scientist, Covenant, Church of God/Anderson, Indiana, Full Gospel, Open Bible and Unitarian, among many others. There's even something called The Church of the Mind, and in freewheeling Takoma Park, Md., there's a listing for The Metaphysical Chapel.

The Washington area's international character is also reflected in the way it worships. Throughout the region you'll find Korean Baptist and Greek Orthodox churches, Islamic mosques, Buddhist, Hindu and Sikh temples and less formal congregations representing religious practices from every corner of the globe.

Metro Washington was founded by WASPs — British Anglicans, to be exact — and the Protestant influence is still the driving religious force in the region, especially in Northern Virginia. There are, however, some interesting dynamics here that newcomers should be aware of. In Washington, D.C., for instance, there is a large contingency of black Catholics, perhaps even rivalling the number of Baptists. And in Maryland, a state that was founded as a haven for persecuted Catholics, the Catholic heritage is still very strong. In addition, Jewish families traditionally have migrated to the Maryland suburbs. These factors partly explain why Maryland and Washington historically have been more ethnically diverse than Virginia.

The religious and ethnic gap is closing, however, as the metro area continues to become more politically, economically and socially integrated.

In this brief chapter, we want to introduce you to some of the more colorful, provocative and historical houses of worship in Metro Washington. Our purpose is to entertain, not recommend or list churches to attend. We'll leave that to ministers and the Yellow Pages. At the end of the chapter, however, we have listed some phone numbers of religious umbrella groups and associations that might help you get started in finding a specific church, meeting house, temple or synagogue in your area.

Washington's Spiritual Legacy

Washington, D.C.'s most prominent spiritual icon is also one of the city's newest churches. Well, it's new in the sense that it was recently completed — after 83 years in the making. Construction of the awe-inspiring Washington National Cathedral, at Wisconsin and Massachusetts avenues NW, was begun in 1907, with the laying of the first cornerstone, and completed in 1990. Worship services, concerts and recitals have been going on here since the presidency of Theodore Roosevelt, however. Although officially known as the Cathedral Church of St. Peter and St. Paul, and affiliated with the Episcopal church, the National Cathedral is truly an interdenominational place of worship, serving as host for an array of Protestant, Catholic and Jewish services.

The cathedral, the seventh largest in the world, is widely revered as "the last of the great cathedrals," a church built in the Old World fashion — stone by stone. The 14th-century, Gothic-style structure sits atop Mount Saint Alban, the highest point in the District of Columbia. The cathedral's commanding perch above the city skyline affords not only great views from its ornate bell towers but allows for the massive structure to be seen from miles around. On a clear day, one can make out the 200-yard-long cathedral from as far away as Fort Washington, Md., some 15 miles to the south.

Among the interred in the cathedral are the bodies of President Woodrow Wilson, Admiral George Dewey, Helen Keller and her teacher Anne Sullivan Macy, as well as Mabel Boardman, former head of the American Red Cross, and Cordell Hull, secretary of state during World War II. For tour and event information, call (202) 537-6247.

The oldest church in Washington is St. Paul's (Episcopal), established in 1719. It's located in the middle of Rock Creek Cemetery, at Rock Creek Road and Webster Street NW. (Despite the street and cemetery name, the church is several blocks from Rock Creek Park.) On the grounds is one of the most artful and poignant sculptures in Washington: a bronze statue of a young women by Augustus Saint-Gaudens. Henry Adams commissioned the memorial in 1890 in honor of his wife who had committed suicide. Noted critic Alexander Wolcot called it "the most beautiful thing ever fashioned by the hand of a man on this continent."

A dominating presence in the Northeast quadrant of the city is the National Shrine of the Immaculate Conception, the largest Roman Catholic Church in the Western Hemisphere. The Romanesque- and Byzantine-style shrine, noted for its blue-domed roof, sits adjacent to Catholic University, a fascinating destination in itself. The National Shrine's bell tower, reminiscent of St. Mark's in Venice, contains a 56-bell carillon. Carillon concerts are held year round on Sunday at 2:30 PM. For tour information, call (202) 526-8300.

The greatest concentration of houses of worship in Washington can be found along 16th Street in Northwest, one of the city's major north-south arteries and a boulevard that has come to be known as the "Street of Churches." Among the eye-catchers here is First Baptist Church, at 16th and O streets, built in 1955 in a pseudo-Gothic style. Harry Truman and Jimmy Carter frequented First Baptist while in office.

At 16th and P streets, Foundry Methodist Episcopal Church was founded by Georgetown businessman Henry Foxall, owner of the Foxall-Columbia Foundry on the Potomac River. Today, the congregation is one of the largest, wealthiest and most integrated in Washington.

The Jewish Community Center, a block away at 16th and Q, is an 83-year-old limestone structure built in the classical style. For several years the building was owned by the University of the District of Columbia but was repurchased by a local Jewish group in 1990 and returned to its original use.

At the southeast corner of 16th and Corcoran streets is the Church of the Holy City, a French Gothic-influenced building with a tower built in homage to the one that overlooks the entrance to Magdalen College in Oxford, England. The 98-year-old Episcopal church is graced by some rather intimidating gargoyles.

The Scottish Rite Temple, at 1733 16th St., was designed by John Russell Pope and modeled largely after the Mausoleum of Halicarnassus in Greece. Pope, you may remember, was the same man who designed the Lincoln Memorial, another classical Greek structure. The temple serves as the headquarters of the Supreme Council of the Southern Jurisdiction of the Thirty-Third Degree of the Ancient and Accepted Scottish Rite of Freemasonry. Try saying that two times real fast.

Also not to be overlooked on 16th Street at Harvard Street is All Souls Unitarian Church. The church, whose parishioners include some of the leading African-American powerbrokers in Washington, was built in 1924 as a reproduction of London's St. Martin's-in-the-Fields.

Nearby, at 16th and Columbia Road, stands the Washington branch of the Unification Church, a denomination that was started by the eccentric South Korean Rev. Sun Myung Moon, who is also the owner of *The Washington Times* newspaper. Up until 1975, however, the church housed the Mormon Washington Chapel. The chapel was designed in the 1930s by Don Carlos Young, the grandson of Brigham Young.

At one time or another it seems that just about every church in Washington has been honored by the presence of an important politician, statesman or celebrity. We've already mentioned the case of First Baptist, which now is frequented by President Clinton and family. Teddy Roosevelt was a regular at Grace Reform Church (Dutch Reformed), at 15th and O streets NW. His wife and family, however, attended services at St. John's Episcopal Church, located right across the street from the White House, at 16th and H NW. St. John's houses an extensive collection of Roosevelt memorabilia, and to this day remains the church most visited by presidents.

St. Matthew's Cathedral (Catholic), downtown on Rhode Island Avenue NW, was where President Kennedy attended services and was the site of his funeral mass. Herbert Hoover, a devout Quaker, worshipped at Friends Meeting House, 2111 Florida Ave. NW.

Frederick Douglass, abolitionist, journalist and scholar, was part of a congregation of free blacks and slaves who made up the Metropolitan African Methodist Episcopal Church, 1518 M St. NW, sometimes called the National Cathedral of African Methodism.

The first synagogue ever built in Washington was the Old Adas Israel. President Grant attended the dedication in 1876. The building nearly fell victim to the wrecking ball before being moved to its present location at 3rd and G streets NW, where it is restored as the Lillian and Albert Small Jewish Museum.

One of the most intriguing facades in Washington is that of the Islamic Mosque and Cultural Center, 2551 Massachusetts Ave. NW. Located in the thick of Embassy Row, the long white building and its 160-foot-high minaret are the religious and cultural focal point of the Washington area's growing Islamic community, which now totals about 70,000 people. Visitors are welcome, but proper attire is the rule here and that means arms and legs (and, yes, women's heads) must be covered. For information, call (202) 332-8343.

Virginia's Colonial Churches

Across the river in Northern Virginia, one can peek into the world of colonial worship at Christ Church and the Old Presbyterian Meeting House in Old Town Alexandria. Built in 1773 by city founder John Carlyle, Christ Church was the regular place of worship for George Washington and, later, Robert E. Lee. The English country-style church sits in the center of Old Town, at 118 N. Washington St. (also known as the George Washington Memorial Parkway). Its courtyard is graced by 200-year-old poplar and oak trees that provide natural shelter for the graves of several Confederate soldiers who died in Alexandria hospitals. Just about every president has attended services at this historic Episcopal church.

Alexandria's Scottish forefathers also built the Old Presbyterian Meeting House at 316 S. Royal St. George Washington's funeral services, originally scheduled for Christ Church, were held here because icy roads made the trip to the center of town impossible. Buried in the cemetery behind the meeting house is the Unknown Soldier of the American Revolution.

Probably the most distinguishable building in Alexandria is the George Washington Masonic National Memorial, located atop a hill at 101 Callahan Dr., between King and Duke streets. The memorial, modeled after one of the Seven Wonders of the Ancient World — the lighthouse at Alexandria, Egypt — contains a collection of Washington artifacts, including the clock from his bedroom at Mount Vernon, which, interestingly enough, was stopped at the moment of his death. For tour information, call (703) 683-2007.

Where Latter-Day Saints, American Saints and Midshipmen Pray

Suburban Maryland has its share of spiritual landmarks, but none is more imposing than the Washington Temple of the Church of Latter-Day Saints, which looms Disney-esque above the Capital Beltway in Montgomery County. The $15 million marble temple, quite a sight at night, is off-limits to non-Mormons (although public tours were given for a short time after construction was completed). However, a visitors center on the grounds, at 9900 Stoney Brook Dr., in Kensington, is open to the public and guided tours of the shrine's perimeter are offered. For information, call (301) 587-0144.

Literary buffs may want to venture up to Rockville, the Montgomery County seat, to view the grave sites of F. Scott Fitzgerald and his wife, Zelda, at the cemetery at St. Mary's Catholic Church, at Viers Mill Road and Rockville Pike. Their remains were moved here in 1975 from their original graves in Rockville Cemetery.

Moving farther up north, to Frederick County, one can visit the National Shrine of St. Elizabeth Ann Seton in the village of Emmitsburg. Mother Seton, who lived in this area in the early 19th century, founded the Sisters of Charity and the first parochial school system in the United States. She was canonized in 1975 by Pope Paul VI, becoming the first American Saint. Slide presenta-

Insiders' Tip

Washington's rich spiritual heritage is probably best represented by the incredible cross section of churches, temples and synagogues found along 16th Street in Northwest. Sunday afternoons along this grand avenue take on an almost festive air.

tions, exhibits and interpretive programs are available at the visitors center. For more information, call (301) 447-6606.

Take the time and you'll soon discover that some of the most interesting spiritual sites in Metro Washington are found in unusual locations. Case in point is the dramatic Naval Academy Chapel in Annapolis. You can't miss the place. Its copper-green dome towers above all other buildings on this majestic campus, or "grounds," as Midshipmen like to say. The chapel dates back to 1904 and bears a striking resemblance to Les Invalides, in Paris. Heroes of the sea are honored in its Tiffany stained-glass windows, and a 12-foot model of a 15th-century Flemish ship hangs above the rear choir loft. The most moving site here is actually beneath the chapel, where lies the crypt of John Paul Jones, the American naval hero of the Revolutionary War. The ark-like marble sarcophagus is adorned with carved dolphins and inscriptions of the ships commanded by Jones, the father of the U.S. Navy, and the man who gave us the seminal battle cry, "I have not yet begun to fight."

We, on the other hand, have yet begun to scratch the surface of Metro Washington's fascinating spiritual landmarks. The rest, as they say, is for you to explore.

Worship Resources

Council of Churches of Greater Washington, 411 Rittenhouse Rd. NW, Washington, D.C. 20011, (202) 722-9240

Interfaith Conference of Metropolitan Washington, 1419 V St. NW 20009, Washington, D.C., (202) 234-6300

Protestant

African Methodist Episcopal/ Second Episcopal District, 1134 11th St. NW, Washington, D.C. 20011, (202) 842-3788

Baptist D.C. Convention, 1628 16th St. NW, Washington, D.C. 20001, (202) 265-1526

Christian Churches (Disciples of Christ)/Capital Area, 8901 Connecticut Ave., Chevy Chase, Md. 20815, (301) 654-7794

Church of the Brethren/Mid-Atlantic District, 300 N. Montague St., Arlington, Va. 22203, (703) 524-4100

Episcopal Diocese of Washington, Washington Cathedral/ Mount Saint Alban, Washington, D.C. 20016, (202) 537-6555

Evangelical Lutheran Church of America/Metro Washington, D.C. Synod, 212 E. Capitol St. NE, Washington, D.C. 20003, (202) 783-7501

National Capital Presbytery, 4915 45th St. NW, Washington, D.C. 20016, (202) 244-4760

Society of Friends (Quakers), 4119 Davis Place NW, #101, Washington, D.C. 20007, (202) 483-3310

United Church of Christ/Office of Communications, 2000 M St. NW, Washington, D.C. 20036, (202) 331-4265

United Methodist Board of Church and Society, 100 Maryland Ave. NE, Washington, D.C. 20002, (202) 488-5600

Roman Catholic

Archdiocese of Washington, P.O. Box 29260, Washington, D.C. 20017, (301) 853-3800

Jewish

Jewish Community Council of Greater Washington, 1522 K St. NW, Suite 920, Washington, D.C. 20005, (202) 347-4628

Mormon

The Church of Jesus Christ of Latter-Day Saints/Washington Metropolitan Area Regions, 529 14th St. NW, Suite 900, Washington, D.C. 20045, (202) 662-7480

Islamic

The Islamic Center, 2551 Massachusetts Ave. NW, Washington, D.C. 20008, (202) 332-8343

Photo: Washington Convention and Visitors Association

The Mary McLeod Bethune Statue honors her contributions to the civil rights movement.

Inside Metro Washington Parks and Recreation

Metro Washington may be at the southern terminus of the Eastern megalopolis, but much of the region feels and looks far removed from most peoples' big-city expectations. Green buffers are everywhere, from small leafy plots of land in Washington's inner city, to the giant state and regional parks found in the suburbs.

According to the World Resource Institute, an international environmental policy group, Metro Washington is among the nation's "greenest" urban communities, largely because of the pervading parks and woodlands found here.

Aside from the aesthetic and environmental advantages, the parks and the wealth of recreational opportunities they provide make for a vital aspect of the area's high quality of life.

This chapter presents a brief survey of the national, state, regional and local park systems within the national capital area and follows with a listing of some unusual — as well as vintage Washington — recreational pursuits.

National Parks

No other American urban area can claim as many National Park Service properties as can Metro Washington. It's one of the many perks of being in or near the Nation's Capital.

The Park Service's domain begins with the National Mall, that "vast esplanade" as envisioned by the capital city's designer, Pierre Charles L'Enfant. The three-mile expanse of green extends westward from the foot of Capitol Hill to the Lincoln Memorial and Potomac River. It contains the highest density of museums and monuments in the world.

The Mall, as you've probably discovered, is every bit as humble as it is inspiring. It was designed to be used by the people, and used it is. Informal games of soccer, volleyball, softball and touch football are almost as common a sight here as the museums and monuments. From spring through fall, Capitol Hill staffers, among others, use the Mall for their various athletic leagues.

The Mall is also the site of some of the nation's most important public gatherings. In 1963, for instance, Dr. Martin Luther King, Jr. led one of the largest public demonstrations in U.S. history on these hallowed grounds. Every four years, the East Mall, at the base of the Capitol Building, is the site of presidential inaugural swearing-in ceremonies. Regardless of your political affiliation, the ceremony and the setting make for an unforgettable Washington experience.

The city's second most visible greenspace is Rock Creek Park (202-426-6834), located in the center of Northwest and covering nearly 2,000 acres of rolling hills, woods, meadows and the namesake boulder-strewn creek. This is one of the world's largest urban parks, and its amenities are plentiful: vast hiking, biking and bridle trails; picnic areas; an equestrian center; golf course; tennis courts; and a historic mill. (See our chapters on Hidden Nooks and Crannies and the Civil War for some other interesting sites within this urban forest.)

In the 1800s, the Chesapeake & Ohio Canal was built to link Washington with the western reaches of the Potomac River. It stretches 185 miles from Georgetown to Cumberland, Md., passing through 74 lift locks. In 1971, the entire length was declared a national park and today the C&O Canal and Towpath (202-472-4376) is one of Washington's and Suburban Maryland's most coveted recreational retreats. Tree-lined gravel pathways extending along the route provide excellent biking and jogging trails; the canal itself, meanwhile, makes for gentle canoeing and kayaking.

Metro Washington sits amid a region of beautiful and fragile wetlands. At the Kenilworth Aquatic Gardens (202-426-6905) in Northeast, naturalists can spend an afternoon traversing 14 acres of preserved pools and marshes and inspecting the national park's 40 species of pond and marginal plants, including water lilies, lotuses and hyacinths.

The nearby National Arboretum (202-475-4815), also in Northeast, showcases a lush variety of plants, flowers and trees. The 444-acre park bursts into an incredible blaze of color during the spring azalea and summer rhododendron seasons, prime times to plan a visit.

The National Park Service has been equally generous to Washington's suburbs. In Northern

Insiders' Tip

Insiders...

Know where to go to catch rainbow trout inside the Beltway. Every March, the parks authority in Arlington County stocks several sections of Four Mile Run (an unusually pristine urban stream) with thousands of trout in anticipation of opening day of the Virginia trout season. Remember to get a state fishing license and trout stamp before making that first cast.

A couple strolling through one of the many parks in Metro Washington.

Virginia, the George Washington Memorial Parkway and its adjacent Mount Vernon Trail provide spectacular riverside hiking and biking trails extending from the river banks opposite Theodore Roosevelt Island southward 17 miles to Mount Vernon.

Farther to the south, in Prince William County, Prince William Forest Park (703-221-7181) covers 16,000 acres of dense forests and meandering creeks. In northern Fairfax County, meanwhile, Great Falls Park (703-285-2966) touts one of the most impressive natural sights in Metro Washington: The cascading Great Falls of the Potomac plunging (in some places more than 35 feet) through a series of jagged rocks and gigantic boulders that make up Mather Gorge. The falls can also be viewed from the Maryland side of the river at the C&O National Historical Park (301-739-4206).

Also in Suburban Maryland, Greenbelt National Park (301-344-3948) defies its highly urban setting just off the Beltway in Prince George's County with acres of wooded trails and special interpretive nature programs for kids.

State Parks

Both Virginia and Maryland are blessed with large state park systems, including generous tracts of preserved wilderness in land-scarce suburban Washington.

Northern Virginia's Mason Neck State Park (703-339-7265) in Fairfax County and Leesylvania State Park (703-670-0372) in Prince William County offer precious access to the Potomac River. Mason Neck is home to several bald eagles that nest among its towering pines and hardwoods. Leesylvania sits on land that was once owned by Revolutionary War hero "Light Horse" Harry Lee and later the Fairfax family.

George Washington's Gristmill State Park (703-339-7265), also in Fairfax County, is an interpretive historical site that offers tours of a reconstructed mill once used by the first president who resided just down the road at Mount Vernon Estate.

While not technically in Metro Washington, Fauquier County, Virginia's Sky Meadows State Park (703-592-3556) drapes over the rolling foothills of the Blue Ridge Mountains and connects with the famed Appalachian Trail. Arts benefactor Paul Mellon, who resides in nearby Upperville, donated this one-time dairy and horse farm to the state. Just 60 miles from downtown D.C., Sky Meadows attracts weekend campers and hikers.

Maryland, a small and populous state, is proud of its open spaces and rightly so. In Montgomery County, Seneca Creek State Park (301-924-2127), near Gaithersburg, affords hundreds of acres of outstanding hiking and fishing opportunities almost within eyesight of suburban housing developments. Prince George's County's Patuxent River (301-627-6074) and Cedarville (301-888-1622) state parks offer glimpses into the tranquil world of Tidewater Maryland, while Anne Arundel County's Sandy Point State Park (410-757-1841) boasts the closest saltwater swimming beach to downtown Washington. Sandy Point is located adjacent to the western terminus of the Chesapeake Bay Bridge near Annapolis. Its manmade rock jetties are popular with anglers.

Regional Park Authorities

Over the years, the regional park authorities in Northern Virginia and Suburban Maryland have acquired thousands of acres of invaluable lands and preserved them for recreational use — no small feat in our increasingly urbanized area.

The Northern Virginia Regional Park Authority (703-352-5900), for instance, has set aside 9,000 acres of park land in Arlington, Fairfax and Loudoun counties and the cities of Alexandria, Fairfax and Falls Church. Some of the largest and most visited parks in the system are Algonkian Regional Park (703-450-4655) along the Potomac in Loudoun County, Bull Run Regional Park (703-631-0550) in western Fairfax County, not far from Manassas National Battlefield Park, and Pohick Bay Regional Park (703-339-6100) in southeastern Fairfax County. Like neighboring Mason Neck State Park, Pohick is home to nesting bald eagles.

In Suburban Maryland, the regional park authority is known as the Maryland-National Capital Park & Planning Commission, which works in conjunction with the Montgomery County Department of Parks (301-495-2525) and the Prince George's County Department of Parks & Recreation (301-699-2407). Two of the largest and most scenic parks in this highly regarded system are Little Bennett (301-972-9222) and Black Hill (301-495-2525) regional parks, which together cover more than 5,000 acres of rolling countryside in upper Montgomery County.

County and City Park Authorities

The city parks of the District of Columbia and the county parks of Northern Virginia and Suburban Maryland are often overshadowed by the region's vast network of national, state and regional parks.

Nevertheless, they play a vital role in the community, providing urban sanctuaries ranging from the simple neighborhood park and playground to comprehensive athletic and recreation centers, swimming complexes, gardens, historic sites and instructional facilities. All of the park authorities offer a full slate of recreational courses, cultural programs and even special fitness activities for small children, seniors and physically challenged residents.

For a complete list of local parks and activities in your neighborhood, we suggest you call the following:

District of Columbia

District of Columbia Department of Recreation and Parks, (202-673-7671).

Northern Virginia

Alexandria Department of Recreation, Parks and Cultural Activities, (703-838-4340).

Fairfax County Park Authority, (703-246-5700).

Arlington County Department of Parks, Recreation and Community Resources, (703-358-3323).

Loudoun County Department of Parks and Recreation, (703-777-0343).

Prince William County Park Authority, (703-792-7060).

Suburban Maryland

Montgomery County Department of Parks, (301-495-2525).

Prince George's County Department of Parks & Recreation, (301-699-2407).

Insiders' Tip

To find out if your neighborhood or community has a Little League baseball program, go straight to the source — call Little League International in Williamsport, Penn. at (717) 326-1921.

Anne Arundel County
Recreation and Parks
Department, (410-222-3600).

Youth Sports

The best sources we know to get your kids launched into youth athletic programs — whether it's baseball, softball, basketball, football, soccer, gymnastics, golf, tennis or swimming leagues — is by calling your respective city or county park authority information office which we've listed above. Note that many of these activities aren't confined to the kids. Adult and senior programs are a vital part of most park authority programming.

Recreation

We could go on for years listing and describing the thousands of park and recreation programs available to residents throughout Metro Washington. Instead, we thought we'd take the time here to tell you about some of the offbeat and obscure activities as well as those you probably never dreamed existed in our fair region. For the more conventional programs, activities and special classes available through the county and regional parks, contact them directly and they will gladly send you literature, usually in the form of seasonal guide booklets.

Bungee Jumping

No, it's not from the top of the Washington Monument. At least not yet. But a company in Fairfax County called Sky Jam Bungee (we're not sure if that name promotes confidence) will take you out to the hinterlands, tie you to a hot air balloon with a huge bungee-like cord and drop you over the side. Moonlight jumps and group rates are available, too. Think we're kidding? Give them a call at (703-255-4708).

Camping

Wilderness camping inside the Beltway? Surely you jest. At Greenbelt National Park (301-344-3948) in Prince George's County you can pitch a tent in densely forested woods that obscure both the sight and sound of the Capital Beltway that hums less than two miles from the campground. Expect crowds on holiday weekends and anytime the Grateful Dead is in town.

Within 10 miles outside the Beltway you can find several great spots to spend a night under the stars, beginning with Fairfax County's serene Burke Lake Park (703-323-6600). Over on the Maryland side, Cosca (301-868-1397) and Watkins (301-249-9220) regional parks in Prince George's County and Wheaton (301-949-4006) and Cabin John (301-299-4555) regional parks in Montgomery County all have clean, safe and scenic campgrounds.

Kayaking

For those who survived the balloon bungee jump, the next step is tackling the turbulent rapids of the Potomac River below Great Falls. This is some of the most exciting whitewater in the East and it's less than 15 miles from the White House. But please, take a lesson first. Adventure Schools (301-770-0551) in Suburban Maryland can get you started off right.

Fishing the Potomac

Thirty years ago, the Potomac River was on the brink of a painful death, the victim of decades of untreated sewage dumping and unchecked urban and agricultural pollution runoff. Thanks to the Clean Water Act and a heavy dose of civic pride, the Nation's River, while still not pristine, is considered one of the healthiest urban rivers in the U.S. So much so, that it is now a premier bass fishery, both above and below Great Falls. It's even possible to land three- to five-pounders within the shadows of the Memorial and Wilson bridges. For a special day on the river, contact Potomac bass guru Ken Penrod and his Outdoor Unlimited guide service (301-937-0010) whose clients have included former President Bush and Supreme Court Justice Sandra Day O'Connor.

Rock Climbing

Metro Washington is deceptively hilly and at several points along the bluffs of the Potomac the terrain can be downright rugged. You can learn to scale these and other rock faces by taking a climbing course. The Fairfax County Park

Photo: Nat. Capital Parks, U. S. Dept. of the Interior

Construction of the Equestrian Statue, Arlington Memorial Bridge, in 1951.

Authority (703-246-5700) offers some of the best around.

Sailing

The Washington Sailing Marina (703-548-9027), about a mile and a half south of Washington National Airport in Alexandria, will rent you a cute little Sunfish sailboat by the hour. There's something to be said about coming about with a view of the monuments.

Of course, the serious sailor will want to head to Annapolis, the self-proclaimed sailing capital of the East. Boat charters here are nearly as abundant as the tourists, but we suggest you contact the friendly folks at the Annapolis Sailing School (410-267-7205).

Shooting

We're talking about the legal kind, of course. And you can take aim at those clay pigeons at the Bull Run Regional Park Skeet and Trap Shooting Center (703-830-2344) in Fairfax County and at the Prince George's County Trap and Skeet Center (301-577-7178) in Glenn Dale, Md.

Softball on the Mall

How do those terminally intense Capitol Hill aides unwind — besides patronizing Pennsylvania Avenue's famed watering holes? Many of them, men and women, take to the field and the open spaces of the National Mall for a friendly but competitive brand of nonpartisan (sometimes) softball. You needn't be a Hilltopper to caucus on the diamond. For full disclosure on this non-federally funded activity, call (202-544-3333).

Golfing on the Mall

The East Potomac Park Golf Course (202-863-9007) is located in the namesake park that is considered part of the National Mall. Within a short walk from the Jefferson Memorial, the 18-hole course (commonly referred to as the Hains Point course) also features a driving range. An adjacent miniature golf course is a perfect diversion for the kids.

Horseback Riding in D.C.

You can jump in the saddle at the Rock Creek Park Horse Center (202-362-0017), located in the heart of Washington's largest park. The National Park Service offers trail riding on miles of bridle paths, lessons and year-round boarding. On the bridle paths keep an eye out for deer. Yes, there's a herd right in the thick of Washington.

Inside Metro Washington Volunteer Opportunities and Social Clubs

Never let it be said that Metro Washingtonians don't have any free time for themselves or, more importantly, for others. Sure, we're considered by many to be among the hardest-working, most career-oriented and, all too often, most stressed-out folks on the planet. But you've got to draw the line somewhere, and when that line is finally drawn, many people are passionate about volunteering and joining social clubs.

But wait. We're going to cut you a break here. This chapter is mercifully short. Just consider it something of an abridged version of a summary of an overview. But for good reason. It would be next to impossible to try and assemble any sort of comprehensive listing of the literally thousands of outlets for wannabe volunteers and socializers in Metro Washington. If attempted, we'd probably give the Oxford English Dictionary and the federal budget a run for the money in terms of sheer volume, not to mention tick off our publisher for quadrupling the size of this book.

Instead, we hope to merely give you some places to start as well as touch on a few of the opportunities that only residents of Metro Washington are able to experience. For many residents, newcomers in particular, this area can be a pretty daunting place to live. Volunteering and exploring social outlets not only help to bring this sprawling metropolis down to a more human scale, but they also provide excellent networking opportunities for anyone in search of employment or looking to take their career in a new direction.

Those with the volunteer spirit already know the rewards that can be reaped from donating time, energy and skills without receiving monetary compensation. And if it's variety you're looking for, Metro Washington is sure to please.

As with most any area of this size, a good way to get a feel for the multitude of volunteer opportunities is by perusing telephone directories, community handbooks and other free and easily accessible resources for lists of charitable organizations, social agencies and a vast array of other groups that welcome, and indeed cherish, volunteers. On the civic side, it's as simple as A-B-C: Authorities, Boards and Commissions galore, at the state, county, city and town levels, rely heavily on volunteer help. Citizen participation, whether it's voicing an opinion, voting or volunteering, is essential to the function of a democratic society, and governmental involvement can be particularly satisfying for citizens yearning for an inside look at how some of their tax dollars are spent.

For more information on volunteering for government-related positions, contact the public information or citizens assistance offices for your county, city or town, or the clerk to the board, council or whatever governing body oversees your jurisdiction. For telephone numbers, please refer to the "Government Services/Utilities" chapter.

If you can't stomach getting up-close and personal with government, consider teaching or tutoring, working in a library, a homeless shelter or with Special Olympians. Or perhaps delivering meals to elderly or handicapped shut-ins, fighting fires, or bringing paramedic assistance to the injured and the ill. And remember the hospitals and other health-care centers that are seemingly always in need of volunteer help. Consult the "Health Care" chapter for a listing of area medical facilities and their telephone numbers.

The American Red Cross is of course a major user of volunteer services, particularly in times of disaster or other especially busy periods. Contact the nearest chapter for more information.

Alexandria: (703) 549-8300
Anne Arundel County: (410) 760-9600
Arlington County: (703) 527-3010
Fairfax County: (703) 876-0700
Loudoun County: (703) 777-7171/689-1114
Montgomery County: (301) 588-2515
National Capital Region (Washington): (202) 728-6401/6460
Prince George's County: (301) 559-8500
Prince William County: (703) 368-4511/631-9548

For volunteer experiences that are uniquely Washington, consider the Smithsonian Institution – an institution in more ways than one. Founded in 1846, the Smithsonian has become the world's largest museum complex, with 14 museums (including the most-visited one in the world, the National Air and Space Museum) and the National Zoo. In addition to informing and entertaining the public at large, the Smithsonian conducts vital research and is dedicated to national service and scholarship in the arts, sciences and history.

One of the primary areas of volunteer participation is through the Smithsonian's Docent Program. Docents are volunteer teachers who provide group learning experiences in the form of museum tours or instruction in special areas. Volunteers are also needed for various clerical and administrative duties during normal office hours and to serve as greeters, ushers and assistants at lectures, seminars, films, walking and bus tours and other activities.

For more information on volunteer activities with the Smithsonian, call (202) 357-2700/3256, or write to: Smithsonian Information, Smithsonian Institution, SIB 153, MRC 010, Washington, D.C. 20560.

A host of volunteer opportunities are also available through another Washington institution, yet one with a much greater presence around the country: the National Park Service. Volunteers in Parks, or VIPs, work in nearly all of the 350 or so properties in the National Park Service system, including about 30 here in the National Capital Region. VIP duties range from staffing information desks and presenting living-history demonstrations dressed in period costumes, to light grounds and maintenance work, patrolling trails and writing and designing brochures.

For more information, call (202) 619-7077, or write to the National Park Service's National Capital Region, 1100 Ohio Dr. SW, Washington, D.C. 20242.

If you have some time to give for volunteering but don't know or can't decide how to use it, fret no more. Simply call or stop by the central volunteer office in your community. There, staff members will identify your skills, interests and time available, refer you to agencies where your talents might best be used, and follow up to assure that you found an appropriate position.

Following are the main volunteer clearinghouses for the Metro Washington jurisdictions covered in this book. In some cases, individual cities and towns within these jurisdictions may also have volunteer offices, but these umbrella groups are good places to start.

District of Columbia

Volunteer Clearinghouse of the District of Columbia, 1313 New York Ave. NW, #303, Washington, D.C. 20005, (202) 638-2664

Virginia

Alexandria Volunteer Bureau, 801 N. Pitt St., #102, Alexandria, Va. 22314, (703) 836-2176

The Arlington Volunteer Office, 2100 Clarendon Blvd., Suite 314, Arlington, Va. 22201, (703) 358-3222

Voluntary Action Center of Fairfax County Area, Inc., 10530 Page Ave., Fairfax, Va. 22030, (703) 246-3460

Loudoun Volunteer Center, 30-B Catoctin Cir. SE, Leesburg, Va. 22075, (703) 777-0113

Voluntary Action Center of the Prince William Area, 9300 Peabody St., Suite 108, Manassas, Va. 22110, (703) 369-5292

Suburban Maryland

Anne Arundel County Office of Community Services, Volunteer Program, Arundel Center, P.O. Box 2700, Room 230, Annapolis, Md. 21404, (410) 222-1530

(Note to new residents of Annapolis or Severna Park: Two clubs you may find of interest are the New Annapolitans (410-280-0703) and the Severna Park Newcomers (410-987-0703 or 544-2598).

Montgomery County Volunteer and Community Service Center, 50 Monroe St., #400, Rockville, Md. 20850, (301) 217-4949

Prince George's Voluntary Action Center, Inc., 6309 Baltimore Ave., Suite 305, Riverdale, Md. 20737, (301) 779-9444

When it comes to social clubs, we again suggest you turn to community handbooks, telephone directories and the like for an overview, particularly if you're seeking out Lions, Optimists, Masons and Shriners, newcomer's groups, assorted women's and men's clubs, musical groups and professional societies. And don't forget churches, community centers, friends and co-workers as prime sources of information on meeting people who share your interests.

With such a large transient population, Metro Washington is a hub for state societies and college alumni associations, not to mention groups affiliated with entire nations (see the "International Washington" chapter for a list of some of the major embassies and their phone numbers).

Returning to the Smithsonian for a moment, the institution's wildly popular Resident Associate Program is a good way to learn something, be entertained and meet people all at the same time. The group sponsors a wide variety of lectures, seminars, films and other cultural events throughout the year at different Smithsonian venues. Call (202) 357-3030 for more information.

Since being on the move is something of a habit for many Metro Washingtonians, one group in particular that we'd like to plug is the Washington Airline Society, an organization of air-transport enthusiasts who meet monthly at the National Air and Space Museum.

Formed in 1978, the group is involved in such activities as preserving historical information and artifacts, hosting guest speakers from all segments of the air transport industry, hosting debates and discussions, and sponsoring field trips to aviation-related destinations. Annual dues of $15 include the group newsletter, "Eye on the Sky." All meetings are open to the general public. For more information, call (301) 593-2242 or (703) 920-6477, or write to the Washington Airline Society, 805 Malta Lane, Silver Spring, Md. 20901.

Bottom line with the legion of volunteer opportunities and social clubs in Metro Washington: the outlets are there en masse. If you want to get involved, you can. It's just a matter of time.

Inside Metro Washington Government Services & Utilities

You've pulled up stakes and made the big move to Metro Washington. The job, the home and the neighbors are great. There's so much to see and do, you can't wait to get started. But hold on a minute. Somewhere along the way you'll have to spend precious time taking care of the more mundane yet important aspects of getting settled. Water, electricity, telephone and cable TV hookups, voter registration, car registration . . . the list reads like a sure-fire recipe for boredom. Still, it's got to be done.

Now we're not about to promise that this chapter will help make these and other such tasks enjoyable. Instead, we hope to make them less of a hassle by guiding you along — and preferably around, whenever possible — the sometimes confusing path to understanding which agency is responsible for what in a particular jurisdiction.

You'll note that at the very beginning of the Suburban Maryland and Northern Virginia sections, we've included the information about obtaining a driver's license and auto tags since these are state functions that apply to all the various municipalities within. The listing for "Local Auto Registration" applies to the windshield decals that individual counties, cities and towns require. Their purchase is often based on payment of personal property tax for each vehicle.

And speaking of other jurisdictions, there are literally dozens and dozens of small towns and cities — some largely rural and with just a few hundred residents — located within the Suburban Maryland and Northern Virginia counties (Arlington being the sole exception) featured in this book. Cities generally function almost wholly separate from the surrounding county. Towns, even though they too are self-governing, generally have a closer relationship to the county and in some cases enjoy many county-provided services and facilities (police and fire protection, utilities, schools, etc.). Although, it comes with a price: town residents typically pay both town and county taxes. Still, you don't hear too many people around here complaining about how local government functions or delivers the myriad facilities and services to its constituents. If only the feds would take notice.

By now you may be completely nonplused trying to figure out this inter-jurisdictional thing. But that's perfectly understandable, especially if you've moved here from a place where the political and geographic layers are more easily defined. For simplicity's sake, in this chapter we've included only those intra-county cities and towns that we consider to be the major "sub-jurisdictions," if you will. You'll certainly know it if you've taken up residence in a distinct municipality within a county, but should you have any doubts as to who is responsible for what, read on.

For virtually any question you might have as a newcomer regarding government services, utility hookups and the like, probably the best place to call before venturing any further is your town/city/county Citizens Assistance or Public Information office — or whatever it may be called in your particular community. Or simply a call to the main switchboard at the town/city hall or county government center will do the trick. The folks who staff these places are trained to handle inquiries on a wide variety of topics. And if for some reason they don't have the answer at hand, they can surely refer you to someone who does. The main numbers for each jurisdiction are listed at the beginning of each overview.

Of course, real estate agents — particularly those who specialize in out-of-town relocations — neighbors and co-workers can also be valuable sources of information on some of the intricacies of Metro Washington living.

District of Columbia

(Note: Unless shown otherwise, all phone numbers listed are within the local 202 area code.)

The District Building (City Hall)

1350 Pennsylvania Ave. NW

General Information 727-1000
City "Help" Line 832-4357

Washington is presided over by a mayor and 13 City Council members, each serving four-year terms. Eight council members represent the city's eight political wards while five serve at-large. Elections (held in even-numbered years) are partisan.

The city has enjoyed this limited "home rule" system of local government since Jan. 1, 1975. Still, as a federally chartered and subsidized city, the buck doesn't stop at the mayor's desk; the U.S. Congress has final say on all local laws, budget appropriations and revenue measures. In addition to the Council members, District residents vote for U.S. president, vice president and a delegate to Congress.

Council meetings are held the first Tuesday of each month at 10 AM in Room 500 of the District Building.

Animal Control 576-6664

Auto Registration and Inspection/ Driver's Licenses 727-6680

Vehicle registration fees are collected annually and cost between $50 and $83, depending on weight. A one-time excise tax ranges from 6 to 7 percent of price or retail value,

Springtime at the U.S. Capitol.

depending on weight. Vehicles must be inspected annually at one of two inspection stations. The cost is $5.

Residents who drive in the District must obtain a license — good for four years — within 30 days of establishing city residency. A valid license and Social Security card are required, plus a $15 fee ($7 for learner's permit). A written exam and vision test are also mandatory. The minimum driving age is 16. Front-seat occupants of all vehicles must wear seat belts or face a possible $15 fine.

A separate exam and road test are required for motorcycle drivers. The cost is $15, $7 for learners.

Fire and Rescue Services

Emergency	*911*
Non-Emergency	*462-1762*

Police

Emergency	*911*
Non-Emergency	*727-1010*
Trash Collection	*727-4825*
Voter Registration	*727-2525*

Utilities

Cable TV: D.C. Cablevision	*727-0424*
Electricity: Potomac Electric Power Co. (PEPCO)	*833-7500*
Natural Gas: Washington Gas	*(703) 750-1000; 624-6049*
Telephone: C&P Telephone Co.	*346-1000*
Water and Sewer: D.C. Department of Public Works	*727-5240*

Northern Virginia

(Note: Unless otherwise stated, all phone numbers listed are within the local 703 area code.)

Driver's Licenses/State Auto Tags and Inspection

Upon establishing state residency, new residents have 30 days to apply for a Virginia operator's permit and vehicle registration. The minimum age for drivers is 16, with parental signature required until 18; a road and classroom education course is required for those under 18. The license fee is $12 for five years. A learner's permit — obtainable at 15 years, eight months — is good for one year, but only applies to in-state driving when accompanied by a licensed driver.

The titling fee for each vehicle is $10. The annual state registration costs $26 for passenger cars weighing up to 4,000 pounds, $31 for those over 4,000 pounds.

All vehicles must be inspected annually at official inspection stations (gas stations, dealerships, etc.) for a fee of $6. In Northern Virginia only, an annual emissions inspection costing $12.50 is also required for all cars dating from 1969. New models have a one-year exemption. The inspection is good for two years.

Virginia law requires all children under the age of 4 or weighing less than 40 pounds to travel in an approved safety seat if the vehicle is registered in Virginia and driven by the child's parent or guardian. Another state safety law requires that all front-seat passengers in any vehicle use their seat belts.

For more information, contact the state Department of Motor Vehicles' 24-hour information line at 761-4655.

City of Alexandria

City Hall

301 King St.

General Information	*838-4000*

Alexandria is governed by a City Council consisting of a mayor and six council members. The city manager is in charge of day-to-day operations.

Animal Control	*838-4775*
Local Auto Registration	*838-4777*

Fire and Rescue Services

Emergency	*911*
Non-Emergency	*838-4600*

Police

Emergency	*911*
Non-Emergency	*838-4444*
Trash Collection	*751-5130*
Voter Registration	*838-4050*

Utilities

Cable TV: Jones Intercable	*823-3000*
Electricity: Virginia Power	*359-3568*
Natural Gas: Northern Virginia Natural Gas	*750-9500*
Telephone: C&P Telephone Co.	*876-7000*
Water and Sewer: Alexandria Sanitation Authority	*549-3381*

Arlington County

One Courthouse Plaza

2100 Clarendon Blvd., Arlington

General Information	*358-3000*

Arlington — the smallest (25.8 square miles) county in the U.S. that's self-governing — is headed by a Board of Supervisors featuring a chairperson plus five supervisors, all serving staggered four-year terms. The top administrator is the county manager. The Board meets on designated Saturdays at 9 AM at One Courthouse Plaza.

Animal Control	*931-9241*
Local Auto Registration	*358-3081*

Fire and Rescue Services

Emergency	*911*
Non-Emergency	*358-3365*

Police

Emergency	*911*
Non-Emergency	*558-2222*
Trash Collection	*358-6570*
Voter Registration	*358-3456*

Utilities

Cable TV: Cable TV Arlington	*841-7700*
Electricity: Virginia Power	*359-3568*
Natural Gas: Northern Virginia Natural Gas	*750-9500*
Telephone: C&P Telephone Co.	*876-7000*
Water & Sewer: Arlington County	*358-3636*

Fairfax County

Fairfax County Government Center

12000 Government Center Pkwy., Fairfax
General Information 324-2000/4636

The county is governed by a 10-member (including the chairperson) Board of Supervisors, nine of whom serve specific districts. The chairperson holds an at-large seat. All members serve concurrent four-year terms. The Board meets on designated Mondays (usually twice a month) at 9:30 AM at the Government Center.

Animal Control 830-3310

Local Auto Registration 222-8234

Fire and Rescue Services

Emergency 911
Non-Emergency 246-2126

Police

Emergency 911
Non-Emergency 691-2131

Trash Collection 324-5040

Voter Registration 222-0776; 324-4700

Utilities

Cable TV: Media General Cable of Fairfax 378-8411
Media General provides cable TV service throughout the county — including the incorporated towns and cities located within — except in the Reston area where residents subscribe to the service provided by Warner Cable Communications (471-1749).

Electricity: Virginia Power 359-3568

Natural Gas: Northern Virginia Natural Gas 750-9500

Telephone: C&P Telephone Co. 876-7000

Water and Sewer: Fairfax County Water Authority 698-5800

City of Fairfax

City Hall

10455 Armstrong St. 385-7855

The city is run by a council-manager form of government (mayor and six City Council members).

Animal Control 385-7924

Local Auto Registration 385-7901

Fire and Rescue Services

Emergency 911
Non-Emergency 385-7940

Police

Emergency 591-5511
Non-Emergency 385-7924

Trash Collection 385-7981

Voter Registration 222-0776; 324-4700

Utilities

Cable TV: Media General Cable of Fairfax 378-8411

Electricity: Virginia Power 359-3568

Natural Gas: Northern Virginia Natural Gas 750-9500

Telephone: C&P Telephone Co. 876-7000

Water and Sewer: Residents are served by either the City of Fairfax (385-7915) or the Fairfax County Water Authority (698-5800).

City of Falls Church

CITY HALL (HARRY E. WELLS BUILDING)

300 Park Ave.

General Information 241-5001

Falls Church is governed by a mayor and six City Council members.

Animal Control 241-5053

Local Auto Registration 241-5090

FIRE & RESCUE SERVICES

Emergency 911
Non-Emergency 532-2672

POLICE

Emergency 241-5050
Non-Emergency 241-5054

Trash Collection 241-5080

Voter Registration 241-5085

UTILITIES

Cable TV: Media General Cable of Fairfax 378-8411

Electricity: Virginia Power 359-3568

Natural Gas: Northern Virginia Natural Gas 750-9500

Telephone: C&P Telephone Co. 876-7000

Water and Sewer: City of Falls Church 241-5071

Town of Herndon

TOWN HALL

730 Elden St.

Public Information 435-6800

Herndon is governed by a mayor and a six-member Town Council, each elected at-large for two-year terms.

Animal Control 830-1100

Local Auto Registration 435-6800

FIRE AND RESCUE SERVICES

Emergency 911
Non-Emergency 437-1233

POLICE

Emergency 437-1118
Non-Emergency 435-6846

Trash Collection 435-6853

Voter Registration 222-0776; 324-4700

UTILITIES

Cable TV: Media General Cable of Fairfax 378-8411

Electricity: Virginia Power 359-3568

Natural Gas: Northern Virginia Natural Gas (750-9500) serves most town residents, but a small number are served by Commonwealth Gas (631-5363).

Telephone: C&P Telephone Co. 876-7000

Water and Sewer: Town of Herndon 435-6814

Town of Vienna

TOWN HALL

127 Center St.

Public Information 255-6300

Vienna is governed by a Town Council consisting of a mayor and six council members, all elected at-large.

Animal Control 255-6377

Local Auto Registration 255-6323

Fire and Rescue Services

Emergency	911
Non-Emergency	938-2242

Police

Emergency	938-4900
Non-Emergency	255-6366

Trash Collection 255-6382

Voter Registration 222-0776; 324-4700

Utilities

Cable TV: Media General Cable of Fairfax 378-8411

Electricity: Virginia Power 359-3568

Natural Gas: Northern Virginia Natural Gas 750-9500

Telephone: C&P Telephone Co. 876-7000

Water and Sewer: Town of Vienna 255-6381

Loudoun County

Administration Building

18 North King St., Leesburg

General Information 777-0100

Loudoun County is governed by a Board of Supervisors consisting of a chairperson and eight Board members. A county administrator oversees the day-to-day operations of the county. Supervisors meet on the first and third Tuesdays of each month at 9 AM at the Administration Building.

Animal Control 777-0406

Local Auto Registration 777-0280

Fire and Rescue Services

Emergency	911
Non-Emergency	777-0333

Police

Emergency	911
Non-Emergency	777-0407

Trash Collection
(Contracted privately, by jurisdictions or homeowners associations.)

Voter Registration 777-0380

Utilities

Cable TV: Cablevision of Loudoun (430-8200) and Multivision Cable TV of Leesburg (777-4700)

Electricity: Virginia Power 359-3568

Natural Gas: Northern Virginia Natural Gas 750-9500

Telephone: C&P Telephone 876-7000

Water and Sewer: County of Loudoun 771-1095

Town of Leesburg

Municipal Government Center

25 West Market St. 777-2420

The Town of Leesburg is governed by a mayor and a six-member Town Council, all elected at-large. The mayor serves a two-year term, council members four years.

Animal Control 882-3211; 777-0406

Local Auto Registration 777-2717

Fire and Rescue Services

Emergency	911
Non-Emergency	777-1343

Police

Emergency	911

Photo: Washington Convention and Visitors Association

***U.S. Supreme Court** — The judiciary branch of the American government is based in this famed marble-columned building across from the U.S. Capitol.*

Non-Emergency	*777-3122*
Trash Collection	*771-2790*
Voter Registration	*777-0380*

UTILITIES

Cable TV: Multivision Cable TV of Leesburg	*777-4700*
Electricity: Virginia Power	*359-3568*
Natural Gas: Northern Virginia Natural Gas	*750-9500*
Telephone: C&P Telephone	*876-7000*
Water and Sewer: Town of Leesburg	*771-2750*

Prince William County

ONE COUNTY COMPLEX CT.

Prince William

General Information *792-6000*

Prince William County is governed by an eight-member Board of Supervisors, with each member serving concurrent four-year terms. The Board meets the first three Tuesdays of each month at 2 PM at the County Complex.

Animal Control	*792-6465*
Local Auto Registration	*335-6730*

FIRE AND RESCUE SERVICES

Emergency	*911*
Non-Emergency	*792-6810*

POLICE

Emergency	*911*
Non-Emergency	*792-6650*

Trash Collection
(No county service is provided. Homeowners must contract privately.)

Voter Registration *792-6470*

UTILITIES

Cable TV: Cablevision of Manassas (368-4227) is the prime provider of cable services to Prince William residents. A few residents are served by Westgate Cable (369-6213) and Columbia

Cable *(730-2225).*

Electricity: County residents are served by either Northern Virginia Electric Cooperative (335-0513) or Virginia Power (494-5111).

Natural Gas: County residents are served by either Northern Virginia Natural Gas (800-223-9452 or 750-9500) or Commonwealth Gas (361-3181).

Telephone: GTE of Virginia *680-8822*

Water and Sewer: County of Prince William *335-7900*

City of Manassas

City Hall

9027 Center St. *335-8200*

A mayor and a six-member city council govern Manassas. Members serve four-year terms, with half the council up for election every two years.

Animal Control *361-2812*

Local Auto Registration *257-8200*

Fire and Rescue Services

Emergency *911*
Non-Emergency *368-6211*

Police

Emergency *911*
Non-Emergency *257-8000*

Trash Collection *257-8200*

Voter Registration *257-8230*

Utilities

Cable TV: Most city residents are served by Cablevision of Manassas (368-4227), a few by Westgate Cable (369-6213).

Electricity: City of Manassas *257-8219*

Natural Gas: City residents are served by either Northern Virginia Natural Gas (800-223-9452 or 750-9500) or Commonwealth Gas (361-3181).

Telephone: GTE of Virginia *680-8822*

Water and Sewer: City Water and Sewer Utility *257-8219*

City of Manassas Park

City Hall

1 Park Center Ct. *335-8800*

Manassas Park elects a mayor and six-member City Council. All members serve four-year terms.

Animal Control *361-2812*

Local Auto Registration *335-8835*

Fire and Rescue Services

Emergency *911*
Non-Emergency *335-8845*

Police

Emergency *361-1136*
Non-Emergency *335-8844*

Trash Collection
Residents are eligible for private collection using city-issued containers. Call (800) 234-1305 for information.

Voter Registration *335-8806/8800*

Utilities

Cable TV: Cablevision of Manassas368-4227

Electricity: Northern Virginia Electric Cooperative *335-0513*

Natural Gas: Residents are served by either Northern Virginia Natural Gas (800-223-9452 or 750-9500) or Commonwealth Gas (361-3181).

Telephone: GTE of Virginia	*680-8822*
Water and Sewer: City of Manassas Park	*335-8805*

Suburban Maryland

Driver's Licenses/State Auto Tags and Inspection

A Maryland driver's license must be obtained within 30 days of establishing state residence. The minimum age for licensing is 16; applicants 16 to 18 must present a certificate showing they have passed an approved driver's education course. Learner's permits can be obtained at 15 years, nine months. The cost for a four-year license is $20 for the first one issued; renewals are also good for four years and cost $6. Motorcycle drivers are subject to the same regulations and fees.

Annual registration for cars is $27 (up to 3,700 lbs. gross vehicle weight) and $40.50 (over 3,700). Vehicles (except those with diesel engines) must be inspected biannually at certified stations for emissions unless the vehicle is over 15 years old. The testing fee is $9; the late fee is $5 per month.

For information, call the state Motor Vehicle Administration at (301) 768-7000.

Anne Arundel County

(Note: Unless otherwise stated, all phone numbers listed are within the local 410 area code.)

The Arundel Center

44 Calvert St., Annapolis

General Information	222-7000

Anne Arundel County is governed by a county executive — elected countywide for a four-year term — and a seven-member County Council. Council members represent a specific district and serve four-year terms. Council meetings are held the first and third Mondays of each month at 7:30 PM at the Arundel Center.

Animal Control	222-6690
Local Auto Registration	950-1682

Fire and Rescue Services

Emergency	911
Non-Emergency	987-4010

Police

Emergency	911
Non-Emergency	222-8050

Insiders' Tip

Insiders...
Call on the citizens assistance office of their town, city or county to get a handle on the scope of government services.

Trash Collection 222-6100

Voter Registration 222-6600/6611

Utilities

Cable TV: Three companies serve most county residents. United Cable Television (268-7551 or 858-5156) is the provider for Annapolis and homes south of Route 50; those who live north of Route 50 can receive Jones Intercable (987-3900), North Arundel Cable Television (987-5811), or both.

Electricity: Baltimore Gas & Electric 224-3000

Natural Gas: Baltimore Gas & Electric 224-3000

Telephone: C&P Telephone Co. 224-1900

Water and Sewer: Anne Arundel County 222-7500

City of Annapolis

City Hall

160 Duke of Gloucester St.

Public Information 263-7940; 269-0138

Annapolis is governed by a mayor along with eight city aldermen who are elected by district or city ward. The mayor is elected at-large.

Animal Control 222-6690

Local Auto Registration 950-1682

Fire and Rescue Services

Emergency 911

Non-Emergency 263-7975

Police

Emergency 911

Non-Emergency 268-9000

Trash Collection 263-7967/7949

Voter Registration 222-6600/6611

Utilities

Cable TV: United Cable Television 268-7551 or 858-5156

Electricity: Baltimore Gas & Electric 224-3000

Natural Gas: Baltimore Gas & Electric 224-3000

Telephone: C&P Telephone Co. 224-1900

Water and Sewer: City of Annapolis 263-7970

Montgomery County

(Note: Unless otherwise stated, all phone numbers listed are within the local 301 area code.)

Executive Office Building

101 Monroe St., Rockville

General Information 217-1000

Information and Referral Office 217-6500

The Montgomery County Council consists of a chairperson plus eight members. The day-to-operations of the county are managed by the county executive. Council meetings are held each Tuesday at 9:30 AM in the Hearing Room of the Council Office Building.

Animal Control 217-6999

Local Auto Registration 950-1682; 948-3177

Fire and Rescue Services

Emergency 911

Non-Emergency 217-2442

Police

Emergency	*911*
Non-Emergency	*279-8000*
Trash Collection	*217-2410*
Voter Registration	*217-6450; 424-4433*

Utilities

Cable TV: Cable TV of Montgomery 294-7600

Electricity: PEPCO (202-833-7500) serves the majority of county residents. A small northeastern section is serviced by Baltimore Gas & Electric (685-0123) while the extreme northwestern portion is served by Potomac Edison (800-492-7020).

Natural Gas: Washington Gas	*(703) 750-2500*
Telephone: C&P Telephone Co.	*852-9900*
Water and Sewer: Washington Suburban Sanitary Commission (WSSC)	*699-4000*

City of Gaithersburg

City Hall

31 S. Summit Ave.

General Information	*258-6300*

Gaithersburg is governed by a mayor and a five-member council. Elections are non-partisan, and council members serve staggered four-year terms.

Animal Control	*258-6343*
Local Auto Registration	*258-6320*

Fire and Rescue Services

Emergency	*911*
Non-Emergency	*217-2442*

Police

Emergency	*911*
Non-Emergency	*258-6400*
Trash Collection	*217-2410*
Voter Registration	*217-6450; 424-4433*

Utilities

Cable TV: Cable TV of Montgomery	*294-7600*
Electricity: PEPCO	*(202) 833-7500*
Natural Gas: Washington Gas	*(703) 750-2500*
Telephone: C&P Telephone Co.	*852-9900*
Water and Sewer: City of Gaithersburg	*258-6370*

City of Rockville

City Hall

111 Maryland Ave.

General Information	*309-3000*
Public Information Office	*309-3322*

Rockville is governed by a mayor and a four-member Council. Elections are non-partisan, and members serve concurrent two-year terms.

Animal Control	*309-3115*
Local Auto Registration	*309-3293*

Fire and Rescue Services

Emergency	*911*
Non-Emergency	*217-2442*

Police

Emergency	*340-7300*
Non-Emergency	*309-3100*
Trash Collection	*309-3094*
Voter Registration	*217-6450 or 424-4433*

Utilities

Cable TV: Cable TV of Montgomery 294-7600

Electricity: PEPCO (202) 833-7500

Natural Gas: Washington Gas (703) 750-2500

Telephone: C&P Telephone Co. 852-9900

Water and Sewer: City of Rockville 309-3093

City of Takoma Park

Municipal Building

7500 Maple Ave.
General Information 270-1700

Takoma Park is governed by a mayor and six-person Council. Elections are non-partisan, and members serve two-year terms.

Animal Control 217-6999

Local Auto Registration 270-1108

Fire and Rescue Services

Emergency 911
Non-Emergency 217-2442

Police

Emergency 911
Non-Emergency 270-1100

Trash Collection 217-2410

Voter Registration 217-6450; 424-4433

Utilities

Cable TV: Cable TV of Montgomery 294-7600

Electricity: PEPCO (202) 833-7500

Natural Gas: Washington Gas (703) 750-2500

Telephone: C&P Telephone Co. 852-9900

Water and Sewer: WSSC 699-4000

Prince George's County

(Note: Unless otherwise stated, all phone numbers listed are within the local 301 area code.)

County Administration Building

14741 Governor Oden Bowie Dr.
Upper Marlboro
General Information 952-3000; 350-9700

Prince George's is governed by a County Council featuring a chairperson plus eight members. All serve concurrent four-year terms. The chief administrator is the county executive. Council meetings are held each Tuesday at 10 AM in the County Administration Building.

Animal Control 499-2828

Local Auto Registration 952-5025

Fire and Rescue Services

Emergency 911
Non-Emergency 925-5200

Police

Emergency 911
Non-Emergency 336-8800

Trash Collection 952-4750

Voter Registration 627-2811

Utilities

Cable TV: Metro Vision Inc. (499-1980) serves county residents south of Central Avenue. Multivision Cable of Maryland (731-5560) serves those living north of Central Avenue.

Electricity: County residents are served by either Baltimore Gas and Electric (234-5000) or

Potomac Electric Power Co. (PEPCO) 202-833-7500.

Natural Gas: County residents are served by either Baltimore Gas and Electric (234-5000) or Washington Gas (703-750-1000).

Telephone: C&P Telephone Co. 851-4000

Water and Sewer: Washington Suburban Sanitary Commission (WSSC) 699-5600

City of Bowie

City Hall

2614 Kenhill Dr.
General Information 262-6200

The City of Bowie is governed by a mayor and a six-member Council, all of whom serve concurrent two-year terms. Elections are non-partisan.

Animal Control 262-6200

Local Auto Registration 262-6200

Fire and Rescue Services

Emergency 911
Non-Emergency 925-5200

Police

Emergency 911
Non-Emergency 336-8800

Trash Collection 262-6200

Voter Registration 627-2811

Utilities

Cable TV: Multivision Cable of Maryland 731-5560

Electricity: Residents are served by either Baltimore Gas & Electric (234-5000) or PEPCO (202-833-7500).

Natural Gas: Residents are served by either Baltimore Gas & Electric (234-5000) or Washington Gas (703-750-1000).

Telephone: C&P Telephone Co. 851-4000

Water and Sewer: City of Bowie 262-6200

City of College Park

Administration Building

4500 Knox Rd.
General Information 864-8666; 779-5526

College Park is governed by a mayor and an eight-member council, all of whom serve concurrent two-year terms. Elections are non-partisan.

Animal Control 864-8877

Local Auto Registration 277-4286

Fire and Rescue Services

Emergency 911
Non-Emergency 925-5200

Police

Emergency 911
Non-Emergency 336-8800

Trash Collection 864-8666

Voter Registration 627-2811

Utilities

Cable TV: Multivision Cable of Maryland 731-5560

Electricity: City residents are served by either Baltimore Gas & Electric (234-5000) or PEPCO (202-833-7500).

Natural Gas: City residents are served by either Baltimore Gas & Electric (234-5000) or Washington Gas (703-750-1000).

Telephone: C&P Telephone Co. 851-4000

Water and Sewer: City of College Park 864-8666

City of Greenbelt

Municipal Building

25 Crescent Rd.

General Information 474-8000

The City of Greenbelt is governed by a mayor plus five-member council. Elections are non-partisan, and council members serve concurrent two-year terms.

Animal Control 474-7200

Local Auto Registration 474-1552

Fire and Rescue Services

Emergency 911

Non-Emergency 925-5200

Police

Emergency 474-5454

Non-Emergency 474-7200

Trash Collection 474-8004

Voter Registration 627-2811

Utilities

Cable TV: Multivision Cable of Maryland 731-5560

Electricity: Residents are served by either Baltimore Gas & Electric (234-5000) or PEPCO (202-833-7500).

Natural Gas: Residents are served by either Baltimore Gas & Electric (234-5000) or Washington Gas (703-750-1000).

Telephone: C&P Telephone Co. 851-4000

Water and Sewer: City of Greenbelt 474-8000

Inside Metro Washington Media

It's been said that information is a fundamental component of power. That being the case, then residents of Metro Washington could justifiably be considered some of the most powerful people in the world. And indeed, many are just that. No. 1 on the list, in fact, lives at 1600 Pennsylvania Ave. NW.

This chapter isn't about political players but rather the awesome presence of the information players. There are few places beyond Washington where the incoming and outgoing stream of information — specifically the written and spoken products of the print and electronic media — is as intense or has the potential to affect more people. And there are few places beyond Washington where the citizens have as much interaction with and exposure to the conveyors of that information, the roughly 12,000 reporters, editors, correspondents, broadcasters, freelance writers and others of that ilk from around the globe who ply their trade here. It's the highest concentration of journalists anywhere on earth, a staggering testament to the sphere of influence of the so-called "Fourth Estate." It's also a downright scary thought to many people (at least until they realize how many lawyers are here!), all those nosy journalists running around, but it's a situation to be expected since Washington plays a dual role of capital of the nation and capital of the free world.

Living in Metro Washington, you soon get accustomed to the fact that much of the "local" news is also national and international news. Call it a blessing or curse, but that's reality. It's what happens when reporters have beats that include not only city hall, the county courthouse and the school board, but also the White House, Capitol Hill, the Supreme Court, the Pentagon and other focal points of the federal establishment.

Beyond the newspapers, magazines, radio and TV stations and other media based in Metro Washington, nearly every major (and some not-so-major) news outlet in the world has a presence here, whether it's a full-blown bureau with two dozen staffers and a complement of high-tech machinery or a lone correspondent holding court at the National Press Building with little more than a desk, telephone and typewriter. This diverse legion of workers affiliated with non-local press entities contributes greatly to the 12,000 figure mentioned above.

Metro Washington is home to such media giants as The Washington Post Company, publisher of not only one of the world's most influential newspapers, but also *Newsweek* magazine; Gannett, proud parent of "The Nation's Newspaper," *USA Today*, and a host of other print and broadcast properties; United Press International, the venerable but financially troubled wire service that nearly went out of business in 1992 before an 11th-hour buyout; and the National Geographic Society, an American publishing institution (along with the likes of *Life* and *Time* magazines and the long-defunct *Look* magazine) that not only produces great magazines, but also terrific maps, globes, books and TV specials. And of course there are the numerous trade associations based here that represent the press in one form or another.

Washington media certainly move to their own beat, but in recent years that beat has been muted somewhat with the demise of no less than four local magazines, one of the more painfully tangible signs of the economic upheaval that has manifested itself in different ways around the nation. Stopping their presses for good were *Regardie's*, a feisty journal that catered to the elite of Washington business and real estate; *Dossier*, which chronicled the significant society and party circuit in the nation's capital; *Museum & Arts Washington*, an outstanding monthly that focused on the city's impressive arts and cultural scene; and *New Dominion*, a Northern Virginia lifestyle/business magazine.

On a more positive note, the late 1980s and early '90s also saw the start-up of one publication and two radio stations. *Washington Flyer*, the nation's first in-airport magazine and an official product of the Metropolitan Washington Airports Authority, launched at Washington National and Washington Dulles International airports. Taking to the airwaves were WCXR (105.9 FM), whose "classic rock" format has become one of the radio industry's hottest, and WTEM (730 AM), Washington's first all-sports station which promptly went and out-bid WMAL (630 AM) for the rights to broadcast all Redskins games starting with the 1992-93 season. It was quite a coup — and an expensive one at that — for the new kid on the block; WMAL had been the team's radio home for more than 40 years.

Whether it's scanning the radio or TV dial or flipping through a newspaper or magazine, Washington media are diverse to say the least. Another result of the region's global influence is the availability of foreign and domestic publications that neighborhood 7-Elevens, bookstores, libraries or streetside newsstands don't stock. News junkies, students, academicians and homesick transplants will be relieved to know that there are numerous other sources for out-of-town reads, and the District is home to three of the area's best: American International News, 1825 I St. NW (202-223-2526); The News Room, 1753 Connecticut Ave. NW (202-332-1489), which also carries scholarly journals and bilingual directories; and One-Stop, 2000 Pennsylvania Ave. NW (202-872-

1577). Sometimes, it doesn't even require leaving home. Several major newspapers based elsewhere, such as *The New York Times* and *The Wall Street Journal,* offer same-day delivery to certain areas of Metro Washington. Virginians wanting to keep close tabs on events in their state capital can pick up a current copy of the *Richmond Times-Dispatch,* one of the South's oldest and most respected newspapers, at some area newsstands; the paper also maintains an active Washington bureau. Marylanders, meanwhile, can receive *The Capital,* the daily digest of happenings in and around Annapolis, through the mail if they don't mind getting it a day or two late.

As with some other topics covered in the book, this chapter is intended as an overview, not an encyclopedic compilation. We've avoided for the most part mentioning any personalities and other details that can quickly become outdated. And while we've tried to be as current as possible, bear in mind that publication titles, radio and TV formats and the ownership of such entities do indeed change as well as cease to exist, often with little warning. I guess that's one of the risks we run by including this information in a book, but then, it would sure be cumbersome to do it all by fax.

Newspapers

Like many American cities, Washington has witnessed the death of a major metropolitan newspaper, in this case it was the popular afternoon daily, *The Washington Star. The Washington Times* has strived mightily since 1982 to fill the void, but it just hasn't been the same. Yet. *The Washington Post* has long been and remains the undisputed king of the local media hill. While aggressive and forthright in its effort to provide a conservative option to the liberal *Post,* the *Times* continues to lag greatly in virtually every category, from circulation and ad pages, to classified listings and, perhaps most prominently, stature.

The only other local dailies are the *Journal* chain, which publishes Monday through Friday and focuses almost exclusively on news and events in Northern Virginia and Suburban Maryland, and *The Capital,* which publishes seven days a

Insiders . . .
Watching Redskins games on TV often choose to turn down the sound and turn up the radio and listen to the entertaining broadcast team of Frank Herzog, Sam Huff and Sonny Jurgensen on WTEM. Herzog, a longtime sports broadcaster on local television, handles the play-by-play; former Redskins and Hall of Fame members Huff (linebacker) and Jurgensen (quarterback) do the color commentary.

Insiders' Tip

week and covers Annapolis and surrounding areas of Anne Arundel County.

While TV and radio have come a long way since their inception in delivering the news with unprecedented speed and, in the case of television, amazing visual impact, they will never supplant the newspaper when it comes to expansive coverage and an overriding sense of permanence. Case in point: Excluding commercials, the average half-hour TV newscast is actually about 22 minutes long, and if written down, the words wouldn't even fill the front page of a major newspaper.

THE WASHINGTON POST

1150 15th St. NW
Washington, D.C. 20071 (202) 334-6000

Scan virtually any list of the most influential newspapers in the nation, even the world, and *The Washington Post* is surely to be included, ranking up there along with other domestic powerhouses such as *The New York Times, The Wall Street Journal* and *The Los Angeles Times.*

Whether you appreciate, despise or merely tolerate its unabashedly liberal bent, the *Post* is an amazing study in what a top-notch major newspaper should be, given its wealth of resources, a worldwide presence and an immense staff replete with Pulitzer Prize-winning reporters, editors, photographers, even a cartoonist (the inimitable "Herblock"). After all, this is the paper that broke the Watergate scandal, propelling two formerly obscure reporters, Bob Woodward and Carl Bernstein, to international notoriety and forever changing the face of investigative journalism.

Living in Metro Washington and reading the *Post* day in and day out, you come to expect what readers of many other papers do not: In-depth analysis and commentary, from both sides of the political fence, on a broad range of topics; reprints of the entire text of presidential speeches and news conferences; its own Sunday magazine; stories and photos from the farthest reaches of the world provided by *Post* staffers, not wire services; heavy coverage of national and international news to complement the coverage of local goings on; in-depth special series; and stimulating editorial and op-ed pages. That the *Post* does all of this in black and white for the most part is a testament to its market dominance. It doesn't feel a need to try and compete visually with the color-rich, contemporary, award-winning design of *The Washington Times.*

But the *Post* goes beyond the daily newspaper in flexing its formidable muscle throughout the community. Since early 1990 the paper has operated Post-Haste, a free information service accessible by touch-tone telephone. The system, which grew from 34 incoming phone lines to 88, has handled more than 20 million calls and evolved into what the paper calls "an increasingly important link between *The Post* and its readers." Calls come in now at the rate of some 800,000 per month!

The plethora of information available through Post-Haste includes stock quotes, mortgage rates and other financial data, updates in news, sports and special events (such as national and local elections), lottery results for the District, Maryland and Virginia, sound bites of popular music reviewed by *Post* staffers, weather reports, ski conditions, additions to the bestseller lists that appear in the Book World section, soap opera plots, recycling policies of local jurisdictions, and public services offered by the *Post* such as guided tours of its headquarters.

Calls to Post-Haste are free within Washington's local dialing area. After reaching the main number, (202) 334-9000, callers are asked to enter a four-digit code for the kind of information they want. A directory of Post-Haste categories and their respective numbers appears in the paper each day.

The Washington Times

3600 New York Ave. NE
Washington, D.C. 20002 (202) 636-3000

If nothing else, *The Washington Times* gives conservatives a loud, colorful voice of their own. Plucky and aggressive, the *Times* (which also publishes a weekly news magazine, *Insight*) has been a seven-day-a-week daily only since September 1991, but you wouldn't know it from the way it challenges the *Post* toe-to-toe in its marketing strategies and daily news coverage.

The *Times* distinguishes itself not only by its strong right-wing tilt, but by its owner: the Rev. Sun Myung Moon's Unification Church. Debates linger over how much influence — if any — the controversial church and its leadership have over the paper's day-to-day operations or its editorial decisions. But perceptions are often more damaging than reality, and in the case of the *Times*, this is one monkey that'll be nearly impossible to get off its back.

Controversy and circulation figures aside, the *Times* has come a long way in just over 10 years in making Washington a two-newspaper town again and in convincing people to give them a try. With a wealth of talented staffers of their own, many of them former *Star* employees, the *Times* has earned praise for its visual appeal, outstanding sports and business sections (the stat- and detail-rich sports section in particular more than gives the *Post* a run for its money), hard-hitting investigative instincts and for hustle, gumption and chutzpah in the face of a David and Goliath type of rivalry with the *Post*.

In an effort to woo readers from its cross-town rival, the *Times* has even gone so far as printing with a special ink that resists rubbing off onto readers' hands (it actually

Insiders . . .
Rely on the numerous community newspapers — many of which are free — for coverage of local events, people and places that they won't get from any other publication.

Insiders' Tip

works) and publishing its weekend section on Thursdays as a service to those who like to have their days off planned by the time Friday rolls around. A novel idea indeed.

As long as the money supply never runs out, the *Times* will continue to be the proverbial fly in the *Post's* ointment and the darling of the conservative establishment. The *Times/Post* battle is good old-fashioned newspaper competition at its finest.

The Journal Newspapers

2720 Prosperity Ave.
Fairfax, Va. 22034 (703) 560-4000

The *Journal* publishes separate editions Monday through Friday in five area jurisdictions: The City of Alexandria plus the counties of Arlington, Fairfax, Montgomery and Prince George's.

Suburbanites have come to depend on the *Journal* for in-depth coverage of their communities beyond that which is provided by the *Post* and the *Times*. It takes a full-time presence in the suburbs, and the *Journal* certainly has that, although it's hard to be timely with weekend happenings if you don't have Saturday and Sunday editions.

The chain does a respectable job of covering its own turf, particularly in the areas of news, sports and features, and has been known to scoop its two major competitors in stories involving such bread-and-butter categories as local government, crime and the courts.

The *Journal* also produces two smaller weekly supplementary papers in Fairfax and Prince William counties.

The Capital

P.O. Box 911
Annapolis, Md. 21404 (410) 268-5000

The Maryland Gazette

P.O. Box 567
Glen Burnie, Md. 21060 (410) 766-3700

One of two major community papers in Anne Arundel County, *The Capital* publishes every day and offers intensive coverage of Annapolis and the immediate area.

The Capital's sister publication, *The Maryland Gazette*, is based in Glen Burnie and comes out on Wednesday and Saturday.

Residents of Metro Washington have dozens of other community news outlets. The weekly chains in particular are vast, with virtually every enclave in the District, Northern Virginia and Suburban Maryland having some sort of newspaper to call its own.

Many of the publications are free and distributed either by mail or doorstep-to-doorstep based on Zip code zone. As two writers who cut their professional teeth in community journalism, we know the important role such papers play.

Among the District's smaller media offerings are *The Washington Blade*, a free weekly for the gay and lesbian community; *City Paper*, a free weekly covering culture, the arts, music, nightlife and related topics; *Roll Call*, a biweekly (Monday and Thursday) covering Capitol Hill and distributed to all House and Senate offices; the *Washington Afro-American*, a weekly for the black community; and the *Washington Business Journal*, a weekly that, as its name suggests, examines the local business scene.

Maryland's community weeklies include the *Potomac & Bethesda Almanac* (published by Alexandria-based DCI Publishing), the *Charles County Times/Crescent*, the *South County Times*, and the *Gazette Newspapers* of Bethesda, Gaithersburg, Germantown, Damascus, Olney, Potomac and Chevy Chase. Anne Arundel County publications include the *Crofton News Crier* and two Annapolis freebies, *Alive!* and *The Publik Enterprise*, which in some ways are the Maryland capital's answer to Washington's City Paper.

Back across the Potomac River, Arundel Communications has a huge stake in Northern Virginia. Links in this vast chain include the *Loudoun Times Mirror*, the *Eastern Loudoun Times* and the Times Mirror papers in the Fairfax County communities of Burke, Chantilly, Herndon, Reston, Vienna and Springfield. A bit farther removed from Metro Washington are the *Fauquier Times Democrat*, the *Clarke Courier* and the *Front Royal News*.

JGF Media Inc. owns Northern Virginia's weekly *Sun/Gazette* newspaper that serves Great Falls, McLean, Vienna and Oakton, the small daily (Monday-Friday) *Northern Virginia Sun*, and a monthly in Loudoun County, *Middleburg Life*.

DCI's Northern Virginia presence is felt in Alexandria and the counties of Fairfax and Prince William with the *Alexandria & Franconia Gazette Packet*, the *Mount Vernon Gazette*, *Centre View* of Centreville and Chantilly, *The Connection* papers of Burke, Fairfax, Springfield, Reston/Herndon/Fairfax West and McLean/Great Falls/Vienna/Oakton/Tysons, and the *Manassas Weekly Gazette*.

There's also the *Herndon Observer* and the *McLean-Providence Journal*.

Magazines

As we mentioned earlier, Washington's magazine roster has shrunk considerably in recent years. But if there's one local constant with a reach that extends far beyond our area it's the National Geographic Society (202-857-7000), publisher of the esteemed *National Geographic* as well as *National Geographic Traveler*. NGS's Explorer's Hall at 17th and M streets NW makes for a fascinating stop on a local touring itinerary. The gift shop sells great maps, globes and books on a variety of topics. NGS also offers a fascinating film and lecture series. Call (202) 857-7700 for information.

Insiders . . .
Seeking an inexpensive form of amusement like to compare same-day editions of *The Washington Post* and *The Washington Times* to see how their disparate political leanings influence such things as the placement of major stories and the photos and headlines that accompany them.

Insiders' Tip

Another locally produced magazine with distribution beyond the immediate area is *Mid-Atlantic Country* (301-220-2300), a monthly that was formerly headquartered in Old Town Alexandria but now makes its home in Greenbelt, Md. This beautifully designed, edited and written lifestyle magazine is targeted to residents of the Atlantic Seaboard region that stretches from New Jersey to North Carolina.

Two major players (excluding *The Washington Post Magazine*) remain on the local magazine front. *Washington Flyer* (703-739-9292), a glossy bimonthly based in Old Town Alexandria, covers a range of topics pertinent to business and leisure air travelers— locals and out-of-towners alike. With complimentary distribution at Washington National and Washington Dulles International airports, the magazine occupies a unique market niche with impressive demographics and a high pass-along rate. Just four years old, the *Flyer* also produces a supplementary publication, *Here!*, that focuses on the arts, culture, fashion, shopping and dining.

The area's true city magazine — although its readership base is predominantly suburban — *Washingtonian* (202-296-1246) is a slick, thick monthly known for its "Best Of" lists, dining/shopping guides, maps of the stars' homes, interesting features and personality profiles and the occasional hard-hitting investigative piece. High paid-circulation numbers, a well-heeled readership and a large and talented staff have helped *Washingtonian* maintain its enviable position in the local magazine market.

Radio

Turn on you car radio and push the "scan" button and barely two seconds will pass before you lock onto a station. Push it again and again and you'll get the same result. Metro Washington is by no means New York or L.A. in terms of market size or listening choices, but it does offer over 50 AM and FM stations with a wide range of formats.

Here's a look at what's offered around the dial.

Adult Contemporary/Soft Adult Contemporary

♪ WLTT 94.7 FM
♪ WASH 97.1 FM
♪ WGAY 99.5 FM
♪ WMMJ 102.3 FM
♪ WRQX 107.3 FM
♪ WFMD 930 AM
♪ WAGE 1200 AM

Classical

♪ WGMS 103.5 FM
♪ WETA 90.9 FM (also information/National Public Radio)

Country

♪ WMZQ 98.7 FM/1390 AM
♪ WFRE 99.9 FM
♪ WRCY 107.7 FM
♪ WQSI 820 AM
♪ WPWC 1480 AM

Easy Listening

♪ WMJS 92.7 FM

Jazz

♪ WPFW 89.3 FM (also community radio)

♪ WDCU 90.1 FM (also talk/gospel)

News/Talk/Sports/Information

♪ WMAL 630 AM

♪ WCPT 730 AM (audio simulcast of CNN's "Headline News")

♪ WWRC 980 AM

♪ WNTR 1050 AM

♪ WMET 1150 AM

♪ WTOP 1500 AM

♪ WPGC 1580 AM

♪ WAMU 88.5 FM (also folk and bluegrass music; National Public Radio)

♪ WJFK 106.7 FM/1300 AM (also jazz)

Oldies

♪ WBIG 100.3 FM

♪ WNAV 1430 AM (Annapolis station also has news, Navy sports)

♪ WXTR 104.1 FM

Religious/Inspirational/Gospel

♪ WABS 780 AM

♪ WCTN 950 AM

♪ WUST 1120 AM

♪ WFAX 1220 AM

♪ WDCT 1310 AM

♪ WYCB 1340 AM

♪ WAVA 105.1 FM

Rock

♪ WIYY 97.9 FM (hard-rock Baltimore station with D.C. overlap)

♪ WHFS 99.1 FM (modern/alternative rock)

♪ WWDC 101.1 FM (album rock)

♪ WCXR 105.9 FM (classic rock)

Soul/Talk

♪ WOL 1450 AM

Sports-Only

♪ WTEM 570 AM

Top 40/Contemporary Hits

♪ WPGC 95.5 FM

♪ WZYQ 103.9 FM

♪ WINX 1600 AM

Urban Contemporary

♪ WKYS 93.9 FM

♪ WHUR 96.3 FM

Other

♪ WILC 900 AM (contemporary Latin)

♪ WNTL 1030 AM (international/ethnic)

♪ WWDC 1260 AM (personality/Middle of the Road)

♪ WMDO 1540 AM (Latin music/news)

♪ WMOM 1560 AM (MOR)

Insiders . . .
Check *Washingtonian* magazine and the weekend sections of the *Post* and the *Times* for interesting guides to local dining, shopping, nightlife and assorted recreational diversions.

Insiders' Tip

♪ WMUC 88.1 FM (progressive)

♪ WGTS 91.9 FM (educational/cultural)

Television

Virtually anything a television viewer wants is available in Metro Washington. Along with all the major networks, numerous independent stations and of course literally hundreds of cable channels are at your fingertips in the local area.

Most residents of Metro Washington are now able to get cable TV, although there remain pockets where service has yet to be provided and may never be for various reasons. Surprisingly, the District is a fledgling cable community, with the first cable franchise having been awarded only in the last several years. Consequently, the number of households with cable service is comparatively low. Media General Cable of Fairfax, a subsidiary of the Fortune 500 publishing and broadcasting conglomerate Media General, has been operating since the early 1980s and is far and away the largest local cable provider with nearly 200,000 subscribers in Fairfax County.

Cable offerings for local residents run the gamut, from local public-access channels that offer community and civic information to the major players such as premium movie channels (HBO etc.), CNN, Discovery, MTV, ESPN, TNT, Chicago and New York "super stations" and of course C-SPAN (Cable-Satellite Public Affairs Network) and C-SPAN II, which offer live coverage of the U.S. House of Representatives and U.S. Senate, respectively, and related programming. For some strange reason these channels seem to be especially popular around here.

The following companies provide cable TV service to residents of Metro Washington. Information on specific services and other details is included in the "Government Services/Utilities" chapter.

- City of Alexandria: Jones Intercable, Inc.
- Anne Arundel County: Three companies serve most of Anne Arundel County. United Cable Television is the provider for Annapolis and homes south of Route 50; residents north of Route 50 can receive Jones Intercable or North Arundel Cable Television, or both.
- Arlington County: Cable TV Arlington
- District of Columbia: D.C. Cablevision
- Fairfax County: Media General Cable serves the vast majority of county residents. Reston residents

Insiders' Tip

Insiders . . .
Count on the National Geographic Society's Washington headquarters as a prime source for great maps, books and other items relating to places, people and animals of the world.

subscribe to the service provided by Warner Cable Communications.

- Loudoun County: Cablevision of Loudoun and Multivision Cable TV of Leesburg
- Prince William County: Cablevision of Manassas and Columbia Cable
- Montgomery County: Cable TV of Montgomery
- Prince George's County: Metro Vision Inc. and Multivision Cable of Maryland

WASHINGTON'S MAJOR LOCAL TV STATIONS AND THEIR NETWORK AFFILIATES:

WRC Channel 4 (NBC)
WTTG Channel 5 (Fox)
WJLA Channel 7 (ABC)
WUSA Channel 9 (CBS)
WDCA Channel 20 (Independent)
WETA Channel 26 (PBS)
WHMM Channel 32 (PBS)

OTHERS:

WMPT Channels 22 and 67 (Independent)
WFTY Channel 50 (Independent)
WNVT Channel 53 (Independent)
WNVC Channel 56 (Independent)
WTKK Channel 66 (Independent)

BALTIMORE STATIONS AVAILABLE TO MANY RESIDENTS OF METRO WASHINGTON:

WMAR Channel 2 (NBC)
WBAL Channel 11 (CBS)
WJZ Channel 13 (ABC)

Photo: Calvert County, Maryland, Tourism

Drum Point Lighthouse in Prince Frederick, Maryland.

Inside

From the Blue Ridge to the Bay: A Day Trip & Weekend Sampler

Let's not kid ourselves. Scores if not hundreds of books have been written about daytripping and weekend frolicking in and around the Nation's Capital. And for good reason. Few areas in the United States can boast of the inexhaustible array of scenic, cultural, historic and recreational attractions within an honest day's drive and back from an urban region as can Washington, D.C.

Our point here is not to rewrite what already has been inked. We don't have the room or the patience. Instead, we want to take you to some of our favorite nearby destinations — places we proudly put on our "must-see" itinerary for visiting families and relocating friends eager to discover the rich environs and folkways beyond the Beltway.

When we say "beyond the Beltway" what we really mean is away from the metro area but close enough to more than justify a day's outing or a weekend mini-vacation.

What a palette we have to work with. From the ancient, forest-covered Blue Ridge Mountains to the tranquil majesty of the Chesapeake Bay, the world's largest and most productive estuary, to all those points in between, the storybook quality of the Mid-Atlantic countryside and all that it offers is the stuff of inspiration, rejuvenation and endless repeat visits. It is part of the cultural fabric of being a Washingtonian.

We've divided the chapter into three broad parts: The Blue Ridge, The Bay and the Beaches, and Points In Between. Of course, from time to time, we may meander beyond our geographic parameters. After all, we couldn't, in good conscience, omit such special places as the Dolly Sods Wilderness of West Virginia or the Victorian charm of Cape May, New Jersey, just because they didn't fit into our thematic scheme. We'd be cheating ourselves and doing a disservice to you.

So come along, weekend warriors. Put the maps in the glove box, check the fuel gauge and fasten those seatbelts. It's time to let your imaginations and frontiers soar.

The Blue Ridge

Named for their pervasive blue haze, the result of a complex photochemical reaction involving trees, light and moisture, the Blue Ridge Mountains are the nation's easternmost range, running from north Georgia to southern Pennsylvania, with Virginia claiming the largest stretch.

To give you an idea of their proximity to Metro Washington, D.C., residents of western Fairfax County can see the mountains on a clear day while driving along busy Route 28. Conversely, Skyline Drive in Shenandoah National Park got its name because in earlier times one could make out the Washington skyline from its eastern overlooks.

Oh, Shenandoah!: The National Park

This is it. The Big Kahuna, the Grand Poo-bah of the Virginia Blue Ridge. Stretching more than 130 miles along the spine of the mountains, from Front Royal south to Waynesboro, Shenandoah National Park (703-999-2229) is a naturalist's paradise.

Each year, nearly two million people flock to the park and its famed Skyline Drive to take in dramatic vistas of the Appalachians and the rolling, fertile farmland of the Shenandoah Valley and the Piedmont. Don't let those numbers scare you, though: The park contains over 195,000 acres and once you venture off of Skyline it's possible to hike, fish and camp for several days without seeing another human. The same can't be said about wildlife, however. Bobcat, deer, fox, turkey and bear, among other critters, are prevalent in these parts. In fact, the density of deer and black bears is among the highest anywhere in the United States, so if you plan to go backcountry camping be sure to check in at the Ranger Station to get briefed on safeguarding your camp.

For a less rugged but equally woodsy experience, try one of the park's four drive-in campgrounds — Big Meadows, Lewis Mountain, Loft Mountain and Matthews Arm — or two modern lodges, Skyland and Big Meadows (both 800-999-4714).

Aside from the fabled Appalachian Trail, which runs the distance of the park, excellent hiking opportunities can be had on dozens of peaks that comprise the highest mountain range between the Catskills and the Smokies. We highly recommend a day-climb on venerable Old Rag Mountain (elevation 3,291 feet), a favorite of Virginia's legendary statesman Harry F. Byrd, who regularly made the trek up until his 80s. A hike on the less-strenuous but taller Hawksbill Mountain (4,049 feet) is another favorite of

Insiders' Tip

Insiders...
Order a lunchbox from Sutton Place Gourmet before heading out for an afternoon sail on the Chesapeake Bay.

daytrippers, especially in late October when the park's thick, deciduous forests turn into a technicolor fantasyland.

Above all, Shenandoah is chock-full of wonderful hidden nooks and crannies. Things like abandoned settlers' cabins, cascading waterfalls and virtually untouched trout streams brimming with native brookies are just some of the treasures awaiting those with a penchant to get off the beaten path. A personal favorite is the five-mile hike to Camp Hoover, President Herbert Hoover's "summer White House" and austere fish camp built along the banks of the pristine Rapidan River, one of the best trout waters in the Old Dominion. Each year around August 10, the anniversary of Hoover's birthday, the National Park Service hosts a "Hoover Days" weekend in which the public is allowed to visit the camp and learn a bit about the president's leisure habits and the interesting guests who frequented the remote enclave. During this weekend, you have the option of taking a bus ride down the mountain or hoofing it on foot, both of which begin at the park's Byrd Visitor Center, Skyline Drive at milepost 51.

"Little Washington," the "Little Apple" and the Caverns

Blue Ridge Mountain towns move to their own whimsical, unpretentious beat. Folks still wave to strangers and shopkeepers are gracious even if you're just browsing. Surprises abound here, sometimes bordering on the surreal.

For instance, in tiny Washington, Virginia, off Route 211, sits one of the nation's most highly acclaimed restaurants and country inns — the Michelin five-star Inn at Little Washington (703-675-3800). Well-healed guests have been known to come from as far away as New York and Atlanta to dine on the restaurant's Nouveau French cuisine and spend a night in the tastefully furnished rooms. On any given Sunday morning, "Little Washington," the oldest of 28 towns in the U.S. named for our first president, probably could claim the world's highest concentration of Jaguars and Mercedes-Benzes. The inn, quite honestly, is out of this author's financial league but a drive through this early 18th-century, Quaker-influenced village is encouraged for those of all means.

Down the road from Little Washington and at the base of Shenandoah National Park lies perhaps the busiest hamlet in all of Virginia. Sperryville, the self-proclaimed "Little Apple," is an enterprising apple-farming village-turned-gift-shop mecca that almost dares you to drive through without picking up mountain crafts, antiques or fresh-squeezed cider from places like the Sperryville Emporium or Wolf Mountain Store.

Across the mountain from Sperryville, the Shenandoah Valley town of Luray is home to the much-hyped but nevertheless worthy Luray Caverns (703-742-6551). Go ahead, take the tour. It's an hour long and you'll see some of the most stunning stalactites and stalagmites in the East. Housed in the same complex as the caverns is the Historic Car and Carriage Caravan, an exhibit of antique cars, carriages and coaches. Rudolph Valentino's 1925 Rolls Royce is even here. Like we said, surreal.

Of Patsy Cline, Drive-ins and Barbecue

If the pressures of the big city start turning you a tad cynical, take a spin out to the northern Shenandoah Valley and rediscover vintage Americana. Winchester, the region's largest city, is home to dozens of historical attractions, including the western frontier command office of young General George Washington and the Civil War headquarters of Thomas "Stonewall" Jackson. Civil War buffs may remember that Winchester changed hands at least 70 times during the war, far more than any other community.

It is also in Winchester that the spirit of native daughter and country music legend Patsy Cline lives on. Cline, who gave us such heartfelt renditions of "I Fall to Pieces" and "Sweet Dreams" died in a plane crash in 1963 at the age of 30. She was buried at the Shenandoah Memorial Cemetery on Route 522, also known as the Patsy Cline Memorial Highway. Her mother still lives in town.

Just south of Winchester is Stephens City, home to a rapidly disappearing American icon — a drive-in movie theater. During the spring and summer months it's not uncommon for Washingtonians to pack up the car and head west to the Family Drive-In (703-869-2175). Where else can you sit in your car waiting for "Lethal Weapon III" to start and watch the sun set over the mountains? The setting alone is worth the 70-minute drive from Washington.

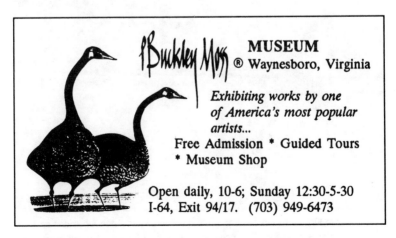

Foxhunting in Virginia's hunt country, in the areas of Loudoun and Albemarle counties and the countryside around Richmond, features some of the most scenic landscape in America. These nationally recognized hunts take place from October until March.

Virtually all the towns of the northern Valley are riddled with antique stores, but Strasburg, at the foot of towering Massanutten Mountain, takes the cake. Here you can find nearly 100 dealers in the downtown Strasburg Emporium (703-465-3711), which houses furniture from every American era, as well as intricate chandeliers, rugs, quilts, lace, old carousel horses and pottery. Top it off with a gourmet meal at the Victorian-inspired Hotel Strasburg (703-465-9191) or, for a more down-home experience, try a platter of hickory-fired ribs and chicken at Bad Water Bill's Barbecue (703-465-4988), also worth the drive alone.

On the Wild Side of Front Royal

Between Strasburg and Front Royal, the heavily trafficked gateway to Shenandoah National Park, lies one of the region's truly undiscovered natural gems, the Elizabeth Furnace Recreation Area (703-984-4104). Situated off of twisty Route 678, in the heart of the sprawling George Washington National Forest, this rugged gorge country of spiralling limestone outcroppings and the swift-moving Passage Creek is more akin to the wilds of West Virginia than to the gentle Shenandoah Valley. It also was the site of many a clandestine military operation during the Civil War. Creekside campsites are available at the Recreation Area, and hikers are encouraged to make the day-climb to the summit of Signal Knob, with its commanding views of the valley.

The Generals' City

The legacies of Stonewall Jackson and Robert E. Lee pervade their beloved Virginia, but nowhere is their presence felt more than in the scenic Shenandoah Valley town of Lexington in beautiful Rockbridge County. Here, you can tour the only house Jackson ever owned and walk the hallowed grounds of the Virginia Military Institute where he taught natural philosophy to Confederate cadets. At the VMI Museum (703-464-7207)) displays include such objects as Jackson's bullet-pierced raincoat and a taxidermy of his favorite war horse, Little Sorrel. Within earshot of VMI is the impressive Washington & Lee University and Lee Chapel (703-463-8400), the still-used shrine to Jackson's confidant and the final resting place of the South's greatest hero. Don't leave Lexington without visiting the office Lee inhabited while assuming the presidency of W&L after his defeat in the Civil War. It's in virtually the same state as

Insiders...
Like to cruise Skyline Drive during the winter months when the roads are virtually empty and the air is at its clearest.

Insiders' Tip

he left it in 1870. Buried nearby on campus is Lee's favorite mount, and maybe the most famous war horse in American history, Traveller.

A Tale of Two Mountain Resorts

Lodging is in no short supply in the Virginia upcountry. However, two of the more interesting spots to rest and recreate are Mountain Lake Lodge, near Blacksburg, and the queen of mountain resorts, The Homestead in Hot Springs.

Still best known as the filming site of the hit movie "Dirty Dancing," Mountain Lake Lodge (800-346-3333) sits nearly 4,200 feet up in the Allegheny Mountains of Giles County. Semi-rustic in nature, although a far cry from earthy, Mountain Lake caters to families in the summer and has developed quite an extensive package of theme weekends during the off-season, including, of course, a "Dirty Dancing" weekend. Isolated yes, but once you get there expect a slew of indoor and outdoor activities such as a full spa, great hiking trails, excellent fishing in the natural spring-fed pond, and plenty of interpretive programs like the one we saw on Appalachian folk art.

Up the mountains to the north, The Homestead (703-839-5500) is consistently rated by international travel writers as one of the world's top resorts. *Conde Nast Traveler* magazine recently placed it No. 22 in the world! This plush but relaxed setting is a favorite of the corporate-retreat set (as well as of members of Congress and other segments of Washington officialdom) but also is frequented by couples and families looking to pamper themselves in the resort's five-star spa, restaurants, stables and golf courses. Golf legend Sam Snead, who grew up in the area, considers the Homestead's Cascades course one of the finest in the South. A bit on the pricey side — double occupancy during the popular month of October starts at $220 a night — The Homestead nevertheless is something to be experienced if just once. Our advice is to start saving now.

A Tale of Two Rivers

The mighty Shenandoah and Potomac rivers meet in Harpers Ferry, West Virginia, site of abolitionist John Brown's raid on the U.S. Arsenal, the spark that ignited the Civil War. Now operated by the National Park Service (304-535-6223), this perfectly restored village provides an excellent journey into days past, with influences spanning not only the Civil War but the found-

Insiders' Tip

Insiders...
Know they can call the Virginia Office of Tourism in downtown Washington (202-659-5523) to book a room at any B&B in the Commonwealth.

ing of the nation including a healthy dose of period architecture and steep, narrow cobblestone streets. Craft shops abound as do glorious views of the Blue Ridge and the wild, crystal-clear rivers running below the hilltop city. At just over 400 feet in elevation, Harpers Ferry marks the lowest point in the state of West Virginia.

When the summer steam descends on Washington, head to Harper's Ferry for a day of tubing or whitewater rafting. Trips can be arranged through River & Trail Outfitters (301-695-5177) in nearby Knoxville, Maryland. If the hour-plus drive back to town seems much too formidable after an exhausting day on the rivers, bunk down at our favorite spot, the Hilltop House (304-535-2132). Looking like something out of "Petticoat Junction," the aptly named Hilltop is a bit creaky and cracked in places, but that's all part of the charm. When you factor in atmosphere and sheer coziness, you won't find a better lodging deal in the Blue Ridge.

After a night's rest, head up the road to Shepherdstown, the second-oldest burgh in the state and home to the gracious Bavarian Inn and Lodge (304-876-2551) with its knoll-top perch above the Potomac. Shepherdstown has one of the nation's highest concentrations of 18th-century buildings, making it an ideal spot to just meander. Make sure to duck into O'Hurley's General Store (304-876-6907), known throughout the East for its wonderful crafts, antiques and curios. The store also has a big wonderful black Lab who sits on the porch and nonchalantly greets guests.

Maryland's Quiet Corner

North of the Potomac from Harpers Ferry lies Washington County, Maryland, home to the Civil War's Battle of Antietam, the deadliest clash of the war and one of the bloodiest days in American history. It's amazing to think anything so brutal could happen in this quiet, bucolic setting of dairies, wheat fields and vineyards. But it did and you can read more about it in our chapter on the Civil War.

On a more upbeat note, Washington County, the first such jurisdiction named for George, is home to four of Maryland's best state parks. At Washington Monument State Park (301-432-8065), high atop South Mountain, you can view the first monument built in the president's honor. Originally constructed by the residents of Boonsboro, Md., in 1827, the stone tower has been rebuilt twice since. Climb the monument's 34 steps to take in spectacular views of the Cumberland Valley.

Moving south along the mountain, you'll hit Gathland State Park (301-791-4767), which includes the ruins of Gapland, the country home of Civil War and Reconstruction journalist George Alfred Townsend. Near the entrance to the park stands the imposing War Correspondents Arch, a 50-foot high structure Townsend built to honor the documenters of the great war. Joseph Pulitzer and Thomas Edison contributed to the $5,000 building fund.

Just up the road from both Gathland and Washington Monument is Greenbriar State Park (301-791-4767) and its sparkling spring-fed pond that one national magazine cited as among the clearest in the nation. Camping, fishing and hiking are popular activities here as well as across the county at Fort Frederick State Park (301-842-2155). Nestled along the banks of the Potomac and containing a stretch of the Chesapeake and Ohio Canal, Fort Frederick was originally built as a defense outpost on the western frontier. Still standing, although in a carefully preserved state, the fort survived the French and Indian, Revolutionary and Civil wars and is now honored through a series of historical re-enactments each spring through fall.

The President's Mountain

Largely overshadowed by Shenandoah National Park, Maryland's Catoctin Mountain Park (301-663-9388) is an ideal place to beat the crowds, especially during the autumn months when its 10,000-acre forest of beech, hickory, poplar, oak and maple trees turn to brilliant shades of red, orange and gold. Catoctin is probably most famous for housing Camp David, the

Photo: Washington Convention and Visitors Association

The Chesapeake and Ohio Canal extends 185 miles from Georgetown to Cumberland, Maryland.

woodsy presidential retreat. Don't expect the Clintons to wave you on in, though. The compound is well-hidden and security, as you can imagine, is tighter than a drum. You can, however, spend the night at the park's Owens Creek Campground or in a rustic cabin at Camp Misty Mount. Catoctin's numerous trails and wild trout streams make it a great place for families and novice campers. From the park, you're also within a short drive from the history-rich towns of Gettysburg, Pennsylvania, and Frederick, Maryland. Also, near the park entrance is the quaint railroad town of Thurmont and immediately to the south is Cunningham Falls State Park (301-271-7574), with it gorgeous namesake waterfall.

Maryland's Last Frontier

High in the Allegheny Plateau, in the westernmost reaches of the Free State, sparkles Maryland's Deep Creek Lake. A fishing and boating dream land (it's possible to catch walleye, bass, catfish and trout in the same day), Deep Creek also affords weekend travelers with a number of lakeside cabin, cottage and chalet rentals. A&A Realty/Better Homes & Gardens Rentals (800-336-7303) can arrange for overnight or extended stays. With 65 miles of shoreline, Deep Creek is best seen

Insiders...
Appease their kids, or simply get their quota of thrills, with a daytrip down to King's Dominion amusement park in Doswell, Virginia, just north of Richmond.

Insiders' Tip

from the deck of a sailboat or motorboat. Rental boats are available, but escalating insurance costs have made them an expensive option. Our advice is to bring your own boat or make friends with someone who has one. In all honesty, though, it's possible to enjoy the plentiful attractions of host Garrett County without ever dipping a toe in the lake. In nearby Oakland you can hop on the Western Maryland Scenic Railroad (800-TRAIN-50) or arrange for an afternoon of whitewater rafting on the Cheat and Youghiogheny rivers. And no trip to Western Maryland would be complete without a stop along the boulder-strewn banks of the aptly named Savage River, site of the 1989 World Whitewater Canoe/ Kayak Championships and the 1992 U.S. Olympic Trials.

Wild, Wonderful West Virginia

The Mountain State just may be the best-kept secret in the nation. Its rugged terrain and inspiring mountain vistas seem to defy its proximity to the Eastern megalopolis. Within a day's drive of Metro Washington one can be in country as remote and beautiful as Montana or Idaho. The state's laid-back tenor and affordability are attracting increasing numbers of tourists, but don't ever worry about being crowded out here. In the Dolly Sods Wilderness Area (304-257-4488), near Petersburg, you can walk the land of the Seneca Indians, through patches of wild orchids and blueberries, and huge granite boulders that afford hikers views in excess of 100 miles.

About 20 miles south of Dolly Sods is Seneca Rocks (304-567-2827), a gray wall of ancient sandstone that juts 1,000 feet above the floor of the South Branch Valley. For the truly adventurous, take a mountain-climbing lesson through Seneca Rocks Climbing School (304-567-2600) or Blackwater Outdoor Center (304-259-5117). For those who want to keep their feet firmly on the ground, take a drive up to the Canaan Valley, the highest valley east of the Mississippi River. Spend a night or two in the cozy lodge at Canaan Valley State Park (304-866-4121), a woodsy retreat and conference center that boasts, and rightly so, the best fall colors in the U.S.

For the romantic woodsman, you can always head to the super-expensive and super luxurious Greenbrier Resort in White Sulphur Springs. The Greenbrier (304-536-111) is considered even more upscale than The Homestead, so know what you're getting into. But, if you can afford it, the experience is well worth the cost. Closer to home and easier on the pocketbook, Coolfont Resort (304-258-4500) near Berkeley Springs is the spa of choice among the Washington stress set. Former Bush drug czar William Bennett kicked his cigarette habit here and Vice President Gore has been a loyal customer for years, even once setting off a mini panic by getting lost in the woods with Tipper!

For a taste of true West Virginia Gothic, check in at the intimate and oh-so-isolated Cheat Mountain Club (304-456-4627) near

Durbin. Hosts Norm and Debbie Strauss will see to it that you're fed three delicious squares a day; between meals you can walk out the lodge's back door and catch native brook trout or swim in a natural pool on Shavers Fork Creek. Henry Ford and Harvey Firestone visited the place, which just goes to prove that not all of the great American industrialists were high-fallutin' snobs. This macho-leaning lodge is as down-home as it gets.

A Downhill Run

Snow skiing around here? Okay, the Appalachians aren't exactly the Rockies, but then again most of us aren't Alberto Tomba either. Point is, one can get in some decent skiing in these parts without having to break the bank for a trip out West. In Virginia, you have the option of Wintergreen (800-325-2200), the Homestead (703-839-7721), Bryce (703-856-2121) or Massanutten (703-289-9441). West Virginia's Snowshoe (304-572-1000) and Canaan Valley (304-866-4121) are popular with the more experienced skiers while Pennsylvania's Ski Liberty (717-642-8282) and Whitetail (717-328-9400), both just above the Maryland line, are less than 90 minutes from downtown D.C., making them easy day-ski destinations. Wisp Resort (301-387-4911), near Deep Creek Lake, is Maryland's lone downhill ski area.

The Bay and The Beaches

The Chesapeake Bay

Legendary Baltimore journalist and social commentator H.L. Mencken once called the Chesapeake Bay a "great big protein factory" on account of the inordinate amount of fish, crabs and oysters found in its brackish waters. If Mencken were alive today he would probably amend his definition to include the amount of people who regularly find sanctuary on the fabled body of water. Of course, the bay is a different creature today than it was during Mencken's time. In some ways better, in other ways worse.

Ecologically, the bay is being tested from human's heavy hand. Pollution and urban sprawl have been blamed for historically low levels of oysters and some fish. Chesapeake watermen, for centuries the life and blood of the region, are slowly dying off as real estate prices escalate and competition heats up in the global seafood industry. How-

Insiders...
Love to visit the Virginia, Delaware and Maryland beaches in the off-season, especially during those freaky 70-degree February and March weekends, when lodging rates are typically half those of the summer months.

Insiders' Tip

ever, to speak of the bay and its rich traditions in the past tense would be foolish. New conservation efforts, such as those of the Chesapeake Bay Foundation, have elevated awareness of this vital natural resource. As the Chesapeake, divided nearly equally between Maryland and Virginia, continues to attract record numbers of tourists to its pleasant shores and peaceful waterside villages, one can only hope that we will continue to find the energy and courage to save the bay.

"The Shore"

You may have heard it called Delmarva Peninsula. Washingtonians know it as the Eastern Shore. To locals, it's simply "the Shore." For the uninitiated, it is the land found on the eastern side of the Chesapeake Bay Bridge. This fertile coastal-plain peninsula contains the entire state of Delaware, a good chunk of Maryland and a sliver of Virginia, thus the name Delmarva. Bounded by the bay and the Atlantic Ocean, the Eastern Shore is the land of proud watermen, of Canada geese and duck blinds, sprawling farms, colonial villages and what seems like more water than land.

To experience the true flavor of the Chesapeake — which inspired James Michener's novel of the same name — it's imperative to "cross the bridge." Maybe you've already seen the bumper stickers proclaiming "There is No Intelligent Life West of the Chesapeake Bay." A bit parochial, sure, but once you catch the spirit of the place you just might start agreeing with the notion.

On the Waterfront

After crossing the bridge — the Chesapeake Bay Bridge that is, think about getting off of Route 50. There's nothing particularly exciting about this highway unless you're into strip centers, boat yards and liquor stores. Our advice is to take the slower-moving but scenic Route 213 and head north to Chestertown, Md., on the banks of the Chester River. On the way, you'll pass through Centreville, government seat of Queen Annes County and site of the oldest courthouse, c. 1792, still in use in Maryland. Chestertown, with its 18th-century waterside Georgian mansions, is best discovered on foot, like during the Candlelight Walking Tour each September. Stroll through the grounds of Washington College, the 10th-oldest college in America and the only one to which George Washington personally granted the use of his name.

From Chestertown, backtrack on Route 213 and connect with Route 50 (but just for a short 20 miles) south to Easton. Now you're in the heart of Talbot County, undeniably Maryland's most aristocratic jurisdiction. Easton is the site of the massive Waterfowl Festival held each November, in which the world's finest wildlife artists, woodcarvers and sculptors gather to strut their stuff along with tens of thousands of migratory Canada geese. Easton's fabled Tidewater Inn (410-882-1300) and Gross' Coate (410-819-0802) accommodate sportsmen (including their hunting dogs), sailors, antique hunters and the occasional diplomat. Nearby, you can visit Third Haven Friends Meeting House, c. 1682, believed to be the oldest frame building dedicated to religious meetings in America.

Heading west, take a spin through St. Michael's, a waterfront hamlet that fooled the British Navy one evening during the War of 1812 when citizens placed lamplights in the tops of trees, thus giving the illusion that the village sat on a hill. The British ships fired at the tops of the trees and missed the town altogether. You won't want to miss an outdoor crabfeast at The Crab Claw (410-745-2900) overlooking the harbor, or a walk through the Chesapeake Maritime Museum (410745-2916), with its signature 100-year-old "screwpile" lighthouse.

From St. Michaels, you're just a few minutes' drive from Tilghman Island, a working waterman's community, and Oxford, arguably the most scenic town in Maryland. Tilghman is crab and oyster docks, colorful watermen and rusted boats. It's authentic Eastern Shore. The most colorful lodging on the island can be found at Harrison House (410-886-2121), a traditional Chesapeake fish camp that specializes in regional cuisine and hassle-free fishing trips.

Oxford, on the other hand, is glistening million-dollar sailboats, painstakingly restored Federal-style homes and charming B&Bs such as The Robert Morris Inn (410-226-5111). Head into Oxford from the north and cross the placid Tred-Avon River aboard the Oxford-Bellevue Ferry, the oldest ferry still in use in the U.S. The 10-minute trip across the river is well worth the nominal fee, especially if you're into lowering the old blood pressure.

Don't leave the region without a stop down the bay in Cambridge, hometown of American hero Harriet Tubman, founder of the Underground Railroad. Tubman was born on a plantation outside of town and single-handedly made her way to freedom in the North. But that didn't stop her from venturing to the South at least 20 times in her life to help free hundreds of other slaves during the Civil War era.

Islands in Time

Near the geographic center of the Chesapeake Bay lie two of the most intriguing islands in North America. Smith Island, Md., and Tangier Island, Va., are indeed places that have defied the encroachment of modern society. Both is-

Insiders' Tip

Insiders...
Try to avoid Interstate 95 during major holiday weekends (when the whole world, it seems, is daytripping), instead opting for off-the-beaten path getaways that are easier on their cars and their blood pressure.

lands, just a few square miles large, were settled by the first wave of British explorers to the Chesapeake in the early 17th century. Their descendants, folks with names like Bradshaw, Harrison, Smith and Crosby, still work the water for crabs and oysters, and their speech even today has traces of its Cornish roots. If getting as far off the beaten path as possible interests you, the islands are accessible by U.S. Mail boats (800-521-9189) from Crisfield, Md., along the far southern edge of the Eastern Shore. Closer to home, you can reach Smith Island from Point Lookout, Md., aboard the *Capt. Tyler* (301-425-2771).

The Humble Western Shore

In all fairness, you don't have to cross the bridge to enjoy the bounty of the Bay. While less rustic and authentic as the land to the east, Maryland's Western Shore is doing a pretty good job in balancing suburban growth and retaining some of its maritime character. If you've got angling in your blood but lack the tools to grapple the Chesapeake, like a good solid boat, drive down to Chesapeake Beach's Rod N Real Dock (410-257-2735) and charter a captain for a day or grab a spot on a headboat. Either option will place you with appropriate tackle and bait and a knowledgeable skipper. Fishing on the Bay typically is best in the late spring and fall when bluefish and striped bass are biting. Summer is always good for panfish and the gargantuan red drum.

South from Chesapeake Beach, head down Route 4 to Solomons, the picturesque sailing hamlet that boasts some of the finest seafood dining on the Bay, including The Harbor View (410-326-3202) and Solomons Pier (410-326-2424) restaurants. Within a short drive you can visit the crucifix-shaped Middleham Chapel, c. 1748, the fossil-lined Calvert Cliffs State Park (410-888-1622), and historic St. Marys City, Maryland's 17th-century capital and current site of a large-scale archaeological dig. If you still have energy, drive down to Point Lookout State Park (301-872-5688) on the southernmost tip of Western Maryland and explore the remains of Fort Lincoln, one of the largest Union-run prisons during the Civil War. The park's Civil War Museum is open weekends May through September.

Charm City

In many ways, Baltimore is the ultimate Chesapeake city. The bay's influence is virtually everywhere,

Insiders...
Trek to Solomons Island or any of the winding creeks and inlets around Annapolis, to catch their fill of Maryland blue crabs during the summer months.

Insiders' Tip

The Bushong House in New Market, Virginia, is noted for its involvement in the 1864 Battle of New Market.

from the seafood cuisine (Ralph Waldo Emerson once called the city "the gastronomic center of the universe"), to the thriving Inner Harbor area of shops, museums and hotels, to Fells Point, the rejuvenated harborfront district lined with eclectic pubs, galleries and Federal-style townhomes.

From Fells Point, a variety of sailing trips is available through Schooner Nighthawk Cruises (410-327-7245), including a three-hour buffet moonlight sail, a Sunday champagne brunch sail, a Sunday evening crab cruise and a two-hour midnight mystery cruise on Saturdays. If you're not on the water or at an Orioles game at the showplace Oriole Park at Camden Yards, the next best place to be in Baltimore is the National Aquarium (410-576-3800), with its 7,000 species of aquatic life and probably the best shark tank in the nation. Wrap the day up with an overnight's stay at the cozy Admiral Fell Inn (410-522-7377), overlooking the harbor in Fells Point, and you'll discover why Baltimore is called "Charm City."

Chesapeake (Largely) Undiscovered

Maryland may be for crabs, but Virginia is equally tied to the history, traditions and fortunes of the bay. There's no better starting place to explore the Old Dominion's maritime mystique than the Northern Neck, the verdant, five-county-long jut of land bounded by the bay and the Potomac and Rappahannock rivers.

Less than a three-hour drive from Washington, the tiny Northern Neck village of Irvington has been welcoming anglers, boaters, golfers and antique collectors for generations. The centerpiece of the town has to be the opulent Tides Inn (800-843-3746), a combination resort and conference facility that claims perhaps the top golf course in the state, the world-class Golden Eagle. Overlooking Carter's Creek and the Rappahannock River, the Tides is just a half-day sail from several points along the open bay, including the equally refined resort area of Windmill Point. Sailors can charter a boat for the day, weekend or week at Crockett's Landing Charters (804-438-6559).

Farther north up the Neck lies the sleepy little town of Reedville, a popular stay for B&B lodgers, many who come from as far away as the Carolinas and New England to soak up the quiet Chesapeake atmosphere. On Reedville's shaded Main Street, visitors can choose from the Gables (804-453-5209), a dramatic waterside Victorian mansion, the Elizabeth Anne (804-453-4720), a renovated early 19th-century fish-captain's house, or the Elizabeth House (804-453-7016), another former captain's home.

Just south of the Northern Neck is the Middle Peninsula, a region of wide-open spaces and shadowy coves; it's amazingly undiscovered given its close proximity to Richmond and the Hampton Roads area. One of the more interesting sites on the peninsula is the Rappahannock River town of Urbanna, home to a number of antique stores and perhaps the world's largest oyster festival, scheduled every fall. The nearby communities of Gloucester, with its village green dating back to the early 18th century, and Gwynn, located on post-card-perfect Gwynn's Island, make for interesting sidetrips through the peninsula's fragrant backroads.

The Urban Bay

Rivalling Baltimore in industrial stature is Hampton Roads, a booming metro area that includes the Virginia cities of Norfolk, Hampton, Newport News, Portsmouth, Chesapeake, Suffolk and Virginia Beach. It's a region of hyperboles, beginning with the world's biggest natural harbor, Hampton Roads, and the world's largest naval installation, based in Norfolk. A leisurely bay cruise is mandatory here and one of the best is offered by the *Miss Hampton II* (804-722-9102) in Hampton Harbor. The skipper will bring you up close to some of the nation's most awesome military vessels, including Trident subs and aircraft carriers seemingly the size of Rhode Island. The region is also pocketed with great museums, including the world-class (fine art) Chrysler Museum (804-622-1211) in Norfolk, the Mariners Museum (804-595—0368) in Newport News, the Virginia Ma-

Insiders' Tip

Insiders...
Know they can call the offices of tourism in Virginia (800-VISIT-VA) and Maryland (800-543-1036) to receive complete travel guides to the Old Dominion and the Old Line State.

rine Science Museum (804-425-FISH) in Virginia Beach, the Virginia Air & Space Museum (804-727-0900) and the Casemate Museum (804-727-3971) in Hampton. Be sure to budget time to walk through prestigious Hampton University, one of the nation's first historically black colleges and easily one of the most beautiful academic settings in the Commonwealth.

Those Crazy Beaches

A cultural phenomena strikes Washington every Friday afternoon during the summer. It seems like the whole metro area has gone to the beach, at least judging from the endless snake of traffic along Route 50 or down I-95. Beach-going in these parts isn't a solitary experience, so don't expect the ambience of a deserted tropical island once you get there. The Mid-Atlantic, however, does have its share of perfectly fine beaches, each with its own distinctive personality. To beach his own, in other words.

Assateague Island National Seashore, a favorite place in the sun, is 33 miles of pristine, undeveloped beachfront stretching from nearly Ocean City, Md., to Chincoteague, Va. Much less visited than any other beach in the region, Assateague is best known for the herd of wild horses as well as deer, raccoons and bobcats that roam its shores and from time to time bite or, in the case of equines, kick tourists who routinely ignore National Park Service warnings not to feed or touch the animals. Two campgrounds, one run by the National Park Service (410-641-1441) and one operated by the state of Maryland (410-641-2120), round out the lodging options. A word of advice: Stay away during the months of July and August because if the horse flies don't nail you the mosquitoes surely will. But from April through June and from September through early November, few spots can rival enchanting Assateague.

Five other beaches in brief:

Ocean City, Md., or O.C., is a nice stretch of beach, but extremely commercial both on and away from the water (strip shopping centers, high-rise buildings, etc.). It is, nonetheless, a huge hangout for the young and wild at heart.

Bethany Beach, Del., attracts a much older (late 20s through retirees) crowd than O.C. but is not nearly as developed with high-rises and commercial properties. Parking is a hassle, though; very restricted in residential areas, and options are few so you'll probably end up walking a bit. Still, it's a great weekend destination just for the relaxed set-

Insiders' Tip

Insiders...
With a penchant for Virginia wines can receive information on vineyards, wine tours and festivals statewide through the Richmond-based Virginia Wine Marketing Group, (804) 644-7888.

ting and comparatively pristine beaches.

Rehoboth Beach, Del., is just north of Bethany and similar in many ways, but larger and bit more developed. Plenty of families and older singles can be found roaming Rehoboth's colorful boardwalk.

Dewey Beach, Del., is the recognized "hip" place for the 20- and 30-something weekenders from Metro Washington. It has an active nightlife with lots of incredibly busy bars and restaurants.

Finally, we have to mention Cape May, N.J., on the southernmost tip of the Garden State and a world apart from the urban corridor of the Northeast. A ferry ride away from the Delaware shore by way of the Cape May-Lewes Ferry (302-645-6313), Cape May is a seaside dreamscape of Victorian homes, shops and cottages. At the turn of the century it was a gambling mecca for Southern aristocrats and sea captains but today enjoys a robust trade in tourists who are lured to such timeless hotels as the Inn of Cape May (609-884-3500) and Gothic-style B&Bs like The Abbey (609-884-4506). The entire town is listed on the National Register of Historic Places; it's one of those treasures of the Mid-Atlantic that's not to be missed.

Points in Between

A less than sexy moniker, no doubt, but let's not downplay the importance of the land between the mountains and the bay. After all, we live in this region and are constantly amazed by its diversity, history and scenic beauty. We're not including sites and attractions in the Washington area because you should be getting your fill of those in other parts of this book.

A Hunt Country Tapestry

Just 40 miles west of the bustle of Pennsylvania Avenue is a quiet, rolling green land of Thoroughbred horses, country squires and exquisite stone mansions. This is Virginia Hunt Country and you'll be hard pressed to find a more beautiful setting than the farms and fields of Loudoun and Fauquier counties.

Middleburg, the self-proclaimed "Hunt Country Capital," retains its 18th-century charm but with new twists like gourmet bakeries, five-star restaurants and internationally celebrated antique shops. To the west of Middleburg lie the lovely hill country hamlets of Upperville and Paris, where warehouse-size stables and National Fences seem to outnumber people five to one. Just outside of Paris, meanwhile, is the public's access to Hunt Country living, Sky Meadows State Park (703-592-3556). Once a working plantation, Sky Meadows' 1,100 acres entices weekend warriors with a maze of hiking trails, including a stretch of the Appalachian Trail.

Leesburg, the largest city in the area, is steeped in Virginia history; indeed it was named after one of the most prominent families in the Old Dominion. During the War of 1812, when the British were on their way to burn Washington, the

Federal Archives, including the Declaration of Independence and the Constitution, were hauled through town in 22 wagons on their way to safekeeping in an estate outside of town. Today, Leesburg and the surrounding villages of Hamilton, Lincoln, Waterford, Hillsboro and Purcellville are waging another successful battle for preservation, a concept near and dear to the hearts of Hunt Country residents who consider themselves a few miles but "light years" removed from Washington suburbia.

Mr. Jefferson's Country

You won't live in Virginia, or for that matter in Maryland, a week before someone mentions the word "Charlottesville." For good reason: As home to Virginia's and the nation's most-celebrated Renaissance Man — Thomas Jefferson — Charlottesville is one of the most-cherished sites in the region. Here you'll find Monticello (804-295-8181), Jefferson's captivating hilltop home, and the University of Virginia, one of his many intellectual and architectural achievements.

Charlottesville and surrounding Albemarle County are also about dogwood-lined country roads, hillside vineyards, funky bookstores and sophisticated galleries, museums and restaurants. At the Boar's Head Inn (804-296-2181), just outside of town, you can unwind at a full-service spa and spend the night in one of its many guest rooms.

Farther south, off the Blue Ridge Parkway in neighboring Nelson County, is Wintergreen Resort (804-325-2200). The year round facility claims the best snow skiing in the state and one of the finest golf courses. Here, it's not impossible to ski in the morning and play a round of golf in the afternoon.

Mr. Jefferson's Country is also Mr. Monroe's Country and Mr. Madison's Country. Literally just down the road from Monticello is Ashlawn-Highland (804-293-9539), James Monroe's home, and about 20 miles to the north, in Orange, Va., is Montpelier (703-672-0006), the impressive country estate of James and Dolly Madison.

Maryland's Heartland

Along Interstate 70, in the heart of the Free State, are three of Maryland's most endearing towns. Frederick, New Market and Ellicott City are nationally renown antiquing meccas, but they're also just great spots to unwind and enjoy the simple pleasures of graceful centuries-old buildings, perfectly manicured gardens and friendly denizens. Frederick's 33-block historic district, punctuated by towering church spires, is a must for history and architecture buffs. New Market comes alive virtually every weekend of the year with a bazaar-like setting of antique dealers and craftsmen. Ellicott City's mill-town appearance is enhanced by colorful bohemian artisans living and working alongside yuppie retailers.

The Gray Lady of the Confederacy

The capital city of Virginia, and for a time, the South, is a living, breathing memorial to the Commonwealth. History isn't just a fact of life in Richmond, it's a way of life. Monument Avenue, the South's answer to Pennsylvania Avenue, immortalizes the fallen sons of the Old Dominion through huge statues, tasteful gardens and expansive greens. The street cuts through the heart of "The Fan," one of Richmond's trendiest and most desirable residential areas, a la Georgetown. The White House of the Confederacy (804-649-1861) and many of the original government buildings of the Confederate States of America sit within earshot of downtown skyscrapers and the Virginia State Capitol, yet another building designed by Thomas Jefferson. Here you will also find the office of Edgar Allan Poe (804-648-5523), which also happens to be the oldest building in the city. Richmond is rightfully proud of its premiere museum, the Virginia Museum of Fine Arts (804-367-0844), housing one of the world's largest collections of Fabergé eggs as well as a stunning array of Asian antiquities. Richmonders are also fond of their numerous parks, cemeteries and neighborhoods, some of the most elegant in the South.

Colonial Roots

Before there was Richmond, however, there were Williamsburg, Yorktown and Jamestown. Wedged between the James and York rivers, arguably the Tigris-Euphrates of the South, if not the nation, Colonial Williamsburg (800-HISTORY), Yorktown Battlefield (804-898-3400) and Jamestown Colonial National Historical Park (804-898-3400) represent, quite frankly, the best and worst of Virginia. The worst in the sense that they are obvious tourist traps and you can't help but feel a bit remorseful upon seeing a McDonald's or an outlet shop within a stone's throw from some of the most hallowed ground in North America. The best in the sense that the actual historical parks are run by altruistic foundations, people who strive for class over commercialism. It's hard not to walk out of these shrines feeling like a patriot, or at least a pioneer, and we highly recommend that you budget a full day for each locale. They're easily connected by way of the Colonial Parkway, a gorgeous brick road that winds its way through forests and along the banks of the James and York. The equally impressive James River plantations, proud residences of three presidents and numerous statesmen, are within a 40-minute drive up the panoramic Route 5.

Inside
Spectator Sports: A Region of Champions

Just because government and politics tend to dominate the very character of Metro Washington and outsiders' perceptions of it, don't underestimate the importance of leisure activities — spectator sports especially — to residents. In fact, there's probably a clear and perfectly understandable link between the awesome presence of the governmental/political establishment and the fervor with which we embrace our sporting diversions.

Whatever level of competition is desired, you can find it here, with professional teams, outstanding college and high school action, and much more.

For at least six months a year, playoff and Super Bowl activity excluded, of course, the sports scene focuses intensely on our beloved National Football League team, the Washington Redskins, proud member of the NFL's finest division, the NFC East.

The level of coverage in the local media and the enthusiasm and loyalty of 'Skins fans is astounding, so be prepared. It can seem mystifying to the uninitiated. Example: Another NFL club has claimed the "America's Team" moniker, but who plays at Robert F. Kennedy Memorial Stadium, virtually in the shadows of the Capitol? What could be more American and representative of all the people than that? The *real* America's Team is right here. Case closed.

So you see, after nearly 60 years in Washington and a solid winning tradition fueled by three Super Bowl victories (all under the reign of the inimitable former coach, Joe Gibbs) in five appearances, the team enjoys an almost divine status among the faithful. Getting a ticket to a

Insiders...
Who want to see some of the world's finest athletes in action mark their calendars for the annual Mobil 1 Invitational track and field meet held each February at George Mason University.

Insiders' Tip

home game, however, is another matter altogether. More on this later.

Non-fans, don't despair, though. You'll soon discover that during a Redskins game, with a large part of the local population at home camped before the TV, is an ideal time to go grocery shopping or roam the malls.

Before getting further immersed in Redskins mania (see, we're as vulnerable as anyone around here), Metro Washington's representatives in the National Basketball Association, the Bullets, and the National Hockey League, the Capitals, rate some ink. Conveniently, they both play in the same place, USAir Arena (formerly the Capital Centre), located just off the Beltway and about 25 minutes from downtown Washington in the Prince George's County community of Landover. Built by Abe Pollin, a prominent local businessman and owner of both teams, the 19,000-seat arena is also home to the Georgetown University Hoyas basketball team and serves as the site of a variety of other sporting events, concerts and the like.

One thing's for certain about the Bullets: they play hard and they're fun to watch, winning or not. And winning isn't something the team has done much of since the late 1970s when guys like Wes Unseld and Elvin Hayes were prowling the court and helping bring home an NBA title. These days, Unseld, a Hall of Fame center, wears a coat and tie and prowls the sideline as coach of the Bullets.

The Capitals also boast a high entertainment value and usually with better results than the Bullets. Yet while they've had a long string of playoff appearances, the Caps have yet to put it all together when it counts and capture a Stanley Cup. For what it's worth, they've established themselves as one of the top defensive teams in the NHL and a Patrick Division force to be reckoned with.

Incredibly, Washington has been without a Major League Baseball team since 1971 when the Senators moved out for a second and final time, heading southwest to become the Texas Rangers. A few years earlier, the original version of the Senators left and turned up in Minnesota as the Twins; an expansion version of the Senators played in the interim. Attempts to gain a team either through the recent league expansion (in which Colorado reached new heights with the Rockies and Florida reeled in the Marlins) or perhaps the relocation of an existing team have proven fruitless, but organized efforts to that end will likely persist in one form or another. Fortunately, base-

Insiders' Tip

Insiders...
Looking for a special atmosphere for watching a Redskins game head to Petitbon's, a local restaurant chain owned by the team's coach, Richie Petitbon.

Photo: Virginia Division of Tourism

The Virginia Gold Cup is held each spring and fall at Great Meadow near Warrenton.

ball junkies can get their fix with the Baltimore Orioles, whose home field, the gorgeous new Oriole Park at Camden Yards, sits barely an hour up the road and just blocks from the city's famous and enchanting Inner Harbor.

Devotees of the diamond will also be happy to know that minor league baseball has a strong presence in Metro Washington with the Prince William Cannons, Bowie Bay Sox, Frederick Keys and Hagerstown Suns.

Intercollegiate athletics is a big part of the sports scene as well, and the region's many colleges and universities afford plenty of opportunities for the spectator. Schools with the most prominent athletic programs include the University of Maryland, Georgetown University, the United States Naval Academy, George Washington University, Howard University and George Mason University.

You can also live out your sports fantasies with a variety of other events including horse racing, auto racing, golf and tennis, to name a few. The following provides an overview of spectator sports in Metro Washington; general recreational pursuits are covered in other chapters.

So, having discarded the stodgy, white-collar, work-reigns-supreme label that seems permanently affixed to Washingtonians, let's take a closer look at an abundant roster.

Football

It's only logical to begin with the Redskins. Just how high a pillar do the men in burgundy and gold occupy in the community? Without even getting into the amazing depth of the news coverage, consider that home games have been sold out for nearly 30 years and, with 40,000-plus people on the waiting list for season tickets, will likely remain sold out for the foreseeable future. At least you never have to be concerned about home games being blacked out on local TV — an unfortunate reality in some NFL markets.

Another fact to frame the perspective: it's not unheard of for the fate of season tickets to be determined in divorce court or at a hearing on the estate of the recently departed. Yes, they're that coveted.

But perhaps most compelling is that in a region where people are too often divided by political party, race, gender or socioeconomic status, the Redskins have remained the one unifying force that transcends these and other barriers. It's truly a phenomenon to behold.

Trying to be one of the more than 56,000 fans who jam RFK Stadium for every home game, however, is tough to do when there aren't any tickets available for sale to the general public. A limited number go on sale each summer for the one or two home preseason games in August, but they almost always sell out, too. So you've got to act fast.

If recent talk of building a new, larger stadium somewhere in the region ever turns into action, then the waiting list will certainly shrink a bit. But in the meantime, you've practically got to know someone (preferably team owner Jack Kent Cooke), as the saying goes, to obtain what is truly the hottest ticket in town.

RFK Stadium is located at East Capitol and 22nd streets SE. For more information on events at RFK and the adjacent D.C. Armory, call (202) 546-2222.

When it comes to major college football in Metro Washington, the two teams that come to mind are the University of Maryland and the Naval Academy. Moreover, the University of Virginia, in Charlottesville, while certainly not a local presence in the physical sense, gets fairly thorough coverage in *The Washington Post* and is practically considered a "hometown" team because of the huge local alumni population.

Maryland has struggled mightily to become a winner again, although Mark Duffner, in his second year as head coach, is a good bet to turn things around given enough time. Still, the Terrapins (Terps for short), with a large and loyal following, have become something of a quarterback mill for the NFL since the early 1980s. Superstar Boomer Esiason and the emerging Neil O'Donnell are both alumni, as are Frank Reich, Stan Gelbaugh and Scott Zolak, albeit in less prominent roles. Maryland, a member of the Atlantic Coast Conference — far better known as a basketball power, but that could be changing with Florida State University now in the gridiron mix — plays its home games at Byrd Stadium on the College Park campus in Prince George's County. For ticket information, call (301) 314-7070.

Not since record-setting running back Napoleon McCallum rumbled out of Annapolis and into the NFL has Navy's football program had a whole lot to cheer about (although McCallum's pro career has indeed been disappointing). Without the ability to offer scholarships and thus attract top-drawer high school talent, assembling and maintaining a strong athletic program at a service academy is a tough chore, and this is no exception. But if there's one thing the Midshipmen will always have on their side it's tradition. Whether it's the annual game against archrival Army, in Philadelphia, the thrilling sight of a pre-game jet flyover at Navy-Marine Corps Memorial Stadium, or the overwhelming spirit of the student body, there will always be something special about a Navy game. (As an independent program, Navy football has no conference af-

Insiders' Tip

Insiders...
Driving to RFK Stadium for a Redskins game like to get there about two hours before kickoff so they can beat most of the traffic and have plenty of time to take part in the traditional tailgating festivities.

filiation.) For ticket information, call (410) 268-6060.

Washington's Division I-AA football school, Howard University, is perhaps the nation's finest traditionally black college. But it's not all work and no play. Howard boasts a respected athletic program and has sent several players on to the NFL ranks. The Bison play in the Mid-Eastern Athletic Conference. For ticket information, call (202) 806-7199.

For a truly unique sporting experience, check out a game at Division III Gallaudet University in Washington, considered the nation's preeminent college for the deaf. Football at Gallaudet is played like football most anywhere else except for one thing: players on offense rely on the vibrations emanating from an open-ended bass drum set up on the sideline to know when the play begins. The drum is always hit the same number of times, so the quarterback decides in the huddle on what beat (the second, for example) the center will snap the ball. It's a fascinating scene and still further evidence that one person's "handicap" is another person's challenge to succeed. Call (202) 651-5602 for ticket information.

Basketball

Redskins or no Redskins, for some people, basketball is the only game in town. And it's easy to understand why. Metro Washington, from the public and private high schools on through the college ranks, is a veritable breeding ground for top basketball talent.

Unfortunately, not enough of it has ended up with the Bullets, a one-time NBA powerhouse that has been mired in mediocrity since the glory years of the late 1970s when they captured the NBA title in 1977-78 and returned to the finals the following season in a losing effort. Subsequent years have not been kind to the team, which toughs it out each season in the brutal Atlantic Division where throughout the 1980s the Boston Celtics, Philadelphia 76ers and New York Knicks set the pace.

When they do make the playoffs, the Bullets usually don't advance past the first or second round. Yet, they also haven't finished a regular season with the absolute worst record in the league (although coming close a couple of times) in order to have a better shot at getting a No. 1 or No. 2 pick in the much-coveted draft lottery. They always seem to be somewhere in the middle, which for a pro team is the toughest rut to escape.

Misfortune has plagued the Bullets with cruel regularity, whether it's players succumbing to injuries and eating disorders, bad luck in the lottery or bad luck in the regular draft. A dominating big man (Shaquille O'Neal would have fit the bill nicely), or even a franchise player of a smaller stature who could put people in the seats at USAir Arena, continues to elude the Bullets, hampering their efforts to advance to that next level once again.

Still, the Bullets have taken a step in the right direction in recent years under the stewardship of Unseld and General Manager John Nash, who has orchestrated some major player trades. There is indeed a core of young talent on the team, but it's anybody's guess as to how long it will take to mold them into a consistent winner.

Bullets tickets are priced at $11, $26.50 and $27.50. For ticket information, call (301) 622-3865. If you prefer letters over numbers, that's NBA-DUNK. To place a credit-card order by telephone, call TicketMaster at (202) 432-7328 or (800) 551-7328.

USAir Arena is located at 1 Harry S. Truman Dr., Landover, Md. (Beltway exit 15A or 17A). For general information about USAir Arena and events, call (301) 350-3400.

USAir Arena's other roundball tenant, Georgetown University, has earned a reputation as one of the nation's strongest programs and one that demands players work as hard in the classroom as they do on the court — almost a rarity in major college athletics today. And John Thompson, the physically imposing and highly regarded coach of the Hoyas, deserves much of the credit. Under Thompson's direction, Georgetown has won a national championship, become a regular in post-season play, and remained a power in the formidable Big East Conference.

Georgetown alumni appear on team rosters throughout the NBA. But three names, all products of the Thompson era and all dominating big men, stand out and up: Patrick Ewing, Dikembe Mutombo and Alonzo Mourning. With Thompson at the helm, it's a safe bet that Georgetown will continue to serve as a training school for future stars of the NBA.

Tickets to Hoyas home games can be obtained either through USAir Arena, (301) 350-3400, or the university, (202) 687-4692.

The region's other prominent basketball program is the University of Maryland, which holds court at Cole Field House. Maryland athletics haven't been quite the same since budding star Len Bias died just prior to being drafted by the Boston Celtics in 1986, a drug-induced tragedy that rocked the school and the sports world alike. On the heels of this episode came a shakeup in university administration and the departure of Lefty Driesell, the team's popular and longtime coach who now pilots the basketball program at James Madison University in Harrisonburg, Va.

But recent years have seen a dramatic turnaround in Terps bas-

Insiders' Tip

Insiders...

Who want a first-hand look at the Redskins but don't have high hopes of landing a game ticket always plan a day trip to Dickinson College in Carlisle, Penn., during the short period in August when training camp is open to the public.

ketball, particularly since Maryland alumnus Gary Williams, a proven winner with other major-college programs, took over as coach. Maryland, which produced Walt Williams, a top pick in the 1992 NBA draft, is again making its presence felt in what has long been one of the NCAA's strongest basketball divisions, the Atlantic Coast Conference. With Gary Williams at the helm, the team looks to go nowhere but up. Call (301) 314-7070 for ticket information.

Other Division I-A college basketball programs include the up-and-coming George Washington University Colonials, Atlantic 10 Conference, (202) 994-7411; the American University Eagles, Colonial Athletic Conference, (202) 885-3267; the Howard University Bison, Mid-Eastern Athletic Conference, (202) 806-7199; the George Mason University Patriots (whose home arena, the 10,000-seat Patriot Center in Fairfax, is the only sports/entertainment facility of its kind in Northern Virginia), Colonial Athletic Conference, (703) 993-3270; and the U.S. Naval Academy Midshipmen (does the name David "The Admiral" Robinson, now an NBA center extraordinaire, ring a bell?), also of the Colonial Athletic Conference, (410) 268-6060.

Division II basketball programs include the University of the District of Columbia Firebirds, (202) 282-3174, and the Bowie State University Bulldogs, (301) 464-7710. At the Division III level are the Catholic University of America Cardinals, (202) 319-5286, and the Gallaudet University Bisons, (202) 651-5602.

Baseball

The Washington Senators are long gone, but thank goodness for the Baltimore Orioles.

One of the American League's top teams over the past couple of decades, despite a few stinker seasons along the way, the Orioles hovered around 1st place in the Eastern Division for much of the past two seasons until untimely fall slumps sealed their fate. Still, with a core of talent that includes future Hall of Famer Cal Ripken Jr., Mike Devereaux, Brady Anderson, Ben McDonald and Mike Mussina, the O's look to remain more than competitive for a while.

Going to see an O's game is much easier and more enjoyable than it used to be for Metro Washingtonians. Oriole Park at Camden Yards is a good half-hour closer than Memorial Stadium, the team's home for 38 years, and sits in a wonderful attraction-filled area easily accessible by rail, bus and automobile.

From Northern Virginia, Suburban Maryland and the District, just take the Baltimore/Washington Parkway north into Baltimore and the stadium is right there looming in front of you as you near the downtown area. It's a straight shot and the route is well-marked. You can also take I-95 into Baltimore, which feeds into where the Parkway hits the city, but this route is a bit longer and subject to more traffic hassles. Want to ride the train? Just take Metrorail to Union Station where you pick up a MARC (Maryland's passenger railroad system) train to the Baltimore station located literally right next to the stadium; the trip takes about 45 minutes.

Christened in 1992, the baseball-only Oriole Park at Camden Yards is indeed a mouthful of a name for a stadium. Many people have therefore come to casually refer to it as just Camden Yards, which, along with Oriole Park, was one of the names originally proposed. Team owners apparently couldn't agree on either one, not to mention a slew of other names suggested by fans, so they took the easy way out.

Camden Yards seats about 48,000 people, a perfect size for baseball, and offers a great view from virtually every seat. Modern yet old-fashioned in an architectural sense, this is no boilerplate concrete doughnut of a stadium. It's truly a ballpark designed for the way baseball was meant to be played. There's no artificial turf, no dome and no annoying pillars disrupting the sightlines, but there is wonderful food and drink and a particularly friendly atmosphere. From a fan's perspective, you couldn't ask for more except maybe another World Series title.

Even the stadium's location is interesting. Camden Yards sits in a historic area of downtown Baltimore and masterfully incorporates the 95-year-old B&O Warehouse, which looms just beyond the rightfield wall. The warehouse was refurbished during construction of the stadium and now houses office space for the team along with a cafeteria, bar/lounge and the exclusive, members-only Camden Club. During the early 1900s, a piece of land that now comprises centerfield was the site of a house/watering hole called Ruth's Cafe, operated by the father of baseball's immortal George Herman "Babe" Ruth, a Baltimore native.

Capitalizing on the popularity of the O's in Metro Washington (fans from the area account for a large part of the team's gate receipts, with some estimates as high as 40 percent), there's an Orioles Baseball Store in the District at 914 17th St. NW; (202) 296-BIRD (2473).

Oriole Park at Camden Yards is located at 333 West Camden St. Ticket prices — further evidence that baseball is perhaps the only pro sport that considers the budget realities of everyday fans — are $4, $4.75, $8, $10, $12, $13 and $18;

Insiders...
Attending sporting events in the area understand that the "O" that's often shouted out during the singing of the "Star-Spangled Banner" is intended as a sign of Orioles fan spirit, although it can also be regarded as rude, annoying and disrespectful.

Insiders' Tip

children 12 and under and senior citizens can get in for $1 on selected dates. To order by phone locally, call (202) 432-7328 or (703) 573-7328. For general information, call (410) 685-9800.

To see future Major Leaguers in the making, check out two of the Orioles' farm teams, both in Maryland: the Bowie Bay Sox (410-467-0101) and the Frederick Keys (301-662-0013). The Bay Sox, a Class AA affiliate, play in the Eastern League while the Keys, a Class A club, compete in the Carolina League. The Hagerstown Suns (301-791-6266), meanwhile, are a AA affiliate of the Toronto Blue Jays.

Lest we forget, Northern Virginia also has a pro baseball team in the Prince William Cannons, the Class A affiliate of the New York Yankees. Before becoming the Cannons, they too were called the Yankees, but, local lore has it, George Steinbrenner, the Yankees' colorful and controversial owner, had the name changed because he was envious of their success. We don't really mind, though. Cannons seems much more fitting for a Southern state in which most of the Civil War was fought.

The Cannons play 70 games each season at 6,000-seat Prince William County Stadium on Davis Ford Road in Woodbridge. Opponents include the Durham (N.C.) Bulls, a team made famous by the hit movie "Bull Durham" a few years back that starred Kevin Costner.

Over 45 former Cannons have earned promotions to the Majors (or, as Costner put it, "The Show") including 1989 Manager Stump Merrill, who had a brief stint in that revolving door of a job known as manager of the New York Yankees. Tickets are under $6. For information, call (703) 690-3622 or (703) 590-2311.

And finally, we feel compelled to again stretch the geographical boundaries, this time about 100 miles due south, with a mention of the Richmond Braves, affiliate of the Atlanta Braves and one of the nation's top Class AAA teams. The Braves play at The Diamond, one of the nicest (and most cleverly named) minor-league fields anywhere. For baseball lovers, it makes for an easy day trip to see some of the players being groomed for a move to Atlanta.

For ticket and schedule information, call the Braves at (804) 359-4444.

Hockey

If you thought Washington wasn't a hockey town, think again. While no one is about to mistake the Nation's Capital for such NHL-crazed places as Montreal, Toronto, Minneapolis or even, you guessed it, Tampa, the Capitals have built a strong following since first taking to the ice in 1974. A glance up at the decibel counter in the corner of USAir Arena during a game is strong evidence of the kind of crowds they regularly attract.

The team trophy case has yet to include a Stanley Cup — tough to acquire when the season ends after an early round of the playoffs — but the Caps have nevertheless developed into a consistent winner and post-season contender. Under Bryan Murray, the winningest coach in team history, the Caps posted five consecutive second-place finishes in the Patrick Division during the 1980s topped by a first-place showing in 1988-89. Then, in an odd move that startled many fans, Murray was replaced by his brother, Terry, in the middle of the 1989-90 season. But inconsistency has continued to haunt the team.

Sweeping personnel moves over the years, including some unpopular and questionable trades involving stars such as Mike Gartner and Dino Ciccarelli, have yet to yield the dividends necessary to win it all. Seemingly always on the brink of greatness, the Caps have yet to achieve it.

Ticket prices for Capitals games are $12, $24, $32, $33, $36 and $39. For information, call (301) 386-7080. For credit-card telephone orders, call TicketMaster at (202) 432-7328 or (800) 551-7328.

To see some hockey pros in the making, check out the Capitals' development team, the Baltimore Skipjacks, whose home ice is the Baltimore Arena, 201 W. Baltimore St. Call (410) 727-0703 for information.

Horsing Around

Horse-racing enthusiasts are in luck. Maryland is home to several equine venues (Virginia has approved horse betting as the latest form of gambling, but the first tracks have yet to open; the sport is illegal in the District).

Harness racing is the featured event at Rosecroft Raceway, 6336 Rosecroft Rd., Fort Washington, Md. (just a few minutes from the Wilson Bridge), (301) 567-4000. Thoroughbreds are it at Laurel Race Course, Laurel Racetrack Rd., Laurel, Md., (301) 725-0400. At Baltimore's Pimlico, the showcase event of course is the Preakness, the second jewel in Thoroughbred racing's Triple Crown, held the third Saturday in May. This park is found at 5201 Park Heights Dr., (410) 542-9400.

The Washington International Horse Show takes center stage at USAir Arena for over a week each fall (late October/early November) and features some of the world's top riders not to mention those ever-popular canine show-stealers, the racing Jack Russell Terriers. This is a fun event that the whole family can enjoy. For information, call (301) 840-0281.

Polo fans needn't fret. From April through August, and again

Insiders' Tip

Insiders...
Going to Baltimore for an evening baseball game make a day of it by first enjoying the beautiful Inner Harbor and then heading over to Oriole Park at Camden Yards, just a few short blocks away.

from early September through November, riders saddle up most every Sunday afternoon in West Potomac Park, across from the Lincoln Memorial. General admission is free, but if you can afford to splurge, high-priced box seats are available. For more information, call the National Capital Parks Polo Association/Lincoln Mall Club at (202) 362-3095

Steeplechasing events, usually held in the spring and fall in the Hunt Country of Metro Washington, are as much social gatherings as they are sporting spectacles. Kentucky we're not, yet the influence of the equine industry is astounding in Virginia and Maryland. Entire towns such as Middleburg, Warrenton and Keswick, in Virginia, and Upper Marlboro and Potomac, in Maryland, are dedicated to the care, training and competition of the sport horse. Both states are home to a large number of equine-related organizations and happenings, far too many to list. Check local newspapers, especially the weekend/calendar sections, for times and locations of steeplechasing events.

Golf

Major professional golf tournaments don't appear very often on Washington's sports calendar, so it's understandable why so many local enthusiasts of the game mark off the days in anticipation of one event: the nationally televised Kemper Open, held in May or June at the TPC at Avenel course in Potomac, Md.

Tickets are available to the general public, but they can go fast, especially if some of golf's big names are taking part in the tourney. Call (301) 469-3737 for information.

On the women's circuit, the premier pro event is the Mazda LPGA, held in late spring or early summer at Bethesda Country Club. Call (301) 365-1700.

Tennis

Tennis anyone? Without a doubt the prime contest on local courts each summer (July or August) in Metro Washington is the NationsBank Classic, held at the Washington Tennis Center, 16th and Kennedy streets NW. The lineup usually features several stars of the tennis world in addition to lower-ranked players and some solid local talent. For ticket and event information, call ProServ at (703) 276-9101. USAir Arena also hosts occasional tennis events, often for charity.

Auto Racing

Yes, we even have car racing. To take a vicarious trip around the oval and past the checkered flag, consider:

Old Dominion Speedway & Dragstrip, Route 234, Manassas, Va. Stock car and drag racing are on Friday and Saturday, March-September; (703) 361-7753. Capital Raceway, Route 3 between Baltimore and Washington. Stock car racing is on Saturdays, April-November; (410) 721-7281. Hagerstown Speedway, Route 40, west of Hagerstown, Md.

Stock car racing is featured on Sunday, March-October; (301) 582-0640.

Water Sports

It's free, it's exciting and it's a lot closer than you think.

For a different kind of spectating thrill, head over to Great Falls National Park, located just off Georgetown Pike in the Fairfax County community of Great Falls, and watch gutsy kayakers and occasional canoeists attempt to negotiate the wicked Great Falls of the Potomac River, just north of Washington. Definitely not for the faint of heart.

Even if you show up and don't spot any boaters, you won't have wasted a trip. The water and surrounding countryside are spectacular in themselves and worth a look any time of year.

A little farther removed from the area but also in a beautiful setting, western Maryland's Savage River, in Garrett County near the Pennsylvania and West Virginia borders, regularly hosts national kayaking/whitewater canoe competitions.

And if the water is enough to put you in the mood for looking at some larger and more expensive pleasure craft, keep an eye out for the Washington Boat Show held each February at the Washington Convention Center. Call (202) 789-1600 for details.

The boating mecca of Annapolis, however, lays claim to hosting the world's largest in-the-water exhibition, the United States Powerboat Show, held in October at the City Dock. Boating purists get their due as well in October with the United States Sailboat Show, also at the City Dock. For information on either event, call (410) 268-8828.

Miscellaneous

For sporting events with a distinct international flavor, check out the annual Virginia Scottish Games held for two days each July at Episcopal High School, 3901 W. Braddock Rd., Alexandria. One of the nation's largest Celtic festivals, it features a variety of grueling heptathlon events in addition to less strenuous Highland dancing, bagpiping and fiddling competitions. Canine participants are put through their paces in some amazing sheep-herding contests.

And finally, as we head for the finish line, we've got to mention the Marine Corps Marathon, a fall classic (usually in November). Sometimes referred to as the "People's Marathon," it remains accessible to everyday runners as well as serious contenders. For those who would rather watch than actually attempt to run 26 miles and 385 yards, there are abundant prime vantage points along the course, which begins and ends in Arlington but includes a large section of the National Mall area downtown.

Photo: Washington Convention and Visitors Association

A visitor to Union Station, built in 1907, will be surprised to discover that it houses some great restaurants — as well as flower vendors, boutiques and a lot more.

Inside
Metro Washington Restaurants

New Orleans, fear not. Ditto for New York, San Francisco, coastal Florida, the entire state of Texas and other locales of gastronomic repute. While Metro Washington can comfortably make a claim for history, politics, power, beauty and affluence, cuisine has yet to make its way onto the list. Why? Good question, because for the connoisseur, the adventurous or the merely hungry, there's certainly no shortage of restaurants — either in volume, quality or diversity — from which to choose. They're all here, whether the palate is primed for a five-star gourmet budget-buster, an eclectic ethnic bistro, a hole-in-the-wall, down-home eatery, or something in between.

From Chinatown to Adams Morgan, Capitol Hill to Georgetown, Arlington to Annapolis, Rockville to Old Town Alexandria, and Tysons Corner to Bethesda, a veritable dining world in miniature awaits.

Perhaps one reason why few outsiders deem Metro Washington a dining mecca is that no particular food is strongly identified with the region. The District? Let's see . . . No, the ubiquitous pork that's cooked-up on Capitol Hill, that doesn't count. Maryland? Well, those world-famous crab cakes will certainly do in a pinch. And Virginia? The renowned Smithfield hams are indeed worth squealing about. Still, we're not about to compete on the prominence scale with the likes of Cajun, Tex-Mex and other well-known territorial specialties. But live in Metro Washington, or at least hang around long enough, and you'll begin to realize that whatever cuisine you crave, you're likely to find it here, thanks in large measure to the fact that so many residents are originally from elsewhere.

Fortunately for restaurateurs, Metro Washington offers a customer base of significant stature — a diverse, well-traveled and well-heeled crowd. Suffice it to say that there are plenty of folks here who appreciate good food and who can afford to dine out regularly. And the numbers back it up. Washington ranks No. 4 (trailing only San Francisco/Oakland, Boston and Los Angeles) in the nation among the 10 largest markets in sales at eating/drinking establishments, with more than $2,500 spent per household. That's 28 percent above the national norm and 12 points over the nine-market average.

Before we get into the meat of this chapter, though, a few words about the ingredients.

Foremost to keep in mind: This is in no way an exhaustive listing. We'd probably still be writing if that was the objective! Instead, we've dished up an appetizer, if you will, for a dining menu so diverse as to challenge even the hardiest of restaurant-goers. In fact, we've barely scratched the proverbial surface — or rather, removed that first delicious layer — of what Metro Washington has to offer in the way of calories, carbohydrates and cholesterol.

We're not professional restaurant critics. We couldn't be; I don't think either of us has ever met a (free) meal we didn't enjoy. But we have lived in the area for a combined 40 years or so and done a fair amount of dining around with friends, family and colleagues, so that ought to count for something.

The restaurants that made the cut are a mix of recognized local favorites (in some cases, institutions), very personal choices and a smattering of others located in the District, Suburban Maryland and Northern Virginia. With a few exceptions, none of the major national chain establishments (including fast-food outlets, sandwich/pizza joints and full-service family restaurants such as Bennigan's, Ruby Tuesday, Chili's, Outback Steakhouse, etc.) are represented. It's not that we don't like them, but just that we wanted to instead focus primarily on places you're unlikely to find anywhere else.

The following scale is offered as a very general guide to prices — all of which are subject to change, of course — for a complete dinner for two including appetizers, wine, beer or spirits, and dessert, but excluding tax and tip:

$30 or less	$
$31 to $60	$$
$61 to $100	$$$
Over $100	$$$$

All establishments listed accept most major credit cards.

Restaurants appear alphabetically under each jurisdictional and/or cuisine heading, so don't equate their placement with any quality ranking or preference. Restaurants located in hotels are so noted.

Bon appetit!

District of Columbia

American/Continental

Adirondacks

50 Massachusetts Ave. NE
(Union Station) *(202) 682-1840*
$$$

Maybe it has something to do with its location in the beautifully renovated Union Station, just blocks from the Capitol. Whatever the reason, Adirondacks has been a hit with its contemporary American cuisine (especially beef dishes) served in a gorgeous setting; private dining rooms are available for groups of up to 250.

Blackie's House of Beef

1217 22nd St. NW *(202) 333-1100*
$$

Opened in 1946, Blackie's has used the years wisely to establish itself as a Washington landmark. And it's an easy one to find at that, sitting just off M Street between Georgetown and downtown. Enjoy the beautiful antiques, paintings and the cozy rooms with fireplaces as you dine on generous thick steaks and succulent roast beef.

The Brickskeller

1523 22nd St. NW *(202) 293-1885*
$

Love beer? If the answer's yes, you've just passed The Brickskeller compatibility test. But you may want to bring a small army of friends if the plans include trying to sample the 500 or so brands of brew from around the world offered at this snug, saloon-style eatery, family owned since 1957. Some of the beers are far more palatable than others, but it's an amazing selection never-

Insiders...
Yearning for a meal out on the town but not sure what kind of food they want often head to dining havens such as Arlington, Adams Morgan and Georgetown where scores of restaurants of every description are located within a short distance of each other.

Insiders' Tip

theless (also amazing is the antique beer-can collection lining the walls; you've got to see it to believe it). What to wash down? Try the buffalo steaks and burgers, ribs, spicy chicken wings, seafood, salads and sandwiches, all tasty if unspectacular. Afterwards, head upstairs to Top of the Bricks for some music and maybe even a spin on the dance floor to burn off some of those calories.

CHADWICKS

3205 K St. NW *(202) 333-2565*
$$

It's tough to avoid comparisons with the local Clyde's chain (see subsequent entry), but Chadwicks should view it as a compliment. It's easy to find something to like in this warm, inviting Georgetown saloon/restaurant, be it the atmosphere, a selection from the bar or a menu item, with the latter featuring an array of burgers, seafood, soups, salads, pasta and the like. The only hard part for the uninitiated may be finding this place which sits literally beneath the Whitehurst Freeway near the foot of Wisconsin Avenue.

CHAMPIONS — THE AMERICAN SPORTS BAR

1206 Wisconsin Ave. NW *(202) 965-4005*
$

OK, so this is certainly best known as a casual hangout rather than a dining spot, but it's too appealing not to include. Tucked at the end of a short alleyway in Georgetown near the famed intersection of Wisconsin and M, Champions, as its name implies, is a true sports bar. Expect nothing grand from the menu — the usual saloon beverages and chow — but do expect a sports junkie's paradise, crammed with memorabilia, souvenirs, photos, posters and the like. This is a great place to watch the hometown Redskins, Bullets and Capitals, or any televised sporting event for that matter. At night and on weekends, dancing is *de rigueur* as a DJ spins popular tunes for the 20s and early 30s set. Big crowds are standard.

CLYDE'S OF GEORGETOWN

3236 M St. NW *(202) 333-9180*
$$

Here's a D.C. institution that was smart enough to bring its success to the suburbs. Although all of the locations outside the Beltway have proven to be a hit, none have quite the charm as this original street-front saloon in the very crux of trendy Georgetown. Beyond the irresistible bar area, Clyde's beckons with fresh pasta and seafood, its own brand of award-winning chili, steaks, salads, sandwiches and homemade desserts. A fun, dependable place with broad appeal, patrons are just as likely to include grad students as yuppie couples and old-line establishment types.

DUKE ZEIBERT'S

1050 Connecticut Ave. NW *(202) 466-3730*
$$$

More a place to see and be seen than a dining spot of grand repute, esteemed Duke's claim to fame is, well, the famous: a magnet for local celebrities, powerbrokers, movers and shakers, and the like. Pricey indeed, but known for quality fresh seafood and thick-cut prime rib.

The Guards

2915 M St. NW (202) 965-2350

$$$

The low ceilings and fireplace spell intimate with a capital I. Throw in a British decor and you get the picture. Try the steaks and seafood or a mean bowl of French-onion soup.

Hamburger Hamlet

5225 Wisconsin Ave. NW (202) 244-2038

3125 M St. NW (202) 965-6970

$

Ask five people familiar with the local dining scene about where to go for the best hamburgers in town and three of them — no, make that four — are likely to tell you Hamburger Hamlet. They're that delicious and double-H is that popular. Case closed. Oh yeah, and you can also find great chicken, fish, soups, salads, tons of specials and tantalizing desserts. The faithful also flock to locations in Bethesda, Gaithersburg, Arlington (Crystal City) and Alexandria.

The Jockey Club

(at the Ritz-Carlton Hotel)

2100 Massachusetts Ave. NW (202)659-8000

$$$$

Power dining redefined since it opened more than 30 years ago, The Jockey Club was one of Washington's first restaurants to win four stars. Some may not feel comfortable in the high-brow, clubby atmosphere or the tony Embassy Row locale, but it's gracious and elegant nevertheless and you're sure to enjoy what the kitchen produces. You can't go wrong with continental specialties that include Chesapeake Bay crab cakes (superb), chicken salad and dessert souffles.

Metro Grille

(at the Holiday Inn Crowne Plaza)

775 12th St. NW (202) 737-2080

$$

Metro Grille is just another reason to stay at or at least stop by the wonderful Holiday Inn Crowne Plaza. The extensive, reasonably priced menu is decidedly American and decidedly good. Favorites include a range of seafood and beef dishes (especially the New York strip), chicken, burgers and a great variety of salads. This place is a notch above many hotel restaurants.

Insiders' Tip

Insiders...

With a palate for beer like to try one of the tasty regional microbrews such as Virginia's Dominion Lager and Maryland's Wild Goose Amber that are offered at many local bars and restaurants.

Morton's of Chicago

3251 Prospect St. NW *(202) 342-6258*
$$$$

Here's one of the exceptions to our no-national-chains pledge made at the beginning of this chapter. If this legendary steakhouse can't satisfy that hankering for prime dry-aged beef, you might as well buy some cattle and a do-it-yourself guidebook. You will indeed feel a hit in the pocketbook if this is a stop on your Georgetown itinerary, but if you've got the means, Morton's won't disappoint. Those who eschew the red-meat scene can sink their teeth into the likes of fresh Maine lobster, swordfish, chicken or veal. And be sure to inspect the amazing LeRoy Nieman art collection.

Mr. Smith's

3104 M St. NW *(202) 333-3104*
$$

Yet another saloon/eatery with Georgetown roots and a prime M Street location that has found success outside the Beltway. Great for burgers, steaks, seafood, salad and soups and a friendly pub atmosphere, Mr. Smith's also offers a piano bar plus — in warm weather — a wonderful outdoor garden patio in back. It's a prime spot for enjoying a spring or summer evening.

Old Ebbitt Grill

675 15th St. NW *(202) 347-4801*
$$

When they say old, they mean it—since 1856. Old Ebbitt Grill bills itself as "Washington's oldest saloon," and while that may be subject to argument, its stellar reputation and prime location are not. Just two blocks from the White House, this casually elegant establishment long ago made a name for itself with specialties including roasts, steaks, fresh seafood, homemade pastas, soups, burgers, deli-style sandwiches and homemade desserts. With a 3 AM closing time on Friday and Saturday, it's understandably popular with the hungry after-theater crowds.

Old Glory

3139 M St. NW *(202) 337-3406*
$

Incredible barbecue, sandwiches and burgers, a lively, casual atmosphere and fascinating history-rich decor combine to make Georgetown's Old Glory something to shoot fireworks about. Be sure to add this to the list of places to consider for birthday celebrations or other get-togethers with friends and family.

The Palm

1225 19th St. NW *(202) 293-9091*
$$$

The Washington branch of the famed New York City original loses nothing in the transition southward. The Palm has long been and remains firmly synonymous with prime steaks and jumbo Maine lobster and top-notch service that more than justifies the prices. They even offer complimentary valet parking — a nice touch anywhere, but especially downtown where parking is both scarce and absurdly expensive.

Prime Rib

2020 K St. NW *(202) 466-8811*
$$$

A multiple critics' award-winner through the years, the Prime Rib has distanced itself from the competition with a glamorous setting, coat-and-tie dress code and magnificent fare such as prime aged beef, live Maine lobster and fresh seafood flown in daily from Florida. The cocktail bar is one of the hottest in town. Enjoy it all as you listen to the sweet strains of a baby-grand piano. Free valet parking after 6 PM.

1789 Restaurant

1226 36th St. NW *(202) 965-1789*
$$$

Perhaps it's the location, a two-story Federal townhouse in a quiet residential area of upper northwest near Georgetown University. Then, once you treat your palate to the food, that immediately carries equal weight. Whatever the reason, 1789 captivates you with its country-inn charm and elegance and the efficient, first-class service. Although named for the year the university was founded, 1789 offers a truly Modern American menu with such classic treats as pheasant, venison, fish, veal, softshell crabs, lobster and homemade soups. And be sure to leave room for the breads and desserts, all whipped up on-premises in the bakery.

The Tombs

1226 36th St. NW *(202) 337-6668*
$

The Tombs is another neighbor of Georgetown University, but it's a decidedly informal, college-casual gathering spot. It's easy to dine hearty with accessible and tasty fare such as burgers, sandwiches, pizza, ribs and hearty soups. Oh yes, and check out the stunning prints and memorabilia adorning the walls.

Asian (includes Chinese, Japanese, Vietnamese and Thai)

China Inn

631 H St. NW *(202) 842-0909*
$

Lemon chicken, orange beef, stir fry, an ocean's worth of seafood specialties . . . China Inn focuses its efforts on Cantonese-style cooking and the results are clearly impressive. This Chinatown favorite for more than half a century has built a foundation of customer loyalty and rave reviews that newcomers can only dream about.

Germaine's Asian Cuisine

2400 Wisconsin Ave. NW *(202) 965-1185*
$$

With its fashionable upper Georgetown location and a grand atrium dining room, Germaine's has indeed distinguished itself as a beautiful dining spot. The food and open-hearth grill have garnered equivalent raves. Pan-Asian specialties include Peking duck, basil beef, fresh seafood, Vietnamese spring rolls and an assortment of Indonesian creations.

Hisago

3050 K St. NW (202) 944-4181
$$

Renowned contemporary Japanese cuisine in a spectacular setting: the Georgetown waterfront at Washington Harbor. Get the picture? Hisago is dependable for the freshest ingredients and seasonal specialties, not to mention the neat tempura and sushi rooms.

Hunan Chinatown

624 H St. NW (202) 783-5858
$

The competition is fierce in the Asian restaurant-rich H Street thoroughfare, but Hunan Chinatown succeeds in its dedication to the Hunan and Szechuan classics. Indulge in the numerous vegetable specialties, the pan-fried dumplings, and various lobster, chicken, pork, duck and shrimp creations. The service and presentation are further impetus to make this a regular stop on your Chinatown dining excursions.

Japan Inn

1715 Wisconsin Ave. NW (202) 337-3400
$$

Whether prepared at your table or in the kitchen, the authentic dishes of Japan Inn rarely disappoint. Opt for the sushi and tempura, or perhaps assorted temptations featuring scallops, shrimp, steak and chicken. Any way you enjoy it, this is a complete Japanese dining experience. Throw in an elegant Georgetown setting and you've got the ingredients for infatuation.

Ploy

2218 Wisconsin Ave. NW (202) 337-2324
$

Creative Thai cuisine in Glover Park? Indeed, as this modern cafe continues to prove. While the dishes may not be spicy enough to please the most ardent hot-food aficionados, the chef will happily oblige if you desire the temperature cranked up a few degrees. The dim sum and shrimp cakes aren't to be missed.

Star of Siam

1136 19th St. NW (202) 785-2838
2446 18th St. NW (202) 986-4133
$

Competition in the Thai restaurant scene has gotten considerably stiffer in recent years, but Star of Siam hasn't been fazed. It's consistently good, consistently popular and consistently top-rated regionwide. Hard to improve on that. Whether the location is downtown (19th Street), Adams Morgan (18th Street) or in Arlington at 1735 N. Lynn St. in Rosslyn, expect satisfaction at Star of Siam. The fish and curry selections are especially great.

Sushi-Ko

2309 Wisconsin Ave. NW (202) 333-4187
$$

As the name implies, sushi is the word at Sushi-Ko. And few in town do it better: eel, tuna, flounder, shrimp, salmon, even quail eggs and flying-fish roe. Although many people have been converted by the "Try it, you'll like it" urging of their fellow diners, not everyone has embraced the sushi phenomenon. Not to worry. Sushi-Ko also offers such decidedly tasty and non-sushi creations as tempura, teriyaki and a lip-smacking-good seafood soup with noodles.

Tony Cheng's Mongolian Restaurant

619 H St. NW *(202) 842-8669*

$

To be certain, there's no shortage of barbecue joints in Metro Washington, but you'll be hard pressed to find the Mongolian style (yes, Mongolian) offered anywhere but Tony Cheng's. It's as good as it is different, but don't just take our word as gospel. Tasting is believing. Expect generous portions of meat, vegetables and tangy sauces, and if you have trouble deciding, opt for the $13.95 all-you-can-eat deal.

Vietnam-Georgetown

2934 M St. NW *(202) 337-4536*

$$

If you enjoy Southeast Asian food and the high-energy air of Georgetown, then you won't be disappointed. It's that simple with Vietnam-Georgetown.

Caribbean

Cafe Atlantico

1819 Columbia Rd. NW *(202) 575-2233*

$

A taste of the Caribbean, complete with a starry-sky interior, awaits you at Cafe Atlantico. Expertly prepared foods, particularly the various fish selections, have made this Columbia Road retreat into a local favorite. And while you're taking in some nourishment, expect to be serenaded at various times with jazz, new age and Latin music.

Cities

2424 18th St. NW *(202) 328-7194*

$

While we included Cities under the "Caribbean" heading, that's just one of the choices offered at this innovative eatery where a changing ethnic menu affords diners the chance to do some gastronomic globetrotting: Mexican, Thai, Sicilian, Turkish, Italian, you name it. A novel idea indeed. Then again, restaurateurs had better be creative when looking to stay ahead of the game in competitive Adams Morgan.

Fish, Wings & Tings

2418 18th St. NW *(202) 234-0322*

$

As Caribbean as the name sounds, mon. No problem finding good, reasonably priced food here at this tiny carryout where the accent is clearly on the islands. Seafood of course is a biggie. Fish, Wings & Tings is an Adams Morgan landmark and a casual retreat into the world of ethnic dining.

The Islander

1762 Columbia Rd. NW *(202) 234-4955*

$

Again, if you seek accessible and reliable Caribbean cuisine with plenty to offer in the way of treats from the sea, The Islander is a good bet. Creative appetizers, too, all in an informal setting.

Ethiopian

Meskerem

2434 18th St. NW (202) 462-4100
$

National recognition and awards galore have done a lot to enhance the reputation of Meskerem, which some critics rank as the nation's finest Ethiopian restaurant. If you enjoy such dining adventures, one visit will lay any doubts to rest. Enjoy the big floppy crepe-like bread for scooping up the various hot and mild meat dishes including beef, lamb and chicken, the lentils and green vegetables, and all that glorious sauce. And you can't beat the prices. Meskerem would be justified charging more, but it's nice that they don't.

Red Sea

2463 18th St. NW (202) 483-5000
$

Red Sea is also a heavyweight contender in the local arena of award-winning Ethiopian kitchens. Succulent lamb and beef, delicious poultry and seafood, irresistible spices and stews, and an excellent vegetarian menu combine to rank Red Sea as yet another Adams Morgan stalwart. And to enhance what the palate enjoys, traditional music is performed on Friday and Saturday nights.

Zed's Ethiopian Cuisine

3318 M St. NW (202) 333-4710
$

Only the first letter in its name placed Zed's at the end of the list for recommended Ethiopian dining. Although offering less than some of its competitors in the way of setting and ambience, it always scores high where it matters the most for a restaurant: food. In particular, the rich sauces, beef dishes and a unique offering of broiled short ribs help place Zed's ahead of many of its contemporaries.

French

Aux Beaux Champs

(at the Four Seasons Hotel)
2800 Pennsylvania Ave. NW (202) 342-0810
$$$

This is splendid food and impeccable service in a gorgeous setting that happens to be in one of the city's top hotels. Aux Beaux Champs certainly comes out of the blocks with a big lead in many categories. And it's hard to go wrong with nearly anything the kitchen produces. Top it all off with a garden lounge and a live pianist and you've got the makings of a classic. It is.

Dominique's

1900 Pennsylvania Ave. NW (202) 452-1126
$$$

Although there are those who argue that Dominique's is not the restaurant it once was, it's still worth a try in our opinion if for no other reason than to soak up the ambience and try some tasty exotic favorites like rattlesnake, venison, trout and various other denizens of field and sea. Reliable service, a prime location and a fun decor complete with walls full of photos of famous patrons combine to keep Dominique's a step ahead of some of its many rivals throughout the city.

Jean-Louis

(at the Watergate Hotel)
2650 Virginia Ave. NW (202) 298-4488
$$$$

Nothing should bug anyone in the gourmet French-cuisine crowd about this heralded establishment except perhaps its location in the venerable Watergate Hotel, as divine and elegant a setting as it may be. And if you have to ask about prices, you definitely don't belong here. The renowned and acclaimed chef, Jean-Louis Palladin, has made a nationwide name for himself in more ways than one. The freshest ingredients, the painstaking detail in preparation and presentation, the succulent seasonings and flavors, the white-glove service, Jean-Louis offers the consummate fine-dining experience. And don't forget to make reservations. And bring plenty of cash or plastic.

La Chaumiere

2813 M St. NW (202) 338-1784
$$

This country inn/bistro in the heart of Georgetown is a perennial favorite in the competitive, come-and-go world of French restaurants. Farm tools adorning the walls enhance the Old World flavor. Expect attentive and heartwarming service, delicious and reliable veal dishes, soups, mussels, dessert souffles and fruit tarts.

La Nicoise

1721 Wisconsin Ave. NW (202) 965-9300
$$$

French food served by a rollerskating staff? You read right. Georgetown's La Nicoise is nothing if not fun and a refreshing change of pace in a dining category that people sometimes equate — and sometimes rightfully so — with uppity and pretentious. Entertainment aside, you can enjoy some creative beef, veal, lamb, poultry and pasta dishes here, plus scrumptious desserts.

Maison Blanche

1725 F St. NW (202) 842-0070
$$$

The name means "White House" so guess what familiar piece of public property it claims as a neighbor? Prestigious location aside, perhaps the Mobil four-star and AAA four-diamond awards offer you some insight as to the reputation of Maison Blanche, long recognized as one of the city's top-flight French restaurants. Expect classic cuisine served in old-world elegance. The furnishings, the flowers, the crystal, the service, Maison Blanche has put it all together for an unforgettable dining experience. There's complimentary valet parking after 5 PM.

Insiders...
Know that some of the best crab cakes anywhere in the free world are served in the Willard Room at Washington's magnificent Willard Inter-Continental Hotel.

Insiders' Tip

German

Cafe Berlin

322 Massachusetts Ave. NE(202) 543-7656
$

No, you haven't been transported back to Germany, it just feels that way when you step into Cafe Berlin. The hearty fare — good and reasonable priced if unspectacular — and of course the beer selection makes this eatery worth a try for those with even the most Continental of tastebuds.

Old Europe

2434 Wisconsin Ave. NW (202) 333-7600
$$

Praise and popularity are old hat for Old Europe, unwavering in its appeal at the same spot for 45 years. This place, some will contend, embodies all that an old-world German restaurant should be, except maybe for the American locale. Just use your imagination though and enjoy the fresh-fish specials, the various wursts, schnitzels, dumplings, pork and other filling creations, not to mention the homemade pastries and an extensive wine and beer list. And we can't forget the lively, infectious music.

Indian

Aditi

3299 M St. NW (202) 625-6825
$

This Georgetown eatery has firmly established itself as one of the region's top destinations for those in search of outstanding Indian fare. Don't look for anything unusual here. Do look for reliably good curry, vegetable, lamb and chicken combinations, plus accommodating kitchen and floor staffs to boot.

Bombay Palace

1835 K St. NW (202) 331-0111
$$

Yes, this is part of an international chain with several stateside locations, but Bombay Palace nevertheless garners mention for its better-than-usual service, setting and menu. Especially good choices are any of the curries, tandoori prawns and chicken, lamb and various vegetarian selections.

Madurai

3318 M St. NW (202) 333-0997
$

You won't find any meat, poultry or seafood offered here, so what does that leave? That's right, Indian vegetarian. Enamored as you may be with food that walks and swims before making its way to your plate, you're likely to enjoy Madurai as a nice change of pace. Be sure to try the vegetarian "meatballs" and any of the wonderful rice dishes, and it's tough to beat Sunday's $6.95 all-you-can-eat buffet lunch and dinner.

Taj Mahal

1327 Connecticut Ave. NW (202) 659-1544
$

The vegetarian crowd won't have any complaints about this place either, yet Taj Mahal also does right by non-vegetarians with its imaginative selections of Mogul and tandoori cuisine with all the right spices. Warm and elegant, this Dupont Circle-area favorite also lays out a tremendous lunch buffet weekdays. Perhaps the overall appeal has something to do with Taj Mahal's claim to being "Washington's oldest authentic Indian restaurant" (since 1965).

Irish

POWERSCOURT AND THE DUBLINER
(both at the Phoenix Park Hotel)
520 N. Capitol St. NW (202) 638-6900
$$

For a taste of the Emerald Isle without stepping on a plane, head for Capitol Hill. Powerscourt and The Dubliner, located in what is reported to be the nation's only Irish-owned hotel, are considered by many to be the region's most authentic Irish pub and dining experiences. Granted, Irish cuisine anywhere has never really set the culinary world on fire, but the Phoenix Park Hotel has few peers locally when it comes to doing it right. If the plans don't include a meal, just stop by and soak up a bit o' the friendly and lively atmosphere and enjoy some of Ireland's distinctive libations.

Italian

BICE
601 Pennsylvania Ave. NW (202) 638-2423
$$$

Yes, this is yet another exception to our no-chains claim, but for good reason. Honest. (And it's definitely not because so many of the Hollywood glitterati flocked here during the Clinton inaugural hoopla.) There are only a dozen or so branches anywhere of Bice, a Milan-based operation that emphasizes superb decor, food and service. And it didn't take long for Bice to garner critical acclaim and win over new customers shortly after opening in 1991. Now, a few of those same critics say it has lost some of its original luster and appeal, but you wouldn't know it by the clout Bice still carries with lovers of Italian food. The pasta, duck, quail and red snapper are especially good.

GEPPETTO'S
2917 M St. NW (202) 333-2602
$

Imagine a pepperoni topping piled so high that it's hard to see the pizza itself. While such generosity seems terribly wasteful except for perhaps eaters of above-average girth, it's tough for lovers of deep-dish pizza and pasta not to adore Gepetto's. The pleasure begins from the moment you step inside this Georgetown jewel and take in the delightful aroma. From then on, the attentive staff and the heavenly menu work their magic. Just be sure to bring your appetite — and preferably someone else's.

I RICCHI
1220 19th St. NW (202) 835-0459
$$$

Why go to Florence when you can taste the fortunes of her cuisine right here in the District? The chef-owner of i Ricchi has been more than a goodwill ambassador for his native city, as the talk on the street and the rumblings in the restaurant press will verify. The cheeses, the pasta, the olive oil, the quail, veal, rabbit and pork, it's tough to go wrong here. i Ricchi has taken authentic Italian cuisine in a classy setting to new heights.

Marrocco's

1120 20th St. NW *(202) 331-1354*
$$

If you like the style, service and general warmth of a truly family-run operation, Marrocco's fits the bill. And after nearly 50 years, with the third generation at the helm, the food remains consistently good as well. Pick your favorite Italian province and Marrocco's will likely have a selection to match. Look for reliably good homemade pasta and fresh seafood, and assorted dishes featuring chicken, veal and beef.

Paolo's

1303 Wisconsin Ave. NW *(202) 333-7353*
$$

A bit of Italy comes to the heart of Georgetown (as well as Rockville, at 1801 Rockville Pike) with this established favorite. The huge bar of Italian marble, the extensive glasswork, the wood-burning oven, the friendly service, Paolo's brings together all the right elements for irresistibility, food included. It's renowned for its gourmet pizza and fresh pasta and seafood.

Mexican/Tex-Mex/ Southwestern

Austin Grill

2404 Wisconsin Ave. NW *(202) 337-8080*
$

Some of the region's other Tex-Mex establishments may get more ink, but it's hard to understand why. To be certain, those in the know appreciate the authenticity of Austin Grill, and its popularity shows. To be won over merely requires a sample of any of the expertly prepared and presented enchiladas, fajitas, burritos, chili, even the zesty appetizers. Wash it all down with something frosty, sit back, and enjoy the sights and sounds and you'll surely understand why this restaurant's sister operation, Old Town Alexandria's South Austin Grill, became an instant hit.

Cactus Cantina

3300 Wisconsin Ave. NW *(202) 686-7222*
$

Lively crowds flock to this funky Cleveland Park retreat with their sights set on Tex-Mex delights, and Cactus Cantina doesn't disappoint. Standard fare includes generous portions of enchiladas, tacos, ribs and fajitas.

La Fonda Restaurant & El Azteca Cantina

1639 R St. NW *(202) 232-6965*
$ *(202) 232-6969*

For authentic Mexican cuisine of every description, La Fonda and the adjacent El Azteca Cantina continue to stand out in the colorful Dupont Circle area, as they have for over 30 years. Enhancing the flavors are beautiful tiled rooms and outside dining areas.

Red Sage

605 14th St. NW *(202) 638-4444*
$$$

All the rage since its opening in 1992, Red Sage quickly established a distinctive presence at Washington's ever-growing table of dining spots. How did it happen? Quite simply through a compelling combination of superb Southwestern-style food — savor especially the shrimp, tuna and steak offerings — served in what has been called a "showplace" of museum-quality architecture, design and handcrafts. Even the cocktails have drawn raves. (The restrooms can't be far behind, we guess.) If nothing else, Red Sage is worth a try just to see if so many people could possibly be so right in their bountiful praise.

Middle Eastern

Bacchus

1827 Jefferson Pl. NW (202) 785-0734
$$

In the minds of many Washingtonians, the art of Middle Eastern cooking, in this case Lebanese, begins and ends at Bacchus, whether you choose the original location here or the offshoot in Bethesda (7945 Norfolk Ave.). Count on quality and satisfaction in whatever menu selection catches your eye. Bacchus specialties include the creative kebabs of beef, chicken and lamb, savory sausages, stuffed cabbage and baby eggplant.

Lebanese Taverna Restaurant

2641 Connecticut Ave. NW (202) 265-8681
$$

This lively, attractive establishment has served notice as a serious contender in the Middle Eastern market, if you will, a category that seems to either enchant diners or completely turn them away. For the faithful, Lebanese Taverna will surely please with its own brand of "moussaka" (a Greek staple) — sans the usual ground beef — and other delicious eggplant dishes, the spicy sausages, a variety of vegetable kebabs and of course a wood-fired oven that brings out all the right aromas. And be sure to sample the wonderful Lebanese breads. Hard to complain with reasonable prices, good cooking, and cordial and efficient service. (There's also a Virginia location at 5900 Washington Blvd., Arlington.)

Moroccan

Marrakesh

617 New York Ave. NW (202) 393-9393
$$

The seasoned chicken and lamb, the lemons and olives, Marrakesh does justice — and then some — to these and all the other tangy and savory makings of Moroccan cuisine. Admittedly, eating with your hands takes some getting used to, but the waiters are never far away with a bowl for rinsing. The authentically served (and filling) seven-course meals are followed by a belly dancer nightly, folk dancing Saturdays. Marrakesh continues to lead the way in Moroccan dining.

Seafood

The Dancing Crab

4611 Wisconsin Ave. NW (202) 244-1882
$$

A longtime favorite on upper Wisconsin Avenue, The Dancing Crab is just about what you might expect from a veteran of the Washington seafood trade: great, fresh seafood. Hard-shell crabs are the cornerstone, of course, but just about any treat from the briny depths is a good bet here.

GANGPLANK

600 Water St. SW *(202) 554-5000*
$$

It may be Washington's only floating restaurant, but landlubbers needn't worry. You're no more likely to be swept out to the Potomac and beyond than you are to be disappointed with the food. Indeed, Gangplank is a sure bet for fine, fresh seafood as well as assorted beef and pasta selections. Gangplank hasn't cornered the market on waterfront dining in charming Southwest, but its cozy lounges and superb location go a long way it helping it keep pace with the competitors.

GEORGETOWN SEAFOOD GRILL

3063 M St. NW *(202) 333-7038*
$$$

This is perhaps Georgetown's preeminent spot for fresh seafood. No matter the selection, it's can't-miss at Georgetown Seafood Grill. Service with style and grace, and an atmosphere to match. Check out the daily specials, and of course the fabulous Sunday brunch.

HOGATE'S

800 Water St. SW *(202) 484-6300*
$$

Another of the Southwest waterfront's steadfast fresh-seafood outlets, Hogate's has the name recognition to go along with its impressive fare. If such treats as lobster and assorted fishes aren't your style, opt for one of the juicy Kansas City steaks.

MARKET INN

200 E St. SW *(202) 554-2100*
$$

Consistency in ownership can go a long way in determining the success of many restaurants. Market Inn has had the same folks at the helm for nearly 35 years, and it shows — from the dining room to the kitchen. A renowned lobster house, Market Inn touts its "100 varieties of seafood daily," enough choices to please even the most finicky of diners. Turf lovers can look for succulent beef entrees such as prime rib and steaks. Want more? How about an antique bar, live entertainment from noon 'til closing, a New Orleans jazz brunch Saturday and Sunday, and free valet parking.

PHILLIPS FLAGSHIP RESTAURANT

900 Water St. SW *(202) 488-8515*
$$

The "Flagship" moniker is appropriate; this place is huge, and rightfully so for it's the showcase property of the regional Phillips chain. With a gorgeous waterfront setting (there's even a few slips for some hungry boaters to pull up), snappy service, frequent live entertainment and large banquet/reception areas to handle several different and sizeable functions at once, Phillips successfully puts it all together. Oh yeah, and they also serve some world-class fresh seafood and homemade soups. Be sure to sample some of the crab specialties and other Eastern Shore delights.

Spanish

Taberna del Alabardero

1776 I St. NW *(202) 429-2200*

$$$

Taberna del Alabardero stands alone in this category of District dining, and rightly so. In the minds of many critics and everyday patrons alike, it is considered a serious candidate for the title of Nation's Finest Spanish Restaurant. While traditional cuisine from Spain may be a new dining experience for many, one visit will make instant converts. After the rabbit or the lobster or the fish or the duck, or anything for that matter, don't dare miss the sinfully scrumptious desserts.

Northern Virginia

City of Alexandria

Regional

Armand's Chicago Pizzeria

111 King St. *(703) 683-0313*

$

Superb deep-dish pizza, enough to fill an average eater with two or three hefty slices, is most certainly the forte of Armand's. Call it Sicilian-style, Chicago-style or any style, it's delicious pizza by any name. The bread, the tomato sauce, the cheese, the toppings, begin and end any place you like because pizza lovers won't be disappointed. Also great salads and sandwiches. In a hurry at lunchtime? Try the all-you-can-eat pizza buffet, but be sure to sit near the serving area as it tends to get snapped up as quickly as it's put out. Upstairs, The Penalty Box sports bar, owned by a former pro hockey player, is a great place to take in a Capitals game. Armand's also graces Montgomery County with its presence at 1909 Seminary Rd., Silver Spring.

Dixie Pig

1225 Powhatan St. *(703) 836-0605*
6711 Richmond Hwy. *(703) 765-5353*
2818 Beacon Hill Rd.
(carry-out only) *(703) 768-4395*

$

No star or diamond ratings or blue-ribbon awards here. But the three area Dixie Pig locations are proof that tasty and unpretentious "homecooking" can indeed be had along the concrete byways of the Route 1 corridor and the quiet backstreets of Old Town. There's meat loaf, barbecue, mashed potatoes, fresh vegetables, fountain drinks, all at prices from another time. You get the idea. This is local color and flavor at some of its finest.

Generous George's Positive Pizza and Pasta

3006 Duke St. *(703) 370-4303*
6937 Telegraph Rd. *(703) 719-5600*

$

An odd name indeed, but the gigantic portions of superb pizza and pasta are nothing to laugh at. You'll be too busy chewing, swallowing and smiling in between. The quirky, eclectic decor — a true mishmash of the odd, the colorful and the bizarre — and a fun family atmosphere where kids in particular are made to feel special make Generous George's a hit every time. One visit and you'll understand why people gladly sweat the lines on weekends. (There's also a Fairfax County location in Springfield.)

Hard Times Cafe

1404 King St. (703) 683-5340
$

The same high praise for a tantalizing variety of world-class chili served in a casual setting is to be found at this Hard Times. See the Rockville, Md., listing for details.

Kenny's Bar-B-Que

3060 Duke St. (703) 823-3330
$

You wouldn't expect to find such a tasty barbecue joint along the commercial strip of Duke Street, but there Kenny's sits, wedged between an auto-repair place and a doughnut shop. It's not the easiest place to spot if you're flying along, but make the effort to slow down and find it. Grab a chair in the dinky, sparse and often drafty dining area and enjoy the tangy and cooked-to-perfection pork, beef and chicken barbecue sandwiches and platters. And don't forget the side orders such as corn bread, beans, cole slaw and chunky french fries, which are good enough to be main courses.

King Street Blues

112 N. St. Asaph St. (703) 836-8800
$

Here's yet another contender for some of the area's best barbecue. Just a block or so off King Street itself, King Street Blues also serves up some great burgers, salads and soups. Particularly big with the 20- and 30-something crowds of professionals.

South Austin Grill

801 King St. (703) 684-8969
$

The Old Town version is just as much a hit as the D.C. original (see D.C. listing for details). Funky southwestern decor and a hip young crowd complete the scene.

American/Continental

Chadwicks

203 S. Strand St. (703) 836-4442
$

The Old Town branch of this Georgetown saloon boasts a snug waterfront location along with the requisite warm wood paneling and floors and brass accents, perfect complements to the Chadwicks aura of urban yet gracious hospitality and reasonably priced but always-good food. You won't find much in the way of innovation in the menu items (burgers, sandwiches, pasta and the like), but you will find it to be fresh and satisfying. A choice happy-hour destination, with bars on both the upper and lower levels.

The Dandy

Potomac Party Cruises Inc.
Zero Prince St. (703) 683-6076 (reservations)
$$ *(703) 683-6090 (information)*

This Old Town institution takes waterfront dining one step further, transporting customers out *onto* the gentle Potomac River for an approximately three-hour climate-controlled cruise complete with dancing and wonderful views. Lunch and dinner outings are offered daily, but we're partial to the nighttime excursions when the nearby monuments, memorials and urban skyline are awash in lights. The wonderful food — the choice of fixed-price entrees includes seafood, beef and chicken selections — is served in a spirited and unforgettable atmosphere. Groups of up to 200 can be accommodated.

Fish Market

105 King St. *(703) 836-5676*

$$

Like hundreds of other Old Town buildings, the one that houses the ever-popular Fish Market has a storied past, a one-time focal point of the Colonial-era seafaring trade when Alexandria was a port city and market of widespread importance. The city still buzzes here in the lower King Street area, but these days it's centered around the flourishing restaurant and small-retail business. There's still a noticeably fishy air about the Fish Market, but it serves as a tantalizing prelude to the right-off-the-boat-fresh seafood treats awaiting diners. Be sure to sample the spicy shrimp, the delicious oysters on the half shell and any of the thick, rich seafood chowders. The lively and large bar crowds tend to gravitate toward the unbelievably generous "schooners" of beer, but that doesn't mean they don't go nicely with a full dinner, particularly on a steamy summer evening. Waiting in line here is not at all uncommon, especially on weekends, so plan accordingly.

Gas Light

100 King St. *(703) 739-0555*

$$$

One of the newcomers to Old Town's fine-dining scene, Gas Light offers elegant, refined, white-tablecloth service amid the din of Alexandria's heart and soul. On the food front, the continental lineup features a variety of meats and fishes, pasta, lobster, soups and salads.

Joe Theismann's

1800 Diagonal Rd. *(703) 739-0777*

$$

OK, so it is named after a former Redskins quarterback, not to mentioned owned by him, but that's not why it's on the list. Located right smack across the street from the King Street Metro station, Theismann's serves up some respectably tasty burgers, pasta and seafood dishes. A handsomely decorated place with the requisite sports-memorabilia decor adorning the walls. You'll always find a fun happy-hour crowd and prime spot for sports TV viewing.

Portner's

109 South St. Asaph St. *(703) 683-1776*

$$

While it sometimes seems hard to distinguish among some of Old Town's numerous dining spots in beautiful old brick buildings, there's just something about the warmth and friendliness of Portner's that helps it stand out. Of course, it doesn't hurt to offer superb pasta, burgers and a host of grilled specialties, all available for consuming upstairs or down nestled between fine woodwork and antique accessories, or in the beautiful glassed-in atrium or small patio area. And while the bar is a beautiful sight at the end of a long day, don't look for hopping happy-hour crowds but rather a kinder, gentler gathering. As one would expect, service is top-notch as well.

Union Street Public House

121 S. Union St. *(703) 548-1785*
$$

Union Street is clearly one of the area's most popular neighborhood saloons and restaurants. Choose a lively and often-crowded bar scene downstairs, quieter dining upstairs, or something in between with the back-room (and sometimes overlooked) oyster bar. An array of continental and seafood favorites grace the menu, plus 11 draft beers including the house exclusive, the rich and delicious Virginia Native. Union Street's appeal seems to grow with the years.

The Wharf

119 King St. *(703) 836-2834*
$$

As the name implies, The Wharf means seafood. And you won't run aground by choosing this longtime favorite to sample some of the treasures of the sea. Fish, shrimp, lobster, scallops, oysters, clams, The Wharf delivers consistently high marks for food quality, service and ambience.

International

Geranio

722 King St. *(703) 548-0088*
$$

Specializing in northern Italian cuisine, enchanting and award-winning Geranio is yet another jewel in Old Town Alexandria's impressive crown of top-notch streetfront restaurants. The relaxed yet gracious setting is just right for the satisfying menu that includes top-drawer grilled fresh fish and homemade pasta.

Ireland's Own

132 N. Royal St. *(703) 549-4535*
$

Come find fun and frivolity at one of the region's true Irish hotspots. There's live entertainment to go along with pub grub and cold suds. This was a favorite haunt of some of the higher-ups in the Reagan administration.

Le Gaulois

1106 King St. *(703) 739-9494*
$$

The minute you walk in the door and onto the warmth of the hardwood floors at Le Gaulois, you feel as though you're miles from the city bustle — no easy feat for a streetside restaurant. Friendly, quiet and accommodating to the Nth degree, Le Gaulois serves up creative and very reliable French-influenced cuisine at reasonable prices. Personal favorites include any of the grilled seafood, pate and beef selections.

Murphy's

713 King St. *(703) 548-1717*
$

Old Town's other bastion of Irish cheer, Murphy's is a guaranteed good time with live, sing-along music, plenty of tasty saloon fare and a busy bar. This is one of the top night spots in all of Alexandria, and you can believe it's jumping like no other time come St. Patrick's Day.

Terrazza

710 King St. *(703) 683-6900*
$$$

The dignified yellow awning and gleaming white facade announce the presence of Terrazza, truly one of the area's finest Italian restaurants. The reception inside is just as gracious, inviting and pleasing to the senses. The superb service is surpassed only by the outstanding food, notably the various pasta and seafood dishes presented in an air of refined elegance. Ladies making their way through the foyer shouldn't be surprised if one of the staff members hands her a fresh-cut flower plucked from a nearby arrangement. Terrazza is quality and class to the utmost.

Arlington County

Regional

Hard Times Cafe

3028 Wilson Blvd.,
Clarendon *(703) 528-2233*
$

Chili galore. Need we say more — again? (See the Rockville, Md., listing.)

Red, Hot & Blue

1600 Wilson Blvd.,
Clarendon *(703) 276-7427*

Red Hot & Blue Express

3014 Wilson Blvd.,
Clarendon *(703) 243-1510*
$

No matter the location, count on the legendary Memphis barbecue sandwiches and full-blown platters to be lip-smacking delicious. (See the Montgomery County listing for the glowing specifics.)

Rio Grande Cafe

4301 N. Fairfax Dr.,
Ballston *(703) 528-3131*
$$

Rio Grande offers renowned Tex-Mex delights, Arlington style (see the Montgomery County listing for details).

Tom Sarris' Orleans House

1213 Wilson Blvd.,
Rosslyn *(703) 524-2929*
$$

With its wrought-iron railings and antique furnishings, Tom Sarris' Orleans House brings a taste of the famed French Quarter to the heart of Rosslyn. Highlights of the American menu include prime rib and other beef selections, seafood and one of the area's best salad bars that you can try to tackle from end to end with the all-you-can-eat special.

American/Continental

Arlington Cinema 'N' Draft House

2903 Columbia Pike,
Arlington *(703) 486-2345*
$

It's a different theater, but the same atmosphere, similar menu, same fun, offbeat night out. See the Bethesda Theatre Cafe listing for details.

Carlyle Grand Cafe

4000 28th St.,
Shirlington *(703) 931-0777*
$$

One of the cornerstone establishments in the tidy, compact urban village of Shirlington, Carlyle Grand Cafe is convenient city dining without parking headaches (ample, free and convenient spaces nearby). Just a stone's throw from I-395, you won't know it once you're inside and enjoying the fresh, modern and simple decor and the quality food (meats, seafood, pasta, sandwiches, etc.). Choose to dine downstairs, where the popular bar limits the seating and makes for a livelier time, or upstairs where it's decidedly quieter but equally enjoyable.

Tivoli

1700 N. Monroe St.,
Rosslyn *(703) 524-8900*
$$

Looking for delicious and distinguished dining in the heart of a frenetic business hub? Tivoli's has it with a menu that includes fish, chicken, seafood and beef selections. Also wonderful salads and appetizers. The Rosslyn Metro station is next door for the ultimate in convenience.

Whitey's

2761 N. Washington Blvd.,
Clarendon *(703) 525-9825*
$

For a true taste of down-home goodness, head to Whitey's. It's part sports bar, part game room, part earthy watering hole and part compact soundstage featuring live rhythm-and-blues. The eats are strictly of the burger and sandwich pub variety, but the atmosphere is relaxed and unassuming and the beer cold and plentiful.

International

Bangkok Gourmet

523 S. 23rd St.,
Crystal City *(703) 521-1305*
$$

Wonderful Thai food and attentive service greet you in a cozy setting that's practically in the shadows of the concrete, glass and steel of Crystal City. Bangkok Gourmet is close-in and convenient, but far from ordinary.

El Pollo Rico

2917 N. Washington Blvd.,
Clarendon *(703) 522-3220*
$

Among the best of the area's bargain chicken specialty houses, El Pollo Rico (The Rich Chicken — go figure) does a brisk carryout business in competitive Clarendon. A best bet is the house specialty: charcoal-fired rotisserie chicken that's perfectly flavored and practically melts in your mouth.

Nam Viet

1127 N. Hudson St.,
Clarendon *(703) 522-7110*
$

The name may be turned around, but we've figured it's for a reason: that's exactly what you'll be inclined to do after your first dining experience at Nam Viet. Go back again. And soon. The food is as consistently good as the atmosphere is relaxing and unpretentious and the prices reasonable. Don't miss the bon dun and the great selection of soups.

Young Chow

420 S. 23rd St.,
Crystal City *(703) 892-2566*
$

Talk about a great place to kill some time during a long layover at very-nearby National Airport. Young Chow is a mere five minutes away (even less with a little luck), barely a block off Jefferson Davis Highway, but whether you're a local or from way out of town, you can depend on tasty Chinese food of the Szechuan, Hunan and Cantonese varieties. And of course, being in a veritable mecca of corporate and government offices, the take-out business is substantial.

Fairfax County

Tex-Mex/Southwestern

Anita's

9278 Old Keene Mill Rd.,
Burke *(703) 455-3466*
13921 Lee Jackson Hwy.,
Chantilly *(703) 378-1717*
701 Elden St., Herndon *(703) 481-1441*
10880 Lee Hwy., Fairfax *(703) 385-2965*
521 Maple Ave. East,
Vienna *(703) 255-1001*
147 Maple Ave. West,
Vienna *(703) 938-0888*
$

Vienna was the original home of this popular local chain of "New Mexico"-style Mexican food outlets, but the town couldn't keep Anita's to itself for long. Soon, other suburban communities began to experience what they were missing. While the fare may not satisfy Tex-Mex aficionados used to the zestier, eye-watering concoctions, it is nevertheless consistently good and inexpensive, the service efficient and the setting relaxed and inviting. You can't help but overdo it on the wonderful homemade chips and salsa before the entrees arrive, but be sure to leave room for the sweet, puffy sopapillas that begged to be topped with honey.

American/Continental

Ashgrove's

(at the Sheraton Premiere Tysons Corner)
8661 Leesburg Pike, Vienna (703) 448-1234
$$

The cylindrical glass edifice that is the Tysons Corner Sheraton Premiere is a national showcase property for the chain, so it's reassuring to know that they put such a heavy emphasis on quality at Ashgrove's, one of the hotel's two main restaurants. Offering an array of American specialties, Ashgrove's beckons with its lovely atrium setting, comfortable seating and top-notch service. A tremendous brunch buffet is laid out on Sunday as pianists, harpists and other musicians produce relaxing tunes to dine by.

Clyde's

11905 Market St., Reston (703) 787-6601
8332 Leesburg Pike,
Vienna (Tysons Corner) (703) 734-1900
$$

These suburban versions of the original District Clyde's have done well, to say the least. The older Tysons location and the newest one in Reston — a cornerstone establishment in the impressive and still-developing Town Center — have faithful patrons and are wildly popular happy hour and brunch destinations. (See the Washington listing for details.)

Devon Seafood Grill

8330 Boone Blvd.,
Vienna (Tysons Corner) (703) 442-0400
$$

Although tucked in the lower level (at the rear, no less!) of a Tysons Corner office building, just outside the Vienna limits, Devon stands out in a crowded field. Superb seafood selections and raw bar, a spirited happy hour and service to please all make for a pleasant outing no matter how you cut it.

Evans Farm Inn and Sitting Duck Pub

1696 Chain Bridge Rd.,
McLean (703) 356-8000
$$

Set on 40 acres of historic farmland along Route 123 in the shadows of downtown McLean, Evans Farm Inn has been a longtime favorite, particularly for special brunches and dinners with family, friends and business associates. Featuring American cuisine with flair, the specialties include fresh seafood, prime rib, Virginia's own Smithfield ham and other regional fare. The adjacent Sitting Duck Pub is fashioned after a British pub and features Tudor tables, dart boards, copper pitchers and a roaring fireplace in winter.

Falls Landing

774 Walker Rd.,
Great Falls (Village Center) (703) 759-4650
$$$

For years the focal point of seafood dining in Great Falls, the inimitable Falls Landing continues to impress with its wide range of selections, all fresh and expertly prepared and presented by an attentive and thoughtful staff. Standouts include swordfish, shrimp, crab and lobster; outstanding steak and veal are also available.

FEDORA CAFE

8521 Leesburg Pike,
Vienna (Tysons Corner) (703) 556-0100
$$

Fedora Cafe is a truly fun, "elegantly casual" destination for first-rate sandwiches, pasta and salads. A great happy-hour crowd enlivens things weekday evenings while Friday and Saturday nights draw a fair share of the 20s and 30s set.

HEART IN HAND

7145 Main St.,
Clifton (703) 830-4111
$$

A favorite of former First Lady Nancy Reagan, romantic Heart in Hand specializes in American cuisine with an elegant Southern touch. Any of the fish and meat selections are especially tasty. You can't help but get sentimental and warm all over as you're served in a historic building in this tiny and charming one-stoplight community, the heart of Fairfax County's affluent horse country.

HERMITAGE INN

7134 Main St.,
Clifton (703) 266-1623
$$$

Just across the street from the town's other top restaurant, romance also lingers at Hermitage Inn, housed in a former hotel visited by presidents, including Grant and Hayes. The French country cuisine served in a gracious and genteel atmosphere is pricey indeed, but worth it.

J. R.'S STOCKYARDS INN

8130 Watson St.,
McLean (Tysons Corner) (703) 893-3390
$

There's more to the Tysons Corner area than great shopping. Great beef, for instance, at J. R.'s Stockyards Inn. The beef is all fresh from the family-owned packing plant and it's aged and cut in-house. Try their fresh seafood, chicken, lamb chops, barbecue or gourmet salads. A private banquet room for up to 100 is available.

KILROY'S

5250 Port Royal Rd.,
Springfield (703) 321-7733
$$

Great steaks, burgers and pasta, a lively bar, big-screen TV, dancing to a DJ's tunes, and it's all just a few hundred yards off the Beltway. Kilroy's has long been a favorite nightspot for the West Springfield/Annandale crowds and, with Wakefield Park just down the street, an especially popular gathering place for thirsty athletes during the summer softball season.

MARKET STREET BAR & GRILL

(at the Hyatt Regency Reston Town Center)
1800 Presidents St., Reston (703) 709-6262
$$$

The Hyatt Regency looms tall above Reston's impressive Town Center, which makes it easy to find your way to the hotel's first-rate restaurant, the Market Street Bar & Grill. Accented by an open grill and colorful paintings, the attractive dining area serves up some remarkably good pasta, seafood selections and soups. And, as always seems the case in outdoor-crazy Reston, a delightful stroll awaits you in the Town Center afterwards.

The Palm Court

(at Westfield's Conference Resort)
14750 Conference Center Dr.,
Chantilly *(703) 818-3522*
$$

Housed in the gorgeous Georgian-style mansion that is the heart of the Westfield's conference center and hotel, The Palm Court is worth the drive into western Fairfax. Even before you sit down to eat you'll be able to enjoy the rolling, manicured lawns and the building's gorgeous antique furnishings. Expect elegant dining with live piano music, tableside preparation and extensive selections of Continental and modern American favorites, including Caesar salad, lobster bisque, rack of lamb, duck and a bevy of sinful desserts.

Rick Walker's Scoreboard

724 Pine St., Herndon *(703)689-2880*
10334 Lee Hwy.,
Fairfax City *(703)352-8888*
$

Owned by former Redskin tight end Rick "Doc" Walker, the Scoreboard chain has become a hit on the sports-bar scene. When you're not catching the game on one of the TVs, swigging a cold draft beer or grabbing a handful of saloon appetizer, try the great barbecue ribs, burgers, prime rib, steaks or a variety of seafood.

Vienna Inn

120 Maple Ave. West,
Vienna *(703) 938-9548*
$

This place is a local legend, to say the least. Family owned and operated for over 30 years, the Vienna Inn is one of those places that begins to seem like an old friend as the years go by. You can always count on it, and some things will never, ever change. From the wobbly booths and the chipped Formica tabletops, to the loose door handle and the menu items handwritten on the back of paper plates and tacked to the wall, to the delicious but not-so-healthful chili dogs, hamburgers, crispy french fries and ice-cold draft beer at bargain prices, to the sometimes-gruff help and the honor system under which you're often asked by a waitress before paying your tab, "What did you have?" it's easy to see why the Vienna Inn has long been rated by many to be the Metro area's best neighborhood saloon. And if the faithful have their way, little will have changed 30 years from now.

International

Culmore

6037 Leesburg Pike,
Falls Church *(703) 820-7171*
$$

You wouldn't know it from the name, but Culmore is a Persian restaurant, and one of Northern Virginia's finest at that. The casual atmosphere and good service complement the Persian specialties featuring meat and vegetable kebabs, various stews, chicken, beef, lamb and seafood dishes, and of course the wonders of eggplant and zucchini. A real live belly dancer entertains on weekends.

Ho's Dynasty

6003-D Burke Centre Pkwy.,
Burke *(703) 250-8000*
$

Here's further proof that you can get superb Chinese food in the 'burbs — even in a small shopping center in the quiet, wooded, "planned" community of Burke. Hunan, Szechuan and Cantonese specialties are offered in a casual yet refined setting. And as always seems to be the case with Asian restaurants, the service is friendly and first-rate.

Il Cigno

1617 Washington Plaza,
Reston *(703) 471-0121*
$$

Enjoy outstanding pasta and other Italian delights along the shore of beautiful Lake Anne. The elegant setting includes an outdoor dining area in spring and summer. The adjoining cafe offers lighter fare. Afterwards, take a stroll around the lake and check out the Village Center as you burn off some of those calories.

L'Auberge Chez Francois

332 Springvale Rd.,
Great Falls *(703) 759-3800*
$$$

Ignore what few nay-sayers there are and remember this: it's worth the drive. Accessible only by a twisting two-lane road—one of many in woodsy, fashionable and oh-so-affluent Great Falls — L'Auberge Chez Francois continues to reap awards and praise as the years go by yet never seems to falter in its appeal. The divine menu selections, especially the seafood, duck and veal entrees, are made even more inviting with generous portions, a gracious staff and the restaurant's unmistakable country-inn warmth and romance that permeates the soul. Reservations (sometimes a week or more in advance) are nearly always a must, but L'Auberge Chez Francois is the kind of place you anticipate with a smile.

Le Canard

132 Branch Rd.,
Vienna *(703) 281-0070*
$$$

First-rate French dining in quiet, downtown Vienna, that's Le Canard. The intimate restaurant, tucked into the corner of a shopping center just off Route 123, offers superb selections of seafood, fowl and game. Nightly entertainment at the piano bar is a nice touch.

Nizam's

523 Maple Ave. West,
Vienna *(703) 938-8948*
$$

Chalk up another point for little Vienna, home to yet another first-class dining spot. You'll find plenty of people who will argue that Nizam's is the region's best Turkish restaurant. Small, and attractive, Nizam's does wonders with such delicacies as marinated lamb, various beef dishes, stuffed grape leaves and assorted eggplant specialties.

Old Brogue Irish Pub

760-C Walker Rd.,
Great Falls *(703) 759-3309*
$

As reliable as one of those stout beers from the Emerald Isle, the Old Brogue Irish Pub masterfully blends dining and entertainment. A favorite of some of the powerful, rich and famous who call Great Falls home, the cozy Old Brogue serves up great burgers, soups, sandwiches and salads, and beckons further with a dart board and live folk music on two stages — in the front room and in back. And believe it when the regulars tell you to get here early if you want to have any chance of squeezing into the place for the St. Patrick's Day celebration.

TORTILLA FACTORY

648 Elden St.,
Herndon *(703) 471-1156*
$

Other parts of the region will hopefully have a Tortilla Factory to call their own some day, but until then, it's worth a trip to this small town near Dulles Airport. Tacos, fajitas, enchiladas, burritos, nachos, salsa, the Tortilla Factory prepares it all in the zesty Sonoran tradition. And the results are memorable. Plus, you get a ton for the money and the setting is casual and friendly. Let the branching out of the Tortilla Factory begin!

Loudoun County

American/Continental

BARON'S III

(at the Best Western Hotel)
726 E. Market St., Leesburg(703) 777-9400
$$

American favorites — steaks, seafood, sandwiches and the like — at decent prices are the standard fare here. The Best Western Hotel is conveniently located in the heart of Leesburg near the historic district.

BUFFALO WING FACTORY & DELI

45529 W. Church Rd.,
Sterling *(703) 430-9179*
$

Spicy wings and hearty sandwiches beckon at this popular spot in eastern Loudoun. A particularly big draw for the weekday lunch crowds.

THE COACH STOP

9 East Washington St.,
Middleburg *(703) 687-5515*
$$

The Coach Stop has been a longtime favorite gathering spot in Middleburg for the famous and not-so-famous locals alike. Serving breakfast, lunch and dinner seven days a week, the restaurant features homemade specialties such as crab cakes, prime rib, Virginia country ham, seafood and tantalizing desserts. The onion rings and genuine milkshakes are musts, although not necessarily at the same time.

HIDDEN HORSE TAVERN

7 West Washington St.,
Middleburg *(703) 687-3828*
$$

As is the case with many structures in history-rich Middleburg, the one that the seafood restaurant Hidden Horse Tavern calls home has an interesting story all its own. It was a one-time cellar and coal bin for the original building known as the Colonial Inn dating to 1787. During the Civil War, John Mosby and assorted Middleburg residents used the cellar to hide their best horses from Union troops. But seafood lovers will surely want to head straight for the dining room, the outdoor terrace or cozy up to the fireplace.

Johnson's Charcoal Beef House

401 E. Market St.,
Leesburg (703) 777-1116
$$

Filet mignon, prime rib, a range of fresh seafood selections and Virginia country ham dominate the menu at Johnson's Charcoal Beef House. Breakfast, lunch and dinner are offered, capped each day by a nightly special. Be sure to get an up-close look at the extensive antique gun collection.

Mosby's Tavern

2 West Marshall St.,
Leesburg (703) 687-5282
$$

Mosby's Tavern boasts a casual setting, but the contemporary menu is much more involved. From fresh-dough pizza to Tex-Mex delights and a wide variety of appetizers, burgers and sandwiches, Mosby's Tavern has been a longtime favorite in Leesburg and beyond. Daily lunch and dinner specials, Saturday and Sunday brunch and live entertainment are featured. And if you can manage to push yourself away from the table long enough, stop by the game room for billiards and video games. This is also a popular after-race gathering spot for the horsey set.

The Red Fox Inn

2 East Washington St.,
Middleburg (703) 687-6301
$$$

Established in 1728, this country inn and tavern is one of Middleburg's oldest and best-known establishments. A variety of Continental and American cuisine is featured, whether the meal is a country breakfast, a hearty luncheon or a romantic candlelight dinner served in one of seven cozy dining rooms. The wine list boasts many selections from local vineyards.

Tuscarora Mill

203 Harrison St., Leesburg (703) 771-9300
$$

Seafood, beef, poultry and wild game are prime features on the menu at popular Tuscarora Mill, one of Leesburg's oldest and best-loved dining spots. After eating, be sure to leave time to explore some of the town's fascinating nooks and crannies from this convenient starting point.

International

Knossos

341 E. Market St.,
Leesburg (703) 771-9231
$

Some of the best homemade Greek food around can be found at Knossos. Gyros are a specialty. A friendly staff and prompt service help make for a complete dining experience and a welcome change from the ordinary.

Prince William County

American/Continental

Hero's American Restaurant

9412 Main St.,
Manassas *(703) 330-1534*
$

Good ol' American food — burgers, subs, sandwiches, that sort of thing — is the staple at Hero's. Families, lunching office workers, budget-conscious couples, the appeal is widespread and the satisfaction great.

Occoquan Inn

301 Mill St.,
Occoquan *(703) 491-1888*
$$

Occoquan Inn is another of the town's dining stars. Traditional Virginia countryside cuisine is served up by an efficient staff, in an elegant setting, at reasonable prices.

Pilot House

16216 Neabsco Rd.,
Woodbridge *(703) 221-1010*
$$

Steaks and seafood reign supreme at Pilot House. But also look for outstanding soups and salads, tempting appetizers and a dessert selection that will make you want to stay even longer than you'd planned.

Red Hot & Blue

8637 Sudley Rd.,
Manassas *(703) 330-4847*
$

If you're not a fan of Memphis-style barbecue when you walk in, you most certainly will be when you walk out. Red Hot and Blue just has that affect on people. (See the Montgomery County, Md., listing for a complete rundown of what to expect.)

International

Cafe Rochambeau

310 Commerce St.,
Occoquan *(703)494-1165*
$$

With Cafe Rochambeau, the tiny waterside community of Occoquan can proudly boast of having some outstanding country French cuisine. The veal, beef, fowl and seafood selections are most notable. If time permits, make a day of it in Occoquan and explore the neat shops, boutiques and other establishments.

Carmello's

9108 Center St.,
Manassas *(703) 368-5522*
$$

Carmello's gives you Northern Italian cuisine prepared the way it should be. This restaurant is the focal point in the immediate area for pasta and other delicious specialties from afar.

Cervantes

16918 Dumfries Rd.,
Dumfries *(703) 221-7803*
$$$

It doesn't require a drive into the District to taste some fine Spanish food. Cervantes fits the bill just fine, and the prices may surprise you.

Suburban Maryland

Anne Arundel County (Annapolis)

Regional

BUDDY'S CRABS AND RIBS
100 Main St. *(410) 626-1100*
$

If you can get past the superb hickory-fired ribs and the famed Maryland blue crabs, you'll find plenty of other seafood and beef delights at Buddy's. We know it sounds like a tough challenge, but somebody's got to try. This family restaurant also features an excellent raw bar, a Sunday brunch buffet and plenty of TVs (including a jumbo-screen job) strategically placed throughout to keep patrons informed and entertained.

CARROLL'S CREEK
410 Severn Ave. *(410) 269-1406; 263-8102*
$$

For a waterfront location with a superb view of historic Annapolis, head for Carroll's Creek — the restaurant, that is. The regional American seafood here is a clear winner; so are the Sunday brunch, the outside cafe and the free parking.

MARMADUKES PUB
301 Severn Ave. *(410) 269-5420*
$

Sailing World Magazine proclaimed Marmadukes Pub "one of the top 10 sailor's pubs in the world for its food and drink." What more of a recommendation could you ask for in water- and boat-crazed Annapolis? The homecooked beef and seafood dishes are tops, but be sure to at least inquire about the daily specials. On Friday and Saturday, stay around for the Broadway singalong.

MCGARVEY'S SALOON AND OYSTER BAR
8 Market Space *(410) 263-5700*
$

Home of Aviator's beer (in honor of the Naval Academy perhaps?), McGarvey's bills itself as a traditional saloon and oyster bar and that's what you'll find. A full menu is available until 1 AM all week, although you won't be asked to leave until 2 AM Monday through Saturday. Come back Sunday for the brunch.

MIDDLETON TAVERN OYSTER BAR AND RESTAURANT
2 Market Space *(410) 263-3323*
$$

The historic City Dock is rife with diversions for locals and tourists alike, but Middleton Tavern is a standout. After all, this was a favorite haunt of George Washington and Ben Franklin, so it must be OK (not to mention old). Serving traditional Maryland fare in an 18th-century setting, here you'll find atmospheres that range from casual to formal; choose the sidewalk cafe, raw bar or fireside dining. And by all means muster the courage to down a world-famous Oyster Shooter. Live entertainment appears nightly.

Treaty of Paris Restaurant

(at the Maryland Inn)
16 Church Cir. *(410) 263-2641*
$$

You'll be hard pressed not to give in to the temptations at Treaty of Paris, serving up the perfect blend of Maryland cooking and American gourmet cuisine in an 18th-century dining room. Leave room in your plans for the legendary Sunday brunch, maybe the best in all of the Free State.

American/Continental

The Corinthian

(at the Loews Annapolis Hotel)
126 West St. *(410) 263-1299*
$$

Upscale, stylish and elegant, the critically acclaimed Corinthian has been recently renovated, but the food sure didn't need any fixing. Best bets are the steaks and other beef selections as well as the ocean- and Bay-fresh seafood.

Harry Browne's

66 State Cir. *(410) 263-4332*
$

Surf or turf, or something in between, Harry Brown's is a contender for lunch, Sunday brunch, dinner or just entertainment in the lounge. For a change of pace, try the on- and off-premises catering, even for tailgate parties.

O'Learys

310 Third St. *(410) 263-0884*
$$

Some have tagged this as the best seafood restaurant in Annapolis. That, of course, is always open to debate, but no matter the ranking you choose, O'Learys will certainly leave you with a good impression, particularly in the stomach area. The fresh-fish selection changes daily, and the prime rib is the size of a Buick. Pick your preparation be it mesquite-grilled, poached, sauteed, blackened or baked. There are innovative nightly specials to boot.

Rustic Inn

1803 West St. *(410) 263-2626/1983*
$$

The Rustic Inn is not a misnomer. Elegant, warm, intimate and, yes, even rustic, this is a dependable spot for a number of dining options of the American, French and Swiss varieties with gourmet twists. Seafood, naturally, is a popular feature. Expect nothing but wholesome and natural ingredients.

International

Papazee's Authentic Thai Cuisine

257 West St. *(410) 263-8424*
$$

Annapolis isn't all seafood. Or at least not all traditional American seafood. See what we mean by trying Papazee's for creative Thai cuisine in a friendly atmosphere. To be sure, you can indeed find assorted seafood selections including crispy fish and something called hot pot. And if you yearn to learn how to do this sort of thing at home, attend the cooking class offered on Sundays.

Montgomery County

Regional

Bethesda Crab House

4958 Bethesda Ave.,
Bethesda *(301) 652-3382*
$

Famed Chesapeake Bay crabs, yes, but Bethesda Crab House is also a popular late-night dining option; open 'til midnight daily. Virtually any of the seafood selections are winners here, though, so don't think you've got to stick with the crabs. Then again, when in Maryland. . . .

Cottonwood Cafe

4844 Cordell Ave.,
Bethesda *(301) 656-4844*
$$

Cottonwood Cafe showcases cuisine that is truly indigenous to the American Southwest. Expect Tex-Mex fare with a taste all its own. The secret? Traditional herbs and spices combined with an open-grill preparation. It may not be much of a secret, but it helps Cottonwood Cafe stand out in a crowd.

Crisfield's

8012 Georgia Ave.,
Silver Spring *(301) 589-1306*
$$$

If your namesake is the tiny Maryland community that claims to be the crab capital of the solar system, you'd better serve some world-class crabs. Crisfield does, not to mention a trawler's worth of other nautical treasures. Going strong after nearly 50 years in business, Crisfield continues to impress. When in Ocean City, Md., give Crisfield's II a try. Your palate will thank you just the same.

Louisiana Express Company

4921 Bethesda Ave.,
Bethesda *(301) 652-6945*
$

No, you haven't been transported back to "Lew-zee-ann-uh." It just seems that way at Louisiana Express Company, where authentic Cajun treats — crawfish, po' boys, jambalaya, softshell-crab sandwiches, the works — are served up in a down-home atmosphere. Stop by early for a full breakfast, or on Sunday for a knockout brunch.

Rio Grande Cafe

4919 Fairmont Ave.,
Bethesda *(301) 656-2981*
$$

Waiting in line isn't the only thing you can count on at any of the area's Rio Grande Cafe locations. Tex-Mex fare extraordinaire is also in the offing. Old standbys including tacos, enchiladas, burritos and nachos will keep the traditionalists happy, but don't hesitate to leap into selections as diverse as frog legs, shrimp, quail and ribs. Different strokes for different folks, indeed, but satisfaction for all.

American/Continental

Bethesda Theatre Cafe

7719 Wisconsin Ave.,
Bethesda *(301) 656-3283*
$

Here's what you do with an old movie theater: take out the regular seats, add tables, chairs and counters in a tiered format, and serve deli chow (pizza, burgers, sandwiches, chips, etc.) and drink (pitchers of beer), restaurant style, as patrons enjoy the flick at a bargain price — that is, until you include the food and beverage tab. Believe us, we didn't include this one for the cuisine, but rather the unique experience offered both here and at a similar restaurant, the Cinema 'N' Draft House in Arlington. A uniquely fun night out, especially for couples and groups.

Bethesda Metro Center Food Court

3 Bethesda Metro Center,
Bethesda *(301) 652-4988*
$

We include this primarily for its unique setting, combining modern transportation with good eats at semi-reasonable prices. Talk about convenience, the food court features 11 restaurants with an array of international cuisine. Year round entertainment in the center includes dancing under the stars to an orchestra every Friday evening, May through September.

Blair Mansion Inn

7711 Eastern Ave.,
Silver Spring *(301) 588-1688*
$$

Warmth, cheer and history rolled into one — that's the Blair Mansion Inn, where the American cuisine has been prepared under the direction of the Zeender family for over 30 years. Seafood, steaks, pasta and the salads are best bets.

Hard Times Cafe

1117 Nelson St.,
Rockville *(301) 294-9720*
$

Chili, chili and more chili, with a range of varieties and spices to please even the most ardent fan of the delicious brown, tangy concoction. Some are prepared far differently than others, but the constant throughout is quality and taste. Just watch out for those multi-alarmers, though. Be sure to have plenty of beer on hand to extinguish the flames. Whether you're here or at the Old Town Alexandria location, the buzz words are relaxed, casual and anything but a hard time.

Hazelton's

(at the Gaithersburg Marriott)
620 Perry Pkwy.,
Gaithersburg *(301) 977-8900, ext. 6670*
$

There's nothing really to write home about here except that it's good quality food at affordable prices in a casual setting. What more could you ask of a hotel eatery? If you can think of something, the friendly folks at Hazelton's will probably deliver.

Hamburger Hamlet

10400 Old Georgetown Rd.,
Bethesda *(301) 897-8660*
$

Nothing's changed since our first mention of this landmark earlier in this chapter. Hamburger Hamlet remains as revered as ever with the ground-beef crowd. Please refer to the District of Columbia listing for a recap.

Normandie Farm

10701 Falls Rd.,
Potomac *(301) 983-8838*
$$$

You're not far away at Normandie Farm. It just feels that way. This Potomac landmark has lost nothing through the years; you can still count on delicious American cuisine in a gracious, warm and romantic setting reminiscent of a country inn. If you can't decide on a menu selection, try the $16.50 buffet.

O'Brien's Pit Barbecue

387 East Gude Dr.,
Rockville *(301) 340-8596*
$

Casual and inexpensive, O'Brien's boasts some of the tastiest Texas-style barbecue around, especially the beef and chicken. And there's plenty of competition in the rough-and-tumble world of barbecue eateries. It's not uncommon even for Virginians to drive all the way over and enjoy it along with everyone else. Or they could stay closer to home and try the Springfield location.

O'Donnell's Sea Grill

8301 Wisconsin Ave.,
Bethesda *(301) 656-6200*
$$

At O'Donnell's, a Washington tradition for some 70 years, the accent is firmly on fresh seafood, whether it's lunch or dinner, seven days a week. It's hard to resist such specialties as crab imperial, broiled lump crab cakes and other specialties highlighting the shelled delicacy, but the numerous steak and chicken selections don't disappoint either. A bakery on the premises produces treats that make it hard to push away from the table until you've tried one.

Old Angler's Inn

10801 McArthur Blvd.,
Potomac *(301) 299-9097; 365-2425*
$$$

The prices are the most glaring negative of Old Angler's Inn, but then again, when you consider the setting, the service and wonderful menu selections such as lamb, quail, rabbit and scallops, the financial bite seems somehow less painful. This historic restaurant, sitting snugly beneath the trees across the street from the C&O Canal towpath, radiates romance and enchantment, particularly after a lazy walk or a brisk jog along the canal. Cozy up next to the roaring fireplace in fall and winter, and enjoy patio dining in spring and summer. Back inside, the spiral staircase leads to a quiet dining area where the mood continues to captivate.

Silver Diner

11806 Rockville Pike,
Rockville *(301) 770-2832*
$

In a nutshell, Silver Diner is real home cooking at real fair prices. Special features are the all-day breakfast and the early bird dinner specials. The late hours also make Silver Diner a favorite stop of night owls. Open daily, 6:30 AM-2 AM.

Tarragon's

(at the Gaithersburg Marriott)
620 Perry Pkwy.,
Gaithersburg (301) 977-8900, ext. 6671
$$

Hotel dining can indeed be a hit-or-miss proposition; at Tarragon's, it's a hit, but only at dinner because that's all they serve. Surf and turf selections, salads, soups, pastas, seasonal specialties with the freshest ingredients, this is elegant dining in a setting of welcome repose.

International

Andalucia

12300 Wilkins Ave.,
Rockville (301)770-1880
$$$

Rockville has a Spanish star in Andalucia, which serves up consistently wonderful food (emphasizing the gastronomic delights of southern Spain) with the grace and flair of a matador. Don't overindulge in the outstanding appetizers because you have to save room for such specialties as veal, swordfish and snails. Oh yes, and don't overindulge in those entrees either because the desserts — especially the cakes — are a delightful way to top it all off.

Armadilla Grill

8011 Woodmont Ave.,
Bethesda (301) 907-9637
$

Yes, that "a" at the end of Armadilla IS correct. But besides spelling, there's a much more compelling reason why you'll remember this place: its authentic New Mexican, Native American, Southwestern and vegetarian cuisine that has won praise for good reason. And it's casual and inexpensive, two other ingredients that please many diners. Virginians not wanting to make the cross-river trek can enjoy the Fairfax County location at 14201 Sullyfield Cir., Chantilly.

El Caribe of Bethesda

8130 Wisconsin Ave.,
Bethesda (301) 656-0888
$$

Latin American and Spanish fare is the focus at this award-winning restaurant and bar. There's excellent seafood and steaks in particular.

Fellini's

(at the Bethesda Hyatt Regency)
One Bethesda Metro Center(301) 657-1234
$$

It's not a literal translation, but Fellini's means contemporary Italian cuisine. Indulge in pasta, scallops, lamb, veal, artichoke hearts or one of the other memorable specialties. Sorry, but the inhabitants of the 200-gallon exotic-fish tank are not on the menu. And generous helpings mean you actually have to try and leave room for dessert. If you happen to eschew public transportation (Metrorail comes practically to the front door), there's complimentary valet parking.

Flanagan's Irish Pub

7637 Old Georgetown Rd.,
Bethesda (301) 986-1007
$

Grab a brew and a bowl of their award-winning Irish stew and you'll quickly settle into the routine at Flanagan's. Better-than-ordinary pub fare in an enchanting atmosphere spells return trips time and again.

Good Fortune

2646 University Blvd. West,
Wheaton *(301) 929-8818*
$

Good Fortune has earned a name for itself in the local world of Cantonese cuisine. And it's so affordable it's too good to be true. An exhaustive menu may require more time than usual to peruse, but if you lack the patience, you can't go wrong with any of the selections featuring lobster, duck and fish, or the interesting casserole creations and spectacular stuffed mushrooms.

Hunan Pearl

12137 Darnestown Rd.,
Gaithersburg *(301) 330-8118*
$

You'll find consistently good Chinese fare at this convenient location. As crowded a field as it is, Hunan Pearl manages to distance itself just a bit from some of the formidable suburban competition.

Il Pizzico

15209 Frederick Rd.,
Rockville *(301) 309-0610*
$

In the world of restaurants, high quality at low prices seems to be oxymoronic more often than it is true. But not at the cozy and family-like Il Pizzico, where affordable, delicious Italian cuisine are the benchmarks of success and praise. While the menu is not expansive, you can hardly go wrong, especially with the veal, fish and pasta selections. Or ask about the daily specials, the wine list and, lest we forget, the desserts.

Matuba

4918 Cordell Ave.,
Bethesda *(301) 652-7449*
$

For top-notch Japanese cuisine at bargain prices, Matuba can certainly dish it out. Try any of the fabulous sushi or tempura, especially at lunchtime, for a refreshing change of pace. When in Arlington, try them at 2915 Columbia Pike.

Sabang

2504 Ennalls Ave.,
Wheaton *(301) 942-7859/7874*
$

If you enjoy Thai, Vietnamese or virtually any other Asian cuisine, you'll like Indonesian. The trouble is in finding a restaurant that serves it. Well, you needn't look any farther than Wheaton's Sabang for inexpensive, delicious creations in this unique gastronomic genre. Any of the grilled fishes are particularly outstanding as are the seafood, chicken and beef selections.

Sam Woo

1054 Rockville Pike,
Rockville *(301) 424-0495*
$$

Sam Woo's selections are among the area's best Korean cuisine (grilled at your table if you'd like), including main-course soups and casseroles, many that are sure to please seafood lovers. Or, choose from an extensive selection of Japanese entrees including chicken teriyaki, sushi and tempura. Try the weekday buffet for a truly different kind of lunch break.

SEVEN SEAS CHINESE RESTAURANT

1776 East Jefferson St.,
Rockville *(301) 770-5020*
$$

Seafood is the specialty here, and you know it's fresh from the minute you walk in and spot the large fish tank full of ocean delicacies. Serving both traditional Chinese and Japanese fare including Dim Sum and sushi.

SUNNY GARDEN

1302 East Gude Dr.,
Rockville *(301) 762-7477*
$

Taiwanese food seems a likely candidate for that hard-to-find restaurant category, but one visit to Sunny Garden and you'll wonder why. In fact, you'll probably find more familiar items than you expect since Taiwanese cooking incorporates some of the Chinese-American style so familiar to so many people. Seafood (even eel!) and vegetable specialties in particular help make Sunny Garden a bright spot on the list.

TAKO GRILL

7756 Wisconsin Ave.,
Bethesda *(301) 652-7030*
$

Yes, Bethesda, Tako Grill lives up to its billing. Be it sushi, teriyaki, main-course soups, an array of heavy-on-the-vegetables selections or something in between, Tako Grill spans the spectrum of Japanese cuisine.

THAI ORCHID

8519 Fenton St.,
Silver Spring *(301) 587-2192*
$$

Thai Orchid has bloomed nicely since coming to Silver Spring. Creative and savory selections, fair prices, attentive service and comfortable environs join ranks to make a winner.

WURZBURG HAUS

7236 Muncaster Mill Rd.,
Rockville *(301) 330-0402*
$$

Tough to tell what the specialty is here, isn't it? Thoroughly irresistible and thoroughly German, Wurzburg Haus never fails to please with its spirited Bavarian atmosphere and delicious but calorie-laden feasts of veal, beef, venison, pork, chicken and, of course, the potato pancakes, schnitzels, dumplings and strudel. And oh yes, the wonderful German beers. To further the European theme, a real live accordionist entertains on Friday and Saturday nights.

Prince George's County

American/Continental

JASPER'S

7401 Greenbelt Rd.,
Greenbelt *(301) 441-8030*
$

Can't decide? Not to worry. Jasper's offers American, seafood, Italian and Mexican fare, plus homemade desserts to top it all off. Try the Sunday buffet to satisfy the extra-large appetite.

Lamberts

10825 Lanham-Severn Rd.,
Glendale *(301) 262-2206*
$

Seafood is the word at Lamberts. Fresh, delicious and prepared in so many different ways, but all will please.

Red Hot & Blue

677 Main St.,
Laurel *(301) 953-1943*
$

Red Hot & Blue dishes out what many will adamantly argue is far and away the area's best Memphis-style barbecue, and in a memorabilia-packed setting that pays homage to its roots. It's lean, succulent and full of flavor no matter how you slice it: as smoked pork ribs and shoulders, the variety barbecue platters or any of the pulled-pork and chicken sandwiches. Even the side orders such as beans, fries and slaw are worth savoring. Crowds are a given here, especially on weekends, so just sit back, relax and take in the sights, sounds and smells because you know it's worth the wait.

International

Pho 75

1510 University Blvd. East,
Langley Park *(301) 434-7844*
$

This is the prime destination in Langley Park for contemporary Vietnamese cuisine. Reliable, friendly and affordable, like so many of its Asian counterparts, Pho 75 is a welcome change from the fast-food, burger-and-fry joints that call the area home.

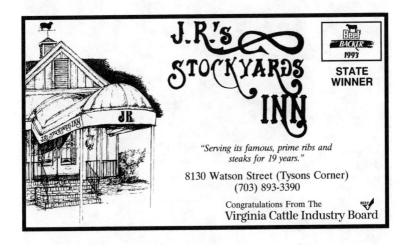

Photo: Willie Redd

Dancing the night away at area night clubs is a favorite activity.

Inside Metro Washington Nightlife

In a place where shuffling papers and climbing corporate ladders could be forms of recreation, and starched shirts and leather pumps are considered *de rigueur* fashions, nightlife may not seem like a top priority for many people. Well, believe it or not, even stressed-out, career-minded Washingtonians know how to have a good time away from the office, embracing the "work hard/play hard" philosophy with ample gusto.

While the nightlife here is plentiful and diverse, don't expect a heavy dose of L.A.-style glitz or New York-style up-'til-dawn bizarreness. Instead, similar to the dining scene, after-hours diversions in Metro Washington include a little bit of everything, from cutting-edge music halls and standup-comedy venues, to funky watering holes, sports saloons, yuppified fern bars and high-energy dance clubs.

First, a few things to keep in mind before venturing out for an evening on the town. As a general rule, the District offers the widest variety of nightlife, but you can almost always expect to pay a bit more for such things as drinks, cover charges and live entertainment. Case in point: single beers approaching the $4 mark are not unheard of, especially at some of the city's tonier clubs. And if they don't get you at the bar, there's a good chance you paid for it at the door. Sometimes, you may get nailed both places, but then, no one ever said socializing was a recommended way to save money. Suburban establishments, meanwhile, are generally a bit less expensive, but in some cases they lag well behind their urban counterparts in the character and atmosphere departments.

"Last call for alcohol," as the saying goes, is typically around 2 AM in the city, 1 or 1:30 in the 'burbs. Some of the downtown haunts may not finish shooing people out the door until 3 or 4 AM.

Incredibly, soft drinks aren't always that much cheaper than booze at many bars and clubs in Metro Washington, although they certainly should be in this age of heightened awareness about the lunacy of drinking and driving. Some places do, however, occasionally offer free unlimited non-alcoholic beverages to the designated driver in a group, so it pays (in more ways than one) to inquire. The drinking age, by the way, is 21 in the District, Maryland and Virginia for beer, wine and liquor. And even those who are well past the legal age but blessed with youthful looks shouldn't be surprised if they're "carded" on a regular basis. The scourge of underage drinking and the increasingly tough penalties levied against those who serve minors have convinced many business owners — grocery, convenience and liquor store operators included — to be extra cautious about who's buying. So take the request for an ID as a compliment, not an insult.

For weekly updates on what's happening on the local nightlife scene, we recommend the "Weekend" and "Washington Weekend" sections of *The Washington Post* and *The Washington Times*, respectively. Both supplements include expansive listings of clubs, shows, special events and other pertinent information. The *Post* publishes its guide on Friday, the *Times's* on Thursday, a strategy that the paper says helps you get a jump on planning those blessed two days of freedom. Whether or not that's true, it sure makes sense to us. We happen to know some people who start thinking about the upcoming weekend on Monday.

As with the dining section, this is far from an exhaustive roundup of Metro Washington night spots, and again for the most part we've avoided listing hotel and chain establishments in an effort to emphasize the local spots, including many of our personal favorites. Entries bearing an asterisk (*) beside their name are also covered in the restaurant chapter, so please refer to that section for more details.

District of Columbia

While areas such as Capitol Hill, Adams Morgan and the F Street corridor have emerged as after-hours destinations in their own right, Georgetown has long been the city's undisputed mecca of nightlife. And that distinction isn't likely to change any time soon.

From the hub at Wisconsin Avenue and M Street NW — the famous intersection where many Super Bowl victory celebrations, Halloween parties and New Year's Eve bashes have spilled into the streets — bars, nightclubs and all manner of other nocturnal destinations radiate in every direction. One of the city's most venerable nightlife establishments sits across from the waterfront beneath the Whitehurst Freeway at 3135 K Street, near the foot of Wisconsin Avenue. With its time-worn brick facade and modest neon sign, **The Bayou** (202-333-2897) is a live-music institution if there ever was one in Washington. This unpretentious, 500-seat nightclub features top-name national rock bands as well as plenty of local talent, but don't always expect to be able to buy a ticket at the door. Convenient parking for The Bayou as well as **Chadwicks*** (202-333-2565), less than a block down the street at 3205 K, can be had curbside, if you're lucky, or at one of the surface lots or numerous garages nearby.

While you're in the neighborhood, wander over to the opposite side of K Street and check out snazzy Washington Harbour where a cluster of shops and restaurants occupies the lower level of a high-priced condominium complex. If nothing else, be sure to take in one of the city's best riverfront views, a sweeping vista with the elegant Kennedy Center looming to the south and graceful Key Bridge linking the city with Rosslyn just to the north. Not surprisingly, outdoor dining and shoreline strolling are prime warm-weather activities here. Nightlife choices at Washington Harbour include **The River Club** (3223 K St. NW, 202-965-3229 or 202-333-8118), an upscale Art Deco dinner-and-dance place that caters to an older crowd with DJ tunes and live jazz, and the more laid back **Jaimalito's Cantina** (3000 K St. NW, 202-944-4400), where you can count on icy margaritas, cold beer and spicy Tex-Mex cuisine.

Heading back up Wisconsin Avenue, the aptly named **Blues Alley** (1073 Wisconsin Ave. NW, 202-337-4141) sits tucked away down an alley just a short ways up on the right. For decades this intimate supper club has been the city's top spot for the best in local and national jazz and blues acts. Reservations are a must, especially on weekends and when top talent is on the bill.

Staying on Wisconsin and crossing M Street, the first alleyway on the left is home to yet another cornerstone of Washington nightlife, **Champions*** (1206 Wisconsin Ave. NW, 202-965-4005), the city's premier sports bar that has sprouted several branches outside the city. DJs provide the music to which hordes of 20- and 30-something patrons drink and gyrate, but TV sports will always be a prime activity here, especially Redskins games and other events of strong local interest. Several blocks up, **Grog and Tankard** (2408 Wisconsin Ave. NW, 202-333-3114) features a wide variety of local music talent, but it's also just a great place to enjoy a beer and some munchies.

For an evening of irreverent, politically charged humor, check out **Chelsea's** (1055 Thomas Jefferson St. NW, 202-298-8222) where the popular local comedy troupe The Capitol Steps appears regularly. No matter who's in the White House or which party controls Congress, this hilarious group of performers never has to worry about a shortage of material.

Wherever you wander in Georgetown, be sure to do some people-watching; it's a target-rich environment to say the least. A few more of our favorites in this part of town include several other denizens of frenetic M Street such as **Mr. Smith's*** at 3104 (202-333-3104), boasting a wonderful piano bar inside and an open-air patio out back; ever-popular **Clyde's*** at 3236 (202-333-9180); **J. Paul's** at 3218 (202-333-3450), where the raw bar is top-notch and the street-front windows open wide during spring and summer; **Paul Mall** at 3235 (202-965-5353), a particular favorite of the 20s set where they boogie to live hard rock and Top 40 tunes; and **Winston's** at 3295 (202-333-3150), a singles magnet with legendary college theme nights.

On the fringes of Georgetown, **The Brickskeller*** (1523 22nd St. NW, 202-293-1885) remains the city's consummate beer-lover's nirvana, offering more than 500 brands from around the world. It's handy for washing down fare like pizza, sandwiches and buffalo burgers. Be sure to check out the unbelievable beer-can collection lining the walls. On the upper level, those with the dancing bug can get their fix as DJs spin rock and pop music. Other popular gathering places in this general vicinity are **Rumors** (1900 M St. NW, 202-466-7378) and**Sign of the Whale** (1825 M St. NW, 202-785-1110), both of which offer great happy hours and are very big with the young-professional set. Sign of the Whale also has a successful location in Falls Church, Va. (see the Fairfax County section).

And speaking of great happy hours, one of the city's best can be found at **Ha'** (pronounced "Hay") **Penny Lion** (1101 17th St. NW, 202-296-8075), an especially big draw for young single professionals. You may forget the strange name but you won't forget the atmosphere on a Friday afternoon. Over on H Street NW, at 1716 to be exact,**Mike Baker's** (202-342-6433) is a longtime popular spot with the college set and young white-collars.

The 15th Street scene has improved remarkably in the past couple of years with the opening of three hot nightclubs. **Club Zei**, yet another alley dweller, located between 14th and 15th, and H and I streets NW (202-842-2445), has become one of the District's hottest dance spots, truly a place to see and be seen. Same goes for **The Spy Club** (805 15th St. NW, 202-289-1779). Meanwhile, the club called **15 Minutes** (1030 15th St. NW, 202-408-1855) dishes out some of the best live and recorded alternative, progressive and cutting-edge rock music in town along with blues and jazz, all in cavernous surroundings practically in the shadows of the White House. Dress down, dress up, whatever, 15 Minutes caters to all kinds. As their catchy radio ad goes, "If you don't judge us, we won't judge you" (or something to that affect).

Two popular nightclubs with two very different personalities are practically neighbors on F Street NW. **The Fifth Column** (202-393-3632), at 915, ranks as one of the city's top dance places. Here, New York meets Washington, with the high-energy music, late hours, interesting mix of people and pricey drinks that would make the Big Apple proud. At 930 F St., **9:30 Club** (202-393-0930) is one of the District's premier venues for live music that doesn't always qualify as merely "alternative" or "progressive." You never know who's going to show up here.

Over at 625-27 E Street NW, **The Insect Club** (202-347-8884), another recent arrival on the nightlife scene, has made its presence felt in a creepy-crawly sort of way. Let's just say you've got to see it to believe it. The interior designer must have double-majored in entomology. Odd decor aside, this place is appealing if only for the informal ambience, pool tables and hip music.

Whether it's variety in music, decor or people you're in search of, you'll probably see it all at **Tracks**

(1111 First St. SE, 202-488-3320). Dancing and socializing are the main events here, with three large dance areas (including one outside) and a customer base that includes gay, straight and everything in between. Dress is decidedly down. A word of caution, though: this place is not in the nicest part of town, so street smarts are indeed in order here.

If your tastes run more toward the Irish-acoustic and folk scene, then you're in luck. **Irish Times** (14 F St. NW, 202-543-5433), **Dubliner** (520 N. Capitol St. NW, 202-737-3773) and **Ireland's Four Provinces** (3412 Connecticut Ave. NW, 202-244-0860) all feature great live music sure to get feet tapping, hands clapping and brogues crooning.

Another sort of ethnic scene unfolds over in Adams Morgan, where African, Latin and Caribbean influences come together to form one of the city's funkiest nighttime atmospheres. **Kilimanjaro** (1724 California St. NW, 202-328-3838) offers some of the best in live reggae, ska and other imported music sure to warm your soul.

And finally, a few words — er, rather chuckles — about Washington's comedy scene. Most clubs feature some good local talent in addition to national acts. Perhaps the biggest stock of laughs in the city is at **Comedy Cafe** (1520 K St. NW, 202-638-5653). Be sure to call ahead about reservations for a Friday or Saturday night show. Other clubs include **Garvin's Comedy Club** (in the Savoy Suites Hotel, 2505 Wisconsin Ave. NW, 202-298-7200), **The Hill** (516 8th St. SE, 202-543-4242) and **The Improv** (1140 Connecticut Ave. NW, 202-296-7008). See the subsequent suburban listings for comedy clubs in those areas.

Northern Virginia

Alexandria

Alexandria's Old Town area is Northern Virginia's answer to Georgetown. That ought to give you an idea of just how rich in nightlife this charming and beautiful area is. And as with Georgetown, a sidewalk stroll along the narrow, sometimes cobblestone streets will reveal a world unto itself. The hub of Old Town's nocturnal activity is located on the river side (east) of Washington Street, also known as the George Washington Memorial Parkway, especially lower King Street and the surrounding few blocks.

One of the most popular night spots, for singles in particular, is **Bullfeathers** (112 King St., 703-836-8088), tucked away from street view, so look for the distinctive maroon awning that announces its presence to passersby. Although some windows would help temper the cave-like ambience, Bullfeathers has long been a preference of Old Town barhoppers. Be prepared for a waiting line to get in on Friday and Saturday nights.

Just across the street, the **Fish Market*** (105 King St., 703-836-5676) is another Old Town institution that regularly draws a crowd. Many come here to dine on some of the best fresh seafood anywhere in town, but the bar is almost always teeming with activity. Dress casually — especially during the steamy summer months when it can be stifling inside — and bring your thirst; you'll need it to finish off one of the legendary "schooners" of beer.

For a more formal setting, including entertainment and great chow to boot, **219's Basin Street Lounge** (219 King St., 703-549-1141) offers live jazz in the elegant 219 Restaurant*. Live music also takes center stage in the cozy upstairs portion of **The Wharf*** (119 King St., 703-836-2834), where there's not a bad seat for watching local and national rock, blues and R&B artists kick up a storm. Downstairs, you can feel the beat, but it won't keep you from enjoying the excellent seafood in the main restaurant or a cold drink in the nautically themed wood-paneled bar.

A few blocks away, **Portner's*** (109 S. St. Asaph St., 703-683-1776) is popular with the 30s-plus crowd that flocks here for lively happy hours, a gorgeous setting and an ambience that's conducive to — surprise! — the lost art of carrying on a conversation.

Down closer to the river, **Chadwicks*** (203 S. Strand St., 703-836-4442) is as inviting as the Georgetown original, with bars upstairs and down. At **Seaport Inn** (6 King St., 703-549-2341) you can enjoy superb seafood and then retire to the adjoining **George Washington's Tavern** for live acoustic music in a cozy pub setting.

Union Street Public House* (121 S. Union St., 703-548-1785) has long been one of Old Town's most popular singles spots, and there seems to be no end in sight for the accolades. Crowded? Yes. But the wait that's not unusual during prime time is worth it, if only for the spirited bar ambience, the terrific beer selection and the friendly help. If the front bar is too much, try the often-overlooked oyster bar in back. It's smaller and less lively, but the beer is just as good and it's easier to find a seat or a quiet corner.

Elsewhere in Old Town, the **French Quarter Cafe** (808 King St., 703-683-2803) is the most openly gay of any establishment in Northern Virginia. Although it caused quite an uproar in the conservative community when it opened a few years ago, the bar/restaurant — often referred to simply by its street address — has encountered few problems since. In fact, save for the telltale inverted pink triangle (a sign of gay pride) posted by the door, you'd never know there was anything unique about the place. Other than being accepted into the community, perhaps the French Quarter Cafe's biggest victory was successfully challenging an archaic Virginia law that prohibited liquor from being served to gays.

Fans of live Irish-themed acoustic music, Irish food and, of course, Irish drink can get their fill at **Ireland's Own*** (132 N. Royal St., 703-549-4535) and **Murphy's*** (713 King St., 703-548-1717).

The Laughing Lizard (1322 King St., 703-836-7885), meanwhile, offers live rock music, standup comedy and other entertainment in a casual setting. For live country and bluegrass music, try **GW's** (1319 King St., 703-739-2274).

Metropolis (1755 Duke St., 703-519-9400), on the fringes of what is generally considered the Old Town area, suffers from something of an identity crisis, being housed in a large office building away from most of the action in the city. Still, it's a fun place to get away to, with pool tables, recorded music, good food and plenty of space to relax in.

Some of the most popular nightlife destinations outside of Old Town include the **Birchmere** (3901 Mount Vernon Ave., 703-549-5919), located in an area known as "Arlandria" (Arlington/Alexandria border). This has become one of the top venues in the nation for bluegrass, country, folk, pop and blues performers, all in a cozy, unpretentious setting. Standing-room-only crowds are not uncommon. A variety of live music is featured at **Nick's** (642 S. Pickett St., 703-751-8900), located in the far western reaches of the city near the Fairfax County line.

Looking for some laughs? Standup comedy can be had at **Garvin's/Alexandria**, at the Ramada Seminary Plaza Hotel (I-395 and Seminary Road, 202-298-7200; a branch of the D.C. original, hence the D.C. phone number) and at **Headliners**, at the Radisson Plaza Hotel (5000 Seminary Rd., 703-379-4242).

Arlington County

Arlington is tiny, but it's an intensely urban county, and it shows by having some of the best and most interesting night spots in all of suburbia.

Bad Habits (5444 Columbia Pike, 703-998-5808) could pass for one of those classic college bars, with live music (heavy on the rock), casual dress and an atmosphere that for some reason just seems conducive to beer consumption. Lots of local bands cut their teeth here. The only drawback: it's located in a tiny shopping center, so convenient parking can be scarce on busy nights.

A more recent entrant in the college-bar genre is **Bardo's** (2000 Wilson Blvd., 703-527-9399). If you drive by too fast you may miss it, so just look for the old Plymouth sticking through the front window. The car isn't just for looks, though; it houses the CD jukebox. One glimpse of this sort of offbeat decorating idea and you instantly know that this is a place that doesn't take itself too seriously. Housed in a former car dealership, Bardo's is garage-rock informal, from the 100-plus selections of beer on tap (including microbreweries, imports and even some stuff made on the premises), to the spraypainted wall decorations, the progressive music, the T-shirt-and-jeans casualness and the hip crowd. Oh yeah, and there's a decidedly politically correct air to the place as well with the visible recycling efforts and the vegetarian menu choices. If you get the feeling you actually are in somebody's garage, there's good reason for it; a big part of Bardo's takes up what used to be the car dealership's service bay. Take the time to walk around and you'll see the beer-making process up close and personal.

There aren't a ton of pool halls to choose from anymore, but one of the best is **Champion Billiards** (2620 S. Shirlington Rd., 703-521-3800), where enjoying a few games, drinking beer and listening to the CD jukebox make for a welcome alternative to the traditional night out. Non-pool shooters in particular will appreciate the video arcade.

Arcade games, live music, casual setting — it all comes together at **Whitey's*** (2761 N. Washington Blvd., 703-525-9825), another Arlington neighborhood watering hole that oozes with character. The hole-in-the-wall, sports-themed charm of suburbia was never better represented than here. Live rock 'n' roll and R&B help keep the place jumping.

Rounding out the Arlington scene are **Cowboy Cafe North** (4792 Lee Hwy., 703-243-8010) and **Cowboy Cafe South** (2421 Columbia Pike, 703-486-3467), where, as the name implies, country & western music is king; **Little Cafe** (2039 Wilson Blvd., 703-471-5212), for comedy; and **Luna Park Grille** (5866 Washington Blvd., 703-237-5862) and **O'Carroll's** (2051 Wilson Blvd., 703-524-5066) for a variety of live music.

Fairfax County

The nightlife picture has brightened dramatically in Fairfax over the past decade or so, no doubt a reflection of the continued growth, development and prosperity in Metro Washington's largest jurisdiction. And while after-hours establishments here will never be able to fully shed their suburban image cloak, the scene from one end of the county to the other is nothing if not rich with variety.

Beginning in Annandale, **Caldwell's** (7131 Little River Tnpke., 703-750-0777) has long been a popular singles spot, albeit in the classic strip-shopping-center vein. The small but lively bar area, dance floor and combination of live music and DJ tunes provide the ingredients for a true local hangout.

In some ways, the Tysons Corner area is to Fairfax what Crystal City is to Arlington: A hub of business activity during the day, but nearly void of life after hours — save for the massive shopping malls. Fortunately, there's **Champions** (8201 Greensboro Dr., McLean, 703-442-0877), nestled in the lower level of — what else? — an office building amid the concrete, steel and glass sprawl. When it comes to 20- and 30-something crowds, lively tunes and a first-class bar, this version is as popular and enjoyable as the Georgetown original.

Like its D.C. and Alexandria counterparts, **Garvin's/Tysons**, at the Westpark Hotel, (8401 Westpark Dr., 202-298-7200) is always a good bet for a few laughs, although, there's something about a hotel setting that lacks the appeal of a true comedy club. The same could also be said for **Comedy Zone**, at the Springfield Hilton Hotel (6550 Loisdale Rd., Springfield, 703-971-8900.)

Two other popular night spots in downtown Springfield include **Deja Vu** (6710 Commerce St., 703-971-4200) — perhaps the biggest singles bar/dance club anywhere in the county — and **Gus'** (6531 Backlick Rd., 703-451-4556), a much smaller bar/restaurant that features live music, a DJ, karaoke and great happy hours.

In the area known as West Springfield, **Kilroy's*** (5250 A&B Port Royal Rd., 703-321-7733) is king. Don't be fooled by the location in the very-suburban and very-subdued Ravensworth Shopping Center. Singles, softball teams and other groups with a propensity for frequenting bars long ago discovered that Kilroy's is a reliable source for mingling, dancing, acoustic and recorded music, and a general good time. Just down the road a ways at Rolling and Old Keene Mill roads — the crossroads of West Springfield —**Zaxx** (6355 Rolling Rd., 703-569-2582) is the closest thing the area has to a decent-sized concert hall. Local and national rock acts appear regularly before the bluejean-clad, 20-something crowds.

Over near George Mason University, **Fat Tuesday's** (10673 Braddock Rd., Fairfax, 703-385-8660) is another major force in live rock, R&B and blues music, though in a much smaller setting. Take pitchers of beer, hot music, a casual setting and a location in a place called University Mall and you get the idea of what kind of atmosphere to expect at Fat Tuesday's virtually any day of the week.

The long-popular **P.J. Skidoos*** (908 Lee Hwy., Fairfax City, 703-591-4515) has become something of a contemporary disco when it comes to music and the pretentious dance aura, but it still boasts a great bar and rates as a prime spot for singles in their 20s and 30s, not to mention anyone with a hankering for good food.

Another longtime Fairfax City favorite, **T.T. Reynolds** (10414 Main St., 703-591-9292), offers live music in a smaller pub setting.

In the northwest Fairfax community of Reston, it's easier to find lakes, trees and jogging trails than great nightlife, but **Fritzbe's** (2334 Hunter's Woods Plaza, 703-476-4400) is an admirable option, although fairly sterile as bars go. (Fritzbe's also has a location in Annandale at 7050 Columbia Pike, 703-354-4560.)

In nearby Herndon, **Rick Walker's Scoreboard** (724 Pine St., 703-689-2880) benefits from having a former Redskin as its founder and namesake, which is perhaps why it ranks up there as a great local sports bar and singles hangout. Downtown

Insiders' Tip

Insiders...
Appreciate the fact that, on weekends especially, a car can be a definite liability in such traffic-choked nightlife hubs as Georgetown and Old Town Alexandria, so carpooling and park-and-walk strategies are preferred.

Herndon's Ice House Cafe (760 Elden St., 703-471-4256) is friendly, fun and reliable, some things that every community bar/restaurant ought to be.

A few minutes away in Great Falls, **Old Brogue Irish Pub*** (760-C Walker Rd., 703-759-3309) offers great live acoustic music in two rooms and one of the coziest atmospheres anywhere in the county. Somehow, with a pint of Harp lager in your hand, a table full of friends and foot-tapping songs to enjoy, life seems that much more enjoyable.

Other recommended nightlife destinations in the county include **Joe Theismann's*** (5912 Leesburg Pike, Baileys Crossroads, 703-379-7777), another place with Redskin roots that offers great sports viewing, plus karaoke; **Sign of the Whale** (7279 Arlington Blvd., Falls Church, 703-573-1616), for the singles scene; and the venerable **Vienna Inn*** (120 Maple Ave. West, Vienna, 703-938-9548) for cheap beer, cheap eats, blue-collar informality, an undeniable sense of yesteryear and to confirm why this place consistently finishes near the top of local surveys ranking the region's favorite neighborhood saloons.

Loudoun County

Loudoun's primarily rural character is evident in its dearth of nightlife, but then, that's not why people settle in this beautiful county. Her charms and attractions are decidedly less commercial. Still, Loudoun isn't void of after-hours haunts.

In Leesburg, **The Black Orchid II*** (1500 East Market St., 703-771-9200) features a mix of live music, including jazz, '30s and '40s nightclub tunes, and mellow guitar, along with casual and fine dining. The crowd ranges from 30-somethings to senior citizens.

Also in Leesburg, the **Limelight Restaurant** (107 Loudoun St. SW, 703-777-7492), in the town's historic district, features singers/ classical piano, guitarists and other laid-back entertainment.

Shenanigan's (538 East Market St., 703-777-2454) caters to the young crowd with dancing to tunes spun by a DJ. **Tuscarora Mill Restaurant** (203 Harrison St. SE, 703-771-9300), in the enchanting Market Station section, is known primarily for its great bar ambience. Enjoy a drink in a wonderful setting and forget about what you may be missing elsewhere. Another Leesburg favorite is **Tulipano Ristorante** (37 Catoctin Cir. SE, 703-779-0090).

In the Countryside area of booming eastern Loudoun County, **JD's American Bar and Grill** (20921 Davenport Dr., Sterling, 703-444-2853) caters to young professionals with a lively bar and occasional live music.

In bucolic Purcellville, **Stonewall Tavern** (on Route 7, 703-338-2850) serves up a coffeehouse-style atmosphere with live acoustic music and an extensive beer selection. There's also the **Breezeway Bar and Grill** (721 E. Main St., 703-338-1964).

In Middleburg, heart of the county's famed Hunt Country, the esteemed **Red Fox Inn*** (2 East Washington St., 703-478-1808) is not only a great restaurant, but a nice quiet place for drinks and conversation.

Prince William County

Most of the nightlife in Prince William County is centered around the Manassas and Woodbridge areas, so it's there where we'll focus

The scene in Manassas includes**Addy's** (10820 Balls Ford Rd., 703-368-0194), which features a DJ on Fridays and Saturdays; **The Admiral's Inn** (8630 Mathis Ave., 703-368-3600), which also has a DJ spinning tunes on the weekend; **Applegate's** (10800 Vandor Lane, 703-335-0000), with live music every day except Sunday; **Brady's** (8971 Center St., 703-369-1469), with live music in the heart of the historic district; **Hero's American Restaurant*** (9412 Main St., 703-330-1534), boasting an extensive beer selection; **K.C.'s** (9411 Main St., 703-361-2400), with live music on Wednesday evenings and a DJ on Tuesday, Thursday, Friday and Saturday; and The **Sports Break** (9550 Center St., 703-335-8105) where sports junkies can get their fix and live-music fans can enjoy the performances Thursday, Friday and Saturday.

In Woodbridge, there's **Bar J Restaurant** (13275 Gordon Blvd., 703-491-3271), featuring live tunes on Thursday, Friday and Saturday; **Kilroy's** (14633 Jefferson Davis Hwy., 703-494-4800), like the Springfield original is a haven for singles and TV sports-watching, and also features live music on Thursday and a DJ on Tuesday, Wednesday, Friday and Saturday; and **The Pilot House** (16216 Neabsco Rd., 703-221-1010), boasts live music Wednesday, Friday and Saturday.

Suburban Maryland

Anne Arundel County

Annapolis is the focal point of Anne Arundel, so naturally that's where much of the county's nightlife is centered. Many of the city's famed eating establishments double as destinations for enjoying live music, dancing, or merely hoisting a few cold ones at the bar. **Armadillo's** (132 Dock St., 410-268-6680) is one of the most popular spots for live rock, pop, R&B and oldies tunes. **Griffin's** (20-22 Market Space, 410-268-2576) doesn't offer live music, but instead the draw is its huge mahogany and marble bar where great drinks and pub grub are served up in a lively atmosphere.

Another favorite along the Annapolis waterfront is **McGarvey's Saloon*** (8 Market Space, 410-263-5700), which boasts the famed Oyster Bar room. Fans of true local watering holes will relish in that there's nothing fancy or pretentious here. It's just a traditional American saloon atmosphere, complete with Tiffany lamps and a tin ceiling, all enclosed in a century-plus-old building.

Middleton Tavern* (2 Market Space, 410-263-3323), considered by many to be the standardbearer of the local tavern scene, dates back more than 240

years. Or at least the building does. The tavern itself, which opened in 1968, also seems to get better with age. Beginning with the huge front porch — ideal for sitting and sipping as the world goes by — there's a lot to like about this place. Live folk and acoustic performances are featured every night downstairs, while upstairs, the Arundel Room (open only on weekends) offers an even quieter alternative with its romantic piano bar.

Ram's Head Tavern (33 West St., 410-268-4545) could be considered the Annapolis version of D.C.'s famed Brickskeller, although instead of some 500 labels of beer, you'll have to settle for around 130 (but no Budweiser). Chili and assorted seafood creations top the list of bar munchies. Progressive jazz tunes courtesy of a CD player offer a backdrop that's a nice change of pace from the din that seems indigenous to many bars.

One of the top local venues for live acoustic music is **Reynolds Tavern** (7 Church Circle, 410-626-0380), where the weekends come alive with the sound of folk singers and Irish balladeers.

Outside Annapolis, **A.L. Gator's** (8501 Fort Smallwood Rd., Riviera Beach, 410-255-2132/5533) could make a strong claim as the county's premier night spot. This legendary singles hangout is where it all comes together: dancing, sports, live music, and of course the socializing of the sexes in a setting that reminds you of one of the ultimate Florida beach bars. In other words, just about anything goes. The allure of this multi-level barfly's dream ranges from its "junky chic" decor (auto parts and other assorted salvaged pieces of civilization) to the dozens of different beers, live progressive, R&B and rock music nightly in the Wreck Room, and recreational diversions such as pool tables, a sand volleyball court, and air hockey and pinball machines. A.L. Gator's is a must stop on any tour of Anne Arundel County nightlife.

Another favorite is Dorsey's own **Timbuktu** (1726 Dorsey Rd., 410-768-4331), which attracts an older (30s and up) crowd with terrific drink and food selections and a live keyboardist and vocalist Tuesday through Saturday. For those who can't wait for the weekend, there are numerous early-in-the-week specials.

Montgomery County

Bethesda has grown into the "downtown" of Montgomery County, so it's not surprising that this urban-style suburban core of activity offers its share of nighttime diversions.

One of the county's top live-music showcases is **Durty Nelly's** (4714 Montgomery Lane, 301-652-1444), where rock, oldies and R&B artists rule the roost. Entertainment aside, some folks come just for the informal club-style ambience and youthful energy. For surroundings that are a bit more on the mellow side, **Flanagan's Irish Pub*** (7637 Old Georgetown Rd., 301-986-1007) features acoustic and folk music in a comfy pub setting.

Malarkey's Cafe & Saloon (7201 Wisconsin Ave., 301-951-9000) offers DJ-provided music with a heavy emphasis on progressive and classic rock Friday and Saturday. The appeal extends even further with an extensive beer selection, plenty of elbow room and tasty pub-style chow.

DJs also supply the entertainment at **Nantucket Landing** (4723 Elm St., 301-654-7979), with rock tunes and dance music among the favorite themes. Beach parties and other summer specials are big here as are audience-participation games and various specials. Although it has operated under several different names throughout the years, the present-day Nantucket Landing has developed into a consummate suburban watering hole.

The same could also be said for **Shootz** (4915 St. Elmo Ave., 301-654-8288), which represents the growing nightlife category of contemporary billiards halls. No longer just smoke-filled retreats where the guys hang out, drink beer and show off their pool-shooting skills, places like Shootz appeal to a much larger audience these days. Still, if all you have in mind is hanging out, drinking some beer and showing off your pool-shooting skills, Shootz fills the bill nicely.

Over in Rockville, **Fatty's** (51 Monroe St., 301-762-4630) has become synonymous with live music, especially rock and R&B, and so has **Outta The Way Cafe** (17503 Redland Rd., 301-963-6895), where the emphasis is on R&B. Another favorite is **Manny's** (4828 Boiling Brook Pkwy., 301-881-7868).

Elsewhere in Montgomery County, several live-music venues cater to a variety of crowds. At **Armand's** (1909 Seminary Rd., Silver Spring, 301-588-3400), rock and pop take center stage, jazz is the focus at **T.J. Remington's** (1100 Wayne Ave., Silver Spring, 301-495-0080), while **Tornado Alley** (11319 Elkin St., Wheaton, 301-929-0795) offers up some of the best live blues, R&B and classic-rock acts anywhere in the region.

Prince George's County

When it comes to nightlife, what Prince George's County may lack in sheer volume, it makes up for in variety.

Starting in the Camp Springs area, **Cotton Eyed Joe's Saloon** (5859 Allentown Way, 301-449-7500) will make you think you've been transported to another region altogether with the high-stepping country dancing and country music that make this place so popular. Then again, Metro Washington has long held the unofficial title as "Bluegrass Capital of the Nation," although what's defined as bluegrass, country, and country & western music and culture seems open to wide interpretation. Anyway, you get the picture.

Dancing is also the focus at **The Hangar Club** (6410 Old Branch Ave., 301-449-6970), except here most of the dancers are attractive, well-built men wearing skimpy outfits. Yes, this is one of the area's few clubs that caters almost exclusively to ladies. Still, its "decency" level, as some might put it, is a notch above many of the clubs for men featuring female dancers because here they don't take quite everything off, but it's indeed enough to send the female patrons into a tizzy. This cavernous establishment hosts hundreds of bachelorette parties and "girls night out" get-togethers each year. Over 30 brands of beer help keep the whistles wet.

In College Park, home of the University of Maryland, **94th Aero Squadron** (5240 Calvert Rd., 301-699-9400) is a popular singles hangout. Its intriguing aviation/military theme — a nod to the nearby College Park Airport, the nation's oldest in continuous operation — includes a prop plane outside and a World War I ambulance inside. White-collar crowds and of course plenty of students help keep the place hopping. **Paragon** (7416 Baltimore Ave., also known as Route 1, 301-774-3444) is one of the area's top college haunts and features high-energy live music.

For laughs, head to Greenbelt where **Comedy Connection** (6000 Greenbelt Rd., 301-345-0563) offers local and national standup performers each evening. Other favorites in Greenbelt include **Hawthorne's** (8811 Greenbelt Rd., 301-552-3030), where interesting works of art adorn the walls and the diverse appeal of sports, music and dancing come together; and wildly popular **Kangaroo Katie's** (7511 Greenbelt Rd., 301-474-9011), which serves up over 100 brands of beer from more than two dozen nations, more than a dozen wines, offbeat snacks (kangaroo, alligator), and an assortment of recreational diversions.

The community of Laurel also rates as one of the county's prime nighttime destinations. Perhaps the best-known of the bunch is **The Greene Turtle** (14350 Baltimore Ave., 301-317-6650), a decidedly laid-back establishment where the signature T-shirt showing two amorous turtles sharing a private moment has paid big dividends in marketing and promotions. **Oliver's Saloon** (531 Main St., 301-490-9200) features a DJ as well as live contemporary rock on Saturday. This is a true neighborhood pub with a good selection of draft brews, wine by the glass, and steamed-crab specials during the summer. Recently renovated and expanded, it's especially hopping during happy hours and on Friday nights. **Randy's California Inn** (Route 1 and Whiskeybottom Rd., 301-725-4103) is the county's other country-dancing and bluegrass mecca.

Inside Metro Washington Attractions

In a region that has such a wealth of attractions — from the physical to the historical to the cultural — earmarking just one chapter for such a vital and extraordinary part of life in Metro Washington seems almost foolhardy. After all, one could easily write a pretty voluminous book on the subject.

Luckily for us, we've thinned the herd quite a bit by including hundreds of area attractions in other parts of the Insiders' Guide. For instance, the chapters dealing with daytrips, the Civil War, nooks and crannies, spectator sports, parks and recreation, education, worship, nightlife and transportation (who doesn't want to see the Metro system?), to name a few, are sprinkled with what we hope are interesting destinations and attractions.

The purpose of this chapter, then, is to give newcomers an overview of just some of the principal attractions in the Nation's Capital, Northern Virginia and Suburban Maryland — those incredible sites and sounds most Americans already have a semblance of familiarity with. If there's something you think we've left out, try checking the index or scanning the table of contents. Chances are, what you're looking for is mentioned somewhere else in the book.

The descriptions of the attractions are followed by a monthly grouping of major annual events in Metro D.C. These are some of the festivals, shows, fairs, concerts and culinary feasts that we believe best represent the region's distinct lifestyle and its varied ethnic, cultural and artistic heritages.

At the end of the chapter, we've included information on some of the leading commercial tour operators as well as the numerous convention and visitors bureaus and tourism offices of the Washington area.

District of Columbia

Memorials

Jefferson Memorial

Southern end of 15th St. SW (202) 426-6821

Breathtaking at night, marble walls inscribed with Thomas Jefferson's writings surround a 19-foot likeness atop a 6-foot granite pedestal. Looking from the memorial across the Tidal Basin affords an unforgettable illuminated view of downtown Washington. This awesome memorial was built in the style of Jefferson's Rotunda at the University of Virginia and was designed by the same architectural firm that blueprinted the National Gallery of Art.

The National Law Enforcement Officers Memorial

Judiciary Square, between E and F sts. and 4th and 5th sts. NW (703) 827-0518

One of the newest national shrines, the National Law Enforcement Officers Memorial features a tree-lined pathway leading past a granite wall displaying the names of fallen officers. The list, tragically, is expansive, including the first police officer ever killed in the line of duty, back in 1794.

Lincoln Memorial

On 23rd St. NW between Constitution and Independence aves. (202) 426-6895

The somber War President looks past the stairs that have served as a site for many public demonstrations and across the vast Reflecting Pool shimmering with the images of the Washington Monument and the Capitol building two miles away. Completed in 1922, the memorial was modeled after the Parthenon in Athens and its walls are inscribed with the Gettysburg Address and Lincoln's Second Inaugural Address.

U.S. Navy Memorial

8th St. and Pennsylvania Ave. NW (202) 737-2300

This interesting memorial at Market Square features the largest map of the world, inlaid in granite on the plaza. Keeping sentry is the "Lone Sailor," a beautiful Stanley Bleifeld sculpture, and nearby are two walls holding 22 bronze sculpture panels, a representation of American naval history and a salute to those who have served or will serve in the Navy. Inside the adjacent Visitors Center, guests can view "At Sea," a riveting account of life on a naval carrier.

Theodore Roosevelt Memorial

Roosevelt Island
Off northbound George Washington Memorial Parkway (202) 285-2600

This obscure, enchanting monument to America's environmental president is set amid a densely wooded island in the middle of the Potomac River between the Roosevelt and Key bridges. In addition to a giant statue of the gregarious 25th president, the island is laced with over three miles of trails and its shoreline offers excellent vistas of the Washington and Northern Virginia skylines. Open from sunrise until dark, Roosevelt Island is accessible only from the Virginia side via a footbridge.

Vietnam Veterans Memorial

23rd St. and Constitution Ave. NW (202) 634-1568

Located just a short walk from the Reflecting Pool and the Lincoln Memorial, the Vietnam Veterans Memorial, or simply "The Wall," has become the most-visited monument in the city since its controversial opening in 1982, attracting over 1.7 million people annually. Built with private funds, the structure — designed by a young architecture student named Maya Lin — is com-

Photo: Washington Convention and Visitors Association

***Lincoln Memorial** — The 19-foot statue of Abraham Lincoln, sculpted by Daniel Chester French, gazes eastward upon the National Mall.*

posed of simple black granite panels etched (in chronological order) with the names of the more than 58,000 Americans who perished in the war. A few steps away, a bronze sculpture depicts three amazingly lifelike infantrymen; a statue dedicated to the women who served in Vietnam stands nearby as well. Accessible around the clock, The Wall is often the site of some of the most moving personal tributes ever witnessed at a very public place.

WASHINGTON MONUMENT

On the National Mall
At 15th St. NW (202) 426-6840

This 555-foot signature landmark of the Nation's Capital is hard to miss, even for newcomers. Certainly one of the most photographed icons anywhere, the simple marble obelisk — the tallest masonry structure in the world — contains nearly 200 memorial stones from all 50 states and numerous countries and organizations. An elevator ride to the top awards one with an unsurpassed view of Washington and environs. But be prepared for a substantial wait in line.

Federal Washington

DEPARTMENT OF AGRICULTURE

Between Independence Ave. and
Jefferson Dr. SW (202) 447-2791

Trace America's agrarian roots at the Department of Agriculture Visitors Information Center, located in Room 113-A of the Administration Building. Exhibits and displays change regularly. This monolithic agency is housed in one of the largest structures in Washington, just a short walk from the National Mall.

NATIONAL AQUARIUM

Commerce Department Building
14th St. and
Constitution Ave. NW (202) 377-2825

Not to be confused with the centerpiece of Baltimore's Inner Harbor that shares the same name, this is the nation's oldest aquarium yet is one of the city's best-kept secrets, due in part, perhaps, to its basement location. Some 66 tanks house more than 1,000 sea creatures, including those in the Touch Tank, a favorite with children that offers a thrilling hands-on experience with underwater life. Be sure to check on times for the popular shark and piranha feedings.

NATIONAL ARCHIVES

Constitution Ave. between
7th and 9th sts. NW (202) 501-5000

The three most important documents in America — the Declaration of Independence, the Constitution and the Bill of Rights — all make their home in a special display case located in the rotunda of this well-guarded building. To keep the precious parchment out of harm's way, the case is lowered 20 feet into a special bomb- and fire-proof vault each evening. For a totally different experience, trace your family history in the cavernous Research Room.

UNITED STATES CAPITOL

East End of the Mall on
Capitol Hill (202) 225-6827

Perhaps the strongest competitor to the Washington Monument in terms of worldwide recog-

Photo: Washington Convention and Visitors Association

The Vietnam Veterans Memorial preserves the names of the 58,000 members of the U. S. Armed Services who died in the Vietnam War.

nition, the Capitol looms majestically over the city as its tallest building, something that will never change, thanks to the far-sighted vision of early planners of the federal district. Tours of the great halls and the magnificent Central Rotunda of this regal edifice are a highlight of any visit to the Hill. For a peek at the Congress hard at work, obtain a pass through the office of your representative or senator.

Library of Congress

Independence Ave. at 1st St. SE *(202) 707-5458*

Another one of Thomas Jefferson's legacies to Washington, his personal collection was the seed stock for what would become the largest library in the world, totaling some 84 million items in 470 languages. The volumes are rivaled only by the magnificence of the Italian Renaissance structure that houses them. Visitors should start at the Madison Building, 101 Independence Ave. SE, for a 20-minute film presentation followed by a 45-minute tour.

Bureau of Engraving and Printing

14th and C sts. SW *(202) 874-3019*

Few people ever get closer to so much money than they do at the Bureau of Engraving and Printing. A 25-minute self-guided tour, one of the most popular in Washington, offers visitors a look at the fascinating process involved in the production of U.S. currency as well as stamps. Free tickets are issued on a first-come, first-served basis, and early arrival is strongly advised. But forget the cameras; strict security prohibits the taking of any pictures.

Federal Bureau of Investigation

10th St. and Pennsylvania Ave. NW *(202) 324-3447*

A tour of the J. Edgar Hoover Building is as intriguing as the man himself. The free, one-hour excursion through America's top law-enforcement agency offers an inside look at crime-fighting techniques and crime laboratories, a peek at photos of the FBI's Ten Most Wanted Fugitives, and a thrilling live firearms demonstration, viewed safely from behind glass. Like so many of the city's other popular tours, early arrival is advised.

Pavilion at the Old Post Office

Pennsylvania Ave. at 12th St. NW *(202) 523-5691*

This landmark soaring above America's Main Street was built in 1899 as the nation's postal headquarters. Set to be demolished in 1934, it was saved by concerned citizens and has since been masterfully renovated into one of the city's premier shopping, dining and entertainment attractions and site of an annual New Year's Eve gala. Ride the glass elevator up to the tower's 12th-floor observation deck for a dramatic view.

Department of State

22nd and C sts. NW *(202) 647-3241*

This massive agency, responsible for creating and carrying out U.S. foreign policy, is partly accessible to the general public: free tours are offered of the eighth-floor diplomatic reception areas. Call for

Photo: Washington Convention and Visitors Association

The Three Servicemen Memorial — The three servicemen gaze sadly at the nearby Vietnam Veterans Memorial, containing the names of their fallen comrades.

times and required reservations. Written materials about the many interesting aspects of the department are available by calling the Public Information Service at (202) 647-6575.

Supreme Court

1st St. and Maryland Ave. NE (202) 479-3211

The weightiest legal decisions in the land are handed down behind the imposing columned facade of this renowned building. While their work is of paramount importance, the nine justices don't deliberate for a full calendar year, going into session only between October and June. Orders and opinions are typically handed down on Mondays, an exciting time to visit. When the nation's highest court is not in session, free lectures are given on weekdays every hour on the half hour from 9:30 AM to 3:30 PM.

The White House

1600 Pennsylvania Ave. NW(202) 456-7041

Known as the "President's Palace" in its early days, this masterpiece of Federal architecture each year hosts scores of dignitaries, entertainers and other luminaries, not to mention more than 1 million curious tourists. Burned by the British during the War of 1812, the White House has been home to every president and his family except George Washington. No other residence of a head of state is as accessible as the White House, where seven of the 132 rooms are part of a self-conducted public tour offered Tuesday through Saturday. To obtain a free VIP pass that's good for a guided tour, contact the office of your representative or senator.

The Smithsonian Institution

On the National Mall

The Castle

1000 Jefferson Dr. SW (202) 357-2700

One look at its imposing reddish-brown, Norman-Gothic exterior and you'll know how this building got its name. The Castle has been a fixture on the Mall since 1855 and now almost seems out of place in the company of some of the more modern architecture. But what a story it has to tell. This is the original building of the Smithsonian Institution that now encompasses 14 museums and the National Zoo, making it the largest museum complex in the world and an unparalleled national treasure. An ideal place for newcomers to begin exploring the Smithsonian collection, the Castle houses the high-tech Visitor Information Center as well as the crypt of James Smithson, founder of the institution that bears his name.

National Museum of African Art

950 Independence Ave. SW(202) 357-2700

This is a fascinating highlight on any Smithsonian tour if only for one reason: it's the only national museum dedicated solely to the collection, study and exhibition of the art and culture of Africa. Permanent exhibits are complemented by numerous rotating shows.

Photo: Washington Convention and Visitors Association

Smithsonian Institution — This red brick "castle" on the National Mall was the first of the great Smithsonian Museums.

National Air and Space Museum

6th St. and Jefferson Dr. SW (202) 357-2700

Humankind's insatiable fascination with flight is dramatically underscored by the National Air and Space Museum's status as the most-visited museum in the world. Its 23 galleries — including the magnificent glass-walled lobby where dozens of aircraft hang in suspended animation — showcase the evolution of aviation and space technology. The collection includes history-making planes flown by the Wright brothers and Charles Lindbergh, the Apollo 11 command module, a space station, and the wiry "flying fuel tank" that Californian Dick Rutan flew on his record-breaking nonstop flight around the world. Since the museum no longer has room to accept large items for display, an annex will be built at Washington Dulles International Airport, where several large aircraft wait in storage.

National Museum of American History

14th St. and Constitution Ave. NW (202) 357-2700

American culture, politics and technology are brought to life at the ever-popular National Museum of American History. From gowns of the First Ladies to an original Model T, from Archie Bunker's armchair to Dorothy's ruby slippers and the "M*A*S*H" gang's stage props, the exhibits are as varied and interesting as history itself.

Arts and Industries Building

900 Jefferson Dr. SW (202) 357-2700

This unique collection of Victorian Americana is a re-creation of the 1876 Philadelphia Centennial Exposition. Attractions include working steam engines and other machines and a 51-foot model of the war sloop *Antietam*.

Freer Gallery of Art

Jefferson Dr. at 12th St. SW(202) 357-2700

Recently reopened after an extensive renovation, the Freer Gallery of Art showcases a world-renown collection of Asian, 19th- and early 20th-century American art. The undisputed highlight is James McNeill Whistler's gorgeous "Peacock Room." Many first-time visitors to the Freer find that it isn't long before they're wanting to make a return trip.

Joseph H. Hirshhorn Museum and Sculpture Garden

7th St. and
Independence Ave. SW (202) 357-2700

This striking doughnut-shaped building is yet another hard-to-miss landmark abutting the National Mall. The Hirshhorn showcases modern art including 19th- and 20th-century paintings and sculpture by such greats as de Kooning, Pollock and Rothko. Adjoining and just to the north, the idyllic Sunken Sculpture Garden features works by Matisse and Rodin.

National Museum of Natural History

10th St. and
Constitution Ave. NW (202) 357-2700

You'll know you've arrived at the National Museum of Natural History when you look up and see the colossal stuffed elephant in the rotunda. And it only gets more intriguing from there. This treasure house contains more than 81 million items documenting humankind and the natural environment. Among the highlights: dinosaur skeletons (all the rage since the dawn of Barney-mania and the 1993 success of Steven Spielberg's dino flick "Jurassic Park"), displays of early man, a live insect zoo and coral reef, and the ever-enchanting 45.5-carat Hope diamond.

Arthur M. Sackler Gallery

1050 Independence Ave. SW (202) 357-2700

Distinctively international, the Sackler Gallery features a permanent collection of masterpieces of Asian and Near Eastern art that spans from the beginning of civilization to the present. Works include jades, bronzes, lacquerware, sculpture, paintings and furniture. Many of the exhibits are on loan from various sources.

Off the National Mall

National Museum of American Art and National Portrait Gallery

8th and G sts. NW (202) 357-2700

The National Museum of American Art's permanent collection of more than 35,000 works, including paintings, sculptures and photographs, offers a rich panorama of the nation's artistic heritage, from Colonial times to the 20th century. The Portrait Gallery features likenesses of individuals who have made significant contributions to the development of the nation, including each president.

National Postal Museum

2 Massachusetts
Ave. NW (202) 357-2700

The newest addition to the vast Smithsonian collection, the National Postal Museum opened in July 1993 with great fanfare. Especially excited were philatelists who queued up for several hours just to get one of the special first-day-of-issue commemorative stamps. The museum documents the founding and development of the modern postal system and features interactive displays and the largest stamp collection in the world, including all U.S.-issue stamps since 1847. One thing's for certain: You'd have a tough time shooing Cliff "Cheers" Clavin out the door.

Renwick Gallery

Pennsylvania Ave. and
17th St. NW (202) 357-2700

Leave the outside world and step into the late 19th century. The Renwick Gallery is a showcase of American design, crafts and contemporary arts. The Grand Salon and the Octagon Room boast period furnishings and decorations from the 1860s and '70s.

National Zoological Park

3000 block of
Connecticut Ave. NW (202) 357-2700

Nearly 5,000 animals — including the rare giant panda — call the National Zoo home. Of special interest are the ape house, the big cats and the reptile collection. But be sure to leave time for a stroll through a re-created rainforest in the popular Amazonia exhibit, the newest addition to the zoo. Some of the wild animals on display aren't the only scarce items around here; ditto for parking spaces. Do yourself a huge favor and take Metrorail to the Woodley Park/Zoo station. From there it's a pleasant 10-minute walk up the street.

Museums & Galleries

Capital Children's Museum

800 3rd St. NE (202) 543-8600

Not as well known as it should be, the Capital Children's Museum is nirvana for the kids and a nice change of pace for mom and dad.

Insiders' Tip

Sure, the White House and the Capitol are "must sees" for every tourist and resident, but the No. 1 attraction in the Nation's Capital is by far and away the National Air & Space Museum, with more than 8.5 million visitors each year. Rounding out the top 10 attractions in descending order are the National Museum of Natural History, Union Station, the National Museum of American History, the National Gallery of Art, Arlington National Cemetery, the National Zoo, the Old Post Office, the Kennedy Center and the Vietnam Veterans Memorial. The Capitol, meanwhile, comes in 11th place while the White House edges in at No. 15.

This is a place that should be a big hit with virtually any young one. Learning is made fun with hands-on exhibits, interactive displays and a special emphasis on world cultures.

Corcoran Gallery of Art

17th St. and
New York Ave. NW *(202) 638-3211*

Of all the fine-arts showcases that the nation's capital has to offer, the Corcoran ranks as the largest and oldest private gallery. It boasts an amazing selection of American paintings and sculpture and a smaller collection of European pieces.

Ford's Theatre

511 10th St. NW *(202) 426-6924*
Box Office *(202) 347-4833*

Forever memorialized as the place where President Lincoln was shot by John Wilkes Booth, Ford's is very much a working year round professional theater, restored to the appearance of that fateful night in 1865. A lower-level museum displays Lincoln memorabilia, Booth's diary, and one of his boots that he was wearing during the assassination. Just across the way, at 511 10th St. NW, is the house where Lincoln died.

Frederick Douglass National Historic Site

1411 W St. SE *(202) 426-5960*

Cedar Hill, the beautifully restored Victorian home of former slave Frederick Douglass, is the centerpiece of this slice of tranquility near the banks of the Anacostia River. A visitors center features a 30-minute film and numerous exhibits on the life of the famed abolitionist, editor, orator and advisor to Lincoln. There's also a half-hour tour and a bookstore with volumes on black history.

U.S. Holocaust Memorial Museum

100 Raoul Wallenberg Place SW
(Between 14th and 15th sts.)
(202) 488-0400

As captivating as it is disturbing, the U.S. Holocaust Memorial Museum — another recent addition to the city's cultural roster — documents the horrors of the Holocaust through photographs, film, interactive exhibits and incredible artifacts. Built with private funds and opened in the spring of 1993, the museum occupies a two-acre parcel right next to the Bureau of Engraving and Printing, just off the National Mall. The five-story building itself is a fascinating architectural statement and tribute to the victims. Due to the graphic nature of some of the materials on display, the tour is not recommended for children under 11 years of age.

National Gallery of Art

4th St. and
Constitution Ave. NW *(202) 737-4215*

Actually two buildings, the National Gallery of Art is one of the world's preeminent cultural attractions, housing a collection vast and rich enough to command more than just a brief visit. The West Building, completed in 1941, features some of the best in American and European paintings, sculpture and graphic arts from the 13th through the 19th centuries. The I.M. Pei-designed East Building, completed in 1978, showcases modern art including a giant Calder mobile. The two buildings are connected by a dramatic fountain- and skylight-enhanced underground walkway. Here you'll also find a cafeteria and a great gift shop featuring books and reasonably priced, framing-quality prints.

National Museum of Women in the Arts

1250 New York Ave. NW (202) 783-5000

The works of women artists—including O'Keefe, Cassatt and Le Brun — spanning four centuries are showcased in this the first museum in the world dedicated to women artists. And in what could be the answer to a trivia question, the collection is housed, ironically enough, in a former Masonic temple.

Phillips Collection

1600 21st St. NW (202) 387-0961

Located in the shadows of Embassy Row, the former home of Duncan Phillips features a diverse collection of masterpieces of French Impressionism, Post-Impressionism and modern art. Be sure to inquire about the wonderful free Sunday concerts, gallery talks and tours.

Embassy Row

Along Massachusetts Ave. NW
Between Scott and Observatory cirs.

Nearly 50 of the city's approximately 150 embassies are clustered along this two-mile stretch of prime real estate, hence the designation Embassy Row. From the grand and ornate to the simple but elegant, the homes make for a wonderful walking tour, especially in the spring and fall. Look for the flag and coat of arms that designate each diplomatic mission. Some of the more noteworthy embassies — from an architectural perspective — include those of Brazil, Japan, Britain, Austria, Pakistan and Turkey.

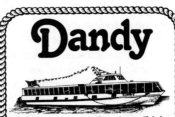

Georgetown

Hub at M St. and Wisconsin Ave. NW
Visitors Center (202) 338-4677

A thriving tobacco port and completely independent Maryland community when Washington was established as the Nation's Capital in the late 1700s, Georgetown is the city's oldest and best-known neighborhood and one that's synonymous with wealth, power and prestige. Locals and out-of-towners alike come here to stroll the narrow, cobblestone streets, view the elegant homes and sample the incredible array of nightclubs, bars, art galleries, restaurants, funky shops and elegant boutiques. The nerve center is at M Street and Wisconsin Avenue NW, through the years the spillover site of some spirited post-Super Bowl, New Year's Eve and Halloween celebrations. Prime attractions include venerable Georgetown University (whose graduates include President Clinton), C&O Canal National Historic Park, Dumbarton Oaks, Georgetown Park (one of the region's toniest malls), the Old Stone House, and Hillwood Museum, former home of cereal heiress Marjorie Merriweather Post and present home of some fabulous French and Russian decorative arts including a priceless collection of Fabergé eggs.

Northern Virginia

Arlington National Cemetery

Memorial Drive, Arlington (703) 692-0931

With its sea of white headstones spread across 612 wooded, hilly acres overlooking the capital city, Arlington National Cemetery is perhaps the most famous burial site in the world. This is the final resting place for more than 175,000 American military personnel who served in conflicts from the Revolutionary War to the present. Among the many famous graves are those of President John F. Kennedy and his brother Robert, President William Howard Taft, Mercury astronaut "Gus" Grissom, and prizefighter Joe Louis. Also located on the grounds are the Tomb of the Unknowns — where the hourly changing of the guard often draws a crowd — and majestic Arlington House, Robert E. Lee's former home that sits high on a hill facing the Lincoln Memorial. Arlington House is also where Pierre Charles L'Enfant, the French architect who drafted the original plans for Washington, is buried.

Gunston Hall

10709 Gunston Rd., Lorton (703) 550-9220

This southeastern Fairfax County landmark was built in 1755 by George Mason, a framer of the Constitution and the father of the Bill of Rights whose namesake university is also in Fairfax. With its 18th-century furnishings, formal gardens and exhibits, Gunston Hall serves as a landmark connection with the region's colonial past. But the home is more than just a museum or monument. It's also a favorite spot for small meetings, parties and receptions.

Iwo Jima Statue

Adjacent to Route 50 at the edge of Arlington National Cemetery

Officially known as the U.S. Marine Corps War Memorial, this is the largest bronze statue in the world and depicts the raising of the American flag on Iwo Jima during World War II. Presented to the nation by members and friends of the Marine

Some 200,000 military veterans and other historical and political figures are buried in Arlington National Cemetery.

Corps, the statue was created by Felix de Weldon based on the famous photograph by Joe Rosenthal. Nearby, the Netherlands Carillon (bell tower) was a gift from the Dutch people in gratitude to America's aid during World War II. In season, a gorgeous field of tulips lies at its base.

Mount Vernon

Southern end of the G.W. Memorial Parkway
Alexandria (Fairfax County) (703) 780-2000

One look at the view from the green expanse of lawn and it's easy to see why George Washington chose this site for his gracious riverside plantation that has become America's most-visited historic house. Washington's final resting place, Mount Vernon offers a wealth of information into the life of the man as well as the turbulent Colonial period. Present-day archaeological digs on the site continue to tell us more. Mount Vernon is easily one of the most popular tourist attractions — especially among foreign guests — in all of Metro Washington.

Oatlands Plantation

On Route 15 near Leesburg (703) 777-3174

Located about six miles south of Leesburg, in Loudoun County, this classic revival home built in 1804 is one of the state's foremost historic plantations. The grounds and architecture are accented by four acres of formal terraced English gardens. Oatlands is the site of various events and gatherings throughout the year.

Potomac Mills

2700 Potomac Mills Cir., Prince William
(Follow signs from I-95 near Woodbridge)

Forget the Civil War sites, historic homes, national parks, even Colonial Williamsburg. Incredibly,

Potomac Mills, located 15 miles south of the Capital Beltway, is Virginia's No. 1 tourist attraction. But for shopaholics and bargain seekers in general, the allure is obvious: hundreds of stores, including numerous upscale retailers, offering superb prices on clothing, household goods, appliances and all manner of other merchandise. It ranks as one of the world's largest outlet malls. When hunger pangs strike, you can choose from over 20 international eateries.

Washington Dulles International Airport

Near Chantilly on the Fairfax/ Loudoun line *(703) 661-2700*

Completed in 1961 and named after John Foster Dulles, President Eisenhower's secretary of state, this was the nation's first airport built for the jet age. Finnish-born architect Eero Saarninen sought to convey the beauty of flight in his dramatic swept-roof design of the Greek temple-like main terminal. And he succeeded, to say the least: in the mid 1970s Dulles was officially recognized by the American Institute of Architects as a masterpiece of 20th-century design. Stroll out to the observation deck along the rear of the terminal for a terrific view of airfield activities. (You may even spot the Concorde since Dulles is one of only two North American gateways for the sleek supersonic jet.) Currently in the midst of a major expansion and modernization project to keep pace with the rapid growth in air service and passengers, the 10,000-acre airport has been chosen as the site for an annex of the filled-to-capacity National Air and Space Museum downtown. The facility will house such aviation gems as a NASA space shuttle, the sinister-looking SR-71 "Blackbird" spy plane and numerous commercial aircraft.

Woodlawn Plantation

9000 Richmond Hwy., Alexandria (Fairfax County) *(703) 780-4000*

Another of southern Fairfax County's architectural icons, Woodlawn Plantation was the Georgian estate home of Nellie Custis Lewis, granddaughter of George and Martha Washington. The richly appointed mansion, a virtual neighbor of Mount Vernon, was designed by William Thornton, architect of the U.S. Capitol. The spacious grounds also feature the Pope-Leighey House, designed by Frank Lloyd Wright in 1939.

Suburban Maryland

Andrews Air Force Base

I-95 at Exit 9, Camp Springs *(301) 981-4511*

Located just off the Capital Beltway (you can't miss the monstrous water tower), Andrews Air Force Base is probably best known as the home of the presidential aircraft fleet. But it's also the official entrance point to the Nation's Capital for foreign dignitaries, heads of states and many other international guests bound for White House meetings and other high-profile events. Andrews was originally established in 1942 by President Franklin Roosevelt as an Army airfield. Tours are available by appointment. The base hosts an annual open house each spring that draws hordes of aviation buffs to the static displays of military aircraft and weaponry.

Beall-Dawson House & Doctors Museum

103 West Montgomery Ave., Rockville *(301) 762-1492*

This authentically-restored brick house, dating to 1815 and furnished in the Federal style, is the headquarters of the Montgomery County Historical Society. The adjacent museum offers fascinating insight into early surgical practices and medical treatments.

C&O Canal Museum/ Great Falls Tavern

Great Falls Park, 11710 MacArthur Blvd., Potomac *(301) 299-3613*

This National Park Service facility — not to be confused with the Virginia side of the park across the Potomac in Great Falls — was built in the 1830s as a traveler's inn along the Chesapeake & Ohio Canal, at that time a major commercial thoroughfare (via mule-drawn barges) between Cumberland, Md., and the District. Great Falls Tavern today houses artifacts and exhibits depicting early canal life. Barge rides are offered between April and October; fall and spring are particularly beautiful times to visit. For a cheap thrill, try one of the footbridges that span the turbulent river.

Chesapeake Bay Bridge

Route 50, Anne Arundel/ Queen Anne's counties (410) 288-8405

Officially the William Preston Lane, Jr. Memorial Bridge, the Bay Bridge, as it's affectionately known, connects Metro Washington with the rural charms of Maryland's Eastern Shore and the Atlantic Coast resorts of the Delmarva Peninsula. The approximately four-mile twin spans offer a spectacular view of the world's largest estuary. Motorists pay a $2.50 toll before heading eastbound.

Maryland State House

State Circle, Annapolis (410) 974-3400

The beautiful Maryland State House is yet another reason to visit the historic sailing mecca of Annapolis. The focal point of Maryland's government, this is the nation's oldest state house in continuous legislative use. It even served as capitol of the U.S. for several months in 1783-84 and is the place where George Washington resigned his commission as commander of the Continental Army and where the Treaty of Paris was ratified, ending the Revolutionary War. Be sure not to miss the great exhibits depicting Annapolis during Colonial times.

National Capital Trolley Museum

1313 Bonifant Rd., Wheaton (301) 384-6352

This underappreciated regional attraction features demonstrations and displays of antique electric streetcars from the U.S. and Europe. There's also an interesting audio-visual show.

National Institutes of Health

Building 10, 9000 Rockville Pike, Bethesda (301) 496-1776

NIH is where doctors, scientists and technicians wage war against some of society's most devastating illnesses including cancer, heart disease, diabetes, AIDS, arthritis and Alzheimer's. This sprawling federal health research complex, perhaps the nation's preeminent medical resource, includes the National Library of Medicine (8600 Rockville Pike; 301-496-6308), the largest medical library in the world that includes a reading room and a department specializing in historic and rare books. The NIH Visitors Center offers a slide show, films and a "working" lab. Tours of the NIH grounds are available Monday, Wednesday and Friday.

U.S. Naval Academy

Bordered by King George Street and the Severn River, Annapolis (410) 263-6933

It's hard not to get a lump in your throat and feel exceedingly patriotic when you set foot on the gorgeous grounds of this National Historic Site where naval officers have been trained since 1845. The academy chapel dominates the scene; below the building lies the crypt of John Paul Jones. Other campus highlights include a museum featuring models, swords and paintings; Bancroft Hall, where the Brigade Noon Formation takes place; numerous monuments dedicated to naval heroes and battles; and Navy-

Marine Corps Memorial Stadium. Tours of the academy are available.

Patuxent Wildlife Research Center

Route 197, Laurel *(301) 498-0342*

A wildlife research facility amid the din of Metro Washington? Indeed. This agency of the U.S. Department of the Interior conducts vital investigations involving a variety of endangered species. Guided tours are available by reservation.

Major Annual Events in Metro Washington

(Please note that for the most part we have omitted dates, times and hours because they so often change from year to year. Instead, you'll find contact numbers for people and organizations who can provide a wealth of detailed information far more accurate then we could have ever hoped to include.)

January

District of Columbia

Martin Luther King Jr.'s Birthday Observance

Lincoln Memorial *(202) 619-7222*

Local choirs, guest speakers and a military color guard salute the memory of the influential civil rights leader at the site where, on a sweltering summer afternoon in 1963, he led one of the largest public demonstrations ever held in Washington. King delivered his famous "I Have a Dream" speech from the memorial steps.

Chinese New Year Parade

H St. NW between 5th and 8th sts. *(202) 724-4091*

The Lunar New Year is a time to close accounts, pay debts, clean house, honor ancestors, prepare exotic foods and thank the gods for a prosperous year. The residents of Washington's Chinatown do it all in style, with traditional firecrackers, drums and colorful dragon dancers that make their way through the streets flanked typically by more than 10,000 onlookers.

Northern Virginia

Robert E. Lee's Birthday Celebration

Arlington National Cemetery *(703) 557-0613*

In tribute to one of Virginia's and the South's greatest military heroes, the door's of Lee's cherished Arlington House open wide for an afternoon of 19th-century music, samples of period food and displays of restoration work.

Suburban Maryland

Annapolis Heritage Antique Show

Medford National Guard Armory, Annapolis *(410) 222-1919*

This giant of an antiques show is set most appropriately in one of the nation's premiere antiquing meccas — Annapolis.

February

District of Columbia

Abraham Lincoln's Birthday (Feb. 12)

Lincoln Memorial *(202) 619-7222*

A wreath-laying ceremony and reading of the Gettysburg Address are the highlights of the 16th president's birthday celebration at his namesake memorial.

Washington Boat Show

Washington Convention Center, 900 9th St. NW *(202) 789-1600*
Admission fee

The latest in pleasure craft and equipment are on display at this annual event which has become a tremendous draw in boat-crazed Metro Washington.

Northern Virginia

George Washington's Birthday Parade (Feb. 15)

Old Town Alexandria *(703) 838-4200*

Old Town plays host to the nation's largest birthday parade honoring a native son and America's first president. Make sure to bundle up.

Mount Vernon Open House (Feb. 15)

Mount Vernon Estate *(703) 780-2000*

After the parade in Old Town, head down to George Washington's lovely estate on the Potomac for an afternoon of period costumes, music and food. A tour of the house on this special day is well worth the wait in line.

March

District of Columbia

St. Patrick's Day Parade

Constitution Avenue NW *(301) 424-2200*

Salute the Irish and sport the green in style during this always-festive downtown parade that features traditional dancers, bagpipers and floats galore.

National Cherry Blossom Festival

The Tidal Basin and various parks and locations downtown *(202) 789-7000*

Perhaps Washington's most visible fete, the National Cherry Blossom Festival honors the extraordinary blooming of the city's 6,000 Japanese cherry trees, surely one of the most beautiful sights in America. The capstone event is the Cherry Blossom Festival Parade (the first Saturday in April), but scores of related parties and ceremonies begin the last week of March. The trees bloom anywhere from late March to early April, depending on how cooperative Mother Nature is. A word to the wise: If at all possible, take Metro into Washington and walk to the Tidal Basin. It's a short jaunt from most stops downtown and you'll save yourself the agony of trying to find a parking space.

Smithsonian Kite Festival

Washington Monument Grounds *(202) 357-3244*

Nothing signals the dawn of spring quite like the sight of multicolored kites dipping and soaring next to the Washington Monument.

Kite makers and flyers of all ages compete for prizes and trophies.

Northern Virginia

St. Patrick's Day Parade

Old Town Alexandria (703) 549-4535

Usually held a day or two before the D.C. parade, Old Town's festivities extend beyond the parade route and into the city's popular Irish pubs, such as Murphy's and Ireland's Own.

Woodlawn Plantation Annual Needlework Exhibition

Woodlawn Plantation
Alexandria (Fairfax County) (703) 780-4000

Needlework crafts from the 18th century to the present day are on display at this lovely plantation, about three miles east of the Mount Vernon estate.

Suburban Maryland

Belair Mansion Annual Quilt Show

Bowie City Hall
(Prince George's County) (301) 262-0738
Admission fee

Heirloom and contemporary quilts are showcased in this benefit to help restore Belair Mansion, one of the most historic homes in Maryland.

April

District of Columbia

White House Easter Egg Roll

The White House, East Executive Ave. NW (Southeast Gate) (202) 456-2200

Children age eight and under, accompanied by an adult, gather on the White House South Lawn for the annual Easter Egg Roll. This is easily the best opportunity in town for youngsters — and for that matter, parents — to play at the president's house.

White House Spring Garden Tours

The White House (202) 456-2200

The gorgeous gardens of the presidential home are open to the public during these annual tours (usually for two days during the second week of the month). Highlights include the Jacqueline Kennedy Rose Gardens and the spectacular West Lawn Gardens.

Filmfest D.C.

Theaters and reception halls throughout the city (202) 727-2396

The Clintons aren't the only ones with Hollywood connections. All of Washington is the focus of the cinematic world during this two-week festival (which spills over into April) of international and American film. Washington, as you probably already know, is one of the top movie markets in the U.S. and one of the most filmed cities in the world.

Smithsonian's Washington Craft Show

Andrew Mellon Auditorium
1301 Constitution Ave. NW
(202) 357-2700

Some 100 juried exhibitors show their original crafts at this wildly popular event featuring fiber, ceramics, glass, jewelry, leather, metal, paper, textiles and wood.

Earth Day (April 22)

National Mall *(202) 619-7222*

The environmentally correct and concerned gather in the "Nation's Frontyard" to learn about ways to keep the planet green.

Northern Virginia

Easter Sunrise Service

Arlington National Cemetery *(202) 475-0856*

An inspiring setting — the cemetery's Memorial Amphitheatre — awaits early morning worshippers.

Historic Garden Week in Virginia

Statewide *(804) 644-7776*

The finest in Virginia homes and gardens are spotlighted during this week-long festival. The above phone number will connect you with tours in Northern Virginia. Our favorites include the gardens at such area plantations as Mount Vernon, Gunston Hall and Oatlands.

Suburban Maryland

Give A Day for the Chesapeake Bay

Statewide *(410) 974-5300*

Marylanders statewide have plenty of opportunities to do their part to help clean up the Chesapeake Bay, America's largest estuary and the Free State's most treasured natural resource. Local activities include tree plantings, stream cleanups and trash removals.

Annapolis Waterfront Festival

Annapolis Yacht Basin *(410) 268-8828*

The capital city honors its maritime heritage during this three-day festival.

May

District of Columbia

Gross National Parade

M and 18th sts. NW *(202) 686-3215*

Washington pokes fun at itself and its offbeat traditions during this annual parade that draws upwards of 100,000 spectators. The festival benefits the Police Boys and Girls Clubs of Washington.

Georgetown Garden Tour

Georgetown *(202) 333-4953*
Admission fee

The private gardens of this famed neighborhood are on display, with proceeds benefiting the Georgetown Children's House. Guided and self-guided tours are available.

Memorial Day Weekend Concert

West Lawn of the Capitol (202) 619-7222

A kick-off to the summer tourist season, this popular concert features the globally acclaimed National Symphony Orchestra in an unforgettable setting under the stars.

Memorial Day Ceremonies

Vietnam Veterans Memorial (202) 619-7222

Speeches, military bands and a keynote address are the centerpieces of this solemn event.

Northern Virginia

Virginia Gold Cup

Great Meadow, The Plains (Fauquier County) (703) 253-5001
Admission fee

Usually held the same day as the Kentucky Derby, Virginia's premier steeplechase has blossomed into one of the largest sporting and social events in Metro Washington. Great Meadow is in the heart of the state's gorgeous hunt country, about an hour west of Washington.

Memorial Day Ceremonies

Arlington National Cemetery(202) 475-0856

Wreath-layings at the John F. Kennedy gravesite and the Tomb of the Unknowns are part of the ceremonies that wind down with a service at the Memorial Amphitheatre. The president usually delivers the keynote address.

Suburban Maryland

Kemper Open Pro-Am Golf Tournament

Avenel Country Club, Potomac (301) 469-3737
Admission fee

The Pro-Am classic features some of the brightest stars on the PGA Tour plus a handful of local celebrities. Redskins quarterback Mark Rypien made the rigorous final cut a few years ago but met his match against the likes of Greg Norman and John Daly.

Chesapeake Bay Bridge Walk

Chesapeake Bay Bridge (Anne Arundel/Queen Anne's counties) (410) 288-8405

Here's your opportunity to take in the magnificent vistas of the Chesapeake Bay — at a leisurely pace. The 4.3-mile walk, enjoyed by thousands of locals and visitors, covers the eastbound span of the Bay Bridge.

Andrews Air Force Base Open House

Andrews Air Force Base, Camp Springs (301) 981-4511

See firsthand how those tax dollars are being spent at this impressive showing of American military and technological might. Andrews is perhaps best known as the home of Air Force One, the president's jet.

June

District of Columbia

Festival of American Folklife

National Mall *(202) 357-2700*

The rich cultural and folklife heritage of the Americas is played out on the National Mall in the form of lectures, concerts, working villages and hands-on exhibits. The festival runs through the 4th of July and attracts upwards of one million people.

Children's Festival

Carter Barron Amphitheatre, 16th St. and Colorado Ave. NW *(202) 619-7226*
Admission fee

Sponsored by the Capital Children's Museum and the National Park Service, this day-long festival includes live music, performing arts and a host of interactive programs.

Dupont-Kalorama Museum Walk Day

Dupont Circle *(202) 387-2151*

D.C.'s most famous arts district extends a gracious welcome through house tours, craft demonstrations and concerts. A shuttle service is provided.

Northern Virginia

Red Cross Waterfront Festival

Oronoco Bay Park, Old Town Alexandria *(703) 549-8300*
Admission fee

One of Alexandria's top summer events, the Red Cross Waterfront Festival brings in a weekend full of music (including some top-name rock, country and reggae acts), ethnic foods, arts and crafts, fireworks, tall ships and, alas, a 10K run to work off those calories.

Antique Car Show

Sully Plantation, Chantilly *(703) 437-1794*

A car-lover's fantasy land unfolds at this historic plantation in western Fairfax County, in the shadows of Washington Dulles International Airport.

Fairfax Fair

Fairfax County Government Center *(703) 246-FAIR*
Admission fee

Not exactly a country fair, but then again Fairfax County hasn't been rural for quite some time. Instead of livestock and produce, you'll get your fill of government service information and community programs. And, of course, there's plenty of music, games and rides along the midway for the kids.

Suburban Maryland

Spirit of America Pageant

USAir Arena, Landover *(202) 475-0685*

This unique telling of American history is played out through patriotic music and skits by the 3rd U.S. Infantry and the U.S. Army Band.

July

District of Columbia

National Independence Day Celebration (July 4th)

National Mall *(202) 619-7222*

Washington fittingly plays host to the nation's largest 4th of July party, with a parade down Constitution Avenue, colonial military maneuvers, concerts at the Sylvan Theatre next to the Washington Monument and an evening performance by the National Symphony Orchestra on the west steps of the Capitol. The day ends with a spectacular 45-minute fireworks exhibit that has been known to draw more than a million onlookers — on both sides of the river.

Bastille Day Waiters' Race

Dominique's Restaurant, 20th St. and Pennsylvania Ave. NW *(202) 452-1132*

To commemorate France's independence, one of Washington's signature French restaurants sponsors this unusual but highly entertaining race in which waiters and customers race along Pennsylvania Avenue carrying champagne glasses on trays for a grand prize trip to Paris.

Latin-American Festival

Adams Morgan and the National Mall *(202) 269-0101*

The music, dance, art, food and theater of Latin America are the focus of a two-day heritage festival that takes place in the eclectic Adams Morgan neighborhood and on the grounds of the Washington Monument.

Northern Virginia

Virginia Scottish Games

Episcopal High School, 3901 W. Braddock Rd. Alexandria *(703) 838-5005*
Admission fee

Northern Virginia shows off its proud Scottish heritage at this weekend fete featuring Highland dancing, bagpiping, fiddling and traditional athletic events. Scottish foods, crafts and genealogy exhibits are also an integral part of the popular festival.

Vienna's Fourth of July Celebration

Waters Field, Vienna *(703) 255-6300*

One of suburban Washington's oldest July 4th celebrations, Vienna presents a viable small-town alternative to the pressing crowds and traffic associated with the downtown D.C. festivities.

Suburban Maryland

Rotary Crab Feast

U.S. Navy-Marine Corps Stadium, Annapolis *(410) 266-7848*
Admission fee

Lovers of Maryland's prized crustacean will want to bring a hefty appetite to this, the world's largest crab feast. The spicy event benefits the Annapolis Rotary Club.

August

District of Columbia

U.S. Army Band's "1812 Overture"

Sylvan Theatre adjacent to the Washington Monument *(703) 696-3718*

Guaranteed to get the patriotic juices flowing, the "1812" gets a dose of firepower from the Salute Gun Platoon of the 3rd U.S. Infantry.

Georgia Avenue Day

Georgia and Eastern aves. NW *(202) 723-5166*

Georgia Avenue, D.C.'s longest business corridor, comes alive with a parade, carnival rides, live music and a wealth of festive foods.

Northern Virginia

Arlington County Fair

Thomas Jefferson Center,
3501 S. 2nd St. *(703) 358-6400*

Arlington's urban multicultural heritage is the cause celebre of this four-day fair typically held the third week of the month.

Civil War Living History Day

Fort Ward Museum and Park
4301 W. Braddock Rd.,
Alexandria *(703) 838-4848*

Fort Ward was one of several Union fortifications that encircled Washington during the Civil War. This living history reenacts Union and Confederate camp life, complete with artillery drills.

Suburban Maryland

Maryland Renaissance Festival

Crownsville *(800) 243-7304*

The Free State slips into a medieval state of mind during this well-attended festival held usually the last weekend of August and extending into October. Jousting events, jugglers, medieval foods and crafts are just some of the many delights that await visitors at this 20-acre "village" located in the heart of suburban Crownsville.

Montgomery County Agricultural Fair

Montgomery County Fairgrounds,
Gaithersburg *(301) 926-3100*
Admission fee

There's still plenty of rural character remaining in this highly urbanized county, as evidenced by the breadth and popularity of this old-fashioned country fair.

September

District of Columbia

National Frisbee Festival

National Mall adjacent to the National Air & Space Museum *(301) 645-5043*

Believe it or not, Washington even has a festival honoring those ubiquitous plastic spheroids. The disc-catching dogs steal the show every year.

Adams Morgan Day

Columbia Rd. and
Florida Ave. NW *(202) 332-3292*

This giant ethnic festival, a salute to Adams Morgan's multicultural character, is a hot ticket with the city's young and hip crowd. Expect to hear great music and sample some of the city's best international cuisine.

Kalorama House and Embassy Tour

Kalorama Neighborhood, north of Dupont Circle *(202) 387-4062*
Admission fee

Historic Kalorama remains one of D.C.'s most exclusive and interesting neighborhoods. It's a great opportunity to visit the Woodrow Wilson House, now a museum property of the National Trust for Historic Preservation.

Rock Creek Park Day

Rock Creek Park *(202) 426-6832*

A slate of environmental, recreational and historical programs are in store during this day-long tribute to one of the world's largest and most beautiful urban parks.

Labor Day Weekend Concert

West Lawn of the Capitol *(202) 619-7222*

The National Symphony Orchestra officially closes Washington's summer tourist season with a rousing selection of classical and patriotic arrangements.

Northern Virginia

International Children's Festival

Wolf Trap Farm Park for the Performing Arts, Vienna *(703) 642-0862*
Admission fee

Kids take center stage during this three-day outdoor festival celebrating the global arts and held at America's only national park dedicated to the performing arts. A variety of performances and educational workshops are presented by national and international groups.

Occoquan Fall Craft Show

Old Town Occoquan *(703) 491-1346*

More than 300 juried artisans, representing 30 states, exhibit their wares in front of some 100,000 shoppers. The weekend fair just might be the largest craft show on the East Coast.

Suburban Maryland

Maryland Seafood Festival

Sandy Point State Park (near Annapolis) *(410) 268-7682*
Admission fee

The bounty of the Chesapeake Bay is presented in a variety of ways — baked, steamed, grilled, sauteed, fried — at this waterside park located adjacent to the western end of the towering Bay Bridge.

Kunte Kinte Heritage Commemoration and Festival

St. John's College Waterfront, Annapolis *(410) 841-6504*

Made into a household name with the screening of TV's "Roots," Kunte Kinte was brought into the harsh New World at the Port of Annapolis. The festival honors his legacy and the rich traditions of generations of succeeding African Americans.

Prince George's County Fair

Prince George's Equestrian Center, Upper Marlboro *(301) 952-1401*
Admission fee

Like neighboring Montgomery County, urbanized Prince George's still holds strong to its rural origins. The county was once a major producer of tobacco, and vestiges of that tradition can still be seen in areas far beyond the Beltway.

October

District of Columbia

Taste of D.C. Festival

Pennsylvania Ave. between 9th and 14th sts. NW (202) 724-4091

Washington's top restaurants lay it on the line in this public tasting, which also includes live entertainment, arts and craft exhibits and games for the kids.

Fall D.C. Antiques Fair

D.C. Armory (301) 738-0360
Admission fee

Nearly 200 dealers from 20 states, Canada and Europe display their heirlooms at this popular show.

Theodore Roosevelt's Birthday Celebration

Theodore Roosevelt Island (703) 285-2702

The scenic urban wilderness sanctuary of Roosevelt Island plays host to this birthday party honoring the nation's first environmental president.

Northern Virginia

Vienna Halloween Parade

Maple Avenue (Route 123), Vienna (703) 255-6300

Vienna claims the region's oldest (since the 1940s) and largest (several thousand strong) Halloween Parade, which wends its way along a healthy stretch of the town's main thoroughfare.

Waterford Homes Tour and Crafts Show

Historic Waterford (Loudoun County) (703) 882-3018

About 50 years ago a group of Waterford residents had the fore-

Photo: Virginia Div. of Tourism

Colorful bagpipe bands are a major feature of the Scottish Christmas Walk, held in December.

sight to set up a preservation foundation to keep this picturesque National Historic Landmark village from going the way of suburbanization. The annual homes tour and crafts fair, which features over 100 juried artisans, benefits ongoing restoration and preservation efforts.

SUBURBAN MARYLAND

U.S. SAILBOAT SHOW/ U.S. POWER BOAT SHOW

Annapolis City Dock *(410) 268-8828*

Held on consecutive weekends, with the sailors going first, these are the largest in-water boat shows in the nation. With zillions of boats and nautical products from the world's leading manufacturers, Annapolis turns into a sort of Woodstock for the water-loving set.

WASHINGTON INTERNATIONAL HORSE SHOW

USAir Arena, Landover *(301) 840-0281*

Equestrian teams from the U.S. and Europe compete in a week-long set of events, with plenty of sideline shows for laymen and kids.

November

MARINE CORPS MARATHON

Downtown D.C. adjacent to the National Mall *(703) 690-3431*
Registration fee for runners

Thousands of world-class runners snake through the streets and parks of downtown in what has become one of the most prestigious marathons in the nation. While most of the running takes place in Washington, the race begins and ends in Arlington.

VETERANS DAY CEREMONIES

Vietnam Veterans Memorial and Arlington National Cemetery *(202) 619-7222*

Both solemn and celebratory, the ceremonies attract thousands of veterans, military VIPs, general spectators and, on occasion, the president.

NORTHERN VIRGINIA

ALEXANDRIA ANTIQUES SHOW

Old Colony Inn, Old Town Alexandria *(703) 838-4200*
Admission

You guessed it, more antiques and crafts from the veritable heirloom gold mine of the Mid-Atlantic.

SUBURBAN MARYLAND

CAPITAL CAT FANCIERS CAT SHOW

Montgomery County Fairgrounds, Gaithersburg *(301) 926-0746*

For fans of felines, this is the cat's meow. Two days of pawing, purring and prized cats.

SUGARLOAF'S AUTUMN CRAFTS FESTIVAL

Montgomery County Fairgrounds, Gaithersburg *(301) 990-1400*

This is it, the granddaddy of all Metro D.C. craft shows, featuring 425 juried artisans. It'll take you two hours just to walk the grounds, let alone browse and shop.

December

District of Columbia

National Christmas Tree Lighting/Pageant of Peace

The Ellipse (directly behind White House) *(202) 619-7222*

The president lights the giant National Christmas Tree and officially kicks off the Christmas season. From early December to New Year's Day, the Ellipse is the site of nightly choral concerts, a Nativity scene, a burning yule log and lighted Christmas trees from each state and territory in the U.S.

Washington National Cathedral Christmas Celebration and Services

Washington National Cathedral, Massachusetts and Wisconsin aves. NW *(202) 537-6200*

Whether you're spiritual or not, the Christmas Eve service here at Washington's answer to the great cathedrals of Europe is simply breathtaking.

Northern Virginia

Alexandria Scottish Christmas Walk

Old Town Alexandria *(703) 838-4200*

A gathering of the clans, bagpipes and all, takes over the streets and alleyways of Old Town for one of the holiday season's most festive events.

Suburban Maryland

Christmas Lights Parade

Annapolis City Dock *(410) 267-8986*

Annapolitans decorate their yachts with Christmas lights for this highly visual, and often chilly, evening on the Chesapeake Bay.

Festival of Lights

Washington Mormon Temple Visitors Center, Kensington *(301) 587-0144*

Tens of thousands of lights adorn the grounds of this Oz-like temple that looms above the Capital Beltway. The temple itself is open only to those of the Mormon faith.

Tour Operators

It takes a while to find your way around any new place, so until you get your bearings straight, what better way to get an overview of all the top attractions than to take a professionally guided tour? It's not just something visitors do, ya know.

The following companies provide regular, scheduled sightseeing excursions for the general public. Except for one, all are Washington-based.

All About Town, 519 6th St. NW, (202) 393-3696

A Scandal Tour of Washington, 1727 Q St. NW, (202) 387-2253

Gold Line, Inc. (Operator of Gray Line Sightseeing), Gray Line Terminal, Union Station, 50 Massachusetts Ave. NE, (202) 289-1995

Old Town Trolley Tours of Washington, 3150 V St. NE, (202) 269-3020

Tourmobile Sightseeing, 1000 Ohio Dr. SW, (202) 554-7950

Wheels Across Washington (Horse & Carriage Tours), 2704 Warrenton Rd., Hartwood, Va. 22405, (703) 752-4763

Convention and Tourist Bureaus/ Tourist Information

We suggest you contact the following agencies to receive comprehensive packets of travel and tourism information.

District of Columbia

Washington, D.C. Convention and Visitors Association, 1212 New York Ave. NE, Washington, DC 20005, (202) 789-7000

Northern Virginia

Virginia Division of Tourism, 1021 E. Cary St., Richmond, Va. 23219, (804) 786-2051

Alexandria Convention and Visitors Bureau, 221 King St., Alexandria, Va. 22314, (703) 838-4200

Arlington Convention & Visitors Service, 2100 Clarendon Blvd., #1, Courthouse Plaza, Suite 608, Arlington, Va. 22201, (703) 358-5720

Fairfax County Tourism & Convention Bureau, 8300 Boone Blvd., Suite 450, Vienna, Va. 22182, (703) 790-0600

Loudoun County Tourist Information Center, 108-D South St. SE, Leesburg, Va. 22075, (703) 777-0519

Prince William County Tourist Information Center, 200 Mill St., Occoquan, Va. 22125, (703) 491-4045

Suburban Maryland

Maryland Office of Tourist Development, 217 E. Redwood St., Baltimore, Md. 21202, (410) 333-6611

Annapolis & Anne Arundel County Conference and Visitors Bureau, 1 Annapolis St., Annapolis, Md. 21401, (410) 280-0445

Montgomery County Conference & Visitors Bureau, 12900 Middlebrook Rd., Suite 1400, Germantown, Md. 20874-2616, (301) 588-8687

Prince George's County Conference & Visitors Bureau, 8903 Presidential Pkwy., Suite 201, Upper Marlboro, Md. 20772, (301) 967-8687

The National Museum of Natural History is home to fossils, dinosaurs and exhibits of American, African, Indian and Pacific cultures. It also houses the world's largest diamond.

Inside Metro Washington Arts

Metro Washington, a vibrant arts community? OK, for those of you who may have responded to this rhetorical question with a snicker, you can stop now and dismiss any notion about the region's undeserved reputation as something of a cultural abyss. Politics, government, big money, high-technology, brains and an international populace, of course. But the arts? In Metro Washington? As sure as you can find a lawyer on K Street.

Part of this perception problem, of course, is that Washington has long been viewed as a consumer of the arts (black-tie galas, high-profile gallery and museum exhibits, film screenings, etc.) but not a creator. It may have taken a while to bloom, but the arts scene here is rich and diverse. From the repertory theaters of 14th Street and the burgeoning artists' colonies of Old Town Alexandria, Adams Morgan, Dupont Circle, Georgetown and Takoma Park, to the esteemed National Symphony Orchestra and such renowned venues as the Kennedy Center and Wolf Trap Farm Park — the nation's only national park dedicated to the performing arts — the cultural landscape of Metro Washington is continually expanding.

But it really shouldn't come as a surprise. It seems to have been overlooked along the way, but Washington has produced more than its fair share of cultural luminaries, especially in the areas of stage, screen and studio. Among those who have (or had) ties to the area, whether by birth or stints working or attending school here, are Ella Fitzgerald, Pearl Bailey, Helen Hayes, Goldie Hawn, Warren Beatty, Shirley MacLaine, Beverly Sills, and guitar virtuosos Danny Gatton and Roy Buchanan.

Metro Washington is one of the most filmed communities in the world, and the city enjoys increasingly close ties to Hollywood. So it only seems logical that film stars John Lithgow, Susan Sarandon and Jon Voight all cut their theatrical teeth at Washington's own Catholic University, whose drama department is among the finest in the nation.

We could go on, but we thought you'd appreciate if we got to the point of this chapter. We naturally can't cover everything, so we've assembled an overview of the major arts elements covering such areas as stage performance (theater, dance and musical concerts), galleries, movie houses and comedy clubs. Some of these areas we cover more in-depth in the Attractions and Night Life chapters, so please refer to those sections of the book for more comprehensive information.

Taking Center Stage

If all the world's a stage and if Washington is indeed the nerve center of the globe, then it stands to reason that the Nation's Capital should have a pretty unparalleled theater scene.

Truth is we don't have the equivalent of the "Great White Way" here. New York is New York and if you want too see the biggest, brightest and best in American theater and dance, Broadway is only 220 miles to the Northeast.

That's not to slight Metro Washington in the least, however. Not only does the region claim a growing theater community, but it also boasts some of the greatest playhouses in the world, starting with the John F. Kennedy Center for the Performing Arts (202-467-4600).

Inside this "living memorial" to the nation's 34th president are no less than six theaters, four of which are regularly used for theatrical productions. The 2,318-seat Opera House occasionally hosts a major Broadway production, such as 1993's popular running of "Phantom of the Opera." The Opera House also hosts performances of the prestigious Washington Ballet Company as well as several national and international dance troupes. The Eisenhower Theater, about half the size of the Opera House, showcases most of the large-scale productions, while smaller shows, like the five-year-running "Shear Madness," are accommodated in the Terrace Theater and Theater Lab.

The National Theatre (202-628-6161), just down the street from the White House, has been bringing stage entertainment to Washingtonians since 1835. In fact, every president since then, with the exception of Dwight Eisenhower, has attended a show here. The National's forte is booking the big musicals, such as "Cats" and "Crazy for You."

Across town on the Southwest waterfront's Maine Avenue, the nationally recognized Arena Stage (202-488-3300) presents a mix of classical and contemporary shows, including the provocative works of David Mammet and August Wilson. The three-theater complex has proven to be a hotbed for up-and-coming talent and for previously untried productions.

The Lansburgh Theatre (202-488-3300), located in a revitalizing section of downtown near the National Gallery of Art, is home to Washington's resident Shakespeare company.

Fans of the master British playwright will also want to venture over to Capitol Hill to the Folger Shakespeare Elizabethan Theatre (202-544-7077), where you can see innovative productions of the Bard's plays put on by the Folger Theater Group. The Folger Consort Group, meanwhile, presents a slate of concerts of medieval, renaissance and baroque music.

One of the most historic and tragic buildings in America, Ford's Theatre (202-426-6927), on 10th Street NW, has been painstakingly

The John F. Kennedy Center for the Performing Arts has six theatres to accommodate a variety of productions.

restored to its condition the night of April 14, 1865, when President Lincoln was shot in the presidential box. Today, Ford's remains an active and immensely popular theater, staging a broad spectrum of family-oriented productions.

Avant-garde and alternative theater are also alive and well in the Nation's Capital, as they should be. All within a five-block section of 14th Street NW are such off- and off-off-Broadway-type enclaves as Woolly Mammoth Theatre (202-393-3939), Studio Theatre (202-332-3300), Horizons Theatre (202-342-5503) and Source Theatre (202-462-1073). In July and August, the Washington Theatre Festival at the Source showcases new plays and playwrights, many from the Washington area.

Some of the finest student theater in the U.S. takes place on stage at Catholic University's Hartke Theater (202-635-5367). CU's dramatic productions often rival some of the best professional theater in the city.

In Northern Virginia, Old Town Alexandria's Little Theatre (703-683-0496) stages a number of traditional and family-oriented community theater productions such as "The Bells Are Ringing."

The West End Dinner Theatre (703-370-2500) in Alexandria and Woodbridge's Lazy Susan Dinner Theatre (703-550-7384) have found a strong niche with the tourist-group market, but also appeal to suburbanites yearning for traditional, not to mention affordable, dramas, comedies and musicals. The meals aren't too shabby either.

Suburban Maryland's best-known playhouse is Olney Theatre (301-924-3400), a converted barn located in the countryside of Montgomery County. Summer theater is the staple here, with quality productions like William Nicholson's Broadway hit "Shadowlands."

Not too far away, The Burn Brae Dinner Theatre (301-384-5800) in Burtonsville leans toward the big musical hits like "The Pirates of Penzance."

A Word About Tickets

The most convenient way to get tickets to Washington area shows is over the phone via TicketMaster (202-432-7328) or Telecharge (800-233-3123). With either service expect a small surcharge. Of course, you can always purchase at the box office, but sometimes finding same-day tickets, especially during the tourist season and for big shows, can be tricky. Best bet is to reserve ahead of time.

If you're like us and place a premium on discount tickets, then head over to Ticketplace (202-842-5387), downtown at 12th and F sts. NW. Here you can find reduced-rate tickets for shows that day only. There are no advanced purchases, and all transactions are done in cash. The outlet is open Tuesdays through Fridays, noon to 4 PM, and Saturdays 11 AM to 5 PM.

The Sound of Music

No one will ever question the fact that the Washington area moves to a different beat. That includes the literal interpretation. Anchored by the Kennedy Center and Northern Virginia's Wolf Trap Farm Park, Metro Washington knows no music unfamiliar to its discerning ears.

The area, after all, has produced its share of musical greats, including jazz legend Duke Ellington, rock 'n' roller Jim Morrison, contemporary songstress Roberta Flack and country sensation Mary Chapin Carpenter.

Live-music aficionados new to the Washington area should find nary a dull moment here. Each week, you can bet you'll uncover at least one major concert that fits your taste or mood—whether it be rock, country and western, opera, classical, bluegrass, R&B or folk.

Washingtonians take great pride in the region's wealth of musical venues, from the massive to the intimate. The Kennedy Center Concert Hall, which from October through April plays host to regular performances by the National Symphony Orchestra (202-785-8100), is recognized worldwide for its impeccable acoustics. Ditto for the center's Opera House, home to the Opera Society of Washington (202-822-

Insiders' Tip

Insiders...

Like to go on Sunday afternoon gallery hops through Dupont Circle, taking in lunch or dinner at one of the neighborhood's many outdoor bistros along or near Connecticut Avenue.

4757) whose season extends from October through March.

D.A.R. Constitution Hall (202-638-2661), near the White House, is an equally impressive venue, serving up its share of classical and pop music performances. It's been said that Vladimir Horowitz, the legendary pianist, prefers to perform in this classy and surprisingly intimate atmosphere.

With the Washington Monument looming in the background, the outdoor Sylvan Theatre (202-485-9666) stages a number of military, big band and pop concerts during warm-weather months. The city's other major outdoor stage, the Carter Barron Amphitheatre (202-485-9666) located in Rock Creek Park, sponsors an annual summer musical festival, including many top names in jazz, soul and R&B.

Downtown, the recently refurbished Warner Theater (202-626-1050), a former vaudeville palace, and George Washington University's Lisner Auditorium (202-994-6800) are two of the area's most coveted pop-music concert sites. Both also play host to jazz, world-beat and other eclectic music and stage offerings.

Due east of the Capitol, RFK Stadium (202-547-9077) is known primarily as the home of the Washington Redskins football team, a cultural icon in itself. The 55,000-seat stadium is also used for those monolithic rock concerts and festivals that seem synonymous with summertime. Acoustically, well, it's a football stadium. But as a host for the often excessive pageantry of rock 'n' roll, RFK plays the role rather well.

Some claim Northern Virginia came of age musically with the opening of Wolf Trap Farm Park (703-255-1900) over 20 years ago. This

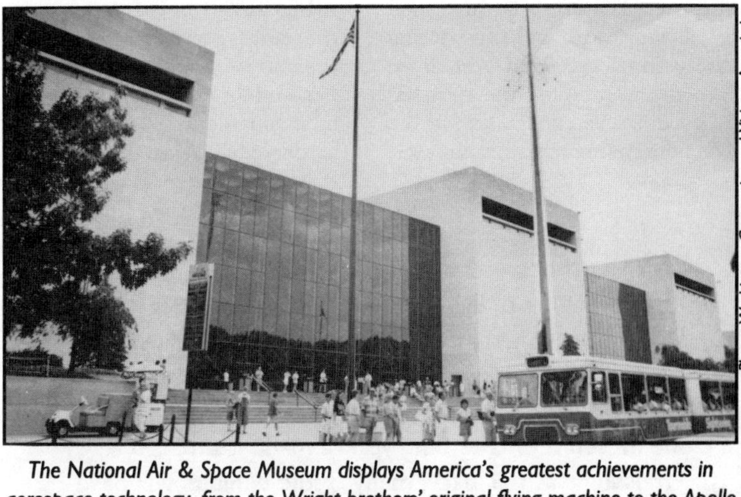

Photo: Washington Convention and Visitors Association

The National Air & Space Museum displays America's greatest achievements in aerospace technology, from the Wright brothers' original flying machine to the Apollo 11 command module.

beautiful National Park Service facility, with its covered wooden pavilion and outdoor lawn seating, brings to the Virginia suburbs some of the world's leading musical entertainers. The park's annual summer concert series is free of musical boundaries. The Moody Blues may perform on a Friday night, followed by a Saturday afternoon Cajun music festival and a Sunday journey through Lake Wobegon with Garrison Keillor. A smaller indoor concert hall, the Barns at Wolf Trap, is used primarily as a showplace for folk and acoustic musicians.

Farther out in Fairfax County, George Mason University's ambitious Center for the Arts (703-993-1400) opened with much fanfare in 1988, some even touting it as the future "Kennedy Center of Northern Virginia." Gracing its stage during the first few seasons were the likes of Andre Watts, Wynton Marsalis, James Galway and George Shearing. The arts, of course, suffered along with industry during the national recession and to be sure the Center for the Arts has toned down its expectations a bit. The bottom line remains, however, that this is one of the finest concert facilities in Metro Washington and one that is sure to reshape the cultural landscape of Northern Virginia in coming years. Literally right next door to the Center for the Arts is George Mason's Patriot Center, used mostly as an athletic arena, but also the site of many pop concerts during the year.

The same applies to USAir Arena (formerly the Capital Centre) in Suburban Maryland. The 20-something facility, located right off the Beltway in Prince George's County, is the largest indoor arena in the region, and is best known as the home of the Washington Bullets basketball team and the Washington Capitals hockey team. The cavernous, 19,000-seat arena, with surprisingly good acoustics, is where some the largest rock, country and pop music acts of the day perform.

Maryland's answer to Wolf Trap is Merriweather Post Pavilion (301-982-1800) in Howard County. While not as polished as its Virginia cousin, this was still one of the pioneer outdoor music halls in the U.S. and its summer rock concert series (harder edged than Wolf Trap's)

Insiders' Tip

Insiders...

Don't let the Smithsonian overwhelm them. One of the biggest perks of living in Metro Washington is having ample time to explore this national treasure. Instead of trying to visit three or four museums during each trip to the National Mall, settle on seeing three or four wings of one museum. By the time you've made it through all the museums at this pace, many of the exhibits will have changed and it's time to start over.

The National Gallery of Art (East Building) houses one of the nation's finest collections of modern art.

attracts huge crowds from the Washington-Baltimore corridor.

In the Galleries

Metro D.C.'s flourishing arts community and gallery scene sometimes gets overlooked by some of the region's more internationally visible art treasures, like the National Gallery of Art, the Corcoran Gallery of Art, the National Museum of Women in the Arts, the Hirshhorn National Museum and the Phillips Collection, to name just a few. We suggest you turn to our Attractions chapter for a complete listing and description of these and other national galleries and museums.

For a tour of private galleries, some of the finest on the East Coast, it's probably best to start in D.C.'s artsy Dupont Circle neighborhood, where you'll find such acclaimed establishments as Veerhoff Galleries (202-387-2333), specializing in antique paintings, and the Foundry Gallery (202-387-0203), an artist's cooperative featuring abstract and experimental contemporary art. Also in the neighborhood are Venable Neslage Galleries (202-462-1800), a collection of American and European paintings, sculpture and paper works, and Affrica (202-745-7272), showcasing the beadwork, masks, textile and pottery of Africa. Local artists, including avant-garde photographers, are the staple of the nearby Jones Troyer Fitzpatrick Gallery (202-328-7189).

Downtown, within a few blocks of the Gallery Place Metro Station, the Franz Bader Gallery (202-393-6111) exhibits the works of three generations of Washington artists, while the Very Special Arts Gallery (202-628-0800) displays some wonderful works by artists with disabilities.

In Georgetown, where taste always seems to run toward the upscale, some of the largest galleries lean toward the traditional. At the Adams Davidson Galleries (202-965-3800), for instance, you'll find American paintings, drawings and sculpture by important artists of the 19th and early 20th centuries, with special emphasis on the Hudson River School and impressionism. Meanwhile, the inspiring works of such 20th-century masters as Chagall, Matisse, Picasso and Renoir are the highlights of the collection found at Galerie Lareuse (202-333-5704).

Northern Virginia's gallery community is perhaps most concentrated in Old Town Alexandria. Here, you'll find the sprawling Torpedo Factory Art Center (703-838-4565), a one-time munitions factory that now houses studio and gallery spaces for more than 175 artisans, including painters, sculptors, glass makers, jewelry makers and potters. Other interesting stops nearby include the Buffalo Gallery (703-548-3338) and Montana Gallery (703-836-6863), which showcase multimedia works by contemporary artists, including those of the American West. In neighboring Arlington County, the Arlington Arts Center (703-524-1494) has its pulse on the ambitious works of regional artists.

One of the more intriguing establishments in Suburban Maryland is the Glass Gallery (301-657-3478). As its name implies, the gallery focuses on blown glass works and multimedia forms of glass sculpture. Lovers of nautical and wildlife art will want to spend an afternoon in Annapolis, where you can browse through a host of specialty shops, including Baruka Gallery (410-268-8300), with its large selection of works by local Chesapeake Bay artists.

At the Cinema

Hollywood has taken a liking to Metro Washington. Not only does the entertainment industry supposedly have a "friend" in the White House, but it also enjoys robust box office support here. The Washington area is one of the largest film markets in the nation, right up there with Los Angeles, New York and Chicago.

The city of monuments and magnificent vistas is also one of the most-filmed locations in the world. Chances are you won't live here long before you spot a movie crew in Georgetown, Capitol Hill, Old Town Alexandria, Annapolis or along the National Mall. In the past few years, such blockbuster hits as "No Way Out," "JFK," "A Few Good Men," "In the Line of Fire," "Patriot Games" and, more recently, "The Pelican Brief" have used Metro Washington as a backdrop.

The region's cinematic riches are buoyed by the presence of the prestigious American Film Institute and the AFI Theatre (202-785-4600) at the Kennedy Center. The AFI, which also publishes a magazine for members, draws heavily among film buffs and purists who regard cinema as a high art form. Each year, more than 600 movies, from the silent years and early talkies to the

Golden Age and avant-garde eras, are screened at the 224-seat theater which doubles as home to special film revivals, festivals and premier showings.

Another straw in Washington's celluloid hat is Filmfest D.C. (202-727-2396), a two-week celebration of American and international film, from the alternative to the mainstream. For two weeks (late April to early May), the city becomes the focus of the movie world, with scores of screenings, seminars and receptions held throughout town.

Unfortunately, as in most areas, the grand movie theaters of the 1920s and '30s are all but gone here, supplanted largely by the antiseptic shopping-mall venues of the suburbs. Nevertheless, there are still some interesting movie houses around, starting with the Uptown Theatre on Connecticut Avenue NW (202-966-5400). Don't let the boxy drab facade fool you; inside it's what you'd expect from the heydays of Hollywood: velvet-backed seats, an ornate and towering proscenium, a plush reception area and a huge screen. It's easily the area's best film-watching venue.

A somewhat similar experience can be had at the six-screen Cineplex Odeon/Wisconsin Avenue (202-244-0880), built in the late '80s with cutting-edge sound and screening technology and a palatial interior that reminds you that moviegoing can still be a memorable event. The refurbished Avalon (202-966-2600), also in upper Northwest, is another great spot to catch some of the most important films of the day.

If your tastes run toward the unconventional, by all means check out the Biograph (202-333-2696) on M Street in Georgetown. The artsy, one-screen theater is known for its obscure retrospectives, animation festivals and provocative repertoire of foreign and classic films.

Just down the street, the four-screen Key Theatre (202-333-5100) gravitates toward the more traditional foreign offerings as well as the more commercial American alternative films.

Imported movies show regularly on screens at the Circle West End Theatre (202-293-3152) near Georgetown and the K-B Janus Theatre (202-232-8900) in Dupont Circle.

Suburban cineastes can take advantage of the Arlington Cinema 'n' Drafthouse (703-486-2345) in Northern Virginia and Maryland's Bethesda Theatre Cafe (301-656-3337) where you can munch on nachos and Buffalo wings and throw back a beer or two while watching second-run movies. While not exactly a unique concept anymore, these off-price movie houses do a brisk business, especially with folks tired of shelling out half their paychecks to see a first-run flick.

Just for Laughs

Washington has always been known to take itself a little too seriously. Thank goodness we've got a burgeoning comedy club scene to loosen up, if just for a few hours, the terminally uptight.

As you might imagine, political satire goes over big here and there's no better practitioners of the art than comedy troupes like Gross National Product and the Capitol Steps. You can catch GNP's improv show at the Bayou (202-783-1212) in Georgetown, a venue mostly known for national touring rock and blues acts. The Capitol Steps, actually made up of Hill staffers, takes its musical parody to benefits and special events throughout the metro area but tends to migrate toward Chelsea's (202-298-8222), also in Georgetown.

Downtown, the Comedy Cafe (202-638-5653) on K Street and the Improv (202-296-7008) on Connecticut Avenue book both established and up-and-coming comedians. In Northern Virginia, you can plant your funny bones at the Comedy Zone (703-971-8900) at the Springfield Hilton, and at Garvin's (202-298-7200), with locations at the Ramada Seminary Plaza in Alexandria and the Westpark Hotel in Tysons Corner. Also nearby are Headliners (703-379-4242), located in the Alexandria's Radisson Plaza Hotel, and the Laughing Lizard (703-836-7885), an upstairs adjunct to Terlitzsky's, a popular Alexandria hangout.

Inside Metro Washington Shopping

For many residents of Metro Washington, shopping is more than just a necessity of life or, as some might declare, a "necessary evil." Rather, it's an avocation, even a consuming passion that, at least for those with more modest standards of living, seems to pose a regular threat to checkbook and credit-card balances, not to mention the stability of a few marriages. Some people have even elevated shopping to a sort of art form, and around here, the inspiration for a masterpiece is never far away.

Metro Washington is no place for shopaholics to try and kick the habit. (That's like asking someone to stroll through the Capitol and not bump into a politician or lobbyist.) The temptations are far too great, whether the consumer is a free-spending millionaire, a penny-pinching college student, or someone in between. Whatever the object of desire, there's sure to be a place in Metro Washington to buy it, from mega-malls, outlet malls and neighborhood shopping centers, to department stores, tony designer boutiques, discount retailers, bulk-buy membership warehouses and antique havens.

Opportunities for priming the economic pump are numerous, and the locals do their part. Per-household retail sales ring up to nearly $23,000 a year here, 15 percent above the national average and about $2,000 over the household average for the nine other top markets in the U.S. Among the nation's top 10 markets, Metro Washington places third in total retail sales (furniture, home furnishings and appliances), trailing only Dallas/Fort Worth and Boston, and ahead of New York, Chicago, Los Angeles and Houston. Meanwhile, the region ranks fourth in sales at general-merchandise and drug stores, automotive dealers, and eating and drinking establishments, fifth at food stores, and sixth at apparel and accessory stores.

Insiders' Tip

Insiders...
Count on the immense Sunday edition of *The Washington Post* for a plethora of coupons, sale supplements and other money-saving resources.

The conspicuous-consumption 1980s certainly were in full swing in the nation's capital. Between 1980 and 1990, retail sales in the Standard Metropolitan Statistical Area doubled to some $31 billion annually! Northern Virginia topped the area with $14 billion, Suburban Maryland was second with $13.5 billion and the District third with $3.8 billion. With an after-tax income base of more than $54,000, area households spent an average of $22,505, or 42 percent of buying income, in the retail marketplace. According to 1990 figures, the top five most popular shopping destinations in the region were the F Street corridor of downtown Washington, Tysons Corner Center in Fairfax County, Potomac Mills outlet center in Prince William County, Landmark Shopping Center in Alexandria, and Fair Oaks Mall, also in Fairfax. More on these and other places to follow.

Still, saving money will always be in vogue. After all, how do you think so many of the rich stay that way? Fortunately, Metro Washington is right in step with the rest of the nation when it comes to offering places where brand-name, first-quality goods can be had at rock-bottom prices. Stores that are especially popular with bargain seekers include membership warehouses such as BJ's, Pace and Price Club, and apparel outlets like Kuppenheimer, Marshalls, NBO, TJ Maxx, Today's Man and Ross. Most of these stores have locations throughout the region.

One of the most recent salvos in the fierce discount wars was fired by Total Beverage (13055 Lee-Jackson Memorial Hwy., in the Chantilly area of western Fairfax County), an innovative concept in retailing that offers terrific prices on beer, wine, soft drinks, bottled water and most any other liquid meant for public consumption — except liquor. In Virginia, unlike Maryland and Washington, the hard stuff is sold only in state-run ABC (Alcoholic Beverage Control) stores.

Beyond grocery items, dollar-stretching Metro Washington shoppers who really do their homework — especially when it comes to purchasing big-ticket items — often turn to *Washington Consumers Checkbook* for objective product reviews and the inside scoop on where locally to find items at the best prices. Think of WCC as a kind of local version of that renowned bible of buying, *Consumer Reports.* The magazine is available by subscription and can also be found at many area bookstores and newsstands. Call (202) 347-7283/9612 for more information.

Insiders' Tip

Insiders...
Look to Metrorail to get them to many of their favorite shopping destinations, particularly during the busy Christmas season and when nasty winter weather hits.

Photo: Washington Convention and Visitors Association

The Old Post Office maintains a wealth of souvenir shops and eateries, located adjacent to the National Mall.

In this chapter we offer something of a shopping tour of Metro Washington, spotlighting the major malls and other retail meccas. As with many other chapters, in no way do we claim to cover all the bases here. When applicable, we've included the name and location of the nearest Metro station, since the rail system is often the most convenient way for many people to get around, especially residents of the District and the close-in suburbs. Yet the great majority of people still take to their cars, trucks and minivans to do their part for the local economy.

A final note before we begin this potentially budget-busting journey into consumer nirvana: While the mega-malls and other shopping hubs of Metro Washington are indeed vital and deserve all the business they can get, keep in mind the small merchants in your particular community when deciding where to spend those hard-earned dollars. Many of them were hit particularly hard during the economic downturn of the last several years and rely heavily on faithful local patrons to keep them afloat. For some items, these places can be just as competitive — and often far more convenient — than their larger rivals. While it wasn't feasible to try and assemble a substantive list of such businesses for inclusion in this chapter, we at least wanted to make a pitch for supporting them whenever possible and to urge shoppers to spread some of the wealth around.

District of Columbia

An interesting and certainly one of the easiest ways to go shopping in Washington is via Metrorail. For the most part, you can forget about nasty weather, parking hassles (including the outrageous prices that so many garages charge), getting lost and other unpleasantries. More often than not in the congested, parking-space-scarce city, Metro is indeed the only way to go. (Please refer to the transportation chapter for information numbers, hours and other details about the Metro system.) Having said that, let's climb aboard.

For simplicity's sake, we'll go alphabetically by Metro stop, start-

Insiders' Tip

Insiders...

Look to stores such as BJ's, Magruder's, Pace, Price Club, Shoppers Food Warehouse and Super Fresh for some of the best bargains in groceries. The bigger chains, including Giant and Safeway, offer terrific savings with bulk foods and products bearing the store's own label. BJ's, Pace and Price Club, three of the growing number of membership warehouse outlets, also carry a huge assortment of other merchandise.

Photo: Washington Convention and Visitors Association

Beyond the historic homes and bustling nightlife of Georgetown lies Washington Harbour, an enclave of shops and restaurants situated on the Potomac River.

ing with the Farragut North station (Red Line), on Connecticut Avenue at K and L streets NW, and the Farragut West station (Orange and Blue lines), on I Street at 17th and 18th streets NW. From a shopping perspective, both stations deposit you in territory ripe with small stores and specialty retailers. The shops and restaurants of **International Square**, at 18th and I, have direct access to the Farragut West station. Farragut North is the best stop for **The Connecticut Connection Mall** (1101 Connecticut Ave. NW), an interesting assortment of shops featuring women's clothing and accessories, fine jewelry, cosmetics, a hair and nail salon, coin and stamp store, specialty food stores and eateries.

From here it's just a short jaunt on the Orange or Blue lines to the Federal Triangle station at 12th Street and Pennsylvania Avenue NW. No, we're not headed for some dank government warehouse, but rather **The Pavilion at the Old Post Office** (1100 Pennsylvania Ave. NW), just across the street from the station. Rescued from demolition in the 1970s and later transformed into a shining star of the city's retail and tourism sectors, this is a don't-miss destination for shoppers, combining history, the second-highest vantage point in the city (take the glass elevator up to the 315-foot clock/bell tower), and of course dozens of shops and restaurants, including a spectacular food court.

Next, take the Red Line north to the Friendship Heights station on Wisconsin Avenue NW at Jenifer Street and Western Avenue, right near the Maryland line. There, follow the exit signs to nearby **Mazza Gallerie**, where 60-plus elegant stores on four levels offer one of the District's most exclusive shopping experiences. High-fashion staples including Neiman Marcus, Ann Taylor, Saville of London and Camalier & Buckley await those whose discretionary income is as generous as their shopping list is long.

Turning in a different economic and geographic direction, head back downtown and transfer to the Yellow, Orange or Blue lines for a trip to the L'Enfant Plaza station at 7th and D streets SW. **The Promenade** area near the station features moderately-priced gift shops, dress shops and costume-jewelry stores as well as great lunch spots.

During most any Metrorail trip through the District on the Blue, Orange and Red lines, you're bound to stop at the massive Metro Center station on G Street at 11th and 12th streets NW, so it's easy enough to hop off and head directly into Woodward & Lothrop or Hecht's, depending on where you exit. Then, stroll a couple of blocks down F Street between 13th and 14th streets NW and check out **The Shops at National Place**, housed in the magnificently restored National Press Building. Here you can choose from over 83 shops including The Sharper Image, Banana Republic, The Limited and Victoria's Secret, as well as numerous eateries.

For the truly "write" stuff, stroll a block or so to**Fahrney's Pens** (1430 G St. NW, just two blocks from the White House). For more than 50 years, this institution has been providing fine writing instruments — Montblanc, Waterman, Cross, et al — to diplomats, statesmen and other well-to-do folks for whom a drugstore ballpoint just doesn't cut it.

For an excursion that will delight shoppers as well as history and railroad buffs, hop back on the Red Line to the **Union Station** stop, located of course at its namesake Union Station (1st Street and Massachusetts Avenue NE, almost in the shadows of the Capitol). This landmark Beaux-Arts building, originally opened in 1908, is another city landmark that was given a new lease on life. Make that many new leases when you consider the more than 120 stores and specialty merchants that make Union Station such an exciting and unusual shopping destination. But don't forget to check out the building itself, especially the ornate gold leaf that adorns the spectacular 96-foot high ceiling in the main hall.

Stores of particular note at Union Station include the U.S. Mint Shop (specializing in unique coin-themed items), The Great Train Store (a trove of railroad memorabilia), Political Americana (American political collectibles galore) and Made In America (brass and pewter Washington-themed desk accessories, patriotic gifts, jewelry and apparel). The station's East Hall is rich in jewelry and art shops. There are also plenty of restaurants including nearly three dozen fast-food outlets, plus a nine-screen theater complex. Despite its additional role as a shopping hub, Union Station chugs on as a working railroad station too, accommodating not only Metrorail but several commuter lines and Amtrak. While the station operates around the clock and the restaurants and theaters stay open fairly late, the stores operate regular mall retail hours. (So much for that 3 AM credit-card fix.) Even if traveling, shopping, eating and movie-watching are the farthest activities from your mind, Union Station is well worth a look if only to admire its stately grandeur. This is what train stations were meant to look like.

Georgetown is the final stop on the city shopping tour, but forget about taking Metro unless you don't mind a substantial walk from the nearest station. Hard to figure, but the rail system never made it to Georgetown—truly one of the city's prized commercial and tourist hubs, and of course home to many of the District's wealthiest and most influential residents. Anyway, there are hundreds of stores to browse, especially along M Street and Wisconsin Avenue NW, from high-end retailers such as Britches of Georgetowne (1247 Wisconsin) to bargain-basement specialists like Sunny's Surplus (3342 M). In the heart of it all is the neighborhood's only true mall, **Georgetown Park** (3222 M St. NW). Sitting smack against the idyllic C&O Canal, this showcase of upscale consumerism offers four levels of 125 stores, boutiques and restaurants. Retailers include J. Crew, Ann Taylor, The Limited and Ralph Lauren's Polo Shop. Thankfully, there's a two-level underground parking garage. During the business day, two hours of free parking are offered with proof of purchase of at least $10 worth of merchandise. For those bound and determined to take Metrorail, the closest you'll get is the Foggy Bottom/GWU station at 23rd and I streets NW. If you'd rather save your energy for the stores, hail a cab or hop a Metrobus.

And finally, any overview of shopping in our Nation's Capital has to include a mention of the city's great museum and gallery shops, particularly those at any of the **Smithsonian's** vast collection of

Photo: Washington Convention and Visitors Association

Georgetown is a vibrant hub of nightclubs, specialty stores, boutiques and restored homes.

properties. These places aren't just for tourists. Locals love them as well, especially for gifts that are hard to find anywhere else including books, jewelry, china, posters and assorted novelties.

Among the most interesting are: Arts and Industries Building (900 Jefferson Dr. SW), for precious reproduction jewelry and novelty foods in old-fashioned packaging; Bureau of Engraving and Printing (15th Street and Independence Avenue SW), for sheets of uncut $1 and $2 bills; Decatur House (1600 H St. NW), for reproduction home accessories of the 18th and 19th centuries; Hillwood (4155 Linnean Ave. NW), for Fabergé-style egg pendants and other items relating to the permanent collection; Hirshhorn Museum (950 Independence Ave. NW), for quirky jewelry, especially earrings; Kennedy Center (Rock Creek Parkway and New Hampshire Avenue NW), for a range of gifts dealing with music, dance, theater and opera; National Air and Space Museum (6th Street and Independence Avenue SW), for freeze-dried ice cream like the astronauts eat, as well as kites and a host of other flight-related objects; National Archives (7th Street and Constitution Avenue NW), for great replicas of the Declaration of Independence, the U.S. Constitution and the Bill of Rights, along with posters and postcards; National Gallery of Art (4th Street and Constitution Avenue NW), for inexpensive prints and postcards of masterpieces that are suitable for framing; National Geographic Society (17th and M streets NW), for superb maps, books and educational children's toys; National Museum of African Art (950 Independence Ave. SW), for textiles, dolls, crafts and jewelry from Africa; Navy Memorial (Pennsylvania Avenue between 7th and 9th streets NW), for small souvenirs and elegant gifts themed to the U.S. Navy, Coast Guard, Marine Corps and Merchant Marines; and, at last, Washington National Cathedral (Wisconsin and Massachusetts avenues NW), for unusual Renaissance and Medieval products such as stuffed gargoyles, stained-glass-patterned scarves and window decorations.

Northern Virginia

Alexandria

When you think of Alexandria, **Old Town** is often the first place that comes to mind. And with Old Town, it's easy to think of great restaurants, pubs and beautiful old homes. But the city's historic district also offers plenty of options for the shop-'til-you-drop crowd. Many of Old Town's 200 or so retail stores are clustered along Washington Street (known as the George Washington Memorial Parkway north and south of the city limits) and east toward the waterfront, particularly along King and Union streets. From clothiers to antique shops, specialty importers to home accessories, Old Town redefines retail variety. And you couldn't ask for a more charming and historic place in which to stroll. Leave the car at home if at all possible, or at least park it as soon as you can. This place is made for walking.

If it's art galleries, clothing stores, eateries and other specialty shops you're after, the prime destination is the Torpedo Factory Art Center and the adjacent mini mall. It all begins on Union Street at the foot of King Street.

Just a few blocks south, Olsson's Books & Records (106 S. Union St.) is another of Metro Washington's local retail institutions, known for its knowledgeable and friendly staff and outstanding selection of many obscure titles. Other shops in Old Town with a charm all their own include Hats in the Belfry (112 King St.), specializing in funky and fun cranial creations; America (118 King Street), where flags, pins, patches, books and other items from all 50 states are sold with patriotic pride; the Pineapple Brass Shop (132 King St.), for authentic colonial reproduction brass pieces by Virginia metal crafters as well as hand-carved duck decoys; Santa Fe Country (1218 King St.), whose treasure trove of American Southwest pottery, jewelry and food stuffs is enough to make natives of Arizona and New Mexico homesick; and the Winterthur Museum Shop (207 King St.), an extension of the Winterthur Museum in Delaware that features elegant American decorative-art reproductions from 1640 to 1860.

Old Town isn't right on a Metro line, but it's only a short bus or taxi ride over from the King Street or Braddock Road Metro stations (both on the Blue and Yellow lines).

Alexandria's only enclosed shopping mall is **Landmark Center** (5801 Duke Street, at I-395), which some residents of neighboring Fairfax County happily call their own as well. Landmark underwent an extensive renovation, expansion and general marketing makeover several years ago that has done wonders for aesthetics and business. The "new" Landmark offers nearly 150 stores and restaurants (no movie theaters, though, surprisingly), including anchors Hecht's, Woodward & Lothrop and Sears.

But for a truly special purchase that you won't find anywhere else, head down the George Washington Memorial Parkway south of Alexandria to Washington's famed **Mount Vernon** estate. For sale in the gift shop is an array of Colonial memorabilia including jewelry patterned after Martha Washington's, and cuttings from the estate's shrubs that date way back to George's time. We're not sure if there are any remnants from cherry trees.

Insiders' Tip

Insiders...
In search of rock-bottom prices on name-brand clothing will check out Marshall's, NBO, Ross, TJ Maxx and Today's Man. There's even an entire outlet shopping mall that caters to the budget-conscious: sprawling Potomac Mills, located just off I-95 in Woodbridge, Va.

Arlington County

True to its predominantly urban character, Arlington is shopper-friendly, with nearly every destination easily accessible by Metro.

Ballston Common (4238 Wilson Blvd., at N. Glebe Road) has become a favorite of shoppers for its central location and great variety of stores. Just a one-block walk from the Ballston Metro station (Orange Line) at Fairfax Drive and N. Stuart Street, the mall features 100 specialty stores on four floors, with an international food court on the ground level. Hecht's and JC Penney are the anchors, but shops such as The Artist's Proof, with antique and other captivating photographs, and A.J. Champions, featuring collectible sports memorabilia, help give Ballston its real appeal.

Over in the concrete and steel maze known as Crystal City, just off Jefferson Davis Highway (Route 1), are **The Underground** (on Crystal Drive, between 15th and 18th streets) and **The Plaza Shops** (corner of Crystal Drive and 23rd Street), two fascinating subterranean shopping experiences linked by a climate-controlled walkway. There are over 125 stores in all, a movie theater, food court and numerous other restaurants. Special stores include Geppi's Comic World and The Invention Store. Both shopping areas are connected to Metro's Crystal City station (Blue and Yellow lines) at 18th Street and Jefferson Davis Highway.

The county's premier retail showcase, however, is the **Fashion Centre at Pentagon City** (1100 S. Hayes St.), which looms across I-395 from its namesake office building. Open only since the fall of 1989, Pentagon City, as it's customarily referred to, is one of the area's most exciting and dynamic shopping showplaces, a visual wonderland complete with towering skylights, palm trees, a sunlit food court, six-screen cinema and four tiers of 130 stores. Anchor tenants are Macy's and Nordstrom; specialty shops include The Nature Company, Victoria's Secret, The Disney Store, San Francisco Music Box Company, Britches of Georgetowne and Britches Great Outdoors. And the Ritz-Carlton Hotel is right next door; in fact, it's joined to the mall and has its own entrance.

On-street parking in this area is very limited, so opt for Pentagon City's own above-ground tiered parking facility. It isn't free, but the price is very reasonable, especially when you consider the convenience. Metro is also particularly desirable since the Pentagon City station (Blue and Yellow lines), at Army Navy Drive and South Hayes Street, brings you literally right inside.

Just a couple of exits south on I-395, **The Village at Shirlington** (2700 S. Quincy St.) is a contemporary urban shopping enclave with a "neighborhood" feel. There are seven theaters plus a bunch of nice restaurants and shops including Kuppenheimer men's clothier.

A "mall" (perhaps "un-mall") of a different sort awaits at **Law's Antique World** (2900 Clarendon Blvd.), a fascinating assortment of some 50 antique and collectible dealers selling jewelry, artwork, furniture, clothes and other goods — all under one roof. There are numerous restaurants nearby, many clustered in Arlington's traditionally Asian and Hispanic neighborhoods that are rich with ethnic cuisine. The Clarendon Metro station (Orange Line), at Wilson Boulevard and N. Highland Street, is just two blocks from Law's.

Fairfax County

When it comes to diversity, selection and high-end retailers, Fairfax County is a little bit Montgomery County and a little bit Washington, but all rolled up into something much bigger. In fact, the county boasts one of the highest concentrations of retail shopping on the East Coast.

One of the four mega-malls is **Fair Oaks**, (intersection of Route 50 and I-66, Fairfax), the centerpiece of a hub of commercial activity in a burgeoning residential area just beyond the Fairfax City line in the western end of the county. The 210 merchants include anchors Hecht's, Woodward & Lothrop and Sears. There's also a freestanding cinema complex that's an attraction in itself.

Springfield Mall (corner of Franconia and Loisdale roads, Springfield) has local bragging rights when it comes to sheer size: an amazing 280 stores, including Macy's and JC Penney, since its extensive renovation and expansion a few years back. But you're never far from a restaurant, including Ruby Tuesday, Bennigan's and a ground-level food court with dozens of walk-up eateries. Due to its convenient location off I-395 near the I-95 interchange in southeastern Fairfax, Springfield Mall is especially big with District residents as well as people from points south including Woodbridge, Fredericksburg and the large military community in Quantico.

To the northwest, **Reston Town Center** (off Reston Parkway between Baron Cameron Avenue and the Dulles Toll Road, Reston) is still in its infant stages of development, but the first phase of this planned community's "urban" core has proven to be a hit with its striking architecture and numerous public gathering spots. Seventy shops — mostly specialty retailers such as The Gap — line the broad avenues. The food scene includes Clyde's and Rio Grande Cafe. There's also office space, some residential units, an 11-screen cinema and, overlooking it all, the gorgeous Hyatt Regency Reston Town Center.

Insiders' Tip

Insiders...

Turn a daytrip into a weekend getaway when visiting some of the popular outlet malls in Pennsylvania, West Virginia, southeastern Virginia and the Eastern Shore of Maryland.

To the east down the Toll Road is the commercial hub of Tysons Corner, the shining jewel in Fairfax County's economic crown that looms like a giant cash register. Shoppers from throughout the region flock to **Tysons Corner Center** (Routes 7 and 123) and its nearly 250 stores including Nordstrom, Bloomingdale's, Hecht's, Woodward & Lothrop, Brooks Brothers and Eddie Bauer. And, of course, the requisite restaurants and movie theaters add to its appeal. Tysons is one of the area's oldest shopping malls (opened in 1968), but you wouldn't know it. Like so many of its peers, Tysons became "new" all over again during the mid 1980s with an extensive renovation and expansion that dramatically reshaped its look, along with its customer-friendliness. Among the most welcome changes were the addition of parking decks and the conversion of underground truck tunnels into rows of specialty shops.

As if "Tysons I" wasn't enough, there's **The Galleria at Tysons II** (2001 International Dr.), just across Chain Bridge Road (Route 123) from Tysons Corner Center and adjacent to the Ritz-Carlton Hotel. This 123-store showplace is upscale to the Nth degree, with Macy's, Saks Fifth Avenue, Neiman Marcus and other posh retailers strutting their stuff. Even many of the food joints are upper crust, with L&N Seafood an especially good bet.

The third major piece of Tysons Corner's retail puzzle is ritzy **Fairfax Square**, which sprouted from what used to be a big parking lot fronting Route 7 across from Bloomingdale's. This place does a formidable Rodeo Drive impersonation with the likes of tenants such as Tiffany & Co., Gucci, Louis Vuitton, Hermes and Fendi. There's also a theater complex and a Chili's restaurant next door.

Beyond the malls, Tysons Corner is home to hundreds of other commercial enterprises, from car dealers, restaurants and hotels to specialty stores and large chain outlets such as Tower Records, Marshalls, Toys R Us and CompUSA, the computer super store.

Farther to the east along Route 7, at Route 50 in Falls Church, **Seven Corners Center** — one of Metro Washington's first regional malls — has long been overshadowed by its bigger and fancier competitors, but

Insiders' Tip

Insiders...
Shopping in Old Town Alexandria know that one of the best places to grab a quick bite of lunch is Deli on the Strand, located on South Union Street. You can't go wrong with the delicious selection of sandwiches served on fresh-baked mini loaves of bread. On nice days, be sure to enjoy your feast by the banks of the Potomac River — just a short stroll away.

Potomac Mills, a discount outlet mall in Prince William County, is a shopper's paradise.

it still presents a nice shopping option with 68 stores that are especially convenient for Arlington residents.

Other smaller shopping areas in the county include the hundreds of local merchants in the towns of Clifton (clustered at Clifton and Chapel roads), Herndon (Elden Street) and Vienna (Maple Avenue and Church Street corridors), Falls Church (Broad Street) and Great Falls ("downtown" at Walker Road and Georgetown Pike).

Loudoun County

You won't find a mega-mall in Loudoun County, but that probably suits many people just fine in this quiet, as-yet-largely-undeveloped area. Yet the small towns and villages are indeed alive with their own brand of retail activity.

Historic downtown Leesburg (intersection of Routes 7 and 15) offers over 100 merchants, primarily specialty retailers stretching along Market and King streets. Leesburg's enchanting **Market Station** (corner of Loudoun and Harrison streets) offers another 100 or so shops while, to the east, more than 250 stores are found in the Route 7 corridor up to the Fairfax County line. This stretch includes the communities of Ashburn, Sterling, and Sterling Park.

Along the western stretches of Route 50, Hunt Country delights are the name of the game in the **Middleburg Historic Shopping District**. The tiny burg offers a fair number (60) of stores for its size, many along Washington and Madison streets. In addition to horsing attire and accessories, Middleburg's retail specialties include antiques, home furnishings, handcrafted gifts, clothing and art. Middleburg Antiques Center (105 West Washington St.) is a haven for period furniture and accessories, fine estate items, rugs, lamps, silver and jewelry.

Prince William County

It says something about the power of shopping when the No. 1 tourist destination in history- and scenery-rich Virginia is **Potomac Mills** (2700 Potomac Mills Cir.), the colossal outlet center near Woodbridge that claims to be the world's largest.

Just 15 miles south of Washington off I-95, Potomac Mills more than lives up to its billing as a paradise for shoppers, especially those with a penchant for savings. The nearly 200 off-price and outlet stores include Ikea, Waccamaw Pottery, Nordstrom Rack (the only one on the East Coast), Nike, Ray-Ban, Eddie Bauer, Guess, American Tourister, Calvin Klein, Levi's and Laura Ashley. Kids and parents alike will love the famous "ball room" at Ikea, where little ones can romp to their heart's delight under adult supervision while Mom and Dad stroll the labyrinth of aisles.

Prince William's other primary shopping areas are **Manassas Mall** (8300 Sudley Rd.), with 125 stores including JC Penney; **Old Town Manassas** (Route 29, 7 1/2 miles off I-66 in the city's downtown area), which features nearly two dozen merchants along with a fascinating museum; and the historic riverfront community of **Occoquan** (just off I-95, about 10 miles south of the Capital Beltway, but also accessible from the extreme southern end of Route 123), with 120 merchants in a charming Victorian setting.

Suburban Maryland

Anne Arundel County

There's no Metrorail system for residents of Anne Arundel County to enjoy, although local bus service is readily available. Whatever the mode of transportation, many residents rely on the county's two major malls for their shopping needs. **Annapolis Mall** (Defense Highway, Annapolis) is anchored by Hecht's, Montgomery Ward and JC Penney and offers some 130 other stores, specialty shops and restaurants. The other mall, **Marley Station** (7900 Ritchie Hwy., Annapolis) features Hecht's and Macy's as the prime tenants along with 135 shops.

For some people, though, shopping begins and ends in Annapolis along Main Street, Maryland Avenue and the City Dock. West Annapolis has much to offer as well (including plenty of free parking) with numerous retailers specializing in arts and crafts, interior design, antiques and apparel. Many merchants in the Eastport area cater to the boating set, with sales of power and sail boats, equipment and nautical artifacts.

Among the favorite Annapolis retailers are the Annapolis Antique Gallery (2009 West St.), a premiere shop with offerings by some of the area's finest dealers. Furniture and decorative accessories are specialties here. Ron Snyder Antiques, Inc. (2011 West St.) specializes in American furniture and accessories from the 18th and 19th centuries. One of the quirkiest shops in all of Annapolis is Heaven on Earth (155-B Main St.), which carries an amazing selection of handcrafted gifts from all corners of the world, such as handpainted fish from Sri Lanka, and Russian crystal.

Annapolis Harbour Center (2472 Solomons Island Rd.) is one of the area's newest shopping destinations; just look for the lighthouse landmark. The center includes stores specializing in home furnishings, apparel, accessories and home-entertainment, and there are plenty of dining spots as well. With roots in Ireland that date back to 1723, Avoca Handweavers (141 Main St.) knows a bit about classic Irish clothing and gifts. And while we're on the international circuit, we have to plug two others of a similar ilk: Treasure of the British Isles (211 Main St.), featuring clothes, books, food, jewelry and other merchandise from England, Scotland and Wales; and Davison's of Bermuda (2 Francis St.), which carries men's and women's sportswear and resort threads with that distinctly proper island look. Apparel specialists in the area include Britches Great Outdoors (City Dock), a Metro Washington institution in its own right; Peppers (133 Main St.), where you can find a huge selection of Naval Academy-themed clothes, hats and accessories; and Sign of the Whale (99 Main St., in The Old Customs House), which offers, as they say, "Unusual Gifts and Women's Apparel," along with items for the kitchen and garden.

Big savings on designer clothes and accessories, home furnishings and other shopping staples are as close as the dozens of shops at outlet centers scattered about the Route 50 corridor. The choices include Annapolis Harbour Center (Route 2, Solomons Island Road, west of Annapolis), Bay Bridge Market Place (South Service Road off Route 50, one mile west of the Bay Bridge), Kent Narrows Factory Stores (on Kent Island, just before the Kent Narrows Bridge at Exit 41 off Route 50), and Chesapeake Village Outlet Center (441 Chesapeake Village Rd., near the Route 50/ Route 301 split in Queenstown).

Montgomery County

Montgomery County's demographics are as impressive as just about any jurisdiction in the nation. One look at the shopping roster only helps confirm this.

Insiders...
Count on Sunny's Surplus stores for great bargains on clothing, equipment and accessories for hikers, campers, hunters, anglers and other outdoor enthusiasts.

Insiders' Tip

Many a retailing fantasy can be fulfilled in the **Chevy Chase** area of the county, which borders upper northwest Washington at Wisconsin and Western avenues. This three-block enclave runneth over with chic department stores, exclusive shops and designer boutiques. The hit parade includes Gucci, Saks Fifth Avenue, Saks Jandel, Rive Gauche, Saint Laurent and dozens of others. And you can even give the chauffeur the day off! Just take Metro to the Friendship Heights station (Red Line), located on Wisconsin Avenue at Jenifer Street and Western Avenue.

White Flint Mall (11301 Rockville Pike, North Bethesda) is another of the county's — and indeed the entire region's — toniest shopping experiences. This three-level, architecturally striking extravaganza of department stores and boutiques includes I. Magnin, Bloomingdale's and Lord & Taylor, plus plenty of places to grab a bite to eat or catch a flick. Take Metro to the White Flint station (Red Line), at Rockville Pike and Marinelli Drive, and the mall is just three blocks away. The walk isn't bad, but if you prefer, opt for the handy shuttle service.

Bethesda's other shopping hub is **Montgomery Mall** (7101 Democracy Blvd.), which has been handsomely renovated and features some 160 stores including anchors Nordstrom — the Seattle-based retailer known for outstanding customer service and an equally outstanding shoe selection — Hecht's, Woodward & Lothrop and Sears.

In the central part of the county, **Lakeforest Mall** (701 Russell Ave., Gaithersburg) offers 160 stores, with its Big Four being Hecht's, Woodward & Lothrop, JC Penney and Sears. There are also 16 restaurants and five theaters.

Wheaton Plaza (11160 Veirs Mill Rd., Wheaton) boasts an entirely new wing, Hecht's, Woodward & Lothrop and Montgomery Ward, plus 120 other stores and the requisite eateries and cinemas. The Wheaton Metro station (Red Line) is just across the street, at Reedie Drive and Georgia Avenue. The station is something of a landmark in itself, boasting the longest escalator (270 feet) in the Western Hemisphere. No. 1 in the world is in St. Petersburg — Russia, not Florida.

In Silver Spring, **City Place Mall** (Colesville Road and Fenton Street) is an outlet-shopper's paradise. For antique lovers, **Antique Row**, along Howard Avenue in Kensington, offers dozens of dealers specializing in everything from accessories to furniture.

And for one truly unique local store that will surely leave you with a taste of the region, check out **The Great Chesapeake Bay Co.** at **Cabin John Mall** (11325 Seven Locks Rd., Potomac), where you'll find a superb collection of Maryland and Chesapeake Bay art, books and other items. And to top it all off, a portion of the proceeds goes toward Bay-related organizations.

Prince George's County

Prince George's may not offer the ritziest of retail experiences compared with some of its neighbors, but the county offers plenty of options to satisfy most residents' shopping needs.

Landover Mall (Brightseat Road and Hamlin Street, Landover) is by far the county's biggest shopping center, offering some 162 stores and specialty shops. Hecht's, Woodward & Lothrop and Sears are here along with six movie theaters and lots of restaurants. The mall is easily accessible by Metrobus from the Landover Metro station (Orange Line) at Routes 202 and 50.

The county's other major shopping destinations include **Laurel Centre Mall** (14828 Baltimore-Washington Blvd., Laurel), with over 120 stores including Hecht's, JC Penney and Montgomery Ward; **Beltway Plaza** (Greenbelt Road, Greenbelt), with 120 stores including Marshalls, Burlington Coat Factory and Sports Authority, as well as 14 theaters; **Prince George's Plaza** (3500 East-West Hwy., Hyattsville), with 113 stores including Hecht's and Woodward & Lothrop; **Iverson Mall** (Branch Avenue, Marlow Heights), where the 80-plus stores include Woodward & Lothrop and Montgomery Ward; **Forest Village Park Mall** (3101 Donnell Dr., Forestville), home to 80 stores such as JC Penney, Kmart and numerous clothing and accessory stores; **Capital Plaza** (6200 Annapolis Rd., Landover Hills), with 73 stores such as Montgomery Ward and Hechinger; and **Free State Mall** (154800 Annapolis Rd., Bowie), anchored by Sears and featuring over 60 other stores including a supermarket and bowling alley.

Outlet Shopping

While we've already touched on a few of the local outlet malls, we wanted to leave you with a few more. After all, once shoppers get used to buying designer goods at up to 70 percent off retail, it's hard not to explore further to see just how many bargains there are to be had. In this list we feature some of the outlets that are well beyond what is considered Metro Washington, but well within an easy few hours' drive for most residents.

First, some recommended reading for bargain hunters, which only seems appropriate since the

Insiders' Tip

Insiders...
Who live in Virginia but think they might save a few bucks by stocking up on distilled spirits at independently operated liquor stores in the District or Maryland are aware that there are limits on the amount of alcohol that can be purchased for transport across state lines. It's a good idea to first check with local authorities to see what the law allows.

entire Mid-Atlantic offers perhaps more outlet choices than any other region in the nation. Topping the list is *The Outlet Shopper: A Guide to Factory Outlet Shopping in Pennsylvania, Maryland, Virginia and the District of Columbia,* by Carolyn Vogel Benson. It's published locally by The Washington Book Trading Co., P.O. Box 1676, Arlington, Va. 22210, (703) 525-6873. For periodical reading that caters to the careful-consumer set, we suggest an interesting newsletter, *The Savvy Shopper,* distributed by Hammer Publications, P.O. Box 860, Tavernier, Fla. 33070, (800) 82-SAVVY.

And remember, state and local travel and tourism offices are also prime sources for shopping info. Few things please these folks as much as suggesting ways for visitors to come and spend money.

Virginia

Berkeley Commons Outlet Center, 5699-48 Richmond Rd., Williamsburg, Va., (804) 565-0702

Massaponax Outlet Center, 5132 South Point Pkwy., Fredericksburg, Va., (703) 891-8676

Williamsburg Pottery Factory, Route 60 West, Lightfoot, Va., (804) 564-3326

Maryland

Perryville Outlet Center, 68 Heather Lane, Perryville, Md., (410) 378-9399

Pennsylvania

Big Mill Factory Outlets, 730 North 8th St., Reading, Penn., (215) 378-9100

The Outlets on Heisters Lane, Reading, Penn., (215) 921-8910/9394

The Reading Outlet Center, 801 North 9th St., Reading, Penn., (215) 373-5495

Reading Station, 6th and Spring streets, Reading, Penn., (215) 478-7000

West Virginia

Blue Ridge Outlet Center, 315 West Stephen St., Martinsburg, W.Va., (800) 445-3993

Tanger Factory Outlet Center, Foxcraft Avenue and West King Street, Martinsburg, W.Va., (800) 727-6885

Inside Accommodations

Finding a room at the inn isn't a difficult task in Metro Washington. Hotels, motels, inns, guest houses, B&Bs and special extended-stay lodgings are almost as common a site in the nation's capital as lawyers and lobbyists...well, almost.

All kidding aside, the lodging industry is a big, big business here. Hotels, motels and inns are the single largest contributor to the region's $4 billion tourism industry. All told, there are about 50,000 hotel and motel rooms in the metro area, ranging from the ultra luxurious to the merely functional.

As one of the world's leading tourism and business centers, Metro Washington is somewhat unique in that its accommodations industry has long been — and always will be — service driven. Competition demands that hotels extend a full slate of added-value perks and amenities. They run the gamut from the simple, like free on-site parking, to the complex, like arranging for tickets to the latest show at the Kennedy Center or even purchasing airline tickets for guests.

What we're getting at here is that you should be choosy, picky even, when selecting a place to stay. Don't compromise your budget and don't ever psyche yourself out. Not every hotel room in Washington commands $120 a night. Most in fact are much less expensive than that.

As a general rule of thumb, hotels in the suburbs, even close-in areas, are priced less than D.C. properties. Of course, that's not always the case but it's pretty safe to say you can find a slew of real values out there as long as you don't mind being a bit off the beaten path. No matter where you stay, the area's comprehensive public transportation system (especially Metro Rail and Bus) does an excellent job linking hotels with business and tourist areas. You'll discover that many hotels also offer their own shuttle and limousine services to destinations around the area.

Another rule of thumb is that the Washington tourism industry reaches its peak in spring and fall. Occupancy rates are at their highest during these months, and so too are room prices. Planning ahead is never a bad idea.

No matter what time of year, Metro Washington hotels do the bulk of their business Monday through Thursday, courtesy the business traveler. Many hotels cut their rates on weekends, sometimes as much as 50 to 60 percent. With that in mind, always feel free to negotiate for the best deal and always inquire about weekend, off-season, holiday and family rates.

The best source we know to keep you informed of the latest seasonal rate discounts and other special hotel package programs is the Washington, D.C. Convention and Visitors Association (202-789-7000). When in town, also be sure to stop by the Washington Visitor Information Center (202-789-7038) at 1455 Pennsylvania Ave. NW, one block from the White House.

We've divided this chapter into several categories, beginning with a section on extended-stay accommodations. For those of you who plan to house hunt in the area, or who might be on short-term assignment, or just simply need a place to call home for a while, the extended-stay section is intended to give you an overview of some of the region's best options. Almost all the choices here include properties that have kitchenettes, with many also having separate living areas.

We follow with a section called "Rooms with a View — and More." This is intended for tourists, newcomers and long-time residents alike who are looking for — or need to recommend — interesting, practical and/or memorable places to spend a night in Metro Washington.

If you look hard enough, you'll find that the District, Northern Virginia and Suburban Maryland all have more than their share of hotel bargains. Some you might even call "steals." To help you along, we've listed some of our favorite values in the "Best for Less" section. Believe us, no one appreciates a bargain more than writers.

A short section on hostels and university inns lists some of the unsung and non-traditional accommodations found only in the District of Columbia.

We end the chapter with a section on B&Bs and small inns, both the country and urban varieties. As a newcomer, you may soon discover that some of the most memorable "getaways" can be had at nearby inns and B&Bs, lodging options that abound in our beautiful and historic region.

While the following lists are by no means exhaustive, we feel they represent some of the best and most viable choices available in each category.

Suite dreams.

Price Key—Average room cost per night based on single occupancy

Under $80	$
$81-120	$$
Over $120	$$$

All hotels listed accept most major credit cards. Virtually every establishment listed also extends some kind of weekend or off-season rate.

Extended-Stay Hotels and Inns

District of Columbia

Capitol Hill Suites
200 C St. SE (202) 543-6000
$$

You can stay a night, a week, a month or a year at this flexible, all-suite property located a short walk from the Capitol, Library of Congress, Supreme Court, Metro and other "Hill" destinations. All 152 rooms have kitchens. It's a popular extended-stay choice among government and private sector workers with ties to Capitol Hill.

Carlyle Suites
1731 New Hampshire Ave. NW (202) 234-3200
$

Affordability and comfort are the key selling points of this art-deco, all-suite hotel located in the trendy Dupont Circle area. All rooms at the Carlyle come with kitchenettes and free on-site parking. From here, you're just a two-block walk from the Dupont Circle Metro station and tons of galleries, restaurants, boutiques and bars. Pets are accepted.

Corporate Suites of Washington
3636 16th St. NW (202) 483-0100

Corporate Suites specializes in month-to-month leases. Furnished studio apartments start at less than $700 a month. Not a bad deal, especially if you need to be in the District and close to everything.

Embassy Row Hotel
2015 Massachusetts Ave. NW (202) 265-1600
$$$

Location, location, location is the theme here. Situated in the city's embassy district, in Dupont Circle, the Embassy Row handles a large, well-heeled international clientele, including newcomers shopping for more permanent residences. The hotel's rooftop bar is a great warm-weather hangout. Many of the recently refurbished rooms come with kitchenettes and mini bars.

Embassy Square Suites
2000 N St. NW (202) 659-9000
$$

Popular with relocating families and executives on short-term assignments, Embassy Square Suites sits in the heart of the downtown business district, about equal distance from the White House and Georgetown. Each suite comes with a kitchenette, and guests are given free reign to an off-premise health club as well as an on-site swimming pool. *USA Today* is delivered to your door each morning. There's also a free continental breakfast and same-day valet service to boot.

Embassy Suites Hotel
1250 22nd St. NW (202) 857-3388
$$$

This tony West End addition to the national chain boasts two-room suites with separate living rooms and bedrooms. The upscale 318-suite property is close to everything: Downtown, Dupont Circle, Foggy Bottom and Georgetown. Guests receive com-

There are five reasons to visit Washington, D.C.

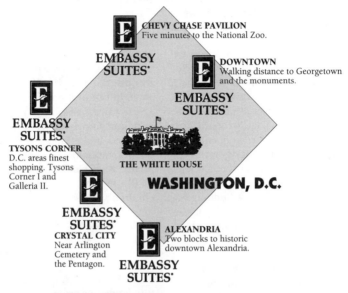

CHEVY CHASE PAVILION
Five minutes to the National Zoo.
EMBASSY SUITES®

DOWNTOWN
Walking distance to Georgetown and the monuments.
EMBASSY SUITES®

EMBASSY SUITES®
TYSONS CORNER
D.C. areas finest shopping. Tysons Corner I and Galleria II.

THE WHITE HOUSE

WASHINGTON, D.C.

EMBASSY SUITES®
CRYSTAL CITY
Near Arlington Cemetery and the Pentagon.

ALEXANDRIA
Two blocks to historic downtown Alexandria.
EMBASSY SUITES®

Six if you count The White House.

Washington, D.C. has a number of wonderful attractions, including the White House. Only five of them, however, guarantee you an enjoyable stay. Spacious two-room suites, free cooked-to-order breakfast and complimentary beverages* nightly, all for the price of a typical hotel room, is reason alone to visit Washington. Not only does Embassy Suites provide great value, all five hotels are convenient to the METRO. So whether your itinerary begins at the Lincoln Memorial or Arlington Cemetery, stay with Embassy Suites and enjoy more of Washington's "other" attractions.

EMBASSY SUITES®

Twice The Hotel® • Call 1 • 800 • Embassy

*Subject to state and local laws.

plimentary cooked-to-order breakfasts. A swimming pool and health club are located on the grounds. This is a popular place with families.

Georgetown Harbour Mews

1000 29th St. NW *(202) 298-1600*
$$

This is an ideal choice for extended stays that require you to be in or near Georgetown. All rooms have full kitchens with dishwashers and microwaves. Irons and hair dryers are also supplied. The 76-room apartment-like setting is frequented by corporate managers and government employees on short-term assignment. The surrounding Georgetown Harbour complex is a stunning waterfront development that also houses restaurants, gift shops, boutiques and the like.

Guest Quarters Suite Hotel/ New Hampshire Avenue

801 New Hampshire Ave. NW *(202) 785-2000*
$$$

Just a half-block from the bustling Foggy Bottom Metro and George Washington University, Guest Quarters/New Hampshire is for those who like their creature comforts. All suites have two color TVs, a kitchen, king- and queen-size beds and a queen-size sofa bed. There's a complimentary health club nearby, and pets are accepted.

Guest Quarters Suite Hotel/ Pennsylvania Avenue

2500 Pennsylvania Ave. NW(202) 333-8060
$$$

Like its New Hampshire Avenue counterpart, this slightly larger Guest Quarters property comes with all the above-mentioned perks. As a bonus, you're just a five-minute walk from the center of Georgetown and all that this fashionable neighborhood offers.

Hotel Anthony

1823 L St. NW *(202) 223-4320*
$$

Somewhat of a sleeper (no pun intended), the Hotel Anthony shouldn't be overlooked. This moderately priced, all-suite hotel is in the middle of downtown, only five blocks from the White House and convenient to monuments, museums and Metro. Kid-friendly, all suites have VCRs, and there's a large stock of children's movies for the asking.

New Hampshire Suites Hotel

1121 New Hampshire Ave. NW *(202) 457-0565*
$$

A small and somewhat unassuming all-suite property, New Hampshire Suites Hotel in the West End is undoubtedly the best bargain in this part of town. Kitchenettes are found in every suite as are stocked honor refrigerators, complimentary coffee and, of course, cable TV. Bring along the jogging shoes and shorts, for you're only a hop and a skip from Rock Creek Park and its miles and miles of gorgeous wooded trails and running paths.

One Washington Circle

1 Washington Circle NW *(202) 872-1680*
$$

All 151 units here include kitchens. Just across the circle is George Washington University and Foggy Bottom Metro. Also within walking distance are the Kennedy Center,

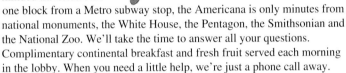

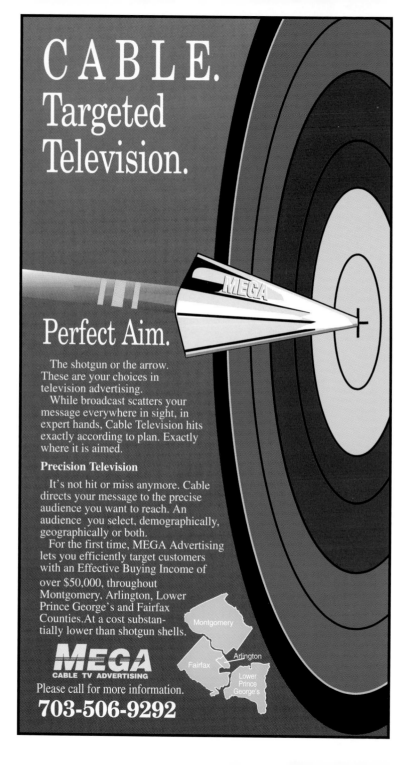

Georgetown, Dupont Circle and parts of downtown. This property is frequented by students and/or their parents.

The River Inn

924 25th St. NW *(202) 337-7600*
$$

It's not on the Potomac, but the river's not too far away. Nor is most of Georgetown and all of Foggy Bottom. All 128 units in this former apartment house are suites, each with a full kitchen. It's a nice place to unwind after an evening at the Kennedy Center, just a couple of blocks away.

St. James Preferred Residence

950 24th St. NW *(202) 457-0500*
$$$

The St. James is an upscale all-suite property that can be checked into for a night, a month or longer. It's located near 24th and K streets, just off Washington Circle and near Foggy Bottom Metro and George Washington University. Georgetown and Dupont Circle are close by.

Savoy Suites Hotel

2505 Wisconsin Ave. NW *(202) 337-9700*
$

Outstanding location and even better prices are the hallmarks of Savoy Suites in upper Georgetown. The 148-room hotel is within earshot of the inspiring Washington National

Cathedral and is largely insulated from the hustle and congestion of closer-in lodgings. Many suites have in-room Jacuzzis and full kitchens. There's also a swimming pool and on-site parking. Truly one of the suite-est deals in the District, it's also a nice place to bunk down for a few days or weeks even if you're shopping for a home in the suburbs.

The State Plaza Hotel

2117 E St. NW *(202) 861-8200*
$$

Don't let the harried urban setting fool you. The State Plaza Hotel, located across from the State Department in Foggy Bottom, is a quiet, self-contained world unto itself. The former apartment building now houses 215 spacious suites featuring separate kitchens and dining rooms. The hotel is often frequented by government employees, especially State Department types, on short-term assignments.

The Watergate Hotel

2650 Virginia Ave. NW *(202) 965-2300*
$$$

The Watergate complex will forever be known best as the site of the infamous "break-in" that ultimately ended the political career of President Richard M. Nixon. There's nothing suspicious about the hotel, however, one of the most luxurious in the District. Gracing the banks of the Potomac River, adjacent to the Kennedy Center, the Watergate has full kitchens, personal valet service, complimentary limousine service, a swimming pool and a health spa. Pricey, yes, but the experience is one that's quintessentially Washington. The Watergate's famous restaurant, Jean-Louis, claims the only 2-star Michelin chef in the United States.

Northern Virginia

Alexandria

Alexandria Lodgings

10 Sunset Dr. *(703) 836-5575*
$

This small inn-like property (two rooms and three suites) is located on the western edge of Old Town, two blocks from the King Street Metro station. You're within a few minutes' walk from any destination in the city's fascinating historic district, including some of its finest restaurants and shops. Guests can expect full kitchens and free on-site parking, which, as you'll soon discover, is at a premium in Old Town. Washers and dryers are also available, a nice touch for extended-stay guests.

The Executive Club

610 Bashford Ln. *(202) 739-2582*
$$-$$$

This all-suite property is located just north of Old Town, and within a couple of minutes' drive of National airport. Various options are available, but the best values are with extended stays.

Guest Quarters Suite Hotel/Alexandria

100 S. Reynolds St. *(703) 370-9600*
$$$

The Alexandria version of the apartment-like hotel is located near Landmark Shopping Center and I-

95 in the highly commercial, far-western reach of the city. Don't expect the quaintness of Old Town; this is concrete canyon territory. Nevertheless, the 225-unit hotel is convenient to most of Northern Virginia and the District. A pool and restaurant are on the premises.

Marriott Suites Alexandria

801 N. Asaph St. *(703) 836-4700*
$$$

One of the newest hotels in Old Town, Marriott commands a superb location and amenities galore. Each suite has a wet bar, refrigerator, coffee maker, iron and ironing board, two remote-control TVs, a VCR in the bedroom, two telephones with call waiting, a pool and a health club. As icing on the cake, you're a 10-minute walk away from lower King Street, the nerve center of Old Town, and maybe a five-minute drive from Washington National Airport.

Arlington

The Virginian

1500 Arlington Blvd. *(703) 522-9600*
$

Specializing in month-to-month suites, the Virginian offers hotel convenience and residential comfort. The Rosslyn location is close to Metro, Georgetown and most of Arlington and Alexandria. Guests receive Metro shuttle service, maid service, cable TV, free utilities and parking, and access to an on-site swimming pool, fitness center and saunas.

Fairfax County

Marriott Suites/ Washington Dulles

13101 Worldgate Dr.,
Herndon *(703) 709-0400*
$$

A turnkey home base for house-hunters in Fairfax and Loudoun counties, Marriott Suites/Washington Dulles is, as the names suggests, close to the airport but also within a few minutes' drive of some of the most desirable suburban neighborhoods in Northern Virginia. In addition to all the perks you'd expect from this national chain, the hotel is adjacent to Worldgate Athletic Club, one of the nation's largest health clubs, and close to Reston Town Center, the D.C. area's newest shopping and nightlife district.

Embassy Suites/Tysons Corner

8517 Leesburg Pike,
Vienna *(703) 883-0707)*
$$$

A Tysons Corner location — about halfway between Washington and Dulles airport — makes this 232-suite property convenient to most points in Northern Virginia. Suites come with refrigerators and minibars and guests can help themselves to free breakfasts. There's also complimentary shuttle service, a fitness center and indoor pool. The hotel is close to one of the world's largest office center and shopping mall complexes, and is within a few minutes' drive of Wolf Trap, the nation's only national park for the performing arts.

Residence Inn By Marriott/Dulles

315 Elden St., Herndon (703) 435-0044
$$

Short- and long-term stays are made easy at this all-suite Marriott property located about five miles east of Dulles airport, in the town of Herndon. One- and two-bedroom suites come with fireplaces. There's also free parking, shuttle to Dulles, and a pool and fitness area.

Suburban Maryland

Montgomery County

Marriott Suites Bethesda

6711 Democracy Blvd., Bethesda (301) 897-5600
$$$

House hunters in Montgomery County and upper Northwest Washington would do well to consider Marriott Suites Bethesda as a temporary command center. It's located near the intersection of the Beltway and I-270, adjacent to Marriott Corp.'s world headquarters and IBM. There's free parking, a swimming pool, health club, restaurant and all the other amenities you'd expect from this service-oriented national chain.

Prince George's County

Budget Host Valencia Motel

10131 Washington Blvd., Laurel (301) 725-4200
$

It may not have the sexiest moniker in this genre, but the Budget Host, as its name implies, is inexpensive (some rooms as low as $30 a night) as well as clean and convenient to the eastern suburbs. More than half the rooms here are suites (43), some with kitchenettes. Families can take advantage of the motel's picnic grove and playground. In addition, you're close to shopping centers and virtually every type of restaurant chain under the sun.

Anne Arundel County

Residence Inn by Marriott

170 Admiral Cochrane Dr., Annapolis (410) 573-0300
$$

The Annapolis version of Marriott's extended-stay, all-suite hotel is accessible to Route 50 and about a 10-minute drive from the city's historic district. All suites have a microwave oven, and non-smoking

Insiders...
Planning a romantic weekend "getaway" often look no farther than some of the in-town and suburban hotels and B&Bs, many of which offer great rates on two-day packages.

Insiders' Tip

rooms are available. An exercise area, outdoor pool, whirlpool and sports court afford plenty of diversions for the kids. A shopping mall with movie theaters is close by, as are plenty of affordable restaurants.

Rooms with a View — and More

District of Columbia

ANA Westin Hotel

2401 M St. NW *(202) 429-2400*
$$

Part of the prestigious Westin Hotels and Resorts group, the ANA is known for its outstanding service. Here you'll find 24-hour room service, an Executive Club floor with business amenities, a 14,000-square-foot fitness center, and kitchenettes in selected rooms. The property borders Rock Creek Park, and Georgetown is a five-minute walk away.

Bellevue Hotel

15 E St. NW *(202) 638-0900*
$$

The Bellevue on Capitol Hill is one of D.C.'s few remaining art-deco landmarks. After a tough day on the Hill you can come back and unwind at the Tiber Creek Pub, a haven for lobbyists and congressional staffers. There's free on-site parking between 4 PM and 9 AM. The 140-room property is two blocks from Union Station, the Capitol and Metro.

The Canterbury

1733 N St. NW *(202) 393-3000*
$$$$

The quiet setting of the Canterbury, just a few strides from the bustle of Connecticut Avenue, only adds to its already exclusive atmosphere. All 99 units are suites. The present-day building sits on the site of what once was the home to Presidents Theodore and Franklin D. Roosevelt.

Capital Hilton Hotel

16th and K Sts. NW *(202) 393-1000*
$$$

The Capital Hilton is a short walk to most points downtown and is just two blocks north of the White House. A massive renovation a few years ago resulted in new guest rooms with multi-line phones and voice mail, business amenities on the top four floors and a new health club. Not surprisingly, the 550-plus room hotel handles a large convention and tourist trade.

Channel Inn Hotel

650 Water St. SW *(202) 554-2400*
$$

This small 104-room hotel is perched right on the Southwest waterfront, with beautiful views of East Potomac Park and nearby marinas. The neighborhood boasts some of the best seafood dining in D.C., starting with the hotel's gourmet Pier 7 restaurant. You're also a short walk to the venerable Arena Stage Theater, the National Mall and the

Smithsonian museums. Free parking is available at the hotel.

Dupont Plaza Hotel

1500 New Hampshire Ave. NW *(202) 483-6000*

$$

The fashionable but unpretentious Dupont Plaza is located right across the street from the Dupont Circle Metro station, within close proximity to some of the city's best art galleries and boutiques. Rooms come with refrigerators, wet bars, remote control TVs and radio alarms. There's a restaurant and gift shop on the premises as well as free parking. Pets are welcome.

Four Seasons Hotel

2800 Pennsylvania Ave. NW *(202) 342-0444*

$$$

Like so many of Washington's premium hotels, the Four Seasons is often frequented by the rich and famous. Rock stars are a common sight here, and a few years ago Donald Trump and Marla Maples staged a much-publicized brouhaha in the lobby. Despite the occasional weirdness, the Four Seasons is all class. Guests of the Georgetown gem can expect some of the best service in Washington, including 24-hour room service, an outstanding concierge, a top-rated restaurant (Aux Beaux Champs) and probably the city's premiere hotel-based fitness center.

Photo: Virginia Div. of Tourism

Briarpatch Bed and Breakfast in Loudoun County offers guests an escape from the fast pace of Washington.

The Georgetown Inn

1310 Wisconsin Ave. NW (202) 333-8900

$$$

If it's Georgetown you want, the Georgetown Inn is the place to be. Right plum in the nerve center of Washington's still most popular nightlife district (and the daylife ain't bad either), this intimate 95-unit inn offers complimentary coffee and *The Washington Post* every morning, overnight shoe shines, turndown service and a secretarial staff. Valet parking is available, an added plus in parking-scarce Georgetown.

The Grand Hotel

2350 M St. NW (202) 429-0100

$$$

True to its moniker, everything about this place is grand, starting with the marble bathrooms and steeping tubs. Most units come with mini-bars, some with kitchenettes. Laundry and dry cleaning services are available to guests as are a swimming pool and health club. Wedged between downtown and Georgetown, the Grand is also close to Rock Creek Park, George Washington University and the Foggy Bottom Metro.

The Grand Hyatt Washington

1000 H St. NW (202) 582-1234

$$$

The Grand Hyatt covers all the bases. It sits across the street from the Convention Center and a half block from bustling Metro Center. Within a short walk are Pennsylvania Avenue and the White House, the National Theater, the Shops at National Place (a shopping mall) and the Smithsonian museums. This gigantic 900-room property is built around a 7,000-square-foot lagoon with an island Baby Grand piano. Camp Hyatt facilities accommodate children, and of course there's a swimming pool and health club. Extra perks include a kosher kitchen and a video check-out service.

The Hay-Adams Hotel

1 Lafayette Square NW (202) 638-6600

$$$

A personal favorite among favorites, this ultra-luxurious, ultra-historic property overlooks Lafayette Park and the White House to the south. Diplomats, statesmen and the who's who of the Washington elite bunk and dine at the Hay-Adams regularly, including former presidents and presidents-elect. It's the ultimate insiders' hotel but always accommodating to all. Valet parking, a full-time concierge, nightly turndown service and butler service are just some of the amenities. Some rooms come with kitchenettes.

The Henley Park Hotel

926 Massachusetts Ave. NW (202) 638-5200

$$$

Although just 10 years old, the Henley Park has emerged as one of the city's leading European-style inns. The 96-room property (formerly an apartment building) is less than two blocks from the Convention Center and near Union Station, Capitol Hill and the National Mall. Guests are treated to express check-ins, mini-bars, complimentary limousine service, overnight shoe shines and health club privileges. A classy British atmosphere pervades.

HOLIDAY INN CAPITOL

550 C St. SW *(202) 479-4000*
$$

A colleague visiting from South Dakota summed this place up best: "Nothing super fancy but a location you can't beat — right up close to the [National] Air & Space Museum." And indeed, the Holiday Inn Capitol knows its market. Tourists take advantage of the moderately priced rooms, restaurant, lobby bar and take-out deli. Kids pack the pool in summer. Not even Fido or Puff will be turned away here.

HOTEL LOMBARDY

2019 I St. NW *(202) 828-2600*
$$

An inn-like hotel for those who want to be near everything, the Hotel Lombardy has 126 rooms, some with kitchenettes, and all with mini bars, free newspapers, VCRs, children's movies and turndown service. Walk to the White House, West End, Foggy Bottom, downtown and the National Mall. Excellent value, especially when you consider location.

HOTEL WASHINGTON

15th and Pennsylvania Ave. NW *(202) 638-5900*
$$$

One of the city's finest older hotels, the Hotel Washington sits

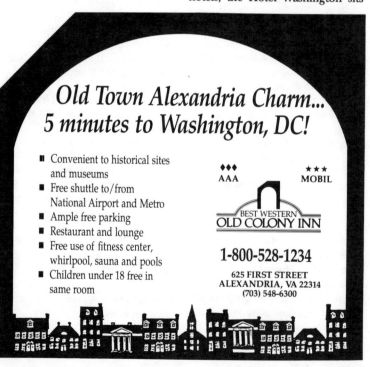

across the street from the Treasury Department and around the corner from the White House. The hotel's Roof Terrace lounge is, bar none, the best place in the city to watch fireworks on July 4th or any of the annual parades along Pennsylvania Avenue. All 350 rooms have been renovated.

Hyatt Regency Washington on Capitol Hill

400 New Jersey Ave. NW (202) 737-1234
$$$

The Capitol Hill edition of this prestigious international chain comes with everything you'd expect: Valet parking, video check-out service, a game room and children's suite, a beauty salon, swimming pool and health club. The massive 865-room property is located a block from the Capitol and two blocks from Union Station. As you can imagine, it commands a huge convention and tourist business.

The Jefferson Hotel

1200 16th St. NW (202) 347-2200
$$$

A small and gracious hotel located amid the hustle of downtown, the Jefferson offers complimentary bathrobes, hair dryers, one-hour pressing, multiline phones, mini bars and VCRs. Some rooms have kitchenettes. Swimming pool and health club privileges are available at the nearby University Club. Pets are acceptable.

JW Marriott

1331 Pennsylvania Ave. NW (202) 393-2000
$$$

Part of downtown Washington's ongoing renaissance, this 1980s entry boasts more than 800 rooms and proximity to The Shops at National Place, the White House and the National Mall. It's big with conventions, tourists and business travelers. There's a swimming pool and health club on the premises.

Loews L'Enfant Plaza Hotel

480 L'Enfant Plaza SW (202) 484-1000
$$$

The Loews L'Enfant is a beautiful, airy hotel located near the pulse of bureaucratic Washington. Within a short walk are the offices of NASA, the Department of Housing and Urban Development, the Transportation and Agriculture departments, and the Federal Aviation Administration. Amenities galore at Loews: All rooms come with VCRs, mini bars, stocked refrigerators, three phones, in-room safes, a TV/radio in the bathroom, swimming pool and health club. Some rooms have kitchens. And pets are allowed. To top it off, the National Mall and monuments are all within an easy, safe stroll.

The Madison Hotel

15th & M Sts. NW (202) 862-1600
$$$

Elegant is the only way to describe this downtown institution featuring 375 rooms appointed with French and Asian antiques. Guests should expect refrigerators and stocked bars in each room, a well as indoor valet parking. Some units come with kitchenettes. The hotel's restaurant, Montpelier, is among the city's best in the gourmet continental genre. Convenient to everything in federal and corporate Washington.

Photo: Washington Convention and Visitors Association

The National Zoological Park is home to the giant panda bear, Hsing-Hsing — always a favorite for kids.

Marriott/Washington

1221 22nd St. NW *(202) 872-1500*
$$$

If you're familiar with Marriott (there's no escaping the chain in the Washington area, its home base) then you already know the routine here. Georgetown is a stone's throw away and there are two Metro stops within three blocks. Guest receive complimentary morning coffee, juice and newspapers. Hair dryers and mini bars are in each room, and pets are accepted.

The Mayflower

1127 Connecticut Ave. NW (202) 347-3000
$$$

This much-revered Stouffer hotel is a Connecticut Avenue landmark, a place to see and be seen. The Mayflower's lobby takes up an entire block, and the property has two restaurants and a lounge. Some of the rooms in this 800-unit-plus hotel have kitchenettes. The White House is only four blocks away. Much of downtown is even closer.

The Morrison-Clark Inn

11th and Massachusetts Ave. NW *(202) 898-1200*
$$$

One of the newer faces to grace the revitalizing eastern edge of downtown, near the Convention Center, the Morrison-Clark nevertheless occupies one of the oldest buildings in Washington. Complementing the mid-Victorian decor are thoroughly modern guest rooms, complete with VCRs and computer data ports.

Normandy Inn

2118 Wyoming Ave. NW *(202) 483-1350*
$$

The Normandy, in upper Northwest, is lodged between the National Zoo and Dupont Circle, and is a short stroll from Rock Creek Park. Underground parking is available as are on-site limousine and car-rental services. Guests receive in-room movies, valet service and a continental breakfast. Pets are accepted.

Omni Georgetown Hotel

2121 P St. NW *(202) 293-3100*
$$

The Omni is more in Dupont Circle than Georgetown, but that's okay — it's close enough to both neighborhoods and their myriad attractions. Guests are pampered with stylishly appointed rooms, a business center, sauna, swimming pool and health club. Some rooms have kitchens. Nearby Rock Creek Park beckons joggers, strollers and the romantics at heart.

Park Hyatt Washington

24th and M Sts. NW *(202) 789-1234*
$$$

Another in a long list of competitive West End hotels, the Park Hyatt has multi-line phones, mini bars and complimentary fresh fruit in all rooms. Some rooms have kitchenettes and about a third of all units are suites. Of course, there's a swimming pool and a health club on the premises.

Phoenix Park Hotel

520 N. Capitol St. NW *(202) 638-6900*
$$$

For a touch of the Emerald Isle right here in Washington, check into the Phoenix Park, America's only Irish-owned hotel. More of an inn than a hotel, it has 90 rooms and is located two blocks from the Capitol and a block from Union Station and Metro. The hotel's Powerscourt Restaurant features Celtic and continental dining, and the Dubliner Pub is widely regarded as one of the best Irish bars in Metro D.C.

Pullman Highland Hotel

1914 Connecticut Ave. NW (202) 797-2000
$$$

The recently renovated Pullman Highland boasts, and rightly so, a full-service business center and meeting rooms. All 143 units are suites, all with honor bars, some with kitchenettes. The hotel is equally accessible to Dupont Circle and downtown.

Radisson Park Terrace Hotel

1515 Rhode Island Ave. NW (202) 232-7000
$$

Wedged between 16th Street and Scott Circle, this 260-room European-flavored hotel is convenient to Metro and embassies. About a fifth of the rooms are suites, many equipped with kitchens. It's located in an interesting neighborhood of graceful old churches, brownstones and funky boutiques, and Dupont Circle is a short walk away.

Ramada Renaissance Hotel-Techworld

999 9th St. NW (202) 898-9000
$$$

Rapidly becoming one of the District's premiere convention and trade show sites, Techworld is located across from the Convention Center, about halfway between the White House and Capitol Hill. Twenty-five retail shops, a fitness center and indoor pool complement the 880 rooms. Pets are allowed.

The Ritz-Carlton

2100 Massachusetts Ave. NW (202) 293-2100
$$$

This Embassy Row landmark is opulence personified. Here you can lounge in your complimentary terry robe after a hot bath in a marble tub. Newspapers are delivered to your door, and shoe shine and limousine services are available. Some rooms come with kitchenettes. As might be expected, the Ritz is popular with CEOs and guests of Washington officialdom. The Jockey Club restaurant is typically packed with stars of industry, government and the entertainment world.

Sheraton Washington

2660 Woodley Rd. NW (202) 328-2000
$$$

This is one of Washington's most beautiful hotels, in an equally gorgeous setting. Rock Creek Parkway is practically in its back yard and the National Zoo is three blocks to the north. Gigantic, the Sheraton Washington offers more than 1,500 rooms, as well as 124 suites, a post office, pool, health club and hair salon. Pets are allowed.

Washington Plaza Hotel

Massachusetts and Vermont Aves. NW (202) 842-1300
$$

A moderately priced downtown hotel, the Washington Plaza offers 340 rooms, a restaurant, lounge, gift shop and free underground parking. Some rooms have kitchenettes. You're five blocks from the Convention Center and close to McPherson Square Metro and the White House.

WASHINGTON VISTA

1400 M St. NW *(202) 429-1700*
$$$

Us tainted locals still know this best as the place where former D.C. Mayor Marion Barry got busted — and videotaped, no less — for using drugs. That's not to knock the Vista, however. This is a fine, centrally located hotel that offers guests three telephones in every room as well as mini bars and refrigerators. The hotel's fitness center comes with a sauna, a nice perk after a long day of sightseeing or business.

THE WILLARD INTER-CONTINENTAL

1401 Pennsylvania Ave. NW *(202) 965-2300*
$$$

Along with the Hay-Adams and a select few other properties, the Willard is among the creme de la creme of Washington hotels. Ironically, this stunning historical landmark almost fell victim to the wrecking ball before it was renovated and reopened in 1986.

With a minute or two walk are the White House, the Treasury Department, the National Theater, the Department of Commerce and the National Mall. The hotel has two elegant lounges, a cafe and a formal restaurant, the Willard Room, which serves perhaps the best crab cakes in the free world.

Wyndham Bristol

2430 Pennsylvania Ave. NW (202) 955-6400
$$$

Service is key at this classic West End hotel that's just a few strides away from Georgetown. The Wyndham offers valet parking, complimentary newspapers, a shoe shine service and rooms with hair dryers and coffee machines. Some units have kitchenettes. Classic English and contemporary decor accentuates an already classy atmosphere.

Northern Virginia

Fairfax County

Holiday Inn Crowne Plaza

775 12th Street NW (202) 737-2200
$$$

Located within a block of the Washington Convention Center, the 456-room Holiday Inn Crowne Plaza features a free indoor health center, meeting and conference facilities and easy access to downtown, Chinatown and Metro Center. In addition to this flagship location there's a similar property on Rockville Pike in Montgomery County (301-468-1100).

Holiday Inn/Fair Oaks

11787 Lee Jackson Memorial Highway, Fairfax (703) 352-2525
$$

Located adjacent to Fair Oaks Mall, one of the region's largest shopping centers, this edition of the national chain comes with exercise facilities, an indoor pool, two restaurants and free transportation to Dulles Airport and Metro.

Marriott Dulles

333 W. Service Rd., Chantilly(703)471-9500
$$

Talk about the Marriott advantage, this is the only airport located on the grounds of Washington Dulles International Airport. A large pond and acres of wooded landscaping almost defy its location, though. There's an indoor/outdoor pool, fitness center and free parking. The terminal is a two-minute drive away, and complimentary shuttle service is provided.

Westfields International Conference Center

14750 Conference Center Dr., Chantilly (703) 818-0300
$$$

Westfields' stately Georgian facade and manicured grounds give the impression of an old established Virginia resort. The lavish, service-driven facility, however, is the product of the boom days of the 1980s. It exudes elegance, from its state-of-the-art conference rooms to its outstanding restaurant and ornate rooms. Dulles airport is seven miles to the north along Route 28. The hotel is also about equal distance from Route 50 and I-66. An ideal venue for a corporate retreat, large and small, a wedding reception or any other special occasion.

Tysons Westpark Hotel

8401 Westpark Drive, McLean (703) 734-2800
$$-$$$

Affiliated with the Best Western chain, the Tysons Westpark Hotel comes with a family restaurant, indoor pool and spa and plenty of free parking. Its central location makes for a natural home base for house hunting in Fairfax County. Its sister property, the Rosslyn Westpark Hotel (703-527-4814) in Arlington, is but a short walk from Georgetown and is largely tourist-driven.

Tysons Corner Sheraton Premiere

8661 Leesburg Pike *(703) 448-1234*

$$$

One of Northern Virginia's most luxurious hotels, the towering Sheraton Premiere (you can't miss it, it's one of the tallest buildings in Tysons Corner) extends to guests such perks as lighted tennis courts, golf privileges, a fitness center, pool and free transportation to Dulles airport. Tysons Corner, a city in itself, is close to I-66 and the Beltway.

McLean Hilton

7920 Jones Branch Dr.,
McLean *(703) 847-5000*

$$$

Another Tysons Corner landmark, the McLean Hilton offers an extensive health club, an indoor pool, minibars in each room and in some suites, bathroom phones. There's a restaurant, bar and drug store on the premises, and you're close to shopping, movie theaters and more shopping at Tysons Corner Mall I & II. Yup, there are two of them.

Alexandria

Old Town Holiday Inn

480 King St. *(703) 549-6080*

$$

A tourist mecca, especially on weekends, the Old Town Holiday Inn offers the best location — and one of the top values — in Alexandria's famed historic district. From here, you're right across the street from the town square, site of the region's most colorful street market (held every Saturday morning), and a short walk from galleries, shops, restaurants and the Potomac waterfront. Colonial-themed guest rooms have hair dryers and speaker phones with computer modem capability. There's also free transportation to National Airport and Metro.

Ramada/Old Town

901 North Fairfax St. *(703) 683-6000*

$$$

With sweeping views of the Potomac and Old Town Alexandria, this Ramada commands a high profile with group tours and the convention crowd. The 258-room property is a five-minute drive from National Airport and is within walking distance of the shops, restaurants and historical attractions of Old Town.

Best Western Old Colony Inn

North Washington and First Streets
(703) 548-6300

$$$

This resort-type property, with a lodge and surrounding motor court, is the northern gateway to Old Town Alexandria. From here, you're maybe a three-minute drive from National Airport and less than 10 minutes to points in D. C. Elaborate conference and banquet facilities make the Old Colony a major player in the meetings and convention market.

Radisson Plaza Hotel at Mark Center

5000 Seminary Rd. *(703) 845-1010*
$$

From I-395, you can't possibly miss the Radisson Mark Center, a tower of concrete and glass that emerges from the surrounding woodlands like a futuristic sentinel. The 500-room hotel, big with convention and conference folks, is surrounded by a manmade lake and about 80 acres of woods — a nice buffer from the traffic and congestion of Alexandria's West End. The property comes with an indoor/outdoor swimming pool, health club and free parking. Some rooms have kitchens. National airport and downtown D.C. are 10 and 15 minutes away, respectively.

Morrison House

116 S. Alfred St. *(703) 838-8000*
$$$

This elegant mansion in the center of Old Town is one of the region's, indeed the nation's, most-celebrated inns. Each of the 45 rooms is individually decorated with Federal-period antiques, and several rooms come with fireplaces and four-poster canopy beds. The inn's cozy restaurant and lounge enhance an already intensely romantic atmosphere. Morrison House is the perfect urban getaway and the site of scores of honeymoons.

Arlington County

Hyatt Regency Crystal City

2799 Jefferson Davis Hwy. *(703) 418-1234*
$$$

Crystal City, a conglomeration of office buildings, fast-food restaurants and big hotels, isn't going to win any awards for aesthetics, but it sure is convenient. Same can be said for the Hyatt Regency here, a 700-unit hotel that offers non-smoking rooms, a health club, an outdoor swimming pool and a lounge. Guests receive complimentary shuttle service to nearby National airport. Crystal City is also close to the Pentagon, downtown D.C. and Old Town Alexandria.

Key Bridge Marriott

1401 Lee Hwy. *(703) 524-6400*
$$$

About as close to Washington as you're going to get in Virginia, the Key Bridge Marriott is a short walk from Georgetown and just two blocks from the Rosslyn Metro. The hotel's riverside location affords spectacular views of the Potomac, the namesake Key Bridge and the District beyond. There's free on-site parking, a pool and health club.

Quality Inn Iwo Jima

1501 Arlington Blvd. *(703) 524-5000*
$$

Popular with tourists, this edition of the national chain is within an easy walk of Arlington Cemetery, the Iwo Jima Memorial, the National Mall and even Georgetown. Rosslyn Metro is three blocks away. The hotel has free parking, laundry facilities and a pool.

The Ritz-Carlton Pentagon City

1250 S. Hayes St. *(703) 415-5000*
$$$

One of the main attractions here is the Pentagon City Fashion Center Mall, one of the region's newest and most popular shopping centers. Typical of the classy Ritz-Carlton, the hotel's public spaces are adorned with a collection of 18th- and 19th-century British art and antiques. The Pentagon, Washington, Alexandria and other points in Northern Virginia are all easily accessible via I-395 and the nearby George Washington Memorial Parkway.

Sheraton National

900 S. Orme St. *(703) 754-2921*
$$

Just a mile from the Pentagon and less than a 10-minute drive from National Airport, this 444-room hotel also offers shuttle service to Metro. Some rooms have kitchenettes and all come with the use of an on-site fitness center and pool.

Loudoun County

Lansdowne Conference Resort

44050 Woodridge Pkwy., Leesburg *(800) 541-4801*
$$$

Located in a resort-like setting north of Dulles airport, Lansdowne attracts a growing share of meetings and conventions, especially among international firms. Luxurious rooms are complemented by an attentive staff, state-of-the-art meetings technology and an outstanding golf course. Lansdowne is part of Loudoun County's burgeoning Route 7 corridor, one of the region's fastest-growing commercial districts.

Carradoc Hall

1500 E. Market St., Leesburg *(703) 771-9200*
$

Carradoc Hall is an affordable country inn on the outskirts of Leesburg. The centerpiece of the property is a colonial mansion built in 1773 and set off by an expansive lawn draped with huge oak and poplar trees. Most of the hotel's 126 rooms are located in separate modern guest rooms. Guests receive free transportation to Dulles and golf privileges at a nearby course.

Suburban Maryland

Montgomery County

Holiday Inn Bethesda

8120 Wisconsin Ave., Bethesda *(301) 652-2000*
$$

It's hard to get closer to the Bethesda Naval Hospital and the National Institutes of Health than here. You're also about equal distance from the Beltway and the District line. Pets are accepted.

Hyatt Regency Bethesda

One Bethesda Metro Center, Bethesda *(301) 657-1234*
$$$

Convenience and elegance abound at the Hyatt Bethesda, located atop the Metro's Red Line in the heart of this suburban community. Both Washington and the surrounding suburbs are just a few Metro stops away. Rooms come with voicemail phone service, and pets are accepted.

Prince George's County

Comfort Inn College Park

9020 Baltimore Blvd., College Park *(301) 441-8110*
$

College Park, home of the 37,000-student-strong University of Maryland, is somewhat of a rowdy college town but we had to include the Comfort Inn for sheer convenience (to the university) and affordability. In addition to the campus, you're close to Greenbelt Park, a 1,300-acre urban wilderness, and NASA/Goddard Space Flight Center, one of the world's largest research facilities. Downtown Washington's 20 to 30 minutes away depending on traffic.

Ramada Hotel/Oxon Hill

6400 Oxon Hill Rd., Oxon Hill *(301) 630-4050*
$

Located right off the Beltway, not far from the Woodrow Wilson Bridge, the Ramada Oxon Hill is convenient to most locations in Prince George's County and even Alexandria, across the river. It's also surprisingly close to downtown D.C. via I-295. There's a tanning salon, pool and full fitness center on premises. Transportation's provided to National airport.

Best For Less

District of Columbia

Allen Lee Hotel

2224 F St. NW *(202) 331-1224*
$

Rooms at the Allen Lee in Foggy Bottom can start as low as $33, which partly explains why it does a brisk business with students and young international tourists. The tidy 85-room hotel is right on the beaten path — close to Metro and six blocks from the White House, the Kennedy Center and the Lincoln Memorial. Ideal for tourists not dependent on a car.

Connecticut Avenue Days Inn

4400 Connecticut Ave. NW *(202) 244-5600*
$

In the city but away from the masses, this edition of the national chain comes with valet service and free on-site parking. It's located in upper Northwest D.C., a safe and exclusive neighborhood, and is made even more convenient by the presence of the Van Ness/UDC Metro two blocks away. Also close by are American University, the National Zoo, Rock Creek Park and the restaurants and shops of Tenleytown and Cleveland Park.

Days Inn Downtown

1201 K St. NW *(202) 842-1020*
$

In the middle of the K Street corridor, close to the Washington Convention Center and Metro Center, Days Inn Downtown is big with vacationing families. During the warm months, guests can laze around the rooftop pool. A multilingual staff accommodates international guests. Chinatown and its wonderful restaurants are a short walk away.

Hotel Harrington

11th and E Sts. NW (202) 628-8140

$

One of downtown's most underrated hotels, the Harrington is for the budget-conscious who want to be in the thick of it. It's a half-block away from Pennsylvania Avenue, about equal distance from the White House and the Capitol. There's free on-site parking and pets are welcome. For whatever reason, the Harrington has always done a strong business with Europeans. More Americans should follow their lead.

Quality Hotel Downtown

1315 16th St. NW (202) 232-8000

$

Right on the cusp of Embassy Row, the Quality Hotel Downtown is also close to the White House and the Convention Center. Guests can expect a complimentary cocktail on arrival, non-smoking rooms, same-day laundry and valet service and reasonably priced parking. For those eying an extended stay, some suites have kitchenettes.

Rock Creek Hotel

1925 Belmont Rd. NW (202) 462-6007

$

A quiet 54-room property, the Rock Creek is convenient to Adams Morgan, a vibrant international neighborhood with great restaurants and some of Washington's best nightlife. You're also in the shadows of Rock Creek Park, the nation's largest urban park and a wonderful destination in its own right.

Windsor Park Hotel

2116 Kalorama Rd. NW (202) 483-7700

$

The Windsor Park, on Embassy Row, is another great European-style bargain. Close to the National Zoo, the inn-like setting is tailor-made for families with small children. All rooms come with a small refrigerator, air conditioning, TV and private bath. The surrounding Kalorama neighborhood is an upscale international district pocketed with interesting shops and quiet tree-lined streets.

Northern Virginia

Alexandria

Towers Hotel

420 N. Van Dorn St. (703) 370-1000

$

If it's important to be near shopping malls and right off the interstate but not too far from D.C., then the Towers should fit the bill. The 186-suite hotel in Alexandria's West End is within striking distance of I-395, one of the region's busiest arteries, and Landmark Shopping Center, a mall that seems to never sleep. D.C. is just nine miles up the road, while Old Town is but five miles east. The area is a fast-food mecca, but you can take solace in the fact that all suites here come with kitchens.

Econolodge/Mount Vernon

8849 Richmond Highway (703) 780-0300
$

Just three miles from Mt. Vernon estate and less than a 20-minute drive to D.C., the Econolodge/Mt. Vernon features all the conveniences you'd expect from this national chain, including free HBO and ESPN, individual room voice mail, sightseeing tours and government, AARP and corporate discounts. From here, the best access to Washington is by way of the Mt. Vernon Memorial Parkway, a scenic and mostly stoplight-free stretch of road that parallels the Potomac River.

Arlington

American Motel

1400 Jefferson Davis Highway
(703) 978-3772
$

From the Americana, you're about equal distance from Georgetown to the north and Old Town Alexandria to the south. This clean and convenient motel is located in tourist-friendly Crystal City, near National Airport, Metro, malls and dining galore.

Travelodge Cherry Blossom Motor Inn

3030 Columbia Pike (703) 521-5570
$

Located on one of Arlington's busiest commuting arteries, the Travelodge offers easy access to Rosslyn, Georgetown, the Pentagon, downtown D.C. and National Airport. Guests receive complimentary on-site parking and a continental breakfast. Metro bus and rail connections are nearby.

Howard Johnson Hotel National Airport

2650 Jefferson Davis Hwy. (703) 684-7200
$

If you've been to one HoJo, you know the routine. This one's in Crystal City, a corridor of concrete, glass and steel that makes up for it by being close to everything, especially National Airport, the Pentagon, Arlington National Cemetery, zillions of shops at Pentagon City Mall and the Crystal City Underground and finally, to the south, Old Town Alexandria. Service is key and guests should expect complimentary shuttle service to National and Metro, as well as laundry and valet service, a health club, pool and free parking. Pets are welcome.

Quality Hotel Arlington

1200 N. Courthouse Rd. (703) 524-4000
$

A huge hotel in an urban setting, the Quality Arlington is near the Court House Metro (complimentary shuttle will take you there) and not terribly far from the Rosslyn business district and Georgetown. A pool, health club and free parking are standard here, and some rooms have kitchenettes. The place is crawling with families during the spring and summer months, testament no doubt to its value and ease.

Prince William County

Home-Style Inn

9913 Cockrell Road,
Manassas *(703) 369-1603*
or (800) 336-8312

This independently owned hotel is located just 10 minutes from I-66 and 15 miles from Dulles Airport, near Old Town Manassas. The Home-Style is favored by families on a budget and other tourists visiting such local attractions as Manassas National Battlefield Park. In-room kitchens and cable TV are de rigueur in all units, and there are also connecting rooms, nonsmoking rooms and a room for the disabled.

Suburban Maryland

Bethesda

Colonial Manor Motel

11410 Rockville Pike *(301) 881-5200*
$

It's not exactly the most scenic place around (this is the land of strip centers and fast-food restaurants), but then again you're not paying for the view. This 171-room motel in North Bethesda is clean, safe and close to White Flint Mall, the epitome of suburban shopping malls. Colonial Manor offers an hourly shuttle service to the National Institutes of Health, so don't be surprised if you see a lot of doctors and scientists running around.

American Inn of Bethesda

8130 Wisconsin Ave. *(301) 656-9300*
$

Much closer to the District than the Colonial, the American Inn is in the middle of downtown Bethesda, about a 10-minute walk from the Bethesda Metro and only a couple of minutes' drive from NIH. For whatever reason, downtown Bethesda tends to get a bad rap (mostly that it's sterile and boring), but the area's restaurant scene is coming on strong, buoyed in large measure by the arrival of the Rio Grande Cafe, a Mexican restaurant that would hold its own in Dallas or Los Angeles. Guests of the American can get microwave ovens upon request and there's a pool to cool off in.

Silver Spring

Holiday Inn Silver Spring Plaza

8777 Georgia Ave. *(301) 589-0800*
$

An easy walk to the Silver Spring Metro and the District line, this Holiday Inn sits in the center of one of Suburban Maryland's oldest and most established neighborhoods. The hotel is a great base for house hunters in Silver Spring or neighboring Takoma Park. Downtown Washington is a good 25-minute drive by way of 16th Street.

Quality Inn Silver Spring

8040 13th St. *(301) 588-4400*
$

Again, it's nothing fancy but this Quality Inn is near much of upper Northwest D.C. and close-in areas of Montgomery County. Walter Reed Army Hospital is a mile to the south, and Takoma Park, to the immediate east, has some interesting Bohemian-tinged shops, restaurants and nightclubs.

Hostels/ University Inns

(All are in the District of Columbia.)

Georgetown University Conference Center

Hoya Station NW *(202) 687-3200*

$$

The nation's oldest Catholic university, the alma mater of President Clinton, is the obvious main attraction of this on-campus hotel. Mostly frequented by guests of the university and seminar participants, the conference center offers some rooms with kitchenettes plus a swimming pool and health club. All of Georgetown, the neighborhood, is within a few minutes' walk and the business district of Rosslyn (Virginia) looms just across Key Bridge. Don't worry about non-stop college parties keeping you up at night; the hotel is located at the far-north end of campus, in a relatively quiet residential area.

The Howard Inn

2225 Georgia Ave. NW *(202) 462-5400*

$

Howard University, one of the nation's premiere historically black colleges, is host to this affordable 147-room hotel. Some rooms have kitchens and there's free on-site parking for all. From here, you're within a 10-minute drive from downtown and Capitol Hill. While security is tight on campus, some of the neighborhoods surrounding Howard have been plagued by violent crime.

The University Inn Hotel

2134 G. St. NW *(202) 342-8020*

$

Located on the campus of George Washington University, this small hotel (83 rooms) is just four blocks from the White House, within earshot of the Foggy Bottom Metro, and just a leisurely stroll from the Kennedy Center and the east end of Georgetown. Guests receive complimentary continental breakfast and a morning newspaper. Pets are accepted.

Washington International American Youth Hostel

1009 11th St. NW *(202) 737-2333*

$

A clean, safe alternative for young travelers on a budget, this 250-bed hostel is located one block north of the Washington Convention Center and easily accessible to the National Mall and most points downtown. There's a large common area for meeting other travelers (lots of Europeans here) plus a huge kitchen for groups. Free movies and tours are available and, as you can image, security is very tight.

Inns/B&Bs

District of Columbia

Bed and Breakfast League/ Sweet Dreams & Toast

P.O. Box 9490
Washington, D.C. 20016 (202) 363-7767
$-$$$

This is a reservation service specializing in B&Bs in Washington's historic districts. All guest houses have easy access to public transportation and offer on-site parking. Some rooms come with kitchenettes.

Bed 'N' Breakfast Ltd. of Washington, D.C.

P.O. Box 12011
Washington, D.C. 20005 (202) 328-3510
$-$$

From budget to luxury offerings, B&B of Washington will connect you with an array of private-home lodgings, guest houses and inns. Some apartments are even available for family groups and extended-stay guests.

Kalorama Guest House at Kalorama Park

1854 Mintwood Pl. NW (202) 667-6369
$

In the lively Adams Morgan neighborhood, just a block from the restaurant district, this elegant 33-room inn is furnished in Victorian antiques. Once inside, expect peace and quiet. There are no TVs or phones in rooms. Complimentary sherry is served in the parlor and garden.

Kalorama Guest House at Woodley Park

2700 Cathedral Ave. NW (202) 328-0860
$

This Victorian townhouse is located in Northwest, in the gorgeous Woodley Park neighborhood. It's close to Washington National Cathedral and the National Zoo. Metro is three blocks away. It is similar in atmosphere to the Kalorama in Kalorama Park.

Swiss Inn

1204 Massachusetts Ave. NW *(202) 371-1816*
$

Each of the six suites in this classy Euro-style inn comes with individual climate control, remote-control TV, private bath, phone and kitchenette. You're just four blocks from the Convention Center and a leisurely walk to the White House and the National Mall. Downtown D.C. is at your fingertips.

Northern Virginia

Alexandria

The Little House

719 Gibbon St. *(703) 548-9654*
$

It's the smallest house in Old Town and maybe anywhere. I doubt if this historic Federal-era, two-story townhome is more than six feet wide. It was originally built as a doll house for the daughter of the owner of the adjoining property. Now it serves as one of the most interesting — and undoubtedly the coziest — guest homes in all of Metro D.C. The Little House comes with a kitchen, living area and upstairs bedroom. All of Old Town is at your fingertips.

Fairfax County

Bailiwick Inn

4023 Chain Bridge Rd., Fairfax City *(703) 691-2266*
$$$

This early 19th-century brick townhouse is wedged in the center of Fairfax City's charming but often overlooked historic district. The Bailiwick has 14 guests rooms, all with feather beds and some with whirlpools and fireplaces. George Mason University and its beautiful new Center for the Arts is right up the road, and the Vienna Metro is less than a 10-minute drive.

Prince William County

Sunrise Hill Farm Bed & Breakfast

5513 Sudley Rd., Manassas *(703) 754-8309*
$

Civil War buffs, naturalists and horse-lovers will fall for this cozy B&B located inside the Manassas National Battlefield Park, just 30 miles west of Washington, D.C. Hiking and horseback-riding trails abound at the national park, and Sunrise Hill will even board your horse. Manassas's historic district, home to the newly opened and much-acclaimed Manassas Museum, is also nearby.

Loudoun County

The Norris House

108 Loudoun St. SW, Leesburg *(703) 777-1806*
$-$$

Right smack in the middle of Leesburg's historic district, the Norris House has guest rooms with canopied beds, antiques galore and fireplaces. It's a nice spot for a romantic night away but also conducive to small meetings and family celebrations. Washington is less than an hour away.

The Laurel Brigade Inn

20 W. Market St., Leesburg (703) 777-1010

$

Rooms here start at $50 a night, making this old colonial stone inn one of the better B&B bargains around. Guests can choose from five tastefully appointed rooms. The house restaurant specializes in Virginia country dining and is reasonably priced.

Red Fox Inn

2 E. Washington St., Middleburg (703) 687-6301

$$$

The Red Fox was built in 1728 by Joseph Chinn, George Washington's cousin. It claims to be the oldest continuously operating inn in America, and just walking into the place makes you feel as though you've stepped back in time. The inn has 19 rooms altogether, six in the main house and 13 in the two annexes. All the shops and attractions of Middleburg, the capital seat of Virginia's blue-blooded Hunt Country, are a short walk away. The peaceful inn and its famed dining room have long been a magnet for Washington yuppies and power brokers.

The Windsor House Restaurant and Country Inn

2 W. Washington St., Middleburg (703) 687-6800

$$-$$$

Perhaps best known for its British pub-style restaurant, the Windsor House in Middleburg also has four distinctive guest rooms. In the Gold Suite, for instance, there's a fireplace and a small kitchen. All rooms in this 169-year-old property come with decanters of sherry and bedside sweets. Middleburg, meanwhile, makes for an excellent destination in the spring and fall when the surrounding countryside is at its most colorful.

Suburban Maryland

Anne Arundel County

Historic Inns of Annapolis

16 Church Cir., Annapolis (410) 263-2641

$$-$$$

This is a group of four historic properties — The Maryland Inn (1776), The Robert Johnson House (1765), The Gov. Calvert House (1727) and The State House Inn (1820) — clustered in the center of Maryland's beautiful capital city. Ultra romantic, we recommend a Saturday night stay followed by a Sunday brunch at the Maryland Inn, a vintage Chesapeake culinary experience perhaps without equal.

Flag House Inn Bed & Breakfast

26 Randall St., Annapolis (410) 280-2721

$

Annapolis is synonymous with the traditions and pageantry of the United States Naval Academy, and you can't get any closer to the spectacle than at the Flag House Inn. Located across the street from the academy's Main Gate, each room comes with private baths, queen-size beds and off-street parking. Football weekends during the fall are always special. Our advice is to book early.

Jonas Green House Bed & Breakfast

124 Charles St., Annapolis (410) 263-5892
$$-$$$

Dating back to the 1690s, the Jonas Green is the second-oldest home in Annapolis. It's within a couple minutes' walk of all the finest restaurants, pubs and shops, including the Middleton Tavern, a watering hole that catered to the likes of George Washington and Benjamin Franklin. Guests have the option of shared or private baths, and all rooms are fully air conditioned.

Harborview Boat & Breakfast

Pier 4 Marina 301 4th St., Annapolis (410) 268-9330
$-$$$

It's only fitting that the sailing capital of the East offers "boat and breakfast" accommodations. One of the best in the genre is Harborview, a coalition of some 20 boats, both power and sail, moored in the Annapolis City Marina. Don't worry about being an experienced skipper; captained waterfront tours are available. In the morning, you can expect a gourmet continental breakfast delivered to your boat.

Frederick County

The Inn at Buckeystown

3521 Buckeystown Pike, Buckeystown (301) 874-5755
$$$

You'd be hard pressed to find a more scenic spot so close to Washington. The century-old Victorian, located in a tiny farming hamlet with gorgeous views of the Catoctin Mountains, has nine guests rooms and a separate cottage with a private hot tub and loft bed. A night's stay here includes breakfast and a five-course dinner.

The Strawberry Inn

17 Main St., New Market (301) 865-3318
$$

In the center of Maryland's most-celebrated antiquing village, the Strawberry Inn, a two-story white frame farmhouse, offers five rooms decorated with Victorian pieces and private baths. This is an ideal spot during the holiday season when New Market's bazaar-like atmosphere is at its peak. Autumn's not a bad bet either.

The Turning Point Inn

3406 Urbana Pike, Urbana (301) 874-2421
$-$$

With Sugar Loaf Mountain and the Frederick County countryside as its backdrop, the antique-filled Turning Point (named because the original proprietors felt that opening a B&B would be a "turning point" in their lives) is everything you'd want in a country inn. It's close to wine country, golf courses and the scores of craft shops in Frederick and New Market. Each of the five rooms in the Edwardian-style home has a private bath. The inn's restaurant is known countywide for its fine seafood dishes.

Inside
International Washington: Life Beyond The Monuments

The original plans for the Nation's Capital were drawn up by a Frenchman, Pierre L'Enfant, so it seems only logical that Metro Washington would develop into a vibrant international crossroads. And you don't have to look far to find some of the ingredients for this melting pot of humanity and heritage.

It's Chinatown, where the spirit of cross-cultural friendship is symbolized in the glittering archway that spans the width of a thoroughfare. It's Adams Morgan, where native Latinos, Ethiopians, Nigerians, Jamaicans and others have forged a neighborhood of extraordinary contrasts, a place where many of the 100 or so restaurants serve cuisine that's indigenous to points scattered around the globe. It's Embassy Row where the diplomatic corps — several thousand strong from over 150 nations — embodies the meaning

Photo: Washington Convention and Visitors Association

Embassy Row is where the majority of the capital's 140-plus embassies are located, on Massachusetts Avenue.

of international communication, cooperation, trade and goodwill. It's Arlington, where Vietnamese, Laotians, Cambodians, Koreans and other Asian groups in particular have prospered as merchants and small-business owners. It's virtually anywhere in the region where you'll find proud people who fled war-torn, famine-ravaged, economically distressed or brutally oppressive homelands to begin life anew here in professions as disparate as cab driver, banker, store clerk, police officer, computer technician, food and maintenance worker, craftsperson, scientist and artist. And it's the presence of institutions such as the World Bank, the International Monetary Fund and the Organization of American States that speaks volumes about living and working in a global economy and a drastically shrinking world.

It's this and much, much more. That's what international Washington is all about.

This chapter is intended to offer a glimpse of Metro Washington's technicolor character. And while touting the "life beyond the monuments," we confess up front that we couldn't help but include a few local landmarks that have especially strong transcontinental ties. Note that diversions such as ethnic dining are not covered here, so please consult the restaurant section of the book for suggestions on gastronomic globetrotting. However, you may notice that we have taken the liberty of duplicating a couple of the international-oriented recreational events that are also found in "Spectator Sports." Forgive us, but they're so good we didn't think you'd mind reading about them twice.

The Allure of Embassy Row

Few aspects of life here are more strongly identified with international Washington than the diplomatic community. The images — stereotypical but fairly accurate in most cases — are easy to conjure up: elegant residences in fashionable neighborhoods, lavish receptions and other "power" social functions, limousine motorcades, large and attentive staffs, instant access to political leaders and other establishment players, and, of course, perhaps the ultimate perk, "diplomatic immunity."

Indeed, ambassadors and their staffs enjoy many special privileges, not the least of which is protection from many of the laws that everybody else has to obey. This isn't to say that diplomats abuse the system and intentionally break laws knowing that they won't have to make amends, but in the event that things do happen, suffice it to say they receive considerations that go beyond the realm of even preferential treatment. And yes, you'll occasionally read stories of a particular embassy that has amassed, let's say, several thousand dollars worth of parking tickets and other minor violations and is being asked by the city to fork over the dough. Don't bet the mortgage on how those cases turn out.

It's tough to explain the degree to which diplomatic coddling is taken, so who better than the U.S. State Department to offer a summary explanation. Quoting Article 29 of the Vienna Convention on Diplomatic Relations, as found in the official Diplomatic List: "The person of a diplomatic agent shall be inviolable. He/she shall not be liable to any form of arrest or detention. The receiving State shall treat him/her with due respect and shall take all appropriate steps to prevent any attack on his/her person, freedom, or dignity." Make of it what you will.

Approximately 150 "embassies" (by law, the private residences of ambassadors and family) and "chanceries" (offices where all the work gets done) are located in Washington including such geographic mind-benders as Burkina Faso, Cape Verde, Myanmar, Benin, Belarus, Mali and the former Soviet republic of Kyrgyzstan. Chanceries are often staid and rather industrial looking while many of the embassies are gracious old mansions, painstakingly restored and complete with manicured lawns and gardens and massive gates. Diplomatic residences are clustered primarily in the historic northwest neighborhood of Kalorama, located north of Dupont Circle, and along Massachusetts Avenue northwest between Sheridan and Observatory circles, thus the common reference to the area as Embassy Row. Coats of arms and flags identify each diplomatic mission, although admittedly, some are much easier to spot than others from the street.

While you're unlikely to have much success walking up to an embassy and asking for a peek inside, some swing open their doors to the public a few times a year during organized tours, many of which serve as important fundraisers for charitable causes. The walking/bus tours are a great way to see some beautiful homes and get a rare up-close look at a unique world insulated for the most part from the general public. One spring event, the Goodwill Embassy Tour, benefits Davis Memorial Goodwill industries. Tour tickets include shuttle-bus transportation. Reservations are required. Call (202) 636-4225 for further information. The Kalorama House and Embassy Tour, held the second Sunday in September, features select homes, embassies and the Woodrow Wilson House, all located in Kalorama. Proceeds benefit the Woodrow Wilson House, a property of the National Trust for Historic Preservation. For details, call Woodrow Wilson House at (202) 387-4062.

Embassies are wonderful, underutilized sources on a nation's culture, history and other facets of

Insiders' Tip

Insiders...
Draw upon the sometimes-forgotten wealth of resources offered by embassies and numerous international organizations in Washington.

their society, as well as on a broad range of information relating to travel and tourism. Many diplomatic missions, particularly some of the larger ones including Canada, Mexico, Australia and many western European nations, offer some wonderful outreach programs, lectures, art exhibits and the like that are open to the public. For example, during one recent two-month period, the Asia Society hosted a series of Aboriginal films at the Australian Embassy. Many of the embassies can also put citizens in touch with area social clubs and other ethnic organizations.

Still, there's no diplomatic outlet in Washington quite like the expansive Japan Information & Culture Center, inarguably the top local authority on all things Japanese. Located at 1155 21st St. NW, the center comes complete with a friendly, helpful staff as well as permanent exhibit space for showings by a wide range of Japanese artists. Call (202) 939-6906.

Unfortunately, there's no central telephone number the public can call for general information on embassies and their resources. So we've listed the chancery address and phone number of 25 of the most prominent diplomatic missions, many with especially large staffs. Public-and/or cultural-affairs personnel can help answer questions or refer you to someone who can. Since the turnover rate in the diplomatic corps is rather high (the Diplomatic List is updated every three months), we didn't include names.

Argentina:
1600 New Hampshire Ave. NW
(202) 939-6400

Australia:
1601 Massachusetts Ave. NW
(202) 797-3000

Brazil:
3006 Massachusetts Ave. NW
(202) 745-2700

Canada:
501 Pennsylvania Ave. NW
(202) 682-1740

China:
2300 Connecticut Ave. NW
(202) 328-2500

Egypt:
2310 Decatur Place NW
(202) 232-5400

France:
4101 Reservoir Rd. NW
(202) 944-6000

Germany:
4645 Reservoir Rd. NW
(202) 298-4000

Great Britain:
3100 Massachusetts Ave. NW
(202) 462-1340

Greece:
2221 Massachusetts Ave. NW
(202) 939-5800

India:
2107 Massachusetts Ave. NW
(202) 939-7000

Israel:
3514 International Dr. NW
(202) 364-5500

Italy:
1601 Fuller St. NW
(202) 328-5500

Japan:
2521 Massachusetts Ave. NW
(202) 939-6700

Mexico:
1911 Pennsylvania Ave. NW
(202) 728-1600
Netherlands:
4200 Linnean Ave. NW
(202) 244-5300
Philippines:
1617 Massachusetts Ave. NW
(202) 483-1414
Russia:
1125 16th St. NW
(202) 628-7551/8548
Saudi Arabia:
601 New Hampshire Ave. NW
(202) 342-3800
South Africa:
3051 Massachusetts Ave. NW
(202) 232-4400
South Korea:
2370 Massachusetts Ave. NW
(202) 939-5600
Spain:
2700 15th St. NW
(202) 265-0190
Sweden:
600 New Hampshire Ave. NW
(202) 944-5600
Switzerland:
2900 Cathedral Ave. NW
(202) 745-7900
Turkey:
1714 Massachusetts Ave. NW
(202) 659-8200

Hurdling Monetary and Language Barriers

Dealings on an international level often require hurdling the barriers of currency and language. In addition to most major banks and airports, local firms specializing in currency include:

• Thomas Cook Foreign Exchange, a subsidiary of the large British-based travel and currency-exchange company, has three locations in Washington: downtown at 1800 K St. NW, (202) 872-1233; on Capitol Hill at Union Station, 50 Massachusetts Ave. NE, (202) 371-9219; and in Georgetown at Georgetown Park, 3222 M St. NW, Suite 322, (202) 338-3325.

• Another large currency-exchange firm is Reusch International, 825 14th St. NW, (202) 408-1200.

• Many American Express Travel Service offices can also provide those francs, pounds, marks and lira. And you don't even have to be a cardmember. There are locations throughout the metropolitan area. For general information, call American Express at (800) 528-4800.

If words, not money, are the problem, there are several major translation services available including:

Insiders' Tip

Insiders...
Realizing that parking is scarce and traffic can be a hassle, take Metrorail or some other form of public transportation to popular annual festivals such as Adams Morgan Day.

• Berlitz Translation Services, 1730 Rhode Island Ave. NW, Suite 1208, (202) 331-1163.

• The Interpreter Bureau, 1660 L St. NW, Room 613, (202) 296-1346.

• The Language Exchange, 1821 18th St. NW, (202) 328-0099.

• Linguex Language Center, 1612 K St. NW, Suite 700, (202) 296-1112.

The nation's capital greets well over a million foreign visitors a year. The Japanese are by far the No. 1 group; also posting large numbers are the British, Germans and Canadians. Fortunately for these folks and other way-out-of-town guests, there's the International Visitors Information Service (IVIS), located at 733 15th St. NW, Suite 300, (202) 939-5566. The service offers a telephone language bank with information in some 45 languages and a reception/information center with bilingual staff and multilingual brochures.

The International Monetary Fund (IMF) operates a Visitors' Center at 700 19th St. NW, (202) 623-6869/7300, primarily to provide information on the IMF and its work. The center includes a bookstore, a reading area with a range of reference materials such as international financial newspapers and magazines, a gallery with three permanent exhibits as well as changing exhibits from member countries, and a 72-seat auditorium, site of a variety of films and lectures relating to the IMF and the international economy. The auditorium also hosts a monthly Economic Forum series and the International Seminar series, an international concert series, documentary and feature films and poetry readings. Other cultural events are offered monthly and advertised in the center's monthly calendar. Something to keep in mind for that special small reception or meeting: the auditorium and gallery are open for use by outside groups and organizations.

By now you may be thinking, fine and dandy, but just what is the IMF? It's an intergovernmental agency with 156 member nations that promotes international monetary cooperation and assists in the expansion and balanced growth of global trade. The IMF also oversees the international monetary system and helps member nations overcome short-term financial problems. An interesting note: before a country can apply to become a member of the World Bank, it must first be a member of the IMF.

And speaking of the World Bank — officially, the International Bank for Reconstruction and Development — its main goal is to promote long-term economic growth that reduces poverty in developing nations. A major way of doing this is by providing loans to those countries and financing investments that contribute to economic growth. The Bank is located at 1818 H St. NW, (202) 477-1234. While not as culturally viable as the IMF, it is indeed a vital and interesting organization and a rich information resource.

Meanwhile, the Organization of American States (OAS), housed in a handsome white marble building at 17th Street and Constitution Avenue NW (just opposite the Ellipse), has a more limited constituency. Formed in 1890, it's the oldest international regional organization in the world, providing a forum for political, economic, social and cultural cooperation among the 35 member states of the Western Hemisphere including nations in North, Central and South America and the Caribbean. Latin American art and antiquities are showcased in the OAS Gallery as well as at the Art Museum of the Americas, an OAS annex located at 201 18th St. NW, between Constitution Avenue and C Street. The museum offers slide sets, videocassettes and publications on Latin American art. Admission is free, and tours are available. Call (202) 458-6016. Free tours of OAS headquarters and its beautiful grounds and gardens are available; the group also maintains a speakers bureau. Call (202) 458-3751.

Ethnic Neighborhoods

Washington neighborhoods not to be missed on any ethnic tour agenda include Adams Morgan, whose hub is at 18th Street and Columbia Road NW. The area is alive with restaurants, bars, nightclubs, shops, boutiques and a host of other attractions, many of which revolve around the community's Caribbean, Latin American and African roots.

Chinatown embraces an eight-block area bordered by H Street and 6th and 9th streets NW, just three blocks from the D.C. Convention Center, seven blocks from Capitol Hill, and sitting conveniently atop the Gallery Place station on Metrorail's Red Line. Again, it's restaurants and shops galore. But the social highlight of the year is undoubtedly the Chinese New Year celebration each January/February. Perhaps the neighborhood's most visible symbol, the glittering jewel-tone Friendship Archway spans H Street at 7th Street. Decorated in the classical art of the Ming and Ch'ing dynasties and featuring four pillars and five roofs, the $1 million project was paid for and jointly built by the D.C. government and Beijing in 1986. It is indicative of more than just Chinese culture and its presence here, however. The two capital cities pledged in 1984 to create a mutually beneficial relationship emphasizing cultural, economic, educational and technical exchanges with a goal to make Washington's Chinatown a world-class center for Asian trade and finance.

Insiders' Tip

Insiders...
Pack a picnic lunch and take advantage of Wolf Trap's spectacular natural setting during the International Children's Festival.

International Landmarks

Landmarks, both natural and manmade, are as much a part of Washington's international landscape as its people. So as promised, here's a quick look at a few of the monuments and landmarks that have a distinct international flavor. In ways large and small, countries from around the world are an integral part of the nation's capital. Among the most prominent influences:

Japanese cherry trees, a gift from the city of Tokyo in 1909. More than 3,000 of these gorgeous specimens dot the landscape near the Jefferson Memorial and the adjacent Tidal Basin. Many can also be found along nearby Hains Point. The original trees were infected by a fungus, so the Department of Agriculture had them destroyed; the replacements arrived in 1912 and were officially welcomed by First Lady Helen Taft and the wife of the Japanese ambassador. Each April, with a little cooperation from Mother Nature, in what is surely one of the most welcome harbingers of spring, the trees sprout their brilliant pink and white blossoms that are enjoyed by thousands of passersby and revered during the weeklong National Cherry Blossom Festival. The dazzling "peak" period lasts only a few days, though, with the weather greatly affecting the arrival, brilliance and longevity of the blossoms.

The Netherlands Carillon, an often-overlooked local landmark with strong foreign ties that looms overhead in Arlington near the Marine Corps War Memorial (Iwo Jima statue) and Arlington National Cemetery. Given to the U.S. in gratitude by the Dutch government after World War II, the 49-bell tower is surrounded by a sea of tulips (in season) and is the site of numerous concerts throughout the summer and on national holidays.

The Washington Monument. Yes, even Washington's most famous landmark has a global influence. The 555-foot obelisk — the world's largest masonry structure — contains nearly 200 memorial stones in its interior walls. Among them are a block of lava from Italy's infamous Mount Vesuvius, a mosaic block from the ruins of Carthage (present-day Tunisia), a stone from the chapel of William Tell in Switzerland, one praising George Washington in Chinese, and a replica stone of the one given by Pope Pius IX. The original stone was stolen by a radical anti-Catholic group in 1854 and dumped in the Potomac. The replacement, a gift to the National Park Service in 1982, is Italian marble inscribed in Latin with the phrase "A Roma Americae" — "From Rome to America."

Heritage Festivals

What better way to honor the diverse heritage of Metro Washingtonians than by parties, parades, festivals and other such events. Just in case you want to mark your calendar, we've selected a generous assortment spanning the entire year.

Chinese Lunar New Year is celebrated each January or February (depending on when the exact day falls) in Washington's Chinatown. Amid the crackle of firecrackers, thousands of spectators line the sidewalks to see traditional lions, drums and dragon dancers make their way through the streets. For the Chinese, the event symbolizes a time to close accounts, pay debts, clean house, honor ancestors, prepare exotic foods and thank the gods for a prosperous year. On H Street NW between 5th and 8th sts. (202) 724-4091 or (202) 638-1041.

St. Patrick's Day has got to be America's favorite heritage celebration, regardless of where you're from. After all, who's going to argue with green beer (as long as it doesn't actually taste like something green), corned beef and cabbage, and that infectious, foot-tapping music. Lucky for those of Irish descent and everyone else, there is no shortage of St. Patrick's Day parades and related events in the Metro area, all happening the week of or actually on March 17.

Old Town Alexandria's official observance usually begins with a parade and also features live music and parties in local restaurants, most notably at Murphy's Grand Irish Pub (713 King St., 703-548-1717) and Ireland's Own (132 N. Royal St., 703-549-4535). For general information, call the Alexandria Convention & Visitors Bureau at (703) 838-4200.

Arlington's St. Patrick's Day celebration takes place at Arlington House in Arlington National Cemetery and features speeches and music to commemorate George Washington Parke Custis, builder of the Georgian mansion and supporter of Irish independence during the 19th century. The ceremony is followed by an open house with period music and food. (703) 557-0613.

In the District, more than 100,000 people have been known to line Constitution Avenue to watch one whopper of a parade. (202) 724-4091.

While the community of Great Falls, Va., doesn't offer a parade, it is home to the Old Brogue Irish Pub, one of the area's most authentic establishments of this genre (great food, drink and atmosphere enhanced by live Celtic music) and host of one of the liveliest St. Patrick's Day celebrations around. One word of advice: get there early. The place is usually packed by early afternoon on St. Patty's Day, and standing in the line that stretches outside can be a bit uncomfortable if the chilly March winds are still blowing. But

Insiders' Tip

Insiders...

In search of a number of international dining options in close proximity to one another give strong consideration to spending an evening in Arlington, Bethesda, Adams Morgan or Chinatown.

don't wait for March to roll around. The Old Brogue is a great destination any time. 760 Walker Rd., just off Georgetown Pike (Route 193). (703) 759-3309.

The British get their due April 24 when the Folger **Shakespeare** Library honors the birthday of its namesake and perhaps England's most famous native son. The Bard's day is filled with music, theater, children's events, food and exhibits. 201 E. Capitol St. SE. (202) 544-4600.

Each May, the **Greek Spring Festival** blooms to life at Saints Constantine and Helen Greek Orthodox Church at 4115 16th St. NW. The celebration features Greek food, music, dances, games, clowns, and arts and crafts. (202) 829-2910.

Contributions that all ethnic groups have made to our nation's diverse heritage are celebrated at the ever-popular **Smithsonian Festival of American Folk Life**, held over a 10-day period in late June/early July, but always including the 4th of July. As one would expect from an event with such a broad focus, the festival brings together an astonishing collection of people, food, arts and crafts, exhibits and performances. On the National Mall. (202) 357-2700. TTY, (202) 357-1729.

It's a bit more tame than the French Revolution it honors, but the **Bastille Day** celebration July 14 along Pennsylvania Avenue offers its own brand of crowds and revelry. The highlight event: a walking race in which "waiters" carry champagne glasses and beer cans on trays for several blocks to compete for prizes that include a trip to Paris compliments of Air France. Sidewalk dining and music add to the merriment. The lunchtime event is hosted by Dominique's Restaurant at 20th St. and Pennsylvania Avenue NW. (202) 452-1126.

Alexandria's Episcopal High School, 3901 W. Braddock Rd., takes on a Highland atmosphere every July when it hosts the **Virginia Scottish Games**. Music, dancing, sporting and animal events and bagpiping are featured alongside Scottish foods, merchandise and genealogy exhibits. (703) 838-4200.

Some 40 countries are represented during the annual **Latin-American Festival** in July, both in Adams Morgan, on 18th Street between Columbia Road and Florida Avenue NW, and on the National Mall near the Washington Monument. Enjoy ethnic food, music, dancing, crafts and theater. (202) 269-0101.

Another popular event is the **African Cultural Festival**, featuring authentic cuisine, music, dance and crafts that celebrate the continent's heritage. At Freedom Plaza, 14th Street and Pennsylvania Avenue NW. (202) 667-5775.

Few events bring together different nations and cultures like the **International Children's Festival,** an annual three-day gala held Labor Day Weekend at Wolf Trap Farm Park for the Performing Arts, just outside Vienna, Va. Wolf Trap, by the way, is America's only national park dedicated to the performing arts. Sponsored by the Fairfax County Council of the Arts, the festival is geared to families and of course children and features an array of performances — dancers, musicians, acrobats and the like — and craft/cultural workshops where children can express their creativity. (703) 642-0862.

Certainly one of the grandaddies of local ethnic festivals, September's **Adams Morgan Day** celebrates the rich character of the Adams Morgan neighborhood of Washington. It's a giant late-summer block party complete with live music, crafts and plenty of good eats that reflects the area's wealth of Caribbean, African and Latin American restaurants. On 18th Street between Columbia Road and Florida Avenue NW. (202) 332-3292.

Thank goodness the Germans invented **Oktoberfest**. The spirited celebration is certainly a fun way to bid goodbye to summer and say hello to fall. If you can't make it to Munich for the real thing, head to Rockville, Md., sister city of Pinneberg, Germany, so you know they get some advice from the experts on doing it up right. Rockville's version of Oktoberfest is held in late September/early October in the Town Center just off Middle Lane. In addition to the requisite food, beer, music and other attractions, there's special entertainment for the young ones as well as a large juried crafts show. (301) 309-3322.

International cuisine is always a highlight at the **"Taste of D.C." Festival**. So forget the diet on this particular October weekend. That way you won't feel as guilty sampling the creations of many area restaurants. Lest you spend all day gorging, there's also entertainment, a special children's area, and arts and crafts. Along Pennsylvania Avenue NW between 9th and 14th streets. (202) 724-4093.

Some of the world's best riders saddle up for the **Washington International Horse Show** every October at USAir Arena in Landover, Md. One of the nation's largest and most prestigious equestrian events, the show features plenty of diplomatic pageantry as a different nation is honored each year and horses are brought in from as far away as Germany and Austria. (301) 840-0281.

Alexandria celebrates its Scottish heritage amid the splendor of the holiday season during the annual **Scottish Christmas Walk** and parade through the charming and history-rich Old Town section. Bagpipers, Highland dancers, children's events and tours of old homes also mark the day. (703) 838-4200.

Photo: Virginia Div. of Tourism

The Waterfront Promenade in Alexandria along the Potomac River leads visitors to urban parks and plazas at the end of King Street and the Torpedo Factory Art Center.

Inside Metro Washington Nooks and Crannies

Metro Washington is a region of magnificent sites and diversions — both of the natural and manmade varieties. We hope we've done an adequate job documenting many of these in our chapters dealing with Attractions, Parks and Recreation, Daytrips, the Civil War and Worship.

But now it's time to turn our attention to those hidden jewels and gems that often get overlooked by tourists and residents alike. No less magnificent than their more notable neighbors, and often no less accessible, these special places and objects are what we like to call the "nooks and crannies." We consider them to be an essential part of the Washington experience. Hopefully you'll have the time and inclination to explore them first-hand and in the process discover your own nooks and crannies.

The chapter is divided into three broad sections: Historic Hideaways, Urban Escapes and Busting the Federal Bureaucracy. The first two are pretty much self-explanatory. The last section sheds a little light on how you can gain access to some of the government's largest and most intriguing complexes.

We should also note that those of you who are passionate about good trivia should by all means consult Bryson B. Rash's *Footnote Washington* (EPM Publications, Inc., McLean, Va.), an engaging and hilarious history sampler that's available at most bookstores throughout the region.

Historic Hideaways

District of Columbia

It seems only appropriate to begin this section with some hidden historical gems groomed especially for children, or at least the kid at heart. At the Daughters of the American Revolution compound on D Street NW, a short walk from the White House, the **Children's Attic** (202-628-1776) is loaded with toys from the Revolutionary period, including a vast assortment of handmade dolls and crafts. There's even a special kids' tour of the fascinating DAR Museum, one of the nation's best exhibits documenting Colonial life.

Across town, at the **Dolls' House and Toy Museum of Washington** (202-244-0024) on 44th Street NW, a tiny world unfolds, tracing the development of homes and home life from around the globe — all from a miniature perspective. Top it off with a trip through the museum's toy shop, and if the trip is part of a birthday celebration the little ones can feast in a special ice cream parlor. Best bet is to book early for parties.

For whatever reason, the **Capital Children's Museum** (202-543-8600) in Northeast, near Union Station, has never really received the attention it deserves. And that's too bad, because this is one of the best "hands on" museums around. The key word here is "touch," and by doing so kids learn how levers and gears work, how machines operate, computers compute, telephones phone and so on. Historical tidbits are mixed with plenty of safe playground diversions including toy cars to drive, ladders to climb, bells to ring and mock sewer pipes to crawl through.

Moving on to more "grown-up" interests, that next trip to the White House might be even more intriguing once you've been briefed on the **FDR Bomb Shelter**. After the Japanese attack on Pearl Harbor, it was decided that President Roosevelt needed a safety escape in case of an air strike on Washington. A tunnel was built below the East Lawn and connected to the Treasury Department safety vault. The vault was transformed into a bomb shelter, and although it was never used it's still there and available for use. Don't expect a tour, though.

Directly south of the White House grounds is an expanse of parkland known as the Ellipse. One of the Ellipse's little-known features is the **Settlers' Memorial**, a granite marker located near 15th Street. Here you will find inscribed the names of the 18 landowners whose corn and tobacco farms ultimately became the land that is today's Washington, D.C.

As you'll soon discover, Washington's east-west streets are designated with alphabetical listings. It won't take long before you notice that there is no **J Street**. Several explanations have been given, but perhaps the most provocative reason has to do with the District's original planner, Major Pierre L'Enfant, a Frenchman. As legend goes, L'Enfant hated Chief Justice John Jay with such a passion that he intentionally left out the letter J in his layout.

On Pennsylvania Avenue, at 7th Street NW, one will stumble upon an unusual fountain decorated with dolphins and a water crane. This is the **Temperance Fountain**, a gift from Dr. Henry Cogswell, San Francisco's first dentist and a staunch supporter of temperance. The ornate structure is supposed to signify the superior qualities of water over alcohol. To this day, a group of professional doctors, lawyers and journalists, collectively known as the Cogswell Society, meet at the fountain once a month for a luncheon. It's doubtful, however, that any present-day group of D.C. doctors, lawyers and journalists could still hold on to the ideals of temperance.

Downtown, at 17th and M streets NW, is the headquarters of the venerable National Geographic Society. In the lobby, you'll find **Explorers Hall** (202-857-7588), a geography and map lover's valhalla. Exhibits, ranging from earth science and cultural geography to environmental and social issues, change regularly and never fail to fascinate. And like so many wonderful attractions in Washington, there is no admission charge.

Almost lost amid the grandeur of Capitol Hill is the historic **Sewall-Belmont House** (202-546-3989), at 2nd Street and Constitution Avenue NW. This 18th-century building now houses the headquarters of the National Woman's Party and contains mementos of the equality movement, including writings and heirlooms belonging to Susan B. Anthony and Alice Paul, the woman who penned the Equal Rights Amendment. The mansion was also once the abode of Albert Gallatin, the treasury secretary who masterminded the finances of the $15 million Louisiana Purchase in 1803.

As you can imagine, Washington's numerous cemeteries are packed with interesting histories. In **Glenwood Cemetery**, near Catholic University, lies the body of Constantino Brumidi, the Italian immigrant artisan who spent nearly a lifetime painting the awesome murals and frescoes found on the walls of the Capitol building.

Mount Olivet Cemetery on Bladensburg Road NE was established in 1858 as a place of rest for Roman Catholics. Among the buried here are James Hoban, designer of the White House, and Mary Surratt, one of the Lincoln assassination conspirators and the first woman ever hanged by the federal government.

As its name implies, **Congressional Cemetery**, on the Anacostia River in Southeast, is a final resting place for members of Congress. Today, more than 60 senators and representatives are buried here as are scores of interesting American personalities, such as John Philip Sousa and J. Edgar Hoover. At Congressional, one can also find the grave of Vice President Elbridge Gerry of Massachusetts, the man who gave us the term "gerrymander," a reference to those oddly shaped political districts so common throughout the nation.

Mt. Zion Cemetery, at 27th and Q streets NW, is one of the oldest black cemeteries in the District, dating back to 1808. Within the three-acre parcel is a burial vault believed to be a way station on the Underground Railroad. Several slaves who died on their way to freedom are supposedly buried in unmarked graves found along the hillside.

Insiders' Tip

Nooks and crannies well worth exploring are those found in the immense Library of Congress. Before you begin your literary quest or investigative research, check out the 18-minute slide presentation and 45-minute tour at the Madison Building, 101 Independence Ave. SE.

Northern Virginia

A leisurely walk through Old Town Alexandria will uncover a multitude of historical treasures. Starting at the **Ramsay House** (703-838-4356) on King Street (now the city's official Visitor's Center), one can peek into the life of William Ramsay, the town overseer, census-taker, postmaster and member of the committee of safety. Ramsay was a close friend of George Washington and it is said that the president spent the night before his inauguration at Ramsay House.

From 1792 to 1933, the **Stabler-Leadbeater Apothecary Shop** (703-836-3713) on Fairfax Street dispensed medicine to Alexandrians, including loyal customers Martha and George Washington. When it closed it was the second-oldest apothecary shop in the nation and the oldest in Virginia. Today, the shop is a museum exhibiting an array of Colonial medical implements and patent medicines. It also contains the most comprehensive collection of apothecary jars in the nation.

Several blocks to the north on Fairfax Street stands perhaps the most impressive home in Old Town — **Carlyle House** (703-549-2997). One of the first houses built in Alexandria, this 240-year-old replica of a Scottish manor home was the residence of John Carlyle and his wife Sara Fairfax. Among other uses, the house served in 1755 as the headquarters of General Braddock, leader of the British forces during the French and Indian War. Guided tours of the home and its terraced garden are encouraged.

The social nerve center of Colonial Alexandria was **Gadsby's Tavern** (703-838-4242) on Royal Street. Noted as "the finest tavern built in the colonies," Gadsby's was the site of numerous balls, meetings and political functions. Among the luminaries who unwound here were the Marquis de Lafayette, John Paul Jones, Aaron Burr, George Mason, Francis Scott Key, Henry Clay and, of course, George Washington. The tavern has been restored to its Colonial condition and is open for tours. Washington's Birthday Ball is still held here every year and is one of the most prestigious social events in Virginia.

Nearby, along the Old Town waterfront on Union Street at the foot of King Street, is the **Torpedo Factory** (703-838-4565), a refurbished 1918 torpedo-shell plant that now houses a thriving arts colony, with more than 200 artists and three stories of studio space. Here you will find an assortment of weavers, painters, sculptors, jewelry crafters, photographers and musical instrument makers. On the third floor sits the Alexandria Urban Archeology Museum, deciphering what Old Town was like before it was, well, old.

A short drive from Old Town places you in **Arlington National Cemetery** (703-692-0931), a veritable gold mine of hidden nooks and crannies. Some of the many overlooked figures buried in this national shrine include 44 non-Americans. One German and two Italian prisoners of war are buried here as are a number of British, Canadian, South African,

Photo: Virginia Div. of Tourism

Guests can relive 18th-century tavern life at Gadsby's Tavern Museum in Alexandria.

Chinese, French, Greek and Dutch troops.

Baseball fans may want to pay their respects to Gen. Abner Doubleday, the man who invented the game and who also fired the first Union gun at Fort Sumter, South Carolina. Doubleday is buried in the cemetery along with thousands of Civil War soldiers, both from the North and South. One interesting but little-known figure buried at Arlington is Lt. Thomas Selfridge, the first person killed in a military plane crash. Selfridge was on a test flight in 1908 with Orville Wright at Fort Myer in Arlington when the accident took place.

Historical nooks also still abound in highly suburbanized Fairfax County. **Sully Plantation** (703-437-1794), situated off of Route 28 in the far western edge of the county near Dulles Airport, was built by Revolutionary War hero Richard Bland Lee in 1793 and reflects a combination of Virginia's prevailing 18th-century Georgian Colonial architecture and the Philadelphia-influenced Federal townhouse style. Lee's wife, Elizabeth Collins, was the daughter of a wealthy Philadelphia merchant, hence the architectural homage. Miraculously, Sully survived the stormy years ahead including the Civil War, thanks in large measure to the Lee women who stayed behind and protected the plantation from Union and Rebel forces.

It's hard to believe that George Washington was considered land poor for his time. **River Farm** (703-768-5700), located off the Mount Vernon Memorial Parkway, was one of four farms Washington added to his fledgling Mount Vernon estate during the 1760s. On these fields he began to experiment with crop rotation, even introducing to the region a Kentucky coffee bean tree. Today, River Farm is the site of the headquarters of the American Horticultural Society.

Much of the southwestern portion of Fairfax County remains green and open, a patchwork of beautiful horse ranches and small produce farms. This is also where you will find the **Town of Clifton**, a hunt-country community that was settled in the early 1800s and still retains a secluded storybook charm. Sites not to be missed here include The Hermitage Inn, a Mobil Four-Star restaurant that was once the presidential retreat for Chester Arthur, Grover Cleveland and Benjamin Harrison. Across the street is the country chic Heart in Hand, a popular dining spot for influential Washingtonians and a favorite getaway of Nancy Reagan's.

A 20-minute drive along the scenic backroads leading from Clifton puts you in the Prince William County village of **Occoquan**. Among the earliest port cities in Virginia, Occoquan gained prominence as a thriving tobacco center. Today, its economy revolves around antiques and you'd be hard pressed to find a greater density of such shops anywhere in Metro Washington. Each September, the riverside village hosts one of the largest antique fairs on the East Coast.

The many legends of George Washington will live on in eternity at the **Weems-Botts Museum** (703-221-3346) in the Prince William community of Dumfries. This restored Colonial home was once the bookstore of Parson Mason Locke Weems, Washington's biographer who created the legend of the cherry tree. Serious students of George won't want to miss this tucked-away treasure.

Heading still farther south along Interstate 95, make sure to budget plenty of time to explore the alleyways and sidestreets of historic Fredericksburg, the hometown of George Washington's mother. At the **Mary Washington House** (703-373-1569) on Charles Street are plenty of original furnishings that belonged to this beloved mom. Ms. Washington was a widow for 46 years and spent the last 17 years of her life in this Colonial cottage. She was buried nearby on land that was once part of **Kenmore Estate** (703-373-3381). Considered one of the most beautiful homes in America, Kenmore was built in 1752 by Colonel Fielding Lewis, who married George Washington's younger sister Betty. Kenmore is renowned worldwide for its 18th-century formal boxwood garden.

Suburban Maryland

Here's one for the trivia minded. Did you know that the **First President's Grave** is in Prince George's County, in an unmarked site? No, we're not talking about George Washington here, but John Hanson of Maryland. Hanson was chairman of the Maryland delegation to the Continental Congress when the Articles of Confederation were approved in 1781. He was elected president of the United States by the Congress under the terms of the Articles and served in that role from 1781 to 1782, thus technically preceding Washington by eight years. A year after his term ended, Hanson became ill and died at his nephew's estate in Oxon Hill. He was buried at the estate, but there's no official record stating the exact location of the grave.

Unmarked graves aren't the only historical curios to be uncovered in Prince George's. Aviation buffs will surely want to visit the **College Park Airport Museum** (301-864-1530), located on the grounds of College Park Airfield, the world's oldest continuously operated airport. Among the "firsts" documented here include the development of the Air Force's initial bomb-dropping devices, the first mile-high flight, the first machine-guns fired from an airplane and the first U.S. Post Office air-mail flights.

Maryland agriculture has long been tied to chickens and turkeys so it shouldn't come as a surprise that the **Poultry Hall of Fame** (301-344-2403) is here. Yes, there is such a bird and it's located in Beltsville, home to the sprawling U.S. Department of Agriculture Research Center. Each year, five poultry phenoms are inducted into the Hall. Wonder if Colonel Sanders has made it in yet?

There once was a time when homicides were conducted in a gentlemanly manner. In Metro Washington, such rituals took place at **Bladensburg Dueling Grounds**, now part of Anacostia River Park in Bladensburg. For nearly 50 years, offended gentlemen settled their arguments here, facing each other at 10 paces with pistols and muskets. The most famous victim of the grounds was Commodore Stephen Decatur, conqueror of the Barbary pirates, who was killed in a duel with James Barron. Congress outlawed the place in 1839, but duels continued at Bladensburg nearly up until the outbreak of the Civil War.

Maryland and horses go way back — back before there even was a Kentucky. In fact, the Bluegrass State owes much of its equine tradition to Maryland, whose finest horses were moved to the Kentucky wilderness by the Rebel cavalry at the start of the Civil War. Today, Maryland boasts more Thoroughbreds per square mile than any state in the union. At **Belair Mansion and Stables Museum** (301-262-6200) in Bowie you can trace the blood lines of some of the nation's most valuable horses to this Colonial plantation. Two horses stabled here — Gallant Fox and Omaha — won the Triple Crown.

It's amazing how many people go to Annapolis and never step foot inside the **Maryland State House** (410-974-3400), the oldest state capital building in continuous legislative use. Its visitor center, museum and short guided tour are excellent primers to Annapolis and all of the Old Line State. One of the many facts you'll learn is that the Continental Congress convened here in 1783, and from November of that year to August, 1784, the Maryland State House served as the Capitol of the United States.

From the mid to late 1700s Annapolis was the principal seaport of the upper Chesapeake Bay (Baltimore was little more than a marshy wilderness) and one of the colonies' largest tobacco centers. These heady years of commerce are captured in the Maritime Museum at **Victualling Warehouse** (410-268-5576), where you can browse through exhibits on trade goods, barrel-making, shipbuilding, sailmaking and other nautical fancies.

Maryland's answer to Thomas Jefferson would have to be William Paca. Like the illustrious Virginian, Paca was a member of the Continental Congress, signed the Declaration of Independence, served as governor of his home state and was an avid gardener. It is this last point that brings us to the **William Paca House and Pleasure Gardens** (410-263-5553) in Annapolis. From the upstairs window of the house one can get the best vantage point of the gardens, where terraces lead down to a wilderness area that contains a two-story octagonal pavilion and a Chinese Chippendale trellis bridge. Both the house and gardens have been restored to their 1765 state of elegance.

Urban Escapes

District of Columbia

The juxtaposition of urban excitement and bucolic serenity is one of the many charms of Georgetown. Amid the noisy drama of M Street lies the **Old Stone House** (202-426-6851), built in 1766 and believed to be the oldest building in the District. Step into the backyard at 3051 M and you'll enter into another world. A quiet garden, maintained by the National Park Service, overflows with seasonal plantings, exotic butterflies and birds. It's a great place for a brown-bag lunch. When you're finished, take a tour of the historic house, which many parapsychologists claim is one of the most haunted buildings in Washington.

A couple of blocks directly south is the Georgetown stretch of the **C&O Canal and Towpath** (202-472-4376), another National Park Service-maintained site that serves as refuge for hikers, bikers, anglers and canoeists. There's even a mule-drawn barge to float on, complete with a historic interpretation by Park Service docents.

In the quiet upper section of Georgetown sprawls **Dumbarton Oaks** (202-342-3200) at 3101 R St. NW, a plantation and garden that lends perhaps the best glimpse into Washington aristocratic life. Also on the grounds is a museum of Byzantine art, operated by Harvard University.

There's probably no better way to escape the congestion of Washington than by paddling a canoe or rowboat across the gentle waters of the Potomac. Boats can be rented reasonably by the hour or day at **Fletcher's Boathouse** (202-244-0461), along Canal Road in Northwest, and at **Thompson's Boat Center** (202-333-4861), on the Georgetown waterfront. Pack a lunch and a fishing pole. The Potomac River, thanks to improved water quality, has become one of the most productive bass fisheries in the nation.

Moving on to one of the highest points (physically) in the city, it's hard not to be inspired by the grandeur of the National Cathedral. On the grounds here one will find the lovely **Bishop's Garden** (202-537-6380), actually a series of gardens consisting of a boxwood garden, a rose garden and a medieval herb garden. The garden's stone-paved walkways, pools and ivy-covered gazebo make for one of the most tranquil settings in the District.

Tranquility is also the order of the day at the **Japanese Tea House** on the grounds of the Embassy of Japan, 4000 Nebraska Ave. NW (202-939-6700). The tea house was imported from Tokyo and sits amid a lush garden that resembles an early 19th-century feudal lord garden. Visitors are given a guide book that explains the elaborate tea ceremony.

The **Botanic Garden Conservatory** (202-226-4082), located on the National Mall in front of the Capitol, may resemble neither a nook nor a cranny, but you'd be surprised how many people overlook this fascinating greenhouse research facility. (That is, except for Congress, which gets its free supply of plants from here.) The conservatory houses a number of experimental plantings that eventually find their way around the Mall, as well as scores of lush tropical plants, ferns, cacti and succulents. Green thumbs will especially like the educational exhibits that typically change with the seasons.

A few blocks east of the Capitol, at 7th and C streets NE, is the always festive **Eastern Market**, an open-air emporium that buzzes with produce and seafood stands, jewelry carts, craft shops and clothing boutiques. Get there early on a Saturday morning and grab a cup of coffee and a croissant at the bakery. It's hard to find a better way to begin the weekend.

New York may have the marvelous Rockefeller Center ice skating rink, but we'll take the less-crowded and more accessible one on the Mall any day. Located between 7th and 9th streets NW, the **Ice Skating Rink** affords the perfect wintertime diversion, and the stately backdrop of federal buildings and museums is hard to beat, even if you're a die-hard New Yorker. They'll rent you skates on the spot and, of course, there's plenty of hot chocolate and coffee to go around.

A couple of miles to the north, in the center of Rock Creek Park, Northwest Washington's vast wilderness area, is **Pierce Mill** (202-426-6832), a fully restored and operational grain mill that dates back to 1820. The mill is situated at the base of a waterfall and surrounded by meadows and woodlands, making it an ideal picnic spot. A short drive away, at the park's Nature Center on Glover Road NW, you can take in the nighttime sky at the **Planetarium** (202-426-6834). Star-gazing programs are offered throughout the year as are special programs for the kids.

The Washington area is a region of great vistas and one of the finest can be had at **Hains Point**, at the far southern end of East Potomac Park. From here you can scan the Southwest waterfront, including Fort McNair and the Navy Yard. To the west, across the Potomac, you can watch planes approach and take off from Washington National

Airport. Picnic spots abound and the fishing, especially in early spring and fall, is consistently good.

A few stone skips away from Hains Point is **Washington Marina** and the myriad boats (many that look like floating mansions) that line the docks. At the Marina shop, you can buy, rent, dock or have a boat repaired. Come the steamy months of summer, the marina is among the coolest and most relaxed spots in town.

Cool, yes, but relaxed, no, best describes the scene at the **Fish Wharf** on Maine Avenue SW, one of the most colorful sites in the District. Dozens of permanently docked flat-boats have been converted into sea-food shops, dispensing everything from Chesapeake Bay blue crabs and Carolina shrimp to Atlantic salmon and Chincoteague oysters. The wharf lets you mingle with real watermen, folks who not only know how to catch fish but can give you invaluable information on how to best prepare their catch.

Northern Virginia

A different kind of urban escape can be had at **Gravelly Point**, where it's practically possible to reach up and touch a jet as it descends into Washington National Airport. Gravelly is really nothing more than a parking lot and a strip of grass located just north of the airport along the George Washington Memorial Parkway in Arlington (accessible only from the north-bound lanes). However, virtually any time of day you can find packs of aviation enthusiasts sitting on the grass or the hoods of their cars taking in the spectacle. A word of caution: Bring some earplugs and limit your stay to less than an hour.

Directly north of Gravelly Point is Columbia Island, better known as **Lady Bird Johnson Park**. In a fitting tribute to a woman who fervently crusaded for the beautification of America's highways and cities, the riverside park is chock full of gorgeous flowers, including Texas wildflowers, and is easily traversed by way of a bike and foot path. Each spring, Lady Bird Johnson Park is among the most beautiful sites in Metro D.C. It's a prime place to just sit on a blanket and stare out at the river and the Washington cityscape.

Two Fairfax County retreats —**The Claude Moore Colonial Farm** and **Gunston Hall** — present radically different perspectives on 18th-century life but are nevertheless similar in their quiet, bucolic appeal. The Moore farm (703-442-7557) in McLean gives a glimpse into the life of a poor Colonial family, complete with a one-room cabin, turkeys, cows, pigs and a vegetable garden. In southeastern Fairfax is Gunston Hall (703-550-9220), the home of Tide-water aristocrat George Mason, author of the Virginia Bill of Rights, precursor to the American Bill of Rights. Gunston Hall's terraced box-wood garden, with plantings dating back to Mason's time, is among the most spectacular sites in Virginia.

Suburban Maryland

In Montgomery County, **Brookside Gardens** (301-949-8230) is famous for azaleas and the two conservatories that each spring feature impatiens, fuscias, caladiums and tropicals set against a towering Bird of Paradise tree. Natural and paved paths lead out to the newer aquatic and butterfly gardens and a tasteful Japanese tea house.

Glen Echo Park (301-320-5331), just above the District line in Montgomery, was once an amusement park but is now a quirky artist colony operated under the auspices of the National Park Service. Artists, sculptor, weavers, writers, dancers and musicians exhibit their work at festivals and open houses throughout the year. They also conduct classes here. For the kids, there is an antique carousel and a theater offering live stage shows on weekends.

Turn-of-the-century rural Maryland is only as far away as **Oxon Hill Farm** (301-283-2113) in Prince George's County. This working farm exhibits the daily activities that go into raising and bringing to market tobacco, produce and livestock. The farm is within earshot of the bustling Woodrow Wilson Bridge but might as well be a century removed.

The Chesapeake Bay just might be the nation's premiere urban escape. Chances are if you surveyed Bay sailors on any particular day, the majority would be from Washington, Baltimore, Philadelphia and Norfolk. Setting sail on the majestic Chesapeake doesn't necessarily require a ton of experience or money. The **Annapolis Sailing School** (410-267-7205) will teach you the ropes of the Bay and put together customized sailing vacations for individuals and families. "Sail Away Weekend" packages include basic sailing courses and hotel accommodations in Annapolis, the self-proclaimed "Sailing Capital of America."

Busting the Federal Bureaucracy

District of Columbia

Cracking the Washington bureaucratic code is a lot easier than you'd probably imagine thanks to the federal government's surprisingly tourism-friendly nature. One of the most accessible and hence popular federal buildings is the **Bureau of Engraving and Printing** (202-874-3019), at 14th and C streets SW. A 25-minute self-guided tour provides a glimpse of the inking, stacking and cutting of U.S. currency. Tickets are issued on a first-come basis, and early arrival (9 AM) is advised.

Across the Mall, at 9th and E streets NW, you can tour the J. Edgar Hoover Building, the nerve center of the **Federal Bureau of Investigation** (202-324-3447). You'll get an insider's look at the FBI's crime-fighting activities, crime lab and gangster guns, all topped off with an unforgettable marksmanship demonstration. Also, be sure to check out the panel of the Ten Most Wanted Fugitives.

If you're interested in the great outdoors and the preservation of land, natural resources and wildlife, then for sure plan to visit the **Department of the Interior Museum** (202-208-4743), at 1849 C St. NW. The museum features exhibits of surveying equipment, maps, historical documents, natural history and American cultures.

The American propaganda machine comes alive on the **Voice of America** tour (202-619-4700), held at the Health and Human Services building, 4th Street and Independence Avenue SW. The tour tells the story of how the VOA's shortwave radio systems and television programs, magazines and books are used to gain support abroad for American policies.

The incredible art and culture of Latin America unfolds at the impressive **Organization of American States** compound (202-458-6016) on 18th Street NW. While in the vicinity, be sure to walk across the street (Virginia Avenue) and take a look at the striking statue of Simon Bolivar, the liberator of much of South America.

The Washington Post, 1150 15th St. NW, isn't a federal bureaucracy, but it's an important bureaucracy nonetheless. To get the inside scoop on how the news is gathered, disseminated, printed and distributed, take a tour of this bastion of American journalism. The guided tours (202-334-7969) are open to adults and children at the fifth grade level and above.

Northern Virginia

There's no denying that the **Pentagon** (703-695-1776) is one massive nook and cranny. With 17.5 miles of corridors housing more than 23,000 Defense Department employees, the 50-year-old Pentagon remains the largest single-structure office building in the world. A 90-minute public tour of this Arlington facility helps scale down the monolith to a more human dimension. Guided tours include the history of the Pentagon's construction, an exhibit of military art and a walk through the Hall of Heroes, where the names of those who have received the Congressional Medal of Honor are listed.

Responsibility for the creation of the daunting American military infrastructure lies with the U.S. Army Corps of Engineers. At the **U.S. Army Engineer Museum** (703-664-6071), at Fort Belvoir in Fairfax County, the story of these efforts is told in dramatic light. Engineering equipment, uniforms, maps and flags are just a few of the items on display as are such curios as the ship's wheel of the U.S.S. *Maine*, a German glass antipersonnel mine and photographs of paramilitary projects constructed in Vietnam.

The Prince William County community of Quantico has the distinction of being the only town in the United States that is completely surrounded by a military base. To gain access to the town and Quantico Marine Base, just head to the **Marine Corps Air-Ground Museum** (703-640-2606) where you'll find an incredible array of aircraft and ground support equipment, much of it displayed in vintage 1920s hangars. Nearby is the **Quantico National Cemetery** which is actually larger — and unfortunately much less visited — than Arlington National Cemetery.

Suburban Maryland

Surprisingly, few fans of the National Air and Space Museum, the most-visited museum in the world, know about the **Paul E. Garber Facility** (301-357-1400) in Prince George's County. And that's a shame because this facility, essentially the aeronautical restoration shop for the Smithsonian Institution, houses more aircraft than Air and Space. Inside the 24-building installation visitors can get up close and personal with actual restoration projects, including work on a British Hawker Hurricane 11C that was employed in the Battle of Britain during World War II, a German Messerschmitt Me. 163 and a SPAD XIII still scarred by German bullets that was flown by ace pilot Eddie Rickenbacker. In addition, there are hundreds of astronautical artifacts on display, such as the nose cone from a Jupiter launch vehicle that carried monkeys into space.

Another often-overlooked gem in Prince George's County is the **Visitors Center at NASA Goddard Space Flight Center** (301-286-3979). A museum traces the history of American rocketry, from its humble beginnings on Robert Goddard's Massachusetts farm in 1926 to the current research involving the Hubble Space Telescope. Tours of the flight center's intricate tracking and communication system — an installation that houses more computers than any other building in the nation — are offered every Thursday at 2 PM.

Photo: Virginia Div. of Tourism

Civil War reenactors enthusiastically taking part in a battle.

Inside
The Civil War

The Civil War was undeniably the most tragic event in the history of the United States. It claimed more than 620,000 American lives and shattered millions of soldiers and families.

For four harsh years, the Washington area was at the epicenter of this tragedy. Even before the first shots were fired at Fort Sumter, S.C., the tense capital city found itself in a most precarious location — 60 miles south of the Mason-Dixon Line and just 100 miles north of Richmond, Va., the Confederate capital. Across the Potomac River in Virginia, the Stars and Bars flew defiantly from homes and shops within eyesight of Union soldiers. Surrounding Washington on the eastern side of the river lay Maryland, the powerful border state whose loyalties shifted from town to town, and oftentimes from house to house.

Even residents of the capital city grappled with the loyalty issue. Not surprisingly, many fled to the join the Confederate cause, while thousands of other Southern sympathizers remained at home, many taking part in clandestine operations under the nose of the Federal war machine.

The war forever changed the complexion of this once sleepy Southern town. Temporary shelters, office buildings, camps, hospitals and supply depots cropped up throughout the city. Each day, 500 new residents flocked to the District. Housing was scarce, crime soared, slums grew up in the shadows of the Capitol and the White House, and public services were virtually nonexistent. Tiber Creek, a marshy tributary now covered by Constitution Avenue, was an open sewer. The unsanitary conditions led to a typhoid epidemic that killed thousands of residents, including the young son of President Abraham Lincoln.

Ironically, for much of the war, Washington was a slave-holding city. Only six months before the Emancipation Proclamation became law did the District ban slavery.

If conditions were tough in Washington, then they were simply torturous in the surrounding countryside of Virginia and Maryland. At the Battle of First Manassas in July 1861, 35,000 Union soldiers under the command of Gen. Irvin McDowell met a Rebel force of 32,000 troops. It was supposed to be an easy Northern victory. So easy that hundreds of Washingtonians rode out to the site 30 miles west of the city to witness the festivities. First Manassas turned out to be anything but a Northern cakewalk. The Confederate army, bolstered by the brave showing of Gen. Thomas Jackson (who earned the nickname "Stonewall" here) crushed the Union advance. By day's end, nearly 900 young men lay dead on the fields of Matthews Hill, Henry Hill and Chinn Ridge. Ten hours of fierce fighting ended any notion that the war would be settled quickly.

First Manassas sent a shockwave through Washington. Forts and gun batteries were erected at a deafening pace, encircling the anxious city that many grew to believe could be overrun by Gen. Robert E. Lee (a native to the area) and his adept Southern army.

And indeed, the South did come close to striking the Union nerve center. At Fort Stevens, in the present-day Rock Creek Park, Confederate Gen. Jubal Early led his troops into the District's northern fringes on a balmy July evening in 1864. President Lincoln was among the many spectators who witnessed the battle that was eventually repelled by the Union.

The Civil War, of course, ultimately devastated neighboring Virginia. In Fredericksburg and surrounding Spotsylvania County, just 50 miles south of Washington, four major battles (Fredericksburg, Chancellorsville, The Wilderness and Spotsylvania Court House) would rage between 1862 and 1864. Over a patch of land no larger than 500 square miles, some 100,000 Union and Confederate soldiers were killed — twice the casualties of the Vietnam War. Tens of thousands more casualties would be claimed in the hundreds of skirmishes and battles, including the bloody Battle of Second Manassas (3,300 killed), that took place within a 60-mile radius of Washington. It is little wonder that more American lives were lost on Virginia soil than have been lost in all other American wars combined.

The single most violent day of the war, however, took place near the rural Maryland hamlet of Sharpsburg, less than 70 miles northwest of the District. Here, on Sept. 17, 1862, at the Battle of Antietam, more than 12,000 Federal troops and 10,000 Confederates were killed in some of the most gruesome hand-to-hand combat ever witnessed. Never in our history have more Americans been killed in one day.

The point here is not to be overly macabre or sensational when describing these events, most of which took place at historic sites so easily accessible to modern-day Washington. Rather, it is to help put into perspective the full tragedy of the war, which quite frankly is sometimes lost amid the crowds and commercialization that inevitably seize the region's battlefields and shrines during the tourist season.

The remainder of this chapter is designed to give a brief glimpse of some of Metro Washington's fascinating Civil War sites. If you're a Civil War buff, this region is your nirvana. If you're simply interested in learning a little more about The War Between the States, the Washington area will prove to be an unequalled instructor.

For those wishing to read more in-depth analyses of the Civil War in Washington, we strongly suggest picking up a copy of *The Insiders' Guide to the Civil War in the Eastern Theater* as well as Richard M. Lee's fascinating book, *Mr. Lincoln's City*.

For the Civil War purist, there's plenty of opportunity to join one of the area's many round-table groups or battle reenactment troupes, clubs that meet regularly at locations around Metro Washington. For more information, contact any of the above- or below-mentioned national battlefield parks.

Sites With Something to See or Do

District of Columbia

Albert Pike Statue

3rd and D sts. NW

One of the most peculiar and controversial statues in Washington, this memorial supposedly was erected to honor the man who headed the Scottish Rite of Freemasonry (the Masons) during the mid- to late-19th century. Little, however, is actually known about Pike, other than his role with the Masons and a career that dabbled in poetry, newspaper publishing and adventuring. It was later learned that Pike served as a general in the Confederate Army.

Consequently, this statue is the only such outdoor fixture in D.C. that honors a rebel military officer. In recent years, there have been protests calling for its removal, but the likelihood of that ever happening (based on similar experiences in this realm) is probably slim.

Blair House

1653 Pennsylvania Ave. NW
Not open to the public

This venerable mansion has served as a guest house for visiting heads of state and other dignitaries since the administration of Franklin D. Roosevelt. It was also where Robert E. Lee was offered the command of the Union Army. As we all know, the invitation extended by Francis P. Blair, a trusted Lincoln advisor, was turned down by the troubled Virginian. Four days later, Lee swore allegiance to his beloved Old Dominion and the rest is history.

Mathew Brady's Photo Studio

627 Pennsylvania Ave. NW
Not open to the public

The upper floors of this Pennsylvania Avenue office building were once used as the gallery and studio of the nation's most celebrated Civil War photojournalist, Mathew Brady. Brady's haunting photographs have done more to unlock the mysteries and nuances of the tragic war than have all the subsequent volumes of written documentation. His studio was frequented by the great and near great of official Washington, including one of Brady's biggest admirers, President Lincoln.

The Capitol

1st St. between Independence and Constitution aves.
Open Daily 8:30 AM to 4:30 PM
Free admission (202) 225-6827

Probably the most visible and accessible building in America, the Capitol is a required stop for anyone visiting or living in Metro D.C. Next time you're in these hallowed halls, consider that during the Civil War the Capitol was used for a variety of functions, including a fort, barracks and hospital for Union troops. Maybe the most unusual function was that of a bakery. Believe it or not, during the early months of the war, some 60,000 loaves of bread were baked each day in cellars under the West Wing. The bread was distributed to hungry soldiers stationed at the nearby forts that protected Washington.

The Old Capitol Prison

Site of the present-day U.S. Supreme Court
1st and East Capitol sts. NE

When the original Capitol was burned by the British in the Battle of 1812, a temporary building was constructed across the street. The interim structure was used for a variety of purposes but was probably most famous as a prison for Southern spies and sympathizers, as well as your garden variety of criminals (both Yanks and Rebs), rogues, drunks, con artists and other suspected misfits. In 1865, the prison was the site of the hanging of Confederate Capt. Henry Wirz, commander of the Andersonville Prison in Georgia, where more than 13,000 Federal troops died of disease and hunger. The Old Capitol was demolished in 1867.

The Confederate Memorial Association

1322 Vermont Ave. NW
Call for appointments (202) 483-5700

The Confederate Memorial Association, a.k.a. "The Confederate Embassy," is one of the oldest social organizations in Washington. In the fledgling moments of the Civil War, the Vermont Avenue mansion served as the South's embassy and in the years following became the Confederate Old Soldier's Home. Today, the building houses one of the area's most expansive libraries and museums dedicated to all things Southern. The association is still very active and claims several members whose ancestors fought for the South.

Ford's Theatre and the House Where Lincoln Died

511 10th St. NW
Open daily 9 AM to 5 PM
Free Admission (202) 426-6924

The night of April 14, 1865, forever changed the face of America. At 8:30 PM, the Lincolns and guests, Maj. Henry Reed Rathbone and Clara Harris, arrived at Ford's Theatre to see a performance of the critically acclaimed production of "Our American Cousin." Less than two hours later, Southern sympathizer and unemployed actor John Wilkes Booth would enter the presidential box and shoot Lincoln and stab Rathbone. As Booth escaped the city, the unconscious president was carried across the street to the

Petersen House, where he died at 7:22 the next morning.

Today, Ford's Theatre, a national historic site, is restored to the condition it was the night of the assassination. It is still a performing theater, with shows scheduled throughout the year. A must-stop here is the lower-level museum exhibiting Lincoln memorabilia (some 3,000 items) as well as Booth's diary and one of his boots. At Petersen House (516 10th St.) one can view the room where the president died.

Frederick Douglass House

1411 W St. SE
Open daily April to Sept. 9 AM to 5 PM; Oct.-Mar. 9 AM to 4 PM
Free Admission *(202) 426-5960*

Former slave Frederick Douglass became a famed abolitionist, editor, orator and advisor to Abraham Lincoln. Douglass's home, Cedar Hill, contains a vast collection of personal items and artifacts from this turbulent period in American history. Visitors can expect a 30-minute film, followed by an engaging 30-minute tour. Cedar Hill, a national historic site, is located in the Southeast neighborhood of Anacostia. It affords a stunning view of downtown to the north.

Fort Dupont Park

Minnesota and Massachusetts aves. SE
Open daily during daylight hours
Free Admission *(202) 426-7745*

Located in the hills of Anacostia, Fort Dupont was one of 68 Union forts and 93 gun batteries that formed a ring around the city. It guarded the vital 11th Street Bridge that linked the Southeast neighborhood with the Federal district of Washington. Although it never saw battle, the fort served as an important sanctuary for runaway slaves, many of whom joined D.C.'s growing community of "contrabands." The guns and barracks are gone, but the fort's earthworks can still be found in the 376-acre namesake park that is run by the National Park Service.

The Rock Creek Park Forts

Rock Creek Park
5000 Glover Rd. NW
Open daily during daylight hours
Free Admission *(202) 426-6832*

Within and around Rock Creek Park, Washington's huge and surprisingly pristine urban forest, one can trample the grounds of a handful of strategic Civil War forts that guarded Washington from the Confederates. Fort Stevens, just to the east of the park at 13th Street and Piney Branch Road, is where Jubal Early's spirited Southern forces squared off against an aggressive Union line in July of 1864. Among the battle's many spectators was President Lincoln, who only after much pleading from a Union commander reluctantly retreated to safer ground. It was the first and only battle the president ever witnessed.

Fort Reno, at Belt Road and Chesapeake Street, no longer remains, but you can check out its key vantage point as the highest point in the District, more than 400 feet above sea level. Fort DeRussey, meanwhile, sits right off a bike path at Oregon Avenue and Military Road, in the heart of Rock Creek. To the west of the park, at Western Avenue and River Road, is Fort Bayard, now a popular picnicking site.

Ulysses S. Grant Memorial

1st Street NW (In front of the Capitol Reflecting Pool)

Sculptor Henry Shrady's memorial to the tireless Union general is one of the most striking images in the District. It was modeled after a sketch made of Grant by a young soldier from Massachusetts during the aftermath of battle at Virginia's Spotsylvania Court House. The general is sitting atop his warhorse, Cincinnati, and his penetrating eyes seem to be surveying the vastness of the National Mall that unfolds to the west. The adjacent bronzed images of cavalry troops in action are some of the most moving combat sculptures ever crafted.

Joe Hooker's Division

Below Pennsylvania Avenue between 9th and 15th sts. NW

Washington's most notorious "red-light" district cropped up during the Civil War, in an area wedged between Pennsylvania Avenue and the National Mall. Houses of ill-repute sprung up to cater to the growing masses of troops and administrators who were flooding into the Northern capital. Along with the soldiers and bordellos came hordes of gamblers, thieves, pimps and other unsavory characters. As legend has it, Gen. Joseph Hooker, a one-time commander of the Army of the Potomac, was responsible for rounding up the city's growing legion of prostitutes (some estimates numbered them as high as 15,000) and confining them to this area that became known as Hooker's Division. Legend also has it that this is where the slang name for prostitutes originated. The once lively district is now the site of the sterile and staid Federal Triangle, a sprawl of government office facilities that includes the Internal Revenue Service, a building some might claim is the biggest of all houses of ill fame.

Lincoln Memorial

The National Mall at 23rd Street NW
Open 24 hours
Free Admission (202) 426-6895

The awesome, marble shrine to the nation's greatest president is loaded with symbolism, from the wall-carved inscription of the Gettysburg Address to the 36 Doric columns representing the reunion of the 36 states at the time of Lincoln's death. Perhaps the most poignant symbol connected with the monument, however, is the nearby Arlington Memorial Bridge. The stately bridge connects the Lincoln Memorial with Arlington House, Robert E. Lee's plantation home that overlooks the monument from the Virginia side of the Potomac River. The symbol suggests not only the healing of the nation but a common linkage between two great Americans.

Old Corcoran Art Gallery

(Now known as the Renwick Gallery)
17th Street and Pennsylvania Avenue. NW
Open daily 10 AM to 5:30 PM
Free Admission (202) 357-2531

During the first three years of the war, the Old Corcoran Art Gallery was the Union's largest supply depot in Washington, dispensing tens of thousands of uniforms, tents and equipment to soldiers fighting in the Virginia countryside. Gen. Montgomery C. Meigs, director of transportation and supply, used the building as his headquarters during the last year of the war.

U.S. Patent Office

(Now occupied by the National Portrait Gallery)
8th and F Sts. NW

Today, the former U.S. Patent Office houses two of the city's greatest cultural treasures—the National Collection of Fine Arts and the National Portrait Gallery. During the war, besides being a place where inventions were inspected, the building was used as temporary barracks and as an Army hospital. It was also here where Lincoln held his second inaugural ball on March 5, 1865, on the eve of the war.

Sherman Monument

15th Street and Pennsylvania Avenue NW

Between the Treasury Department and the Ellipse is a small park area that contains the mounted statue of Gen. William T. Sherman, the Union commander who almost single-handedly destroyed the Deep South. A fierce soldier, Sherman was also a compassionate man who had sincere sympathies for the South. In fact, many of the radical Republicans in the U.S. Senate thought he was too sympathetic, and Sherman later found himself ostracized from the inner circles of power after the war.

Washington Arsenal

Present-day site of Fort McNair
4th and P Sts. SW

The Washington Arsenal was the largest such Federal installment of the Civil War. It was also the nearest rail and water shipping point for ammunition headed to the battle fronts in Virginia. Two days after the assassination of President Lincoln, the conspirators who aided John Wilkes Booth were brought to the arsenal's prison and tried. On July 7, 1865, the four condemned, including Mary Surratt, were hanged here and buried in the adjacent prison yard. Four years later, the bodies were released to their respective families.

Washington Monument

Constitution Avenue and 15th Street NW
Open 9 AM to 5 PM daily; 8 AM to midnight in spring and summer
Free Admission *(202) 426-6841*

Like just about everything else in Washington, the city's most visible landmark was greatly impacted by the Civil War. Work on the monument, which had begun in 1848, came to an abrupt halt during the war. At that time, it stood at only 156

Insiders' Tip

The grandaddy of all area Civil War battle reenactments is held each summer near Manassas National Battlefield Park. The Prince William County Park Authority helps sponsor the event which typically draws participants and spectators from across the nation.

feet high, or less than a third of its completed height (555 feet). One can readily see the point where work stopped on the memorial: The masonry patterns of the last two-thirds of the obelisk are different from the original section. Interestingly, former Confederate prisoners were employed to help build the final stretches of the monument, which opened to the public in 1888.

THE WHITE HOUSE

1600 Pennsylvania Ave. NW
Open for tours 10 AM to noon, Tuesday through Saturday
Free Admission

America's most famous home wasn't all that majestic in the years leading up to and during the Civil War. In fact, just two years before the outbreak of the war, the White House's sewage was still being emptied directly onto the Ellipse (known in those days as the White Lot), the marshy park located immediately to the south. Nearby, at the bottom of 17th Street, stood the city dump which lay adjacent to a polluted, disease-ridden canal. You may remember that Lincoln's son, Willie, died of typhoid fever and the president himself came down with small pox — all no doubt due to the unhealthy surroundings.

WILLARD'S HOTEL

1401 Pennsylvania Ave. NW

Perhaps the grandest of Washington's grand hotels, Willard's (today known simply as The Willard) was the undisputed social center of the nation's capital during the Civil War. Both Lincoln and Grant stayed here during their first nights in the city, and this was the site where Julie Ward Howe penned "The Battle Hymn of the Republic," the spiritual anthem of the North. Ironically, John Wilkes Booth frequented the hotel often during the weeks and days prior to the Lincoln assassination.

Northern Virginia

Alexandria

BOYHOOD HOME OF ROBERT E. LEE

607 Oronoco St.
Open 10 AM to 4 PM Monday through Saturday, noon to 4 PM Sunday
Small admission fee (703) 548-8454

Like George Washington, Robert E. Lee was born on Virginia's Northern Neck, a vast plantation region bounded by the Potomac and Rappahannock rivers and the Chesapeake Bay. And like the first president, Lee would ultimately move north to Alexandria, a bustling port city that was becoming one of the East Coast's leading trade and shipping centers. Lee's father, the Revolutionary war hero "Light Horse Harry" Lee, brought his family to the house in 1812. Young Robert spent 10 years in the large Federal-period home on Oronoco Street in Old Town. Among the home's many distinguished guests was General Marquis de Lafayette, the Frenchman who fought side by side with the elder Lee and Washington during the Revolutionary War. The home was also the site of the 1804 marriage of George Washington Parke Custis (Martha Washington's grandson) and Mary Lee Fitzhugh. Robert E. Lee married their daughter, Mary Anna Randolph Custis, at Arlington House.

Confederate Statue

South Washington and Prince Sts.

At the busy intersection of South Washington and Prince streets stands Alexandria's memorial to its fallen Confederate comrades. The statue is simple enough — a single soldier standing upright and gazing steadfastly toward the south. About four years ago the statue, which stands in the middle of the street, accidentally was knocked over by a speeding motorist, an act that set off a minor controversy. Some folks in the community claimed it was a traffic hazard, an insensitive one at that, and should be removed permanently. A legion of powerful town elders sensed an underhanded Yankee plot to rid the city of part of its history. Johnny Reb was mended and placed back in his original position, a striking reminder that even in the farthest northern reaches of the South, the passions of the Civil War still run deep.

Fort Ward Museum & Historic Site

4301 W. Braddock Rd.
Grounds open 9 AM to sunset daily
Museum open 9 AM to 5 PM Tuesday-Saturday; noon to 5 PM Sunday
Free Admission (703) 838-4831

Named after the first Union officer to be killed in the Civil War, Fort Ward was one of dozens of Union fortifications that suddenly popped up following the North's embarrassing defeat at the Battle of First Manassas, just 30 miles to the west. Armed with 36 guns, it was the fifth-largest fort surrounding the nation's capital. Today, visitors can see much of the same structure as it appeared over 100 years ago. The Fort Ward Museum contains an impressive collection of Civil War artifacts and photographs. The park holds its annual Civil War Living History Day each August, one of the region's better period reenactment events.

Arlington County

Arlington House/ Arlington National Cemetery

Memorial Drive
Open daily 8 AM to 5 PM
Free admission (703) 692-0931

Perched on a bluff overlooking the Potomac River, Arlington House once was the home of Robert E. Lee. When Lee left to command the Confederate forces, the Georgian-style mansion and its several thousand acres of surrounding property were seized by Federal troops and became the headquarters for the Army of the Potomac. Three Union forts were built on the land, and casualties (both Northern and Southern) from local battles were buried here beginning in June 1864. Today, the area is known as Arlington National Cemetery and is one of the most visited burial grounds in the world. The house, also known as the Robert E. Lee Memorial, is completely restored and furnished with Lee family heirlooms. From the front steps of the mansion, one can experience perhaps the most spectacular views of Washington.

Fairfax County

Fort Marcy Park

Accessible from the northbound lanes of the George Washington Memorial Parkway near McLean, Va. (follow signs)
Open to the public during daylight hours
Free Admission

Fort Marcy, or what remains of it, sits atop Virginia's Prospect Hill, about a mile west of Chain Bridge. The Union earthwork defense compound was responsible for securing both Chain Bridge, which spans across the Potomac into northwest Washington, and the vital Chesapeake and Ohio Canal, the main supply link for the war-time capital. During the war, the fort, named for Gen. George McClellan's father-in-law, held 18 guns, including a 10-inch mortar, two 24-pound mortars and 15 smaller cannons. Today, visitors can view the fort's remaining earthworks and take in dramatic vistas from the grounds which sit 275 feet above the Potomac.

Fairfax City

Marr Monument

4000 Chain Bridge Rd. (703) 385-7855

On the lawn of the Old Fairfax Courthouse is a stone monument built in 1904 in memory of Capt. John Quincy Marr, the first Confederate officer killed in the Civil War. Marr was in command of the Warrenton Rifles when, on the night of June 1, 1861, he was killed in a skirmish in Fairfax City with Company B of the Union Second Cavalry. Like all Confederate cannons, those flanking this monument face north. Nearby, in the Fairfax City Cemetery, 10561 Main St., lies a grey granite obelisk marking the graves of 200 unknown soldiers of the Confederacy, including 96 Fairfax County Civil War fatalities.

Prince William County

Manassas National Battlefield Park

12521 Lee Hwy., Manassas, Va.
Open 9 AM to 5:30 PM in winter; 9 AM to 6 PM in summer
Small admission fee (703) 754-1861

Just 30 miles west of the Nation's Capital, Manassas National Battlefield Park looks much the same as it did in 1861. Several square miles of Virginia countryside have been preserved in memorial to the two landmark Civil War battles that took place here — fighting that claimed more than 4,000 lives and 30,000 wounded. In recent years, developers have had their eyes on parcels of land abutting the park, and in one of the more inane proposals, one prominent builder nearly won approval to construct a shopping mall within eyesight of these hallowed grounds. Fortunately, preservationists had more clout on Capitol Hill than did the developers, and consequently Manassas remains remarkably untouched given its proximity to suburbia.

The beauty of the battlefield goes beyond the rich history and graceful monuments. Manassas is a park in every sense of the word, with miles of horse and hiking trails, interpretive roadside tour markers, picnic areas and restored homes. At the Visitor Center, a 15-minute slide presentation and a small museum help tell the story of the two great battles. Make sure to pick up brochures from park rangers that outline some of the more interesting walking and driving tours. No trip to the area should be complete without a stop at the Manassas Museum in the neighboring city's Old Town district, about a 10-minute drive from the battlefield. (See below.)

Manassas Museum

9101 Prince William St., Manassas, Va.
Open 10 AM to 5 PM Tuesday through Sunday
Small admission fee (703) 368-1873

The Manassas Museum (not affiliated with the battlefield park) reopened in 1992 in a modern and spacious building in downtown Manassas. It interprets the history and material culture of the community and the surrounding Northern Virginia Piedmont region. On display here are an array of prehistoric tools, Civil War weapons and uniforms, railroad artifacts, Victorian costumes, quilts and photos that collectively tell the story of this historic part of the Old Dominion. Of special interest are a pair of video programs that describe the settlement of the Manassas area and the legacy of the Civil War. More than anything, the museum helps one understand why two of the most important battles of the war were fought in this otherwise peaceful community.

Confederate Cemetery

Center Street
Old Town Manassas, Va.

Two years after the South's surrender at Appomattox, Confederate veteran W.S. Fewell donated one acre of land in the center of Manassas for a cemetery. A year later, more than 250 Southern soldiers had been reinterred there. The focal point of the cemetery is a red sandstone monument that is capped by a bronze statue entitled "At Rest."

Loudoun County

Ball's Bluff

Located off of Route 15, just north of Leesburg, Va.
Open to the public during daylight hours
Free admission

The viciously fought Battle of Ball's Bluff (Oct. 21, 1861), won by the South, was an event of significant national importance because it raised serious questions in the U.S. Congress as to how the Civil War should be conducted. The Union suffered heavy casualties, a result of a series strategic blunders. Shortly after the battle, Congress established the Joint Committee on the Conduct of the War, an organization charged with reviewing all military procedures and other leadership issues that became politicized through war.

The Village of Waterford

On Route 662, about a 15-minute drive from Leesburg, Va. (703) 882-3018

This tiny and immaculate Hunt Country village traces its roots back to 1733 when it was founded by Amos Janney, a Quaker who had emigrated from Pennsylvania. By the time of the Civil War, the strongly abolitionist residents supported the Union, a very unpopular stance in Virginia. During the war, the village suffered Union harassment because of its location and Confederate harassment because of its Quaker-influenced abolitionist beliefs. As a result of the Confederate backlash, Samuel Means, a resident miller, abandoned his Quaker principles to form the Independent Loudoun Rangers, the only organized troops in Virginia to fight for the Union.

Suburban Maryland

Montgomery County

Cabin John Aqueduct Bridge

Located off the Clara Barton Parkway, in Cabin John, Md.

There's only one place in the nation where the names of both President Lincoln and Confederate President Jefferson Davis appear together. They're inscribed on a plaque on the Cabin John Aqueduct in Suburban Maryland. The aqueduct, the longest stone arch bridge in the world, was commissioned in the 1850s when Franklin Pierce was president and Jefferson Davis was secretary of war. It was designed to transport water from the Great Falls of the Potomac to Washington. A commemorative plaque was placed on the bridge abutment upon completion. When the Civil War broke out, someone discovered Davis's name and it was quickly removed. Years later, under the presidency of Theodore Roosevelt, a new plaque was installed that included the Confederate hero. The bridge and the plaque remain to this day.

Clara Barton House

5801 Oxford Rd., Glen Echo, Md.
Open daily 10 AM to 5 PM
Free Admission (301) 492-6245

Known as the "Angel of the Battlefield," Clara Barton was one of few women allowed behind the lines by the Union Army. She tended to the thousands of wounded at Antietam, the bloodiest day in American history. She was also instrumental in helping locate and identify the graves of more than 22,000 Civil War soldiers scattered throughout eastern and southern theaters. Barton perhaps is best known, however, as the founder of the American Red Cross. This house, now a fascinating museum, was originally built as a warehouse for Red Cross supplies. After Barton made it her permanent home in 1897, the house was expanded to 36 rooms and now is considered an important landmark in Victorian design.

White's Ferry

White's Ferry Road, Poolesville, Md.
Open daily 6 AM to 11 PM;
winter 6 AM to 8 PM
$3.50 roundtrip;
$2 one-way (301) 349-5200

White's Ferry on the Potomac River is the site where Confederate Gen. Jubal Early led 13,000 troops across the river into Maryland in July 1864. Early and troops would eventually make their way into the present-day Rock Creek Park, thus becoming the only Rebel forces to ever come within striking distance of the nation's capital. This was also the site where Robert E. Lee earlier had crossed the river en route to his first large-scale invasion of the North. Today, at White's Ferry, you can load your car onto the *Jubal Early* ferry and ford the river into Virginia. It is the only ferry boat still operating on the Potomac, and is accessible from both the Maryland and Virginia shores.

Prince George's County

Fort Washington Park

Rt. 210 South to Fort Washington Road (On the Potomac River)
Fort Washington, Md.
Free Admission (301) 763-4600

Originally built to guard Washington from the British during the Battle of 1812, this impressive and fully restored masonry fort was the southern lookout for Union troops during the Civil War. In January 1861, it was the sole fort protecting the capital and was manned by just 40 Marines. You can relive these tense moments at the Torchlight Tattoo ceremonies held on Saturday evenings throughout the summer. Breathtaking views of the Potomac and the District in the distance await visitors here.

The Mary Surratt House

9118 Brandywine Rd., Clinton, Md.
Open Thursday-Friday 11 AM to 3 PM; Saturday-Sunday noon to 4 PM; closed January and February
Small admission fee (301) 868-1121

This unassuming tavern and post office was also the home of Mary Surratt, who was charged as a conspirator in the Lincoln assassination. On the day Lincoln was shot, Surratt supposedly left behind a package at the tavern that contained field glasses and some guns for the fleeing John Wilkes Booth. As a result of her involvement, Mary Surratt was hanged along with three other conspirators, thus becoming the first woman ever to be executed by the federal government.

Charles County

Dr. Samuel A. Mudd House

Rt. 232 near Waldorf, Md.
Open Saturday and Sunday Noon to 4 PM; Wednesday 11 AM to 3 PM
Small admission fee (301) 934-8464

After shooting President Lincoln, John Wilkes Booth escaped from the scene by jumping from the president's box and onto the stage at Ford's Theatre. In the process, he badly fractured his leg and this is where the story of Dr. Samuel Mudd comes in. On their escape route through Southern Maryland, a disguised Booth and his accomplice, David Herold, made a stop at the country doctor's farmhouse. Mudd, supposedly not knowing the identity of the assassins, set Booth's leg and even tried to arrange for a carriage for the two men's journey. (Booth and Herold would ultimately leave on horseback.)

Despite his alleged innocence, Mudd was convicted by a military court of aiding and harboring an escaping fugitive. He was sent to Jefferson Prison near Key West, Fla., only to be pardoned later by President Andrew Johnson. While in prison, Dr. Mudd was called on to treat fellow prisoners during an outbreak of yellow fever. After being discharged for his humanitarian efforts, Mudd returned to his Maryland home and became a noted national expert on treating the fever. Today, the Mudd home is a fully restored historic site, complete with period furniture and mementos that detail the doctor's plight to establish his innocence.

Frederick County

Barbara Fritchie House and Museum

154 W. Patrick St., Frederick, Md.
Call for times and days open; generally closed December through March
Small admission fee (301) 698-0630

Forever immortalized in the John Greenleaf Whittier poem bearing her name, Barbara Fritchie was a staunch Union supporter who lived in Frederick, a town of split loyalties during the war. As legend has it, Fritchie proudly flew the Stars and Stripes from her upstairs window as Gen. Stonewall Jackson and his Confederate troops marched in and captured the sleepy Maryland village. Jackson, noting the flag, confronted the 96-year-old patriot about her loyalties. The unfazed Fritchie shouted to the general: "Shoot if you must, this old gray head, but spare your country's flag." Jackson, taken aback by the woman's determination and bravery, proclaimed: "Who touches a hair on your gray head dies like a dog." The house, part of Frederick's large historic district, is filled with Fritchie heirlooms, including a poet's corner dedicated to Whittier's tribute.

Monocacy National Battlefield

Off Route 355 near Frederick, Md.
Open daily during daylight hours
Free Admission (301) 432-5124

It was here that Gen. Lew Wallace's Union forces were defeated by the Rebs under Gen. Jubal Early, who later went on to attack Washington, D.C., at Fort Stevens. Wallace is probably best remembered as the author who penned *Ben Hur*, and most military strategists would claim that he was a better writer than commander. Like Manassas, Antietam and virtually every Civil War battlefield in the nation, Monocacy is under relentless pressure from developers determined to turn the surrounding countryside into condo units and shopping centers. Go figure.

ORDER FORM

Use this convenient form to place your order for any of the Insiders' Guides® books.

Fast and Simple!

Mail to:
Insiders' Guides®, Inc.
P.O. Box 2057
Manteo, NC 27954 *or*
for VISA or Mastercard orders call
1-800-765-BOOK

Name ______________________________

Address ______________________________

City/State/Zip ______________________________

Quantity	*Title/Price*	*Shipping*	
	Insiders' Guide® to the Triangle, $12.95	$2.50	
	Insiders' Guide® to Charlotte, $12.95	$2.50	
	Insiders' Guide® to Virginia Beach / Norfolk, $12.95	$2.50	
	Insiders' Guide® to the Outer Banks, $12.95	$2.50	
	Insiders' Guide® to Williamsburg, $12.95	$2.50	
	Insiders' Guide® to Richmond, $12.95	$2.50	
	Insiders' Guide® to Orlando, $12.95	$2.50	
	Insiders' Guide® to Virginia's Blue Ridge, $12.95	$2.50	
	Insiders' Guide® to The Crystal Coast of NC, $12.95	$2.50	
	Insiders' Guide® to Myrtle Beach, $12.95	$2.50	
	Insiders' Guide® to Charleston, $12.95	$2.50	
	Insiders' Guide® to Virginia's Blue Ridge, $12.95	$2.50	
	Insiders' Guide® to Civil War Sites In The Eastern Theater, $12.95	$2.50	
	Insiders' Guide® to Lexington, $12.95 (Spring '94)	$2.50	
	Insiders' Guide® to Wilmington, NC, $12.95 (Spring '94)	$2.50	

(N.C. residents add 6% sales tax.) GRAND TOTAL ____________

Payment in full (check, cash or money order) must accompany order form. Please allow 2 weeks for delivery

Index of Advertisers

Index

Symbols

A

B

C

D

E

F

G

H

I

J

K

L

M

N

O

P

Q

R

S

T

U

Y

Z